HOW LONG WILL
SOUTH AFRICA SURVIVE?

R. W. Johnson

New York
Oxford University Press

For my friends,
Anne Summers, Margaret Tite, and Gavin Williams
who, in a difficult time, helped

First published in the United Kingdom 1977 by
THE MACMILLAN PRESS LTD
London and Basingstoke

First published in the U.S.A. 1977 by
OXFORD UNIVERSITY PRESS INC.
New York

Typeset in IBM Century by
PREFACE LTD
Salisbury, Wilts
Printed in Great Britain by
BILLING & SONS LTD
Guildford, Worcester and London

Library of Congress Cataloging in Publication Data
Johnson, Richard William.
How long will South Africa survive?

1. South Africa—Politics and government—1961-
2. South Africa—Race relations.   3.   South Africa—
Economic conditions—1961-   4. Africa, Southern—
Politics and government—1975-   I.   Title.
DT779.9.J64   320.9'68'06   77-11919
ISBN 0-19-520012-8
ISBN 0-19-520013-6 pbk.

Contents

Preface

Although this book has been written by someone who works as an academic, it will be evident to the reader that it is not written in the accepted academic style. In part this is because I have wished to keep footnoting to a minimum. I have worked from a plethora of sources, including a vast array of newspapers and periodicals, and did not wish to swamp the reader in attributions. But the book is also written the way it is simply because I wanted to do it that way. It deals with a large and dramatic subject set in a contemporary period. The full truth relating to some of the questions it raises may not be known for many decades, if ever. It would be as foolish to imagine that the Quai d'Orsay will rush to assist future scholars in understanding French intrigues in Angola as it would be to expect that Dr Kissinger's memoirs, when they appear, will reveal the full complexities of US policy towards southern Africa. Properly speaking, then, the materials do not yet exist for a fully academic study of this book's subject, South Africa's development towards its present crisis. If such a study were attempted it would have to be altogether more hesitant and cautious in its approach to a number of burning issues than this book is. But that was, for me, largely the point. They *are* burning issues. I have preferred to take the scholarly risks I have in order to tackle important but speculative concerns rather than leave them alone. The reader will have to judge whether I have backed hunches too outrageously far.

Although an Englishman by birth and now again by residence I enjoyed (and that is the right word) a South African boyhood. I have not, though, attempted to write about South Africa before. In 1976, however, I found myself caught up again by the sheer drama of events in southern Africa. It has been a strange experience to recapture old emotions and excitements in the writing of this book. I have tried to avoid flat value judgments where possible, but I have not minded if some of the excitement showed.

There are a number of people I should like to thank for having helped me. John Winckler was at all times a constructive, supportive and essential contact and friend at Macmillan, and Allan Aslett was unfailingly helpful and considerate there too. I have benefited, as well, from friends at Oxford, not so much in the immediate preparation of the manuscript, but more pleasurably and lengthily through discussions of southern Africa with them over time; from Gavin Williams, Charles van Onselen, Belinda Bozzoli and Stanley Trapido. They all know more than me; I have learnt much from them and have enjoyed doing so.

I am grateful, too, to my colleagues at Magdalen, They have, in the broadest sense, made the college where I have the luck to work a tolerant and stimulating place and I have benefited accordingly.

Finally, my thanks go most of all to Anne Summers, to whom I owe a debt quite above and beyond that acknowledged on the dedication page. She encouraged me from the outset to write; found time from her own writing to read and comment on the first three chapters; was endlessly patient with me; and allowed me to renege shamefully on my commitment to equal shares in domestic and parenthood duties. She also performed the difficult but occasionally necessary duty of preventing Rebecca and Dicken from being other than a comfort and help to me. Neither she, nor they, nor anyone else, should bear any of the blame for whatever errors of judgment this book may contain.

R. W. Johnson

April 1977   Magdalen College, Oxford

NOTE ON CURRENCY

The South African unit of currency, the Rand, was tied to the £ sterling at a rate of R2 = £1 until the 1967 devaluation of the £. From October 1972 the Rand was tied to the $ instead and its value oscillated between $1.40—1.50 with the floating of the $. In June 1975 the Rand was devalued from $1.49 to $1.42 and in September 1975 to $1.15.

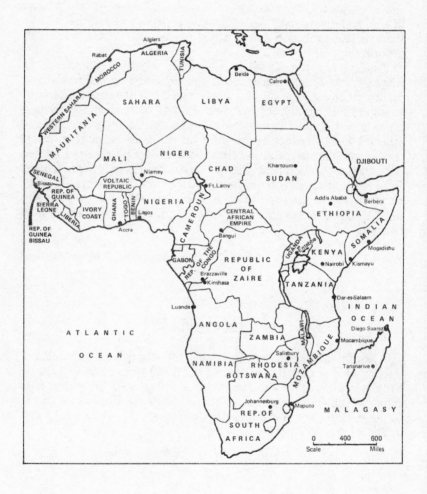

Algiers

Rabat
MOROCCO
ALGERIA
TUNISIA

Beida
Cairo

WESTERN SAHARA

SAHARA
LIBYA
EGYPT

MAURITANIA

MALI
NIGER
CHAD
Khartoum
DJIBOUTI

Niamey
Ft.Lamv
SUDAN

SENEGAL
Bissau
REP. OF
GUINEA
VOLTAIC
REPUBLIC
NIGERIA
Addis Ababa
Berbera

SIERRA
LEONE
GHANA
TOGO
BENIN
Lagos
CAMEROUN
CENTRAL
AFRICAN
EMPIRE
ETHIOPIA
SOMALIA

LIBERIA
IVORY
COAST
Accra
Bangui
Mogadishu

REP. OF
GUINEA
BISSAU
GABON
REP. OF THE CONGO
UGANDA
Entebbe
KENYA
Kismayu

Brazzaville
Kinshasa
REPUBLIC
OF
ZAIRE
Nairobi

TANZANIA

Luanda
Dar-es-Salaam
INDIAN
OCEAN

ATLANTIC
OCEAN

ANGOLA
Diego Suarez

ZAMBIA
MALAWI
Mocambique

Salisbury
Tananarive

NAMIBIA
RHODESIA
MOZAMBIQUE

BOTSWANA

Johannesburg
Maputo
MALAGASY

REP.OF
SOUTH
AFRICA

0   400   600
Scale   Miles

A Political Map of Africa 1977

RADICAL STATES

Algeria

Benin

Republic of the Congo

Ethiopia

Republic of Guinea

Guinea Bissau

Libya

Malagasy Republic

Mali

Tanzania

COUNTRIES WITH TREATIES OF FRIENDSHIP WITH USSR

Angola

Mozambique

Somalia

POLITICALLY AMBIVALENT STATES

Djibouti

Ghana

Mauretania

Nigeria

Uganda

Zambia

CONSERVATIVE PRO-WESTERN STATES

Botswana

Cameroun

Central African Empire

Chad

Egypt

Gabon

Ivory Coast

Kenya

Liberia

Malawi

Morocco

Niger

Senegal

Sierra Leone

Sudan

Swaziland

Togo

Tunisia

Voltaic Republic

Western Sahara

Zaire

WHITE-RULED STATES

Namibia

Rhodesia

South Africa

SOMALIA
Mogadishu

Douala
Banqui
KENYA
Kampala
Libreville
Mbandaka
Kisangani
UGANDA
Entebbe
Nairobi
GABON
REPUBLIC
REP. OF THE CONGO
OF ZAIRE
Mwanza
Mombasa
Brazzaville
Kinshasa
Tabora
Pointe Noire
Zanzibar
Cabinda
Kalemie
TANZANIA
Dar-es-Salaam

Ambriz
Luanda
Quibala
Shaba
Nova
Lisboa
Novo Redondo
Silva Porto
MALAWI
Lobito
ZAMBIA
Benguela
ANGOLA
Lusaka
Blantyre
Mocambique
Sa da Bandeira
Caprivi
Tete
Strip
Salisbury
Mocamedes
R. Cunene
Beira
Okavango
RHODESIA
Swamp
NAMIBIA
Francistowne
Bulawayo
MOCAMBIQUE
BOTSWANA
Namib
Walvis Bay
Windhoek
Gaberones
Kalahari
Pretoria
Desert
Maputo
Johannesburg
Moabane
SWAZILAND
INDIAN
OCEAN
Desert
Bloemfontein
Pietermaritzburg
ATLANTIC
REP. OF
LESOTHO
Durban
OCEAN
SOUTH
AFRICA
East London
Cape Town
Port Elizabeth

+++++ major railways
——— major roads
▨▨▨ Bantustans

0   200   400   600
Scale   Miles

Introduction: Black Pantomime at the Palais des Nations

As Christmas 1976 neared and the Geneva conference on Rhodesia wore on it seemed increasingly clear that the meeting was haunted. To wander in the halls or grounds of the Palais des Nations is, to be fair, a pretty strange experience in its own right. For these are the headquarters of the ill-fated League of Nations and the ghosts of Woodrow Wilson, Clemenceau, and Lloyd George linger quite unmistakably on this hillside overlooking the fair city of Geneva. The buildings themselves awkwardly juxtapose the new brutalism of steel and glass with the palladian echoes of Versailles. To stroll in the gardens is to imagine oneself an extra in *L'Année Dernière à Marienbad*, particularly now that the carefully arcadian and landscaped grounds are dominated by the huge and futuristic monument to Soviet space achievements which the Russians have recently — and mysteriously — insisted on erecting. The combined effect is uncomfortably weird — as if a spaceship has come to rest in the *Petit Trianon*. In these surroundings it is quite impossible not to remember the ill-fated conception, the naïve pretensions, and the impotent failures of the League of Nations. The sad truth was simply that the League was, in a fairly direct sense, a case of infant mortality. Its progenitor, Woodrow Wilson, picked a quite unnecessary fight with the U.S. Senate over it and, on losing, chose to make the League the central issue of the 1920 Presidential campaign. It took very considerable reserves of foolishness and arrogance on Wilson's part to provoke the ambivalent Republicans into principled opposition to the League. But such reserves Wilson did indeed possess and he deployed them to great effect. The ensuing Republican landslide put paid to all prospects of American participation in the League, which was stillborn as a result. Accordingly real power never resided within the Palais des Nations and, inevitably, an element of play-acting quickly overtook the League's proceedings. And now, in 1976, the same thing had happened again. The Conference on Rhodesia was, equally unmistakably, an

1

American child, fathered by Henry Kissinger during his frantic
shuttle-diplomacy of 1976 as the crisis bursting over southern
Africa at last moved to the top of the U.S. State Department's
priority list. But, almost immediately, the American electorate
sabotaged the Conference, just as they had sabotaged the
League. President Ford — and with him Dr Kissinger — was
voted out of office. The only Power able to make the
Conference 'work' was, once again, broodingly absent. Thea-
tricality was, again, the inevitable result.

Not surprisingly, the world's press representatives, eager to
justify their alarming hotel bills to their editors, made the most
of the fact that there was, at least, an interesting cast.
Unfortunately, Mr Ian Smith, the main lead character (and
Rhodesian premier) quit the performance almost immediately.
This was a considerable blow, for the venomous hostility
between Mr Smith and Mr Mugabe, the ZANU (and then
Patriotic Front) guerrilla leader, had provided a great deal of
dramatic tension. The Press had enjoyed the confrontation of
'former fighter pilot' versus 'schoolteacher-turned-guerrilla', a
depiction encouraged by Mr Mugabe's constant use of boxing
metaphors in his press interviews. Under considerable pressure
from the guerrillas not to compromise their all-or-nothing
struggle by his very participation in the Conference, he
reassured journalists that he was only staying on there for 'a
knock-out in round 15'. (Another of the African participants,
Bishop Muzorewa, mixed religion and ringcraft, advising a Swiss
congregation to 'turn the other cheek once only'.) Mr Smith,
returning to Salisbury, was shrewd enough to know the medium
in which he had been involved. 'There is a lot of acting going on
in Geneva at the moment', he said, accurately enough, 'and the
mass communications media seem to have fallen for this.'
Employing the true actor's ultimate insult, he accused Mugabe,
the rival lead, of staginess: 'He's riding around on cloud nine
with a camouflage terrorist uniform. I don't think he has heard
a shot fired in anger in his life, but he is posing as the big
terrorist there and is being mobbed by everybody.'

While Smith's departure was an undeniable blow, he left a
promising understudy in Mr Pieter Van der Byl, his Foreign
Minister. The main significance of this change was that
Rhodesian contempt for the African delegates was henceforth
uttered in Van der Byl's English public school accent rather
than Smith's clipped, man-in-the-street diction. His sense of
theatre was the same, however. The speeches of the Patriotic
Front were, he said, 'almost a parody, a music-hall caricature of
communist invective'. Mugabe was not even a live actor but a

'bloodthirsty Marxist puppet'. Mugabe, for his part, continued to counter in the style of Muhammad Ali at a weigh-in — Van der Byl was 'the foul-mouthed man' and, frightened of the fight, 'that fool who has just run away'. Smith, though off-stage, kept up a derisive running commentary from Salisbury, continually accusing the Africans of 'playing to the gallery'. Indeed, Smith's language echoed that of the theatre more consistently than anyone else's, and even after the Conference's adjournment seemed quite unable to slip out of the idiom. Asked his feelings about Mr Ivor Richard's shuttle-diplomacy, Smith replied that his enthusiasm 'is much the same as if I were asked to the premiere performance at the Fine Arts Theatre of "Swan Lake" and was told Mr Richard was to play the leading part'. This was an unkind cut at the portly Conference chairman who had chosen alternately to play the roles of stately impresario and genial master of ceremonies. He was, in fact, not much beyond the audition stage as a diplomat. His career in British Labour Party politics had been rudely ended when an ultra-safe seat was snatched humiliatingly from him by an anti-corruption independent in 1974. An embarrassed party leadership had kicked him upstairs to the United Nations. His role in Geneva was far from easy. He was perhaps the last of a long line of British chairmen of decolonisation conferences, stretching back over thirty years. But the British pretension to imperial competence in southern African affairs was now, like the settings of the Palais, an artifice, grandiose but empty. The Conference delegates could see this, and disputed Richard's position and authority whenever it suited them. They — and he — were only too well aware that, at most, Richard was Laertes to Dr Kissinger's Polonius. The old King of Denmark, moreover, had been deposed and the new King, an unknown quantity, was still sitting in Plains, Georgia. His name, as he had endlessly informed his future subjects, was Jimmy Carter. Hamlet, as usual, dominated the court by his absence. Nowadays he lived in Pretoria . . . .

With the principal actors off stage almost every scene in Geneva was, inevitably, dominated by the strangely assorted African delegations. The Mugabe faction, for all that its leader was relaxed enough to strike jocular boxing poses for press photographers, remained a mystery. It included several radical black Americans, notably Edison Zvogbo, a Chicago law professor. ('This conference', he told journalists professorially, 'is a load of crap.') More significantly, there was Josiah Tongogara, a *maquisard* cult figure and head of ZANU's military wing until March 1975 when, along with several other

Mugabe delegates, he had been jailed by President Kaunda of
Zambia on a charge of murdering Herbert Chitepo, the ZANU
chairman. Later came his successor, Rex Nhongo, the head of
ZIPA, around whom even larger myths floated. Both men had
originally fought with the FRELIMO guerrillas against the
Portuguese and had been involved in the Rhodesian guerrilla
war since its inception in 1972. As recently as August 1976
Nhongo had been reported killed in action. He and several other
guerrillas certainly came fairly close to death in Geneva when
they were trapped by a fire in their hotel on the night of
December 3—4. The guerrillas voiced cries of arson, pointing to
a mysterious delay of half an hour between the discovery of the
fire and the summoning of the fire brigade. The Swiss police
dismissed such a theory without, however, offering any alternative explanation. The fire had started in Nhongo's room and it
was hinted that he had fallen asleep drinking, leaving his stove
on. The guerrillas, moreover, had virtually clanked with the
considerable quantity of small-arms carried about their persons
(the Swiss police looking hard the other way), and it seemed
not impossible that the cause lay, unmentionably, there. The
press treated the affair as a joke or, not unreasonably, spoke of
the internecine rivalries between the nationalist factions. This
bespoke a short memory. Western intelligence services have a
not unsuccessful record in the assassination of radical African
nationalists, as the cases of Lumumba, Mondlane, and Cabral
attest. Such events do not take place only in Africa. In 1965, in
true Catch-22 fashion, the Moroccan radical, Ben Barka, was
'disappeared' in Paris. The police never found his body or his
murderers. It had even happened in Geneva before — in 1960
the Cameroun nationalist, Félix Moumié, had been poisoned
there. The Swiss police had never solved that affair either. The
hotel fire, in 1976, is likely to remain a mystery too, though
one might add the footnote that while many of his comrades
jumped from their (third-floor) rooms into safety blankets
below, Mugabe stayed in his room, throwing personal papers
out of the windows. A few days later, at the Palais, Smith and
Van der Byl redoubled their denunciations of Mugabe as a
Communist stooge, claiming that their intelligence service had
recently acquired fresh and conclusive documentary proof of
this. While the Rhodesian troops raiding into Mozambique at
this time had certainly returned with much captured documentation, it seems highly unlikely that Mugabe would have left any
incriminating personal papers at the mercy of his enemies and
potential rivals in the camps raided by the Rhodesians. It seems
not impossible that the papers brandished by Mr Smith a few
days later had come from Mugabe's hotel room, thence,

doubtless, to be circulated to the British and Americans. Certainly, the attitude of the British Foreign Secretary, Mr Crosland, seemed to alter sharply at about this time. As Mr Richard's superior he had, naturally, maintained an attitude of diplomatic neutrality as between the African factions. It was, then, a considerable surprise when Mr Crosland, addressing a NATO conference in Brussels (a week after the Geneva hotel fire), made brutally clear his preference for a 'moderate' solution in Rhodesia, as against the Marxist military dictatorship which, he averred, he believed the guerrillas would install.

Mr Crosland's remarks greatly angered Mugabe, but drew no comment from his ally-of-convenience in the Patriotic Front, Joshua Nkomo. The fact was that the Nkomo delegation was thoroughly alarmed by its partners. This was hardly surprsing given the eminently bourgeois, even conservative hue of Nkomo and his men. Nkomo himself had virtually destroyed his popular standing in Rhodesia by his willingness in earlier days to bargain with Smith. Now, in Geneva, he made an incongruous revolutionary. It was difficult to believe that his huge frame, girded in a checked-and-padded suit, was not more at home amidst the material delights of Geneva than in the Rhodesian detention cells in which he had spent a good part of his life. The anomaly of his alliance with the guerrillas was, perhaps, most brutally highlighted by the killings in Rhodesia on December 5 of a nun and two clerics, Mgr Schmidt and Fr Possenti Weggarten. Both of the latter were close friends of Nkomo — Mgr Schmidt had officiated at Nkomo's wedding as far back as 1949 and had travelled with Mrs Nkomo back to Rhodesia only a fortnight before his death. Father Weggarten had also been a personal friend and Nkomo had sent his sons to be educated under him. While the Africans at Geneva all took the line that the killings must have been the work of the Rhodesian army, it seemed more likely that they were victims of guerrillas under Mugabe's banner.[1] Mrs Nkomo publicly mourned the killings with no

---

[1] This is by no means certain, however. The Catholic Commission for Peace and Justice in Rhodesia found it impossible to arrive at any conclusion as to the identity of the killers, noting that the Rhodesian Army was quite normally in the habit of donning guerrilla or FRELIMO uniforms. This ambiguity appeared to have been dispelled shortly afterwards when the Rhodesian security forces produced a lone African willing to admit to all the murders, but it was quickly restored by the accused's immediate escape from custody under mysterious circumstances. A week later, with little attendant publicity, an African Methodist minister, the Rev. Elisha Kuwana, and his wife were both killed in fighting near Umtali. The Rhodesian Army made no attempt to disclaim responsibility on this occasion.

mention of the probable culprits. 'I am really shaken by all this', she said, 'the missionaries are like my parents to me.'

The Nkomo delegation was a strange and colourful ensemble in itself. It included a number of ZAPU old-timers who, like Nkomo, had known years of jail, detention and exile at Smith's hands, as well as the smooth figure of Ariston Chambati (a recent Oxford graduate), an Asian, a Coloured, a host of advisers, secretaries and spokesmen, and several notable whites, including Mr Justice Leo Baron, the Deputy Chief Justice of Zambia, and Professor Claire Palley, a British law teacher. Most remarkably of all it included Mr Garfield Todd, the former missionary and Rhodesian premier. Todd had lost office in 1958 for proposing that a legal maximum of 20 per cent of Rhodesia's Africans should have the vote. Later he had lost his freedom too when Smith placed him in detention on his farm — an event which had led his daughter, Judith, to flit telegenically before the British media to denounce the Smith regime. During the conference Todd returned to Rhodesia to find his daughter (the wife of a white farmer) armed with a rifle against the guerrillas, with whom Todd was now indirectly affiliated. He attempted to instruct white Rhodesians in the merits of his allies — Nkomo was a liberal man, Mugabe was a practising Catholic. This was roughly as profitable as preaching Communism on the grounds that Stalin was a white man. Todd, unbowed, flew on to London to preach the gospel to the Tory Reform Group where he declared that failure of the Geneva talks would put pressure on the pro-Western orientation of Zambia and Tanzania — presumably to the benefit of Mugabe, at whose side Todd was sitting a few days later in Geneva. It is difficult to feel that Todd was out of place in Geneva — there was about him a strong echo of the League. A man of God, moreover, Todd was flanked on all sides by his comrades in prayer, if not in struggle. Rhodesia being a godly country, virtually all the delegates were vocal Christians of various denominations, although this had not prevented them from attempting to jail or murder one another.[1] Their clear spiritual superior was Bishop Abel Muzorewa, the head of the Rhodesian United Methodist Church, who attempted to confirm his status by using terms such as 'the forces of Satan' to describe the Smith regime. It was clear, though, that the forces of light were not on the Bishop's side at Geneva. He had made the mistake of beginning the Conference with a demand for a referendum to

[1] One of Nkomo's chief delegates at Geneva, Mr Jason Mayo, was killed by a parcel bomb in Lusaka five weeks after the Conference adjourned.

choose a new Prime Minister. Since the only African newspapers permitted by Smith in Rhodesia enthusiastically support Muzorewa, and his popular support is correspondingly large, this initiative was roundly condemned as merely 'silly' by other delegates. Nkomo, indeed, wounded by the Bishop's usurpation of his old electoral power, told him to 'stick to his prayers and leave politics to the politicians'. Thereafter Muzorewa made as little impact on the Conference as did his fellow clergyman, the Rev. Ndabaningi Sithole, for all that the latter had his own motley crew of forty delegates.

Towards the end of the Conference Muzorewa was increasingly abandoned by his delegates, who felt the strong gravitational pull of the Mugabe camp. This applied even to several of the divines in the Muzorewa camp, including the wonderfully named Rev. Canaan Banana. At this point a good deal of un-Christian but penetrating commentary was heard from the Conference clergy. The Rev. Banana described Muzorewa as 'irrelevant' and 'gullible' and gratuitously added that the Patriotic Front, which he was now joining, would have no time for Nkomo after the Conference; and that, as for Sithole, none of the delegates took him seriously. Sithole replied, perhaps with the hotel fire incident or ZANU's black American delegates in mind, that a number of Mugabe's delegates were known to have CIA links. Muzorewa added fuel to this fire by labelling one of his deserters to Mugabe a 'security risk'. The Rev. Banana he described as a 'political prostitute'.

At one stage the Zimbabwe guerrillas, commenting on the Conference over Mozambique radio, declared that 'The Kissinger circus is over. The Kissinger joke is about to begin.' The judgment — very much the same as that passed by Smith's regime — seemed not unjustified, given the verbal antics of the delegates. But the Conference also had an extensive fringe of silent, shadowy, and altogether more powerful actors. These generally emerged into discussion when the all-consuming question of the delegates' huge hotel bills arose, as it very frequently did, and prompted endless gossip as to which delegation was in whose pocket. The delegates had early on complained to Mr. Richard about their allowances of £50 per head for nine delegates each. All delegations had many more than nine members and £50 a day did not go far in Geneva. An embarrassed Mr. Richard pointed out that his own allowance was even less, a suggestion apparently borne out by his habit of eating in lowly bistros. Muzorewa warned that he might have to leave the Conference because he could not 'eat grass'. He was later reported to be in negotiation with the Dutch government

on the matter, and the Swedish and Norwegian governments
agreed to help out. Ghana, Mozambique and a few other
African governments were also reported to be making contributions. Not all the potential donors were from the public
sector. A Moral Rearmament team attempted, at least, to make
a deal with the guerrillas. The Vatican, no less, was rumoured to
have proved solicitous of the needs of the Conference's leading
Catholic, Mr Mugabe. Certainly, when the Mugabe delegation,
forced to move to a cheaper hotel, found themselves some
£5000 short on the bill for their first fortnight, an anonymous
donor stepped in to pay the difference with a single cheque.
Undoubtedly, though, the central figure of such gossip was
Mr 'Tiny' Rowland, the former Paddington station porter whose
entrepreneurial career had started from the modest beginnings
of a farm in Rhodesia and had culminated in his dominance
over the giant multi-national, Lonrho. Rowland, attacked by
Mr Heath, the British Prime Minister, in 1973 as exemplifying
the 'unacceptable face of capitalism' was currently under
investigation by the Public Prosecutor in London for the alleged
irregularities of his company's dealings. This event had not
caused the legendary Rowland to break stride in his regular, if
mysterious, trips in his private aeroplane around his Middle
Eastern and African business empire. This empire, it was widely
bruited, had been built on an elaborate structure of favours to
and contacts with all manner of Third World politicians.
Rowland had affably brushed aside the torrents of criticism
aimed at his head and in 1976 had guided Lonrho to a turnover
of over £1 billion, a figure achieved with such speed that it
seemed likely that Lonrho would soon soar into the rarefied
league of the oil giants.[1] Now Rowland was reported to have
made several trips to Geneva. Early on the Nkomo delegation
had alleged that there was a Lonrho plot afoot to install
Muzorewa in power in Rhodesia, and the Zambians (who might
be thought to know) repeated this charge. But it was Nkomo
himself who was most widely reputed to be 'Lonrho's man' (the

[1] Lonrho (originally the London and Rhodesia Mining and Land Company)
is a classic of the conglomerate species. By the end of 1976 it controlled
620 companies and was still acquiring more. Its interests range from
soft-drinks to gold mines, from Château Lafitte vineyards to the patent on
the Wankel rotary engine. It is also involved in textiles, construction,
insurance, publishing, agriculture, general trading and transport (where its
interests include the engagingly titled Watergate Steam Shipping Co.).
Lonrho is considerably larger than life and has recently attracted an
unofficial biography — see S. Cronje, M. Ling, and G. Cronje, *Lonrho.
Portrait of a Multinational* (London, 1976).

two versions are not mutually exclusive), and certainly the
Nkomo delegates lived in great style at the Intercontinental,
Geneva's most expensive hotel, while some of Mugabe's
delegates could not afford taxis to the Conference and were
taking the bus instead. All such gossip was, of course,
inconclusive. In any case, as one visiting American politician
bitterly complained, 'the trouble is, African politicians can't be
bought. But there sure are a lot of them up for rent'.[1]

The most important American in Geneva, Dr Kissinger's
envoy Mr William Schaufele, was not in the habit of giving
interviews, however. An Africanist veteran at the State Department, Schaufele had been continuously at the heart of southern
African affairs in 1976 and had laid the groundwork for
Kissinger's shuttle diplomacy there. At Geneva he sat in only on
secret sessions and was frequently closeted with Richard. He
was only an 'observer' and was virtually invisible to the Press;
but he was the key figure of the Conference, particularly since
it seemed clear that he would retain his role under Mr Cyrus
Vance, Kissinger's successor. The change of government in
Washington also lent significance to the visit to Geneva of
Senator Dick Clark, Chairman of the Senate African Affairs
sub-committee, and of Congressman Charles Diggs, chairman of
the analogous House committee and a leading figure in
Washington's 'black caucus'. Both men had strong links with the
new president and may even have carried messages from him to
Geneva before moving on to tours of southern Africa. In
Dar-es-Salaam Diggs voiced the opinion that, in the event of the
Geneva talks failing, the Rhodesian regime could hold out for
only eighteen months against the guerrillas — or twelve if the
latter received large-scale Cuban help. This was an interesting
estimate, since Diggs had been briefed by US intelligence
officials whose opinion it clearly reflected.

Any remaining air of realism at the Conference was much
diminished by the fact that its most significant voices were
those of these off-stage prompters. In this group, too, must be
included in particular the Mozambiquans, Sr Oscar Monteiro
(Minister of State to President Machel) and Sr Joaquim
Chissano (the Foreign Minister), who were clearly in a position
of great authority with the Patriotic Front leaders. To them one
could add Sr Eduardo dos Santos, the Angolan Foreign
Minister, Mr Salim Salim, Tanzania's UN Ambassador, Mr

---

[1] Quoted by X. Smiley, 'An Imperial Mess', *The Spectator* (London),
30 Oct. 1976. Smiley's articles stand head and shoulders above the rest of
the Conference's extensive press coverage.

Mark Chona, special adviser to President Kaunda of Zambia
and — more doubtfully — Sir Harold Walter, Foreign Minister of
Mauritius.

All this enormous concentration of diplomatic attention in
Geneva was justified by the presence there of the Zimbabwe
guerrilla representatives. Dr Kissinger, on his African shuttle,
had not bothered to meet any of the Zimbabwe African leaders.
They had had no part in the bargain he had struck in Pretoria,
first with Vorster, and then with Smith. It was an extraordinary
omission, for Kissinger had been engaged in promising what the
Africans alone could deliver. Their willingness and ability to
'deliver', and this was the pivot of the entire Conference, rested
upon their relationship — whether real or merely claimed,
nobody knew — with the guerrilla forces on or inside
Rhodesia's borders.

In December 1975 there had been only about 50 guerrillas
operating inside Rhodesia; in February 1976 another 800
entered from Mozambique; thereafter successive waves in May,
October and December had brought the number to perhaps
2000, a ragged little army composed mainly of teenagers. So
critical was the balance of power in southern Africa that this
force — and what it might become — occupied a central position
in the minds of all the Great and many of the minor Powers. It
was this which made Rex Nhongo[1] — a former Salisbury hotel
waiter, aged 28, and of little education — the centre of
attention in Geneva; it was this which gave Mugabe his key
position at the Conference; it was this which led Sithole and
Muzorewa to make continual claims to the allegiances of the
guerrillas; it was this which had forced Nkomo, the father of
Zimbabwe nationalism, to become the dependent ally of the
'unknown' Mugabe.[2]

It was a surreal situation and it was certainly a surreal

[1] In April 1977 Nhongo's murder by poison was widely (though incorrectly)
reported — not the first time that premature 'news' of his violent decease
had appeared.
[2] Nkomo, alone of the Geneva leaders, could make no claim to have his
'own' guerrillas. He and his party, ZAPU, had begun to remedy this
deficiency by launching a series of raids into Rhodesia, from October 1976
on, for military recruits. At the end of January 1977 ZAPU led away 400
schoolchildren into Botswana on one of these military shopping expedi-
tions. Interpretations of this recruiting process, with its clear echoes of
both hijacking and the supermarket, naturally differ. However voluntarily
the recruits left, there was undoubtedly an element of competitive
ambition and sheer acquisition about the raids. The desperation of the
African elites not to be left behind in the race to inherit the new
Zimbabwe is not to be lightly ignored.

Conference. There was even a surreal note to many of the news items which flowed in as the Conference proceeded. President Seretse Khama, one of the 'front-line' leaders, had heart trouble and was receiving treatment in — of all places — Johannesburg General Hospital. President Bokassa of the Central African Republic had declared himself Emperor and had ordered a crown from a Parisian jeweller. It was unclear whether this move would alter his position of (verbal) support for the Zimbabwe guerrillas through the OAU. He was a recipient of both Russian and South African aid.

From Peking came a continual series of revelations of byzantine palace intrigues. This was, potentially, important news for ZANU and the Mozambique government, both of whom relied to a considerable extent on Chinese aid. South Africa, too, had an interest. Pretoria had found herself briefly in alliance with Peking in their joint support of Holden Roberto's FNLA in Angola, and since then leading South African bankers and even the Interior Minister, Dr Connie Mulder, had made no secret of their hopes for closer political and business links with Mao's successors. President Amin of Uganda reiterated his support for the Zimbabwe guerrillas, declared himself King of Scotland, and voiced admiration for Mr Enoch Powell. In London, Sir Harold Wilson, the former premier and veteran of many previous abortive talks over Rhodesia, had just published a book in which he found himself all but overwhelmed by his own achievements.

News of other conferences came in. At Turnhalle, it seemed that South Africa was moving towards a settlement with Namibian conservatives which would entirely exclude SWAPO. In London an IMF team (led by Mr Alan Whittome, who had negotiated a tough loan to South Africa earlier in the year) was locked in similar talks to settle, for the time being, the fate of the British government. Unlike the Geneva delegates, Whittome and his men gave no interviews and booked into hotels under assumed names. International bankers were also locked in negotiation with President Mobutu over Zaire's impending default on its enormous debts. The result could not but bind Zaire more tightly to the West and thus increase Angola's difficulties on its northern border. On the other hand the moguls of OPEC had begun to congregate in Qatar to dictate a new world oil price which could not but have beneficent consequences for Angola, a major producer, and weaken import-dependent South Africa and Rhodesia on its southern borders.

It was a measure of southern Africa's highly integrated position within the world economy, indeed, which made the news of commodity price trends quite as important as anything said at Geneva. The soaring coffee price was good news for Angola. Provided the frost damage to the Brazilian crop proved reasonably lasting the MPLA regime in Luanda stood to make a killing in the market. The copper price continued low, thus keeping the economies of both Zaire and Zambia on the ropes and restricting their influence in the drama unfolding to the south. The tobacco and chrome prices brought little cheer to Rhodesia, particularly with the news of moves in the US Congress to repeal the Byrd amendment (which had legitimised American sanctions-breaking over Rhodesian chrome). The Russians had announced a record grain crop. This was excellent news for South Africa: for a bad harvest there would undoubtedly have necessitated fresh Soviet grain purchases from the USA; these in turn would have necessitated further Russian gold sales, driving down the gold price. As it was, the gold price, all important to South Africa, was showing steady improvement. Particularly interesting in this regard was the news that the Oman Central Bank had been among the successful bidders at the recent IMF gold auction. Did this presage a general Middle Eastern movement of funds into gold? If so, the gold price would soar, making South Africa effectively invulnerable to all outside pressure. Lonhro had what had been gracefully described as 'the management contract for the economy of Oman'. Was 'Tiny' Rowland using his influence there to back yet another South African horse? The answer, it transpired, was merely that Oman had decided to move, monetarily speaking, into the nineteenth century, selling off as silver scrap the Maria Theresa dollars formerly held to back the currency, replacing them with gold. . . .

Inevitably, though, the news which made the greatest impact in Geneva was the flow of military reports from southern Africa. From Rhodesia came reports of intense guerrilla activity. The Conference had been accompanied by a steep increase in casualties on both sides. Some 2600 guerrillas had been killed since the start of the war in Rhodesia, and an unknown further number in Rhodesian raids into Mozambique. The losses of the Rhodesian security forces were mounting fast towards 200. The security forces were, of course, by no means wholly Rhodesian, for large numbers of American Vietnam veterans, Britons, Australasians and South Americans were enrolled with them. These were certainly needed, for the Rhodesian whites, under the stress of the war, had begun to

dribble away — in 1976 the white population fell by 7000.[1]
Meanwhile the guerrilla war had escalated, since June 1976, into
a full-scale border war between Rhodesia and Mozambique,
with the full battery of conventional weaponry increasingly
openly used.[2] Confused reports from inside Mozambique told
of fighting between the various guerrilla factions leading to
frictions between them and the regular FRELIMO forces.
Clearly the whole of southern Mozambique was now involved in
something approaching military anarchy, with Rhodesian army
units, notably the Selous Scouts[3] and Grey's Scouts,[4] penetrating as far as 60 miles into Mozambique.

Reports from further west made mention of increasing
guerrilla incursions into Rhodesia from both Zambia and
Botswana, with a corresponding increase of tension between
regular troops along both borders (and with actual exchanges of
fire across the Zambian border). Inside Botswana the ZAPU
headquarters in Francistown (32 miles from the Rhodesian

---

[1] The Rhodesian Army's principal Recruiting Officer, Major Nick
Lamprecht, indignantly denied any suggestion that mercenaries were being
recruited — foreigners were paid only the normal Army wage. Nonetheless,
the Army's position is hardly easy (Major Lamprecht's own son, Vincent,
is one of many young Rhodesian whites to have fled the country to
avoid military service). The Army is in no position to be choosy amongst
the human flotsam and jetsam which rallies to its cause. One of the first
foreigners to be killed in action, in November 1976, was a Canadian,
Matthew Lamb. Inquiries revealed that he had escaped a charge of double
murder in Canada in 1967 only by being declared criminally insane.

[2] Rhodesia had for several months maintained a tight-lipped front in the
face of reports of Rhodesian air raids into Mozambique. On November 24
Salisbury admitted to damage inflicted on its planes involved in strikes
inside Mozambique. With R.A.F. Hawker Hunters performing victory rolls
over Umtali as they returned westwards the air war was hardly a secret
now. Moreover, four large military air-bases were now under construction
in Rhodesia — with, rumour had it, CIA help.

[3] Named after the trader, hunter and explorer, Frederick Courtenay
Selous, whose career carried many ironic echoes for the contemporary
period. A close colleague of Jameson and Rhodes, he was sent by the latter
to take over Matabeleland in 1890 at the head of a small contingent of
British South Africa Company police, defeating a Portuguese force sent
from Mozambique to stop them. In 1891, leading the Pioneer Column, he
annexed Mashonaland in the same way. In 1896 he acted with great
ferocity to help put down the Matabele rebellion. Invited to Washington by
Theodore Roosevelt, Selous became the President's frequent companion
on big game hunting trips all over the world. The Selous Scouts are a crack
commando unit, somewhat reminiscent of the US Green Berets, several
of whose veterans serve with the Scouts.

[4] Named after George Grey, leader of a cavalry unit against the Matabele
rebellion. The Scouts are a horse-mounted infantry unit of surprising
effectiveness. Every polo team in Rhodesia is represented in their ranks.

border) were blown up by suitcase bombs. ZAPU blamed the
Rhodesians, who blamed rivalries within the nationalist camp
for the incident. Some plausibility, at least, was lent to the
latter interpretation by reports of gang violence in the Salisbury
townships between the partisans of Nkomo and Muzorewa.
From Angola came fragmentary reports of continued fighting
between the MPLA and UNITA in southern Angola, with strong
suggestions of Cuban and South African involvement respectively. Floods of refugees from the area were pouring into
Namibia, Zambia and Botswana. From the north came reports
of increasing tension along the Angolan border with Zaire and
claims by the Luanda regime that President Mobutu had
re-opened a training camp for FNLA guerrillas. Another
two-fronted Angolan civil war appeared in prospect. From
Namibia came reports of clashes between SWAPO guerrillas and
South African security units. From Zaire and Zambia came
reports of mounting economic difficulties, as the cutting of the
Rhodesian and Benguela railway lines (by ZIPA and UNITA
guerrillas respectively) produced large pile-ups of copper
exports unable to gain shipment. Kinshasa, the Zaire capital,
was now dependent for its food supply on food air-lifted by
South Africa — on terms of generous credit.

Finally, from the great heartland of the White South, South
Africa itself, came continuous reports of the African unrest
which had irrupted in Soweto in June 1976, had triggered
large-scale disturbances in the rest of the country, and still
showed little sign of real abatement. By early December the
best unofficial estimates put the number of deaths since June at
370 and the number of arrests at around 5000, with both totals
still mounting. After a few initial concessions Pretoria had
launched a massive police campaign aimed at the elimination of
all the signs and symptoms, if not the causes, of African unrest.
Several thousand Africans, mainly students, had fled from the
onslaught to Botswana and Swaziland. There seemed no reason
to doubt their potential as future guerrillas in the struggle for
Azania, as South Africa is now called by the liberation
movement. The government, for its part, was pushing ahead
with its Bantustan policy.

When the Transkei, the first Bantustan, acceded to independence on 26 October some 50,000 of its citizens had fled across
its borders to escape their new freedom. They were now
camped along the Transkei border in wretched refugee camps in
which, according to conservative medical estimates, 100 babies
were dying every month. How many of those who survived
would one day wear the tattered battle-jacket of the guerrilla?

In the latter half of 1976 key elements of the South African ANC and Communist Party had transferred their base of operations to Maputo in Mozambique, only a few hundred miles up the coast from Durban, South Africa's third city. At the end of November the first four ANC guerrillas, infiltrating at the junction of the Swaziland and Mozambique borders, inflicted casualties on the South African police. A vast manhunt by land and air was launched, without success.

The whole sub-continent was clearly at ignition point. From the borders of Zaire and Angola in the west to Mozambique in the east and to Cape Town in the south came reports of armed violence and unrest. The volcano had not yet erupted; these were merely its advance tremors. But already the colossal proportions of the explosion it might produce were clear. The life and future of the whole southern African region are densely, intricately, and often confusingly inter-connected. Undeniably at the centre of this structure stands South Africa. Even the legendary Dr Kissinger could not bring Rhodesia to the Geneva Conference. Only South Africa could do that, and only South Africa could have forced it to a successful conclusion. South Africa holds the key to Rhodesia, and to much else besides. The economic and military power of its White Establishment means that in Africa as a whole all roads lead, sooner or later, to Pretoria. Beyond even that, South Africa occupies a critical position in the whole Western strategic and economic order.

White South Africa now stands under heavy and increasing pressure. The entire structure of social and political power in South Africa is under stress, utterly taut. Cracks within it have clearly developed. These *may* be contained. If not, if they grow, if the whole structure is brought down, then the consequences are almost incalculable. To ponder the fall of South Africa's White Establishment is to think about the unthinkable. There are, simply, few larger questions one can ask than whether — or how long — White South Africa can survive.

This book is an immodest attempt to ask that question. This it seeks to do by taking account of how South Africa — and southern Africa — has arrived at the present conjuncture. This in turn requires a consideration of the international environment within which South Africa exists and by which she is critically affected. This is worth stressing. In most of the enormous literature on South Africa there is a strong tendency, in which left-wing radicals and Afrikaner Nationalists are at one, to depict South Africa's development as if it were dictated solely by the internal dynamics of her own history. This

assumption is false at least for the whole period since white
settlement in South Africa began in 1652. This is not to deny
the importance of the 'internal dynamics' of the situation, and
these too require our consideration. Black, Indian, Coloured,
and White South Africans will make their own history — there is
no denying that. But they will not make it entirely on their own
terms, nor can they determine the whole of the context and
conditions which will affect and even 'cause' their own actions.
To put our point at its crudest, it is most unlikely that South
Africa's future will be settled by a conference in Geneva. She is
no minor state — like Rhodesia — to be bargained over by
interested third parties. But her future is more likely than not
to be influenced rather significantly by the dealings on the gold
bullion market in Zurich. Moreover, the influence of external
developments on South Africa — or, to put it another way, the
importance of South Africa's integration into a world political
and economic order — has increased and will increase. Thus
while it is possible to give an account of South Africa's last
great crisis — that surrounding the Sharpeville shootings of
1960 — which largely ignores the external context, this is
simply not possible for the South African crisis of 1976.

The most striking feature of the demise of white South
Africa — one too easily forgotten in 1977 — is that it has
constantly been prophesied and that it has not come about. The
opponents of the Pretoria regime have continuously underesti-
mated its formidable resilience and strength, and their wrong
guesses have cost many lives. Our account must, therefore, start
with the Sharpeville crisis of 1960 and the White Establishment's
remarkable recovery from it.

1   The Sharpeville Crisis and the Defeat of Revolution

On 21 March 1960 a crowd of some 10,000 Africans from the Sharpeville location (near Vereeniging, Transvaal) gathered in a noisy demonstration, organised by the PAC, against the South African pass laws. The local detachment of white police panicked and fired into the crowd. When their volleys ceased 67 Africans lay dead and 186 were injured. South Africa's greatest crisis since the Rand revolt of 1922 had begun. The country was gripped by a spreading wave of African strikes, riots and demonstrations. There was more shooting, more deaths. Anyone who lived through the period will not forget the great crowds of stick-waving Africans billowing forth from the locations, like long swarms of angry hornets; the smoke spiralling up from the overturned and burning buses; the Saracen armoured cars rumbling menacingly towards the sound of tumult; the fear and the wild reports, the sheer anger and sheer confusion on all sides. Everyone — black or white — had their own 'story' of Sharpeville and the Emergency which followed.

As events recede into the past they often receive a new — and sometimes spurious — historical dignity. To compare recent events with them becomes strangely sacrilegious, not only in the eyes of those who lived through the brave days and tragic hours of that history themselves.

As time advances further, great events come to support not only myths and political folk-memories, but schools of thought, reputations and careers. Great tragedies and wild tumults alike may be canonised in careful doctoral theses, embalmed in learned journals. We lose the past and are in awe of it.

It takes, then, a certain boldness to suggest that Sharpeville was in many ways comparable with the Russian revolution of 1905. As South Africa entered 1960 it appeared that its Nationalist government had confounded the liberal prophets of doom as thoroughly as Count Witte had once done. For, after the Nationalist victory of 1948 there had been no shortage of voices warning that repressive and authoritarian regimes could

not afford to ride roughshod over the seething discontents of
the helot masses. In South Africa such voices came, pre
eminently, from the tiny (and mainly white) Liberal Party and
from the principal black organisations, the PAC and ANC.[1] The
Africans, they argued, were (like the Russians peasants) treated
little better than slaves, for all the legal fact of emancipation.
South African liberals, like the Russian liberals aghast at the
breaking up of the *mir*, argued that apartheid and the
Bantustans policy would produce an intolerable dislocation of
African social life, and was bound to be economically counter-
productive. Instead, the decade of the 1950s had seen steady
economic growth at an average annual rate of 5%. Foreign
capital had continued to flow in, as had all the foreign (white)
immigrants the government would allow. Such African protest
as there was (the Defiance Campaign, the Bus Boycott) had
annoyed the government but not seriously troubled it. The
government's critics never doubted the moral force of their
criticisms but their predictions of fearful events to come wore
rather thin and vague. Sharpeville was as much a shock to them
as to the government. Indeed, Sharpeville took even the black
opposition groups (the ANC and PAC) by surprise; no less than
1905, when it came, had caught the Russian revolutionaries
unawares.

    In both cases the trouble began with firing upon an unarmed
crowd by the centrally unauthorised command of local government forces. The massive and spontaneous expression of
popular anger and discontent which followed largely by-passed
the unready revolutionary organisations. The ANC and PAC had

---

[1] The ANC was the senior nationalist party on the African continent,
having been founded in 1912. It had a long history of peaceful and
unsuccessful petitioning. From 1952 on it was headed by Chief
Albert Luthuli, a Congregationalist preacher and former teacher. With
the ANC must be bracketed its partners in the Congress Alliance,
which dates from 1955 and which bound together in support of the
common programme expressed in the Freedom Charter: the Coloured
People's Congress, the Indian Congress and the (white) Congress of
Democrats. This last was a front for the Communist Party of South Africa
(CPSA) after the outlawing of the Party in 1950. All of this opposition
must be classed as liberal, if not reformist. The Freedom Charter was a
document for liberal revolution drafted in the spirit of 1776 and 1789, not
of 1917. The CPSA's decision to adhere to the Congress Alliance thus
meant that no independent focus existed to provide a socialist or marxist
perspective on South African affairs. The PAC, under the leadership of
Robert Sobukwe, another ex-teacher, had split from the ANC in 1959 over
the issue of the 'dominance' within it of white communists. It remained
fiercely anti-communist but contracted an informal alliance with the white
leaders of the Liberal Party.

made no plans for such an event, any more than Lenin had prepared to exploit the opening suddenly offered by the hapless Father Gapon. The result, in both cases, was that extraordinary 'chances' were missed. All over rural South Africa small and even medium-sized towns were suddenly denuded of their police, who were rushed to the urban centres. In almost no case did local Africans attempt to exploit the vacuum thus created in the countryside, Even in the large towns the movement was virtually leaderless. In Cape Town, in the biggest demonstration of the disturbances, perhaps 100,000 Africans marched to the city centre. The police, unnerved, produced several PAC leaders and the leading white radical, Patrick Duncan, to address them. They, perhaps oddly, advised the crowd to return to their locations. The crowd, after an initial display of derision, even more extraordinarily did what had been suggested. Only with the benefit of hindsight was it possible to see that this represented the passing of the most threatening moment of the disturbances. The Nationalist regime — and all white South Africa — underwent a severe crisis of confidence. The hated pass laws were suspended and leading voices suggested fundamental reform — Paul Sauer, the acting Prime Minister no less,[1] announced that 'the old book of South African history was closed at Sharpeville'. To his left the new Progressive Party, a fairly pure analogue of the Russian Cadets, suddenly acquired a wholly new significance. Further left still, the ANC, PAC and the Communist Party all felt their hour had struck.

It was not to be. The wave passed. Promises and concessions were reneged upon. The government soon re-imposed the pass laws, just as the Czar had disposed of the Duma. The ANC and PAC were banned, and the work of repression began. The fact was — in South Africa in 1960, as in Russia in 1905 — that the police and military power of the state machine was intact. Bloemfontein still had its garrison, like St Petersburg before it. The grievances which had fired the movement of mass protest all remained but the movement itself, its energy largely spent, faltered and then collapsed under the increasing pressure of the forces of law and order. Only in the remoteness of Pondoland did a movement of peasant revolt continue, and this too was thoroughly crushed by 1961.

[1] Sauer, the Minister of Lands, stepped into the breach when Verwoerd was shot, 19 days after Sharpeville, by an English-speaking farmer, David Pratt. Verwoerd recovered; Pratt was committed to an asylum where he 'hanged himself'; Sauer was not forgiven his incautious hint of liberalism and was rewarded with the deepest political obscurity thereafter.

This left South African revolutionaries in much the same
position as their Russian counterparts in 1906. They re-lived the
heady days of the year before and were loath to believe they
had ended. But now, to survive, their organisations had to go
underground. Ahead lay a period of police repression and mass
quiescence. The best they could hope for was to keep their
organisations intact and be better prepared 'next time'.

It is at this point, however, that parallels between the Russian
and South African situations end. For the South African
revolutionaries now launched upon an ill-judged campaign of
sabotage; the PAC under the guise of 'Poqo', the ANC and
Communists in 'Umkhonto we Sizwe' ('The Spear of the
Nation'), and extreme white liberals in the African Resistance
Movement. In all cases the belief was strong that the era of
non-violent resistance was over, that it had been morally
discredited by Sharpeville. And so activists who had been
schooled in an era of peaceful protest and open organisation now
attempted the hopeless task of turning themselves overnight
into security-conscious underground saboteurs. As if not fully
believing that it had now turned to violent means, Umkhonto
(by far the most significant of the movements) planted its
bombs with careful regard for human life — the only lives taken
by bombs were those of tragically unfortunate civilians in an
explosion at Johannesburg station perpetrated by the (liberal)
ARM.

The campaign of all three movements did virtually no
damage. A Nationalist newspaper office was blown up, a
number of sugar plantations burnt. The real damage was that
done to the revolutionary organisations themselves which were
decimated by the unsurprisingly ferocious reaction of the
police. The government's security forces were launched by
Mr Vorster, the Minister of Justice, on a campaign of mass
repression which was entirely new both in its amplitude and its
sheer ruthlessness. (It was from this period on that reports of
torture in South African prisons became quite routine.) Into
the police net were gathered not only the saboteurs but a wide
penumbra of suspected radicals beyond them. A large number
of often brave and talented lives were, to no end, extinguished
or ruined. The net effect was to eliminate white radicals
almost as a species, and to dispossess the Africans of virtually
the whole of their established leadership. June 1963 provides a
major landmark in South African political history, for it was
then that the police rounded up almost the entire leadership of
the ANC and the Communist Party in a single swoop at Rivonia
(Johannesburg). After Rivonia only a (well-publicised)
mopping-up operation remained. A great many liberals and

radicals eased the process by choosing voluntary exile. Perhaps the main achievement of the sabotage campaign was to promote the political career of Vorster, who emerged as the heroic strongman of Afrikanerdom, overshadowing Verwoerd himself, long before he succeeded him as Prime Minister in 1966.

The radicals had fundamentally misjudged the situation in the wake of Sharpeville. Even by the time the sabotage campaign began the tide had clearly gone out on the forces of revolt. The righteous outrage which Sharpeville aroused did not produce a new or heightened political insight. It gave the radicals the moral confidence to break with the non-violent past, but not a serious rationale for the tactics they then adopted. Not just liberals, for whom such moral considerations were, indeed, accepted political coinage, but the scientific marxists of the South African Communist Party, threw analysis to the winds and reached for their dynamite.

If the sabotage campaign of the early 1960s still casts a long shadow over the South African Left, it also sheds a revealing light on the ANC—CPSA nexus which continues to provide easily the most significant force in radical opposition to the Pretoria regime. The CPSA has long been joined in an almost symbiotic alliance with the ANC, and the top leadership positions are even today still held by the generation which came of age politically in the Defiance Campaign, and which left the country during or after the sabotage campaign. The ANC, the senior of all African nationalist parties (it was founded in 1912) has long included communists in its ranks but has never been a communist organisation. Indeed, elements within its leadership have recurrently attacked the dominance of the (mainly white) CPSA cadres, producing a number of schisms over the years (most notably that from which the PAC was formed). The irony was that the CPSA was, in many ways, merely an off-shoot of South African white liberalism. In the 1950s it pursued a classically Gandhian campaign of non-violence. But it was only when it turned away from non-violence after Sharpeville that it revealed how deeply impregnated with liberal ideas and reactions it was. The Nationalist government has always argued that its liberal opponents are effectively communists; in fact it has been the other way round.

It is worth pausing to emphasise this point. In 1976 Mr Joe Slovo, the leading white cadre of the CPSA, published an essay[1] on the development of the struggle in South Africa in which the

[1] 'South Africa — No Middle Road', in B. Davidson, J. Slovo, and A. R. Wilkinson, *Southern Africa: The New Politics of Revolution* (London, 1976).

CPSA's justification for its part in the sabotage campaign of the 1960s is summarised.

Sabotage, Slovo admits, was not envisaged as 'an ultimate weapon in people's war', nor as a practical means of bringing crisis and collapse in the enemy camp. Instead, it was necessary for the 'political leadership to place before the people new perspectives which would mark a sharp and open break with the politics of non-violent resistance'; to 'demonstrate that responsibility for the slide towards bloody civil war lay squarely with the regime'; and to provide a 'proving ground for establishing which activists of the existing organisations could make the transition to the new (armed) tactics'; the Umkhonto manifesto itself spoke of the need to 'bring the government and its supporters to their senses before it is too late'. It was, quite plainly, the politics of individualist, liberal machismo, an ethos which has deeper roots in South Africa than almost anywhere. It was also the politics of moral frustration, of 'look-what-you've-made-me-do-now'. Talk of 'bringing the government to its senses before it is too late' suggested, dishonestly, a faith in the reformist potential of the White Establishment which the revolutionaries neither had nor wanted to have, while the 'proving ground' argument bespeaks not merely a cynical instrumentalism towards one's own followers, but also a sort of primitive, locker-room wish to separate the men from the boys. Looking back, Slovo thinks that the movement's mistakes were an overestimation of possible external support (from Ghana? Guinea?); a lack of adequate security sense; and a failure in activity with the masses. All true, doubtless, but this hardly answers the question of why, after their 1905, South African revolutionaries should have adopted the tactics of the *pre*-1905 Russian narodniks and anarchists. Any rank-and-file Bolshevik or Menshevik, let alone Lenin or Plekhanov, would surely have been appalled at such pointless and suicidal tactics.

South African revolutionaries came later to refer to the period after 1963 as the 'post-Rivonia stalemate'. This was a euphemism: the revolution had been routed, not stalemated. Given the inherent strength of the Pretoria regime, the defeat of the radicals was perhaps always inevitable once the crisis moment of Sharpeville had passed. The tactics they chose gave an entirely different dimension to that defeat, however. Many of that generation are still in prison and some have died there. Others, luckier, dropped out of politics altogether, and large numbers fled into exile. The PAC effectively ceased to exist, and the exiles who congregated abroad, mainly in London, consisted almost exclusively of CPSA and ANC activists,

together with a few Liberals. There they devoted themselves to
the Anti-Apartheid Movement (which they effectively took
over) and to planning the South African revolution. Deprived of
their home base they became more dependent on their foreign
well-wishers, a motley band of British and Scandinavian church,
trade union, socialist and liberal groups, together with a few
Eastern European governments.[1]

By the later 1960s the forces of the South African revolution
had become almost wholly a movement in exile. Like most such
movements it was racked by internal quarrels, purges and
personal animosities. It had its share of spies and informers, but
it also leaked information freely of its own accord. Such
weaknesses were probably inevitable, but an even more fundamental weakness of the revolutionary exile movement lay in its
failure to make any fresh intellectual start, or even to assimilate
and analyse the experience of 1960—3.

The period from Sharpeville to Rivonia had posed two great
questions for South African radicals. First, what strategy should
they adopt in a situation where they could no longer operate
openly, and where all their attempts to build a mass organisation or a mass following would be systematically prevented
and crushed? The 'right' answer would probably have been to
lie low and attempt to maintain some presence, perhaps even
some organisation, within the country — rather in the manner
of the Spanish and Portuguese anti-fascists under Franco and
Salazar. After 1960 the radicals had, however, been in no mood
for such unrewarding tactics, with their small returns at great
cost. Instead, they had opted for the cathartic satisfaction of a
banzai charge into the cannon's mouth. The full cost of this
tactic only gradually became clear. The PAC, ANC and CPSA
had all virtually ceased to exist inside South Africa. (The
Liberal Party voted itself out of existence a little later on.)
These movements thus effectively abdicated from any significant role in shaping the burgeoning African movements of the
1970s. This new wave — represented by the 'radical' Bantustan
leader, Chief Buthelezi, the 'Black Consciousness' movement,
the striking black workers, the Soweto students — owed virtually nothing to the revolutionary exiles. Indeed, it seemed
increasingly unlikely that any significant movement *could*
emerge within South Africa which had not ignored the dead
hand of emigré political tutelage.

The second question posed for the radicals by Sharpeville was

[1] The East Germans were of particular importance, financing *Sechaba*, the
ANC journal, which was now produced from East Berlin.

even more fundamental. Even if they could maintain an organisation inside South Africa, what strategy should it adopt to channel and exploit the explosive unrest of urban Africans? Co-ordinated and sustained industrial action by African workers (the traditional answer) was hugely difficult in the absence of trade union organisation. In any case, to be effective such a movement would have to move quickly from an industrial stage to an overtly political one. At this point, it seemed quite clear, the massive demonstrations, riots and displays of street power seen during the Sharpeville period would again constitute the chief and spontaneous form of African mass protest in the South African urban setting. It was quite certain (whatever Pretoria's plans to the contrary) that the number of urban Africans would increase; that the conditions under which they lived would make further mass irruptions inevitable; and that the great and growing cities of South Africa would again provide the eye of the storm. It was also quite clear, after Sharpeville, that the Pretoria regime would be more than a match for such irruptions. It had the police, it had the guns. It had, moreover, an army and air force which it had not needed to use whole-heartedly in 1960. The clear prospect was of more and bigger Sharpevilles in time, with even bloodier defeats for movements of African resistance. With the Soweto riots of 1976 the pattern was, indeed, repeated, with many more lives lost than in 1960. There was still no answer.

It would be unfair to criticise the revolutionary exiles for failing to 'solve' this awful conundrum. There was not much sign, however, that they even examined it. Instead, the movement drifted into an equivocal commitment to rural guerrilla warfare, leaving the more important question of urban political action hanging in the air. There was no suggestion that the drift towards this new tactic was rooted in any fundamental new analysis of the South African situation. More influential was the fact that guerrilla warfare had been tried with some success in other parts of the world: it offered the exiles hope of active participation in a new and dramatic form of struggle, if not from London, at least from Lusaka and Dar-es-Salaam; and it had the surpassing merit of being untried and thus of not having failed. The leadership generation reared in the politics of non-violence and passive resistance were living in the age of Fanon and Guevara; they must needs don the new clothes, however bad the fit seemed. Having experimented with the *narodnik* tactics of sabotage, it was not difficult to entertain *narodnik* dreams of the peasantry.

That they had found no panacea was soon painfully evident

in the disastrously brief SWAPO guerrilla campaign of 1965–
6 in Namibia and the Zimbabwe campaign of 1967–8. Further
demoralisation and damage was inflicted by the publication of
reports contrasting the wretched conditions of ANC guerrilla
trainees in front-line camps with the alleged comfort and
corruption of the globe-trotting leadership-in-exile. These latter
spent much of their time arguing their cause in a liberal rhetoric
to Western audiences.[1] There was no sign that the intellectual
confusion of 1960 had really abated, though the terminology
had changed. There was no sign of any fundamental new
analysis of the fast-changing social and economic structure of
South Africa. Indeed, it was clear that any fresh intellectual
start would have to take place outside the ranks of the
revolutionary movement, and in spite of it. There grew up,
principally in Britain, a whole new school for South African
historiography, often heavily indebted to marxism, but owing
nothing to the CPSA.[2] For the latter responded to its dilemma
by putting up the shutters. It became more defensive, more
bureaucratic, ever more reliant on a narrow and empty
dogmatism. It could not provide any new theoretical approach
for it did not encourage theoretical debate. Had the South
African revolution produced its own Lenin he would undoubtedly have been drummed out of the CPSA. Such was the
measure of the defeat inflicted at Sharpeville and Rivonia. Most
of the radical movement had been destroyed; much of the rest
had been lost in the diaspora of exile; what remained was
deformed.

[1] Again, Slovo's essay provides a good example of this genre. Much heavy
going is made of the principled acceptance of violent tactics. Mr Slovo is
well aware that he is addressing primarily a liberal audience, for whom
such questions of moral posture have a highly protestant importance. It
can hardly be a live issue for him — the CPSA, of which Mr. Slovo is a
leading cadre, endorsed such tactics back in 1961.
[2] This school, which has been influential above all amongst academics
working in Britain, sprang up largely in reaction to the liberal capitalist
view that economic change in South Africa would alone be sufficient to
destroy apartheid, and has attempted to view apartheid and racial
discrimination as pre-determined by, and fundamental to, the operation of
a capitalist system in South Africa. Much of the writing of this school is
found in such journals as *Economy and Society* and the *Journal of
Southern Africa Studies*, but it is also represented in such works as F.
Johnstone, *Race, Class and Gold* and the forthcoming book by M. Legassick,
Capitalism and Segregation in South Africa.

2 The Recovery from Sharpeville and the South African Economic Miracle

Had the repercussions from Sharpeville been confined to what African demonstrators and a few hundred saboteurs could do, there would have been little for the Pretoria regime to worry about. But Sharpeville did immensely more damage than that, for it occasioned a deep crisis of confidence in the White Establishment. Just as, in Stevenson's *Kidnapped*, a sheet of lightning suddenly shows David Balfour that he is ascending a staircase towards a sheer drop, so Sharpeville threw into stark relief the great underlying question of the ultimate survival of white power. Foreign investors, the local business community, and indeed white society as a whole suffered a tremendous blow in confidence and morale. Foreign immigration into South Africa virtually ceased, and there was a sizeable net outflow of English-speaking migrants seeking security abroad, particularly in Australia. The Congo crisis had erupted simultaneously with Sharpeville and the newspapers were full of the slaughter, mayhem and rape which accompanied the birth of this nearest black state to have (at that time) received its independence. It was easy to believe, as many whites did, that the Congo represented what they would have to endure if concessions to Africans were made, and that Sharpeville represented what would happen if they were not. It was the devil or the deep blue sea: it was hardly surprising that some chose the boats. Some of one's acquaintances were queueing at the Union Castle office, others were lining up for recruitment to fight as mercenaries for Tshombe. Fear and uncertainty were general.

Sharpeville also brought a major economic crisis. The Johannesburg Stock Exchange index plummeted and fortunes were lost. Most seriously of all, foreign investors had lost all confidence in South Africa, and the country's reserves fell dangerously, bringing enormous pressure on the currency. It was the most severe financial crisis since 1932. It was also a crisis of a unique sort. True, there had been minor financial crises in 1949, 1954 and 1958. South Africa is heavily

26

dependent on international trade (imports and exports combined generally account for 40% of GNP) and has, in particular, a high import propensity. In virtually every year of its history the country had run a deficit on her balance of payments; but this was normally covered, or more than covered, by the large and regular inflows of foreign capital investment. It was only when the deficits got particularly large (as in the three years above) that trouble ensued. It was this which made the economic crisis of Sharpeville unique, for, after the corrective measures taken in 1958 South Africa actually ran extremely healthy trading *surpluses* in 1959, 1960 and 1961. This was the first time that such a thing had ever been achieved. But the outflow of foreign capital caused by Sharpeville was so enormous that by May 1961 the foreign exchange reserves were down to R153 million — and still falling. The extraordinary result was to force the government to impose stringent hire-purchase, import and foreign exchange controls, despite a large and still growing trading surplus. The economy juddered almost to a halt. The South African economy had, until this point, known almost nothing but growth. In the whole period from 1920 to 1960 the country's GNP had grown at an average real rate of around 4.5%. Even allowing for the rapid growth in population this had meant that per capita incomes had grown 1.8% per annum in the whole period since Union in 1911. The shock, then, was all the greater when in 1960–1 growth came to an almost total halt. The situation for the government was extremely frightening. Sharpeville had not only scared investors about the future of their profits but had set up strong political pressures in the West against the whole idea of 'investment in apartheid'. The simultaneous wave of African independence across the continent could only increase such pressures. Even in 1961 there was still some R1 billion of foreign funds invested in stocks on the Johannesburg Exchange. If this money, too, fled in panic there was almost no bottom to the economic chasm yawning beneath. Even the gold mines, the pillar of stability through the Great Depression, were finding it impossible to attract the foreign investment they needed. Harry Oppenheimer, the chairman of the giant Anglo-American corporation, had to negotiate a $30 million loan from American banks. The young police constables of Sharpeville had killed 'only' 67 Africans, and the firing had lasted less than a minute. A year later it seemed that their volleys had torpedoed the whole economy.

The story of the 1960s is very largely the story of how the White Establishment successfully overcame this legacy of

[handwritten margin note: same as today]

disaster. It is a story of amazing resilience rewarded by almost
total triumph. With only slight initial waverings the government
held the political line — an astonishing achievement given that
Verwoerd, its leader, had been shot and very nearly killed at the
beginning of the crisis. Five months after Sharpeville all signs of
African dissent had been repressed and a taut calm returned.
While foreigners remained fearful of fresh investment, the
haemorrhage of funds abroad was staunched by late 1961.
Emigration ceased and some emigrants even began to trickle
back, often complaining, as only South Africans could, that
there were no servants in Australia. White immigration resumed,
first as a trickle, then as a flood. It had taken the white
population from 1936 to 1960 to grow from 2 to 3 million, but
by 1974 it stood at 4.16 million. The Stock Exchange
recovered, to the huge advantage of the Afrikaans financial
institutions which had rushed in to buy stocks at their
post-Sharpeville lows. Gold mining share dividends tended more
and more to stay at home — in 1917 85% of such dividends had
gone to foreigners, by 1963 only 27% did. The share boom of
the 1960s was so spectacular, indeed, that white South Africans
became stock-market conscious to a degree seen hitherto only
in the America of the 1920s.

The economy rested, after all, on the fundamental strength of
gold and mineral production. First it steadied itself and, from
1963 on, it boomed. The old economic growth rate was
resumed and then far surpassed. Soon only Japan had no need
to envy the South African rate of growth. Despite the disastrous
start to the decade GNP growth over the whole period 1960—70
was a real 5.9%, with per capita incomes rising at an
unprecedented 2.9% per annum. At some point around 1970
white South Africans overtook Californians as the single most
affluent group in the world. Their happy position, moreover,
rested not merely on gold mining and the super-exploitation of
African labour, but on a modernised, highly productive agriculture and an increasingly broad and sophisticated industrial base.
The government's problems were those of success — how to
prevent the incoming flood of foreign capital from generating
an unacceptably high rate of inflation. The South African
economy had come to count in 'world' terms; it had the 18th
largest GNP of any state and, by 1974, had in that sense
surpassed such medium-sized European states as Denmark and
Austria. Moreover by the late 1960s South Africa's imports and
exports had risen to a point where they accounted for well over
half her total GNP. She was now the 15th biggest trading nation
in the world. Attempted economic boycotts orchestrated by

anti-apartheid groups abroad were brushed aside, effortlessly.
The government seized the opportunity provided by its economic miracle to arm itself as never before. The defence budget
rose from $63 million in 1960 to $375 million in 1964, $692
million in 1973, and finally climbed over $1 billion in 1975.
The arms embargo decreed against South Africa by the UN in
1963 made as little impact as had the trade boycott attempts.

Meanwhile South Africa's increasingly skilful propagandists
made not inconsiderable strides in winning back at least some of
the ground lost at Sharpeville. The fact was that while
Sharpeville had exacted a high price, it had — apparently —
bought something very valuable, more than a decade of mass
political quiescence. The repression of tiny radical minorities
was greeted with outrage and horror by liberals inside and
outside the country, as the sheer brutality and lawlessness of
the police became ever more pronounced. But the number of
such radicals was small — at times it seemed that the immense
police *apparat* might run out of opponents to consume (this
never happened) — and there was no mass oppositional activity
to parallel the Defiance Campaigns of the 1950s, let alone the
vehement demonstrations of the early 1960s. Moreover, the
Government pushed doggedly ahead with its Bantustan policies,
the fruits of which began to assume a dubious political
legitimacy. However poverty-stricken, however nonsensical in
political and geographical terms, Bantustans did come to exist.
Africans voted in their elections in large numbers and on a
universal franchise, to the embarrassment of the Progressive
Party whose policies would now actually entail the disen-
franchisement of most African voters.[1] And while Bantustan
leaders were clearly Government creations some, at least, came
to represent something undeniably real. Chief Buthelezi of the
KwaZulu Bantustan was, for one, clearly not a mere puppet.
And nor was 'Zulu national consciousness' entirely a figment of
Pretoria's tribal imagination. Little wonder, then, that the
Government's propagandists abroad enjoyed some success.
Above all, Western business and official circles could be deluged
with a steady flow of statistics evidencing (truthfully) a
wondrous affluence and profitability. So fast was the Republic's
economy growing, it could be pointed out, that the defence

---

[1] The Progressive Party (later the Progressive Reform Party), representing
the extreme left wing of (legal) white policies after the Liberal Party's
demise, favoured a unified and multi-racial franchise, based upon property
and education qualifications comparable to those favoured by nineteenth-
century English conservatives.

budget, though soaring, actually *fell* as a proportion of GNP in
the early 1970s. Politically the impression grew abroad that
what had seemed, in 1960, so sharply etched in black and white
was now a grey and dappled picture.

In a sense South Africa hardly needed to advertise, since the
benefits of trade with and investment in the Republic were
palpably clear to foreigners. Over the period 1958—72 imports
to South Africa climbed 109% by volume, while her exports
(excluding gold) rose by 135%. Total foreign investment in
South Africa, which had reached R3 billion by 1960 and which
had, after Sharpeville, actually fallen slightly by 1963, soared to
over R5.8 billion by 1970 and surpassed R7 billion in 1972.[1]
South Africa offered investors an open and rapidly expanding
capitalist economy, a cornucopia of mineral wealth and almost
unlimited supplies of cheap, non-unionised, super-exploitable
labour. The return on capital was frequently as high as 15—20%
per annum, so that investors could often get the whole of their
money back in only 5 or 6 years. Given all this, investors hardly
cared *what* happened in the sphere of white politics (even
Verwoerd's assassination in 1966 caused no change in the
investment climate). The only fundamental consideration was
that Pretoria should guarantee, if only for the medium-term, the
political quiescence of the blacks. If this could be done — and it
was — then investors could neither afford nor really bear to stay
away. In Vorster, the new premier, they had found their
Stolypin — a man whose ruthlessness in the face of unrest none
could doubt; a tough, intelligent, conservative pragmatist, only
too happy to preside over his country's headlong industrialisation on a swelling tide of foreign investment.

For there was no doubt that it was in this huge flow of
foreign capital that the secret of the South African economic
miracle was to be found. Only 12% of the country's growth was
attributable to the increase in the domestic capital stock, a
further 21% from the increased labour supply and a full 67%
from foreign investment. Of this latter category, virtually the
whole effect (60 of the 67%) came from the transfer of new
technology to South Africa via the medium of foreign capital.[2]
It was technology — whether in the form of jet fighters, nuclear

7% to the $

[1] See J. Suckling, R. Weiss and D. Innes, *Foreign Investment in South
Africa: The Economic Factor* (Study Project on External Investment in
South Africa and Namibia, Papers 5—9, 1975). The author is much
indebted to this invaluable collection.
[2] J. Suckling, 'The Nature and Role of Foreign Investment in South
Africa', in Suckling *et al.*, op. cit., p. 23.

power plants, automobile assembly or television manufacture — which South Africa was, in the last analysis, 'buying' by opening her economy to such massive foreign penetration and rewarding such foreigners so handsomely. This represented a notable change in emphasis in South Africa's economic foreign relations. Over the period 1957—70 intermediate goods fell from 48% to 34% of total South African imports, while capital goods (accounting for the bulk of technological inputs) rose from 30% to a dominant 45%. (Consumer goods accounted for a fairly steady 20%.) It is in South Africa's hunger for access to the advanced technology of the West that the dominant characteristic of the economic miracle of the 1960s is to be found.

The economic miracle of the 1960s had hardly less important consequences for the internal political structure of the South African economy. In part this was because the decade saw the culmination of a major social and economic revolution set afoot by the Nationalist governments of the 1950s.

When the Afrikaner Nationalists had won power in 1948 they had confronted the economic legacies of the Boer War which still burnt so bitterly in their memories. Britain had waged and won this war in order to subjugate the Afrikaner nation, to secure control of the Witwatersrand's wealth and to promote the interests of British settlers in South Africa. Half a century later the South African economy was still in a state of colonial dependency on Britain, and the English-speaking South Africans, a 40% minority of whites, still dominated all the commanding

TABLE 1. *Major Market Shares of South Africa's Imports and Exports (excl. gold) 1962 and 1972* (percentage shares by values)

| | IMPORTS | | EXPORTS | |
	1962	1972	1962	1972
UK	29.6	20.9	33.2	26.4
USA	16.2	16.5	9.9	7.3
Africa	6.8	5.4	15.3	15.1
Japan	4.0	9.5	8.3	12.9
EEC Six	18.3	24.8	21.0	20.0
(of which				
W. Germany)	(10.0)	(14.6)	(5.0)	(6.6)
Other	25.1	22.9	12.3	18.3
TOTAL	100.0	100.0	100.0	100.0

Source: Author's calculations, based on figures provided in Suckling *et al.*, op. cit., Tables 5, 6 and 24.

heights of the economy. It was no accident that the populist
resentment of Afrikaner farmers and poor whites centred, above
all, on the giant Anglo-American Corporation, with its strangle-
hold over the country's mineral wealth. For 'Anglo's' (as it was
tellingly abbreviated) symbolised, in its very name and nature,
the belief of many Afrikaners that 'their' country, and certainly
their economy, was run by a British-led condominium, in which
even the minority shares were held not by Afrikaners but by
Americans and the Johannesburg Jewish community. That this
depiction was ridiculed by the dominant English-language press
made little impression for, of course, the press was owned by
the mining houses too. Truth to tell, the Afrikaner populists
had a fair case which, like their American Populist counterparts
of the 1890s, they weakened with anti-semitism.[1]

Afrikaner Nationalism, having captured the state in 1948,
used its power and patronage in the 1950s to build up a series
of   Afrikaans   financial   institutions — Volkskas,   SANLAM,
SAAMBOU and SANTAM. It provided its poor white supporters with feather-bedded employment in a burgeoning public
sector — in the police, the civil service, the post office and,
above all, on the railways.[2] Similarly, the government shifted
large resources into agriculture, assisting a veritable rural
revolution of modernisation and land concentration to the
enormous enrichment of Afrikaans farmers, who became
agri-businessmen on a massive scale. The beginnings of a new
class of Afrikaner urban businessmen and industrialists began to
emerge, best personified by the pragmatic Anton Rupert,[3] the

---

[1] During the Second World War Afrikaner anti-semitism had found
full-blown expression in the pro-Nazi Ossewa Brandwag organisation. (The
young John Vorster was an O.B. militant and went to jail as a result.)
After the war this strain found milder expression in the exclusion of Jews
from Nationalist Party membership and, inevitably, in attacks on the
(Jewish) Oppenheimer family which controlled Anglo-American, the
totality of South African diamond production and hence also the world
diamond market. Sir Ernest Oppenheimer (formerly a German diamond
clerk) was usually depicted in the Afrikaans press as the be-snouted
'Hoggenheimer' — a capitalist pig who didn't eat pork.
[2] The South African Railways and Harbours (SAR&H) swelled to employ
almost a quarter of a million people, half of them white. As many as 1 in
10 or 12 of the entire white labour force, and perhaps 1 Afrikaans worker
in every 5 or 6 worked for it, admittedly in leisurely fashion.
[3] Rupert, who owns more than 250 factories in 16 countries, was a notably
large contributor to Nationalist Party funds, but often sounded like a
Progressive. During the Sharpeville crisis he held meetings with leading
Liberal and PAC militants. His oft-repeated dictum was that 'If they (the
Africans) don't eat, we don't sleep'. Many black militants claimed that
Rupert did not care enough for his sleep to pay his African workers a
living wage, and boycotted his cigarettes.

magnate of Rembrandt Tobacco, whose Rothmans brand became the world cigarette market leader. All of these trends were to continue at quickened pace in the boom of the 1960s.

Nonetheless, this government-sponsored economic and social revolution was still seriously incomplete in 1960. English-speakers still held sway over most strategic points in the private sector of the economy; more important after over a decade of Nationalist rule, the economy as a whole remained firmly anchored to its Anglo-American moorings. Even in 1960 the sterling area accounted for over 64% of all foreign investment in South Africa, with the dollar area accounting for 20% and all others together only about 15%. Virtually the whole of South Africa's foreign assets were held within the sterling area — principally in the (then) Central African Federation. Britain was overwhelmingly South Africa's most important trading partner. Over the period 1955—66 31.7% of all South African imports came from Britain, as against 18.9% from the USA and 7.1% from elsewhere in Africa. South Africa's exports, in the same period, were even more concentrated, Britain taking 35.5%, Africa 20.7% and the USA 9.1%. There was no sign at all of any diminution in South Africa's dependence on Britain — indeed, the proportion of South African exports taken by Britain had actually *risen* from the level of the previous decade, while the share taken by the EEC bloc had fallen from 32.7% to 24.2%. Most of the African share of South Africa's trade was, moreover, directed towards British colonial Africa, often to subsidiaries of British parent companies. The internal changes in South Africa's political economy had, in other words, taken place within an unchanged external environment of almost neo-colonial economic dependence.

It was a key feature of the South African *Wirtschaftswunder* of the 1960s that the Republic began decisively to break free from this old pattern of economic relations — as Table 1 on p. 31 illustrates.

These figures bear a great deal of examination, for they tell not one but several stories. Over the decade South Africa's import needs became more concentrated on the small group of industrialised capitalist states (the EEC, UK, USA and Japan) willing and able to provide her with advanced technology. This was the more striking given that South Africa's dependence on British imports lessened dramatically, even if Britain remained (by a heavily reduced margin) the Republic's most important export market. At any earlier period one might have guessed that the British connection would have declined only inasmuch as the American 'minority share', and economic links with the rest of Africa, grew in importance. In fact, over this period, both British and American shares in South Africa's trade actually *fell* slightly. This phenomenon was all the more notable in view of the world political pressures which mounted in the sixties against trading with South Africa. One might have expected such pressures to operate most strongly on those states with the smallest original stake in such commerce, and to have least effect on those with the strongest vested interest. Our figures suggest that if such pressures had *any* effect, they operated in a precisely opposite direction.

Two of the chief characteristics of the South African boom of the 1960s were, we have argued, the country's hunger for advanced technology and its determined drive to break free from its old, semi-colonial economic relationships. Concomitant with those two trends was a third of equal significance, namely the forging of powerful new links between South Africa and the ebullient, expanding capitalism of the EEC, and particularly with Germany and France. These new relationships were almost wholly a phenomenon of the 1960s, and they developed with an extraordinary dynamism and rapidity.

1. *The Tokyo Line*

As we have seen, South African trade with Japan also developed rapidly in this period. But the relationship stopped there — South African pig-iron and sugar were swopped for hi-fi sets, Hondas and transistor radios. There were no cultural affinities between the two nations — the Japanese were, after all, only 'honorary whites' — and they had few common political interests. Japan provided the Republic with no arms, and invested little there.

In the six boom years of 1967—72 investment in South Africa from the whole of Asia amounted to only R119 million — and not a little of this probably came from Singapore, Taiwan, South Korea and (especially) Hong Kong. In the same period, by comparison, investment in South Africa from the EEC bloc totalled R1675 million. Japan has maintained no embassy in Pretoria and has tended to side with the Afro-Asian bloc at the UN — a very different attitude from that shown by Paris and Bonn. World reaction to the Kissinger Plan for Rhodesia in 1976 provided a similar comparison. The plan, blessed by Vorster, envisaged large-scale multilateral economic assistance to encourage (or compensate) Rhodesian whites in the face of black majority rule. Bonn and London reacted warmly to the plan; Paris was silent; Tokyo gratuitously announced that Japan could see no conceivable reason to

contribute to a fund for these who had benefitted from white
·racism, as opposed to those who had suffered from it.[1]

2. *The Bonn—Pretoria Axis*

In the 1950s it seemed rather unlikely that West Germany
would emerge as a major trading partner with South Africa. In
the period 1947—54 Germany had provided only 3% of South
Africa's imports and taken only 4.4% of her exports — indeed,
the Federal Republic had ranked well behind both France and
Italy as a market for South African goods. Trade expanded in
the 1950s only to be cut sharply after 1957 with the formation
of the EEC and the erection of fresh tariff obstacles. Despite
this, as we have seen (Table 1), Germany's trade with South
Africa increased by leaps and bounds in the 1960s. The
sophisticated and powerful German economy was, in this
period, rapidly turning the EEC into a German condominium
and achieving a breathtaking economic penetration of Eastern
Europe — Brandt's *Ostpolitik* more than fulfilled old economic
dreams of *Mittel Europa*. Germany was expanding everywhere
and was the ideal source of the high technology capital imports
South Africa wanted. In 1973 Germany actually overtook the
USA to become the second greatest provider of imports. In
1974 — quite staggeringly — she overtook Britain at the top of
the importer's league. Britain's relegation to commercial second
place constituted little less[2] than a new epoch for the South
African economy. At the same time German investment in
South Africa grew at a breathtaking pace, from only R70
million in 1965 to over R1000 million in 1970, and over R1500
million in 1972. In a few short years Germany massively
surpassed the USA, which had been the second largest investor
in South Africa for over half a century. In one sense the
German invasion was even more remarkable than such figures
suggest. For the statistics on foreign investment in South Africa,
showing an enormous British and (until recently) American
dominance, are highly misleading. Analysis of the actual flow of

[1] It is important to draw these distinctions. Much of the (normally anti-
apartheid) literature on foreign trade with and investment in South Africa
tends to draw an undifferentiated picture of world capitalism united in
economic support for apartheid. Such a depiction obscures Pretoria's
special relationship with Paris and Bonn.
[2] Perhaps a little less, since the 1974 figures were much affected by the
miners' strike and 3-day week in Britain. In 1975 Britain (narrowly)
recaptured her leading position in the import table, since when the relative
movements of the Deutschmark and the Pound have probably combined
to retain at least British parity with the Germans.

capital movements into South Africa in the 1961—71 period shows that relatively little new money was coming in from either Britain or the USA: almost all the increase in the investment totals (81% of the British increase, 68% of the USA's) was due to the re-investment of profits generated by their original South African investments.[1] In contrast, virtually all the EEC, and especially German, investments were new. Thus, of the over R2.8 billion which flooded into South Africa from abroad in the 1967—72 period, no less than 59.3% came from the EEC bloc and only 12.1% from the USA and Canada combined.

The importance of the new Bonn—Pretoria axis ran well beyond the sphere of economics, however. German politicians and industrialists were not above invoking elements of a cultural and historical community with South Africa. German settlers had, after all, played an important part in South and South West Africa,[2] and the Kaiser's Germany had supported Kruger in a Teutonic alliance against the British. Siemens, the German electrical giant, has in recent years boasted proudly that it made the telephone used by President Kruger. . . . Such cameraderie, unsurprisingly, falls short of exploring one of the major historical ironies of the situation, namely that the most dramatic phase of development in German—South African relations had coincided exactly with the entry into the Bonn government of the Social Democrats in 1966, and that the SPD's period of majority predominance in government (from 1969 on), far from leading to a contraction of links with South Africa, had seen them expand at a record rate. Two men presided over this booming alliance: John Vorster, whose outspoken support for the Nazis and opposition to the war effort against them had earned him two years in jail; and Willy Brandt (the German Foreign Minister from 1966, the Chancellor from 1969), whose opposition to the Nazis and *their* war effort had earned him exile and the deprivation of his citizenship.

Although Herr Walter Scheel, the Vice-President of the Bundestag (and later Foreign Minister) made an official visit to South Africa in 1969, the political dimension to the new relationship remained shadowy, perhaps conveniently for Bonn,

[1] For these calculations I am indebted to Suckling, op. cit., p. 27.
[2] It was on the image of the pioneering German frontiersman that such evocations centred. There were fewer references to the German Jews who had fled to South Africa. By 1970 Germany had again become South Africa's second largest source of white immigrants — a remarkable fact in the context of the Bonn Republic's prosperity.

by virtue of the fact that neither East nor West Germany was a
UN member before 1973. (Switzerland's considerable economic
links with South Africa remain conveniently shaded in the same
way.) Once at the UN Bonn immediately found herself able to
support less than half (15 out of 33) of the resolutions put on
apartheid and decolonisation in the 1973 (28th) UN session. The
other 18, Bonn announced, she could not support 'as they
justified or implied the use of force, or were in contradiction to
our economic interests'.[1]

The Bonn delegation appeared to be deeply (and naïvely)
wounded by the opprobrium such statements earned her.
Throughout the 1960s and early 1970s Bonn had happily
combined stern warnings to Portugal to end her African wars
with the position of largest arms-supplier to Lisbon.[2] Business
was business, politics was something else. Now Bonn found
herself under greater pressure over her relations with South
Africa which, she angrily asserted, had no military or strategic
dimension.

Nevertheless, in 1974, at the same time as it became clear
that German steel manufacturers had been breaking Rhodesian
sanctions, German journalists were allowed to tour the South
African military communications centre in Simonstown. They
reported, with pride rather than embarrassment, that

> All the data coming in here from all horizons and from
> many sources are processed, analysed, correlated to each
> other and computerized uniquely through the use of German
> technology. From the most sophisticated computer down to
> the radar equipment and to simple telex machines —
> everything is 'Made in Germany'.....[3]

Earlier the same year the South African para-statal, UNECSA
(Uranium Enrichment Corporation of South Africa) had
signed an agreement with STEAG (Steinkohlen-und

---

[1] Cited by F. Ansprenger, 'Germany's Year in Africa' in C. Legum (ed.)
Africa Contemporary Record. Annual Survey and Documents, 1974—75
(London, 1975), p. A58. The ACR is, as always, an invaluable source.
[2] Dr. Erhard Eppler, the SPD left-winger and Minister for Overseas
Development (1968—74) issued such a warning to Portugal at the same
time that the Brandt government was authorising a contract for the
outfitting of an ammunition factory (Explosivos da Trafaria) in Portugal in
1972.
[3] Wilderich Lochow of the German Press Agency, writing in *Frankfurter
Allgemeine Zeitung*, 6 Dec., 1974, and cited by Ansprenger, op. cit.,
p. A58.

Elektrizitaets—AG, Essen) on a joint nuclear power construction programme, though only for 'peaceful purposes'.
Eighteen months later, during the political trial of the Afrikaans
poet, Breyten Breytenbach, a state witness related how Breytenbach had told her that Okhela, the secret organisation[1] of
which he was a member, had broken into a South African
embassy abroad and stolen 'some papers in connection with the
atomic program'. Dr Hilgard Muller, the Foreign Minister,
simultaneously announced that he had ordered an investigation
into the disappearance of a secret file from the South African
embassy in Bonn. The same day (Oct. 1, 1975) in Bonn the
resignation was announced of Lieut.-General Günter Rall as the
German representative on the NATO Military Committee who,
it was disclosed, had made an incognito visit, with the
co-operation of the South African Ambassador in Bonn, to the
atomic energy centre at Pelindaba (Transvaal). The implied
official explanation would thus appear to be that a senior
German military officer, regarded hitherto as a sufficiently good
security risk to be entrusted with NATO secrets, decided to
chance his career by conniving with a foreign power to make a
visit abroad, successfully kept secret from the German security
service and government, there to satisfy an entirely private
passion to inspect a civilian installation of no military significance; and that, finally, when his government accidentally
apprehended what had occurred, it was satisfied by his simple
act of resignation; issued no public rebuke to the foreign power
concerned; nor even asked that its offending diplomat be
recalled. Thus, apparently, the official version. Contrary to the
old adage, fiction is quite normally stranger than truth and the
above may be a case in point.

3. *The French Connection*

The relationship which developed in the 1960s between
South Africa and the other major EEC power, France, was a
curious inversion of the relationship with Germany. The latter,
we have seen, was above all an economic relationship whose
military and political dimensions were discreetly, if unsuccessfully, hidden. The French connection, in contrast, was quite
overtly political and military and had a lesser economic

[1] Okhela, the court was told, was the white wing of the ANC and had been
set up by a group of ANC leaders which included the acting President-
General, Oliver Tambo, in order to fight the influence over the
organisation of the London-based CPSA. Tambo has been the nominally
acting ANC leader since 1963 when Nelson Mandela was seized at Rivonia,
tried, and imprisoned for life on the impregnable Robben Island.

component. In 1964 France had had the third largest stake (5.6%) in foreign investment in South Africa, but by 1966 this had fallen to 5.2%. French investment certainly increased in total value thereafter, but France's proportionate share of foreign investment has probably remained static or even fallen. Similarly, while France remained an important trading partner for South Africa (imports from France quintupled between 1962 and 1972, while exports to her doubled), the general growth in South Africa's commerce actually reduced France's role. In 1962 she provided 2.1% of South Africa's imports, in 1972 3.5%; while the share of South Africa's goods going to France fell from 10.7% in 1947—54 to 3.6% in 1962, to only 2.8% in 1972.

In the light of this unpromising economic background the strengthened political and military links developed between France and South Africa seemed oddly gratuitous and idiosyncratic — terms which, of course, were widely used by critics of other areas of De Gaulle's foreign policy. It was, perhaps, understandable that France should have refused, with only Britain for company, to vote for the UN resolution after Sharpeville condemning apartheid as a possible threat to international security. In 1960, after all, France had reason to believe that the same criteria would be applied to her bitter war in Algeria. But this consideration no longer applied in 1963 when, in the same company, she refused to support the UN arms embargo against South Africa; nor did it apply to the many subsequent occasions when she used her UN vote to protect South Africa from an enraged majority in the General Assembly. When Vorster visited Portugal in 1970, there was speculation as to whether the sheer weight of their South African connections would compel London or Bonn to extend an embarrassed invitation to visit them as well. Both remained silent — but Vorster was received in Paris by the French premier. Given the high political costs of 'dealing with apartheid', the attitude of the French, with their minor economic links with South Africa, seemed supremely irrational.

This impression only deepened if the precise nature of these economic links was examined, for they were apparently designed to incur the maximum political cost for the smallest economic gain. Thus when the French construction industry did make a commitment of capital to South Africa, it was not to reap the easy profits of hotel and office development but in order to assist in two massive projects of strategic value — the tunnel under the Fish River and the Hendryk Verwoerd Dam on the Orange River. As the threat of oil sanctions loomed,

Pretoria cast around for a major oil company with the necessary expertise to help her explore for and refine this most strategic of minerals. CFP (Compagnie Française des Petroles — the French member of the 'Seven Sisters') not only joined Shell and BP in exploration but took a lion's share in the State-owned oil refinery. When Pretoria intimated that it was desirable for foreign firms to allow local participation in their enterprises, CFP sold a large block of shares in its South African subsidiary, Total; not just to any businessmen, but wholly to Volkskas, virtually the private bank of the Nationalist Party and government.

Above all, France sold South Africa arms. When the British Labour government announced in 1964 that it would deliver no further arms to South Africa beyond the Buccaneer jets then on order,[1] France moved in to fill this most sensitive gap of all. Hitherto her total arms sales to Pretoria had consisted of just 7 Alouette II helicopters and a small number of second-hand armoured vehicles. Over the next decade, despite a mounting uproar of criticism from almost every side, France supplied (by 1975) 73 Alouette IIIs, 16 Frelons, 20 Pumas and 9 Transalls (all helicopters), a total of 66 Mirage III fighter-bombers (B, C, D, E and R versions), a large number of Matra, Nord, Milan and Exocet missiles, 4 Daphne and 2 Agosta submarines, and a variety of other equipment. Most strikingly of all, France agreed in 1971 to help set up the Atlas Corporation to build up to 100 Mirage F1-A and 1-C fighters under license in South Africa. This followed the successful Franco—South African joint development of Cactus, a surface-to-air missile system. For such a haul as this Pretoria might well have been willing to pay in blood. As it was, she paid in gold which, as was well known, Gaullists preferred.

What made these deals finally incomprehensible was that France had no apparent plans for a defence alliance with South Africa. No pact was signed, publicly at least, and France began to disengage from her naval base in Djibouti (French Somalia) which would clearly have a pivotal position in any French strategy for the Indian Ocean and East African theatres. South Africa's eager suggestion that France might care to use the Simonstown naval base met a disdainful deaf ear in Paris.

[1] The 16 Buccaneers were the centre of a major political storm in Britain which, in the event, they were hardly worth. By 1973 no less than 6 had crashed and the remaining 10 were permanently grounded. S.A.A.F. pilots preferred the Mirage, and regarded the Buccaneer in the same light that their Luftwaffe counterparts regarded the ill-fated Starfighter.

France had endured the wrath of the UN majority in order to furnish Pretoria with armaments sufficient to make her a significant second-order power in world terms. She had, moreover, greatly assisted Pretoria in its drive towards self-sufficiency in arms production (by the mid-1970s South Africa was able to consider exporting arms herself). She had, like Germany (and before that the USA) helped train South African atomic scientists and place the possibility of nuclear weapon production within South Africa's grasp by 1980. All this France had done for no obvious military reason. It made no apparent sense.

France — or rather De Gaulle and his successors — had, however, an eye to a larger game. If France was to deal equally with the two super-powers, she needed to establish a series of special relationships around the world with major second-ranking powers — not only South Africa, but China, Israel, Pakistan, Brazil and Iran. She intended to bring in the Third World to redress the balance of the Second; even where this required adopting a position on the Left (morally supporting Vietnam against the USA) simultaneously with one on the Right (arms for South Africa). France would develop this string of special relationships by making these secondary powers beholden to her in one way or another. She would not, however, compromise her independence by becoming beholden to them, or getting involved so deeply with them that she could not later extricate herself. French national interest might well dictate that she would want to 'drop' them, and quickly. After 1967 this was what she did in the case of Israel. One day it might be necessary to do the same to South Africa. So while France was happy to sell South Africa Mirages (it made production lines longer and more profitable) and happier still to receive the regular consignments of gold bullion for them, she had no desire to become dependent on South Africa as a market or as a source of imports, let alone commit herself to the horrors of large-scale capital investment with all the long term worries that *they* implied. It was all a matter of balance.

The French had an African policy as well as a world policy. They had not come well out of the scramble for Africa. While Britain had taken the plums — Kenya, Zambia, South Africa, Ghana and Nigeria — France had ended up with a large number of small poor states on the West African littoral and enormous expanses of useless, empty desert. While France gathered her clients to her, like children to a mother's skirt, she needed more than the likes of Senegal, Niger or Dahomey if she were to balance the British, let alone the Russian and American influences now penetrating the continent as well. This, in part, she could do by cultivating the abandoned children of others — Libya and Zaire. But such was the growing power of Nigeria (in French eyes still a British client) that France needed more leverage still. Only one other African power could conceivably 'balance' the new giant of West Africa, and that was South Africa. The realism of such conceptions was questioned by many, their boldness by none.

* * * * * * *

In the 1960s the subtleties and nuances underlying the motivations of South Africa's new partners did not seem very important in the eyes of the White Establishment. South Africans were aware that the ships leaving their shores nowadays made for Japan more now than hitherto, and they grew used to seeing the Mirages rumbling overhead. Far more visible was the flood of foreign imports and, above all, the foreign capital which underwrote the country's frenetic growth.

There was an important new feature to the situation, one which had significant results for the entire political economy. For the South African state had begun to play an increasing role in eliciting and directing these capital inflows. In the figures this showed up not only in the rapidly growing proportion of capital imports raised by the government and directly or indirectly invested by it, but also in the period of private foreign indirect investment. By the early 1970s such investment had, for the first time, actually overtaken private foreign direct investment and, indeed, hugely surpassed it. Much of this indirect investment was being 'organised' by the South African government into state-backed (and even state-owned) economic ventures. The state's determination to play such a role was extremely striking. From 1968 on, indeed, a bizarre sight was to be seen on the international financial markets. The South African government, as if not satisfied by the great wave of foreign investment flooding into the Republic or by a double-digit growth rate, began to knock on banker's doors in the Eurodollar and other markets, seeking loans.

Despite a mounting campaign by anti-apartheid movements abroad against such loans, the Republic had little difficulty in securing them. Indeed, over 40 European, American and British banks formed the European-American Banking Corporation which treated South African loan business as a principal *raison d'être* — providing around one-fifth of all loans to South Africa from 1970 on. Not surprisingly, German and French companies and banking houses were prominent among those lending to or investing in joint ventures with the state. Two examples (both from 1974) may stand for many — the R170 million loan extended by a French banking consortium, headed by the Banque de l'Indochine, to the state shipping company, Safmarine, to buy four French container ships, and the DM140 million loan to the SAR & H by the Berliner-Handelsgesellschaft and Frankfurter Bank for aid in the construction of the R500 million Richards Bay port complex.

The fact was that the capital free market would not, if left to its own devices, finance many of the projects a security-conscious government wanted. It was not merely (though it was partly) that Pretoria had developed a consuming passion for such non-productive goods as missiles, tanks and military aircraft. The government was also intent on a drive for economic self-sufficiency. The concrete results of this drive were to be found in the growing industrial empires of the para-statal corporations.[1] Pretoria, in its utter determination to guarantee the survival of its proudly capitalist economic system, built up a state sector whose size would, in other Western countries, have caused even social democrats to wince. The irony was hardly lost upon the South African business community, particularly its dominant English-speakers, who were not slow to recognise that this vast state economic structure also provided the government with the ideal instrument with which to favour the growth of an Afrikaans business class.

English-speaking whites had, indeed, not one, but many grievances. They resented the continuous symbolic assaults by Afrikaner Christian nationalism on their own liberal imperialist sentiments. They had not wanted a Republic, had been appalled at leaving the Commonwealth and were suspicious of the Teutonic theorising about apartheid. They favoured, rather, a benign, ad hoc paternalism — 'white leadership with justice' as the UP (United Party), which they in the main supported, put it. They treated Africans as did the Afrikaners, lifted their skirts

---

[1] Besides Safmarine and SAR & H, these include South African Airways, ESCOM (electricity), UCOR (uranium), ISCOR (iron and steel), SASOL (oil, coal and gas), ARMSCOR (armaments), SOEKOR (oil exploration), FOSKOR (phosphates), NUFCOR (nuclear fuels), SAICCOR (industrial cellulose), Alusaf (aluminium) and Natref (oil refining). The creation of the para-statal sector has been carried through by the Industrial Development Corporation, which systematically sought out gaps in the Republic's primary and secondary industrial structure and attempted to fill them. The IDC is empowered to guarantee domestic and foreign loans.

from the Coloureds — about whom they felt less humane
concern than did the Afrikaners — and disliked the Indians.
Sharpeville had given many a sufficiently bad fright to cause
them to support the Progressives in the 1961 election, but such
sentiments soon waned. Above all, their grievance was that they
were excluded from political power. The frustration inherent in
this situation was keenly felt by each rising elite of English-
speaking youth. This was particularly true of those from the
great private schools of Michaelhouse, Hilton, Bishop's and St
John's, which 'ought' to have provided the country with its
political elite in the way their more famous English counterparts did. Such milieux recurrently provided recruits and leaders
for NUSAS,[1] the Progressives and, until its dissolution, the
Liberal Party. Their elders retreated into political apathy or
even tried to join the Nationalists on an individual basis.

If English-speakers were irritated, they were hardly angry —
they were making far too much money for that. As the 1960s
boom developed some acquired a schizoid 'Prog-Nat' perspective. Their resentment against the government softened
further still with Vorster's accession to power. Verwoerd had
been impossibly dour, remote and, worse, a theorist. Vorster
was hardly 'their' man, but he chain-smoked, told jokes,
preferred to be called 'John', not 'Johannes', played golf with
Gary Player, and was undoubtedly a formidable leader on every
count. As the economic pace quickened and the boom wore on
English-speakers resembled more and more the liberal middle
classes of Wilhelmine Germany, with Vorster their Bismarck.
They had not chosen *their* Iron Chancellor either and still did
not vote for him. But, almost against their will, they admired
him and revelled in the success he had brought.

At the same time a major split was developing within
Afrikanerdom between the reformist *verligtes* and the more
hard-line *verkramptes*, who finally split away to form the
HNP in 1969. Outwardly the split came largely over the
question of South Africa's detente policy with Black Africa (for
which see Chapter 3), but in fact the split was the inevitable
outcome of the growing social differentiation of the Afrikaans
community. The new and still small elite of Afrikaner businessmen and professionals had little in common with the poor
whites they themselves once had been.[2] They disliked many of

---

[1] National Union of South African Students. This entirely English-speaking
organisation was consistently the most radical legal body in South Africa.
[2] By early 1977 the South African best-seller lists were headed by an
Afrikaans book seeking to prove that South Africa was paving the way to

those who manned the NP (Nationalist Party), seeing them as hacks, opportunists and bigots gorged on success. They were tempted to desert the party but were held within it not only by the traditional cohesion of Afrikanerdom but by the knowledge of their own weakness. For there could be no doubt, despite the HNP's lamentable electoral showing, that the majority of Afrikaners shared the conservatives' sentiments.

Vorster himself realised that the NP could hardly afford to lose the key *verligte* elite and sought to protect them from the ire of the *verkramptes.* The best way to do this was to campaign in strongly *verkrampte* fashion himself against the HNP, which he duly did in the 1970 election. The HNP were trounced, but Vorster's 'black peril' campaign rhetoric so alienated the *verligtes* that many abstained, so that, astonishingly, the UP won six seats from the NP.

The 1970 election provided an exact and fitting conclusion to the miracle sixties. The long-present strains within Afrikanerdom had emerged quite openly. Despite the HNP's poor showing (it won no seats) these strains could only grow. They were caused by a continuing process of social stratification among Afrikaners and thus, ultimately, by the sheer fact of economic growth. And nothing seemed more certain than that this would continue. While it did the government would face little real danger from this flank. Indeed, the government was stronger than ever. It had put down rebellion on both Left and Right. There was little sign of overt African discontent. Internally and externally the state was secure and armed as never before. The decade which had begun as the era of African liberation closed very much as the decade of the White Establishment. It was resilient, rich, and getting richer; not merely defiant, but strong and expanding. For, confident and secure, it had already begun to look well beyond its own borders.

Communism via the over-development of the state and para-statal sector. The popularity among literate Afrikaners of such an attack on the employment milch-cows of poor whites was less a testament to the author's compelling sophistication than to the growing social divisions within Afrikanerdom.

3   From Isolation to Detente - and Failure

The 1960s began disastrously for South Africa externally, as they had domestically. Sharpeville had the same profound effect on world public and governmental opinion that it had on foreign investors. In several Western countries a new post-war liberal political wave had begun to manifest itself in such movements as CND (Campaign for Nuclear Disarmament) in Britain and the civil rights campaign in America. Sharpeville affronted the sensitivities of this younger generation in a way that it would have been quite difficult to equal even by deliberate contrivance. The news photograph depicting South African policemen gazing out over a field of corpses strewn to the horizon was printed and reprinted in the world press. Western governments friendly to South Africa loudly condemned her policies. At the UN, South Africa soon found herself 'the polecat of the world', as her delegate, Eric Louw, commented bitterly.

It is possible, nonetheless, to exaggerate the diplomatic damage which South Africa incurred from Sharpeville. The international significance of the event derived less from its intrinsic tragedy than from the contemporaneous accession to independence of the African states to the north. The sheer number of these states (they ultimately accounted for around one-third of all UN members) gave them considerable diplomatic weight. Sharpeville did not change but merely confirmed their attitude towards Pretoria and, from the outset, they attempted to secure her diplomatic isolation. In 1961 they secured a major triumph when South Africa withdrew, under pressure, from the Commonwealth.[1] Britain, very reluctantly, went along with the decision. For both she and the USA were

[1] The crucial actors were the new African states — India, Pakistan and Ceylon had shared Commonwealth conferences with South Africa with only minor qualms till then. The crucial issue was not Sharpeville but African independence — the conference finally broke down over Verwoerd's refusal to allow the new states diplomatic representation in Pretoria.

determined not to lose touch with African opinion for fear of seeing them driven into alliance with the Communist states. This, indeed, had been the central message of Macmillan's famous 'winds of change' speech in Cape Town in 1960. In 1961 the US State Department despatched its Under-Secretary for Africa, Mennen ('Soapy') Williams, on a not dissimilar African tour. Williams, an American politician in the classic tradition, treated the tour as a political campaign, euphorically embracing African nationalism at every opportunity and showering promises about him like confetti. Pretoria was furious[1] — but isolated. Worse, moreover, was clearly to come, for the tide of African nationalism was spreading irresistibly southward down the continent. It was only a matter of time before it was lapping up against Pretoria's borders.

The new states had no sooner acquired independence than they began to speak of carrying the struggle further, to break the power of the White South. Verwoerd might seek to make a virtue out of isolation,[2] but the White Establishment as a whole was disturbed and alarmed at the prospect of playing an embattled Canute. South Africa might have the strength to stand against the tide, perhaps even indefinitely, but isolation was hardly enjoyable and in the long run it could only be threatening.

There were, moreover, economic reasons why South Africa could not accept isolation, reasons which became more compelling as the sixties' boom proceeded. For South Africa was

[1] Macmillan had steered close to the wind in his Cape Town speech, but had managed not to give major offence. In an earlier draft he had, referring to apartheid, quoted Melbourne's dictum that 'Nobody ever did anything very foolish except from some high principle', but in the event he omitted it. After returning from Cape Town Macmillan was, moreover, eager to dissociate himself from the radical implications of his speech. The wind of change was one thing, he said, 'a howling tempest which would blow away the whole of the new developing civilisation' quite another. Williams, by contrast, uttered cries of 'Uhuru' and 'Africa for the Africans' as he whistle-stopped gaily across the continent. More to Pretoria's taste was Viscount Montgomery's alarming promise to 'draw his sword' in defence of the whites.
[2] Verwoerd had returned to South Africa from the fateful 1961 Commonwealth conference to tell 20,000 of his supporters at Jan Smuts airport that, far from being a disaster, South Africa's exclusion from the Commonwealth was a 'miracle', and that it had been directly willed by God. Verwoerd was frequently comforted by the secure knowledge that he was God's instrument — after his election as Prime Minister he had announced that 'I believe that the will of God was revealed in the ballot'. His opponents could only agree that the Almighty moved in mysterious ways.

becoming a mature industrial economy. Traditionally she had
imported manufactured goods and paid for them with raw
materials. This pattern had slowly changed as South Africa
developed a wider industrial base from which to produce her
own manufactures. The Second World War produced a considerable speeding-up of the process as the country was pushed into
import-substitution by the sharp fall in foreign trade. Even so,
the agricultural and mining sectors remained the most important. In 1947—51 their output together stood at 28.2% of GDP,
that of manufacturing at 19.6%.[1] But the manufacturing sector
was by now growing much faster — from 1945 to 1964 it grew
at an annual average rate of 10.6% while the economy overall
grew at 8.3%. The government encouraged import substitution;
the home market was buoyant, nay insatiable; and foreign
investors increasingly poured their funds into the manufacturing
sector rather than mining.[2] By 1967—71 manufacturing
(26.6%) had clearly overtaken mining (11.3%) and agriculture
(9.9%) combined in its contribution to GDP. The government — and   South   Africans   generally — rejoiced   at   the
country's broad and growing industrial strength.

This structural change in the economy created a fundamental
problem, however. South Africa, as we have seen, had simply
shifted its import demands up the technological scale and was in
this respect becoming even more import-dependent than before.
Clearly, in order to pay for these imports South Africa needed
to export more and, in particular, she needed to start exporting
manufactured goods. This she did with some success — between
1959 and 1971 manufactures went from 35% to 49% of all
exports, while mining (excluding gold) fell from 65% to 51%. It
was nothing like enough, though. Her main trading partners
provided only the most competitive — and distant — markets
for such goods, however happy such countries were to buy her
minerals and food. Outspan oranges would always sell, but it
was difficult to buy many Mirages from the proceeds. Moreover,
the world prices for primary products were notoriously subject
to violent fluctuation in a way that the prices of manufactured
goods were not. It was a matter of increasingly urgent necessity
for South Africa to establish larger and more stable markets for

[1] D. Innes, 'The Role of Foreign Trade and Industrial Investment in South
Africa', in Suckling, op. cit., p. 113.
[2] In 1936 66% of foreign investment had gone into mining, in 1960 33%.
By the 1960s well over half of such investment was going into
manufacturing. Suckling, 'The Nature and Role of Foreign Investment...'
in Suckling, op. cit., p. 18.

her goods. There was only one possible answer: she *must* expand her trade with Africa. Here, stretching northward from her doorstep, was a fast-growing market of several hundred million people; people eager for manufactured goods of all kinds which, in the main, their own countries did not produce. South Africa stood in relation to the rest of the African continent very much as the USA did to Latin America. Manifest destiny beckoned.

The whole of the White Establishment felt the pull of the African market. The Johannesburg *Financial Mail* articulated the vision:

> .... a vast sophisticated South African market of the future, stretching from Cabinda in the west to the Tanzanian border in the east — power grids, super highways, and a tourist paradise.[1]

The government spoke of its dreams for an African Common Market, hinting none too subtly at the colonial economic relationships which it desired within it:

> Our economic and political objectives in Southern Africa are to harness all natural and human resources from Table Mountain to the border of the Congo River.... Member countries of the Common Market could complement one another. For example, the Republic of South Africa could manufacture machinery, chemicals and electrical appliances — while the Transkei could produce jute, Swaziland sugar, Botswana beef, and Lesotho water.[2]

In the early 1960s it was hoped that the forging of such economic links might gradually bring a political rapprochement in its wake — the flag could follow trade. But as the decade wore on and the need to break into the African market became more pressing, it was increasingly realised that political rapprochement must have first priority — trade would follow the flag. Detente with black Africa was an economic necessity. It

---

[1] *Financial Mail*, August 1969, cited by R. Weiss, 'South Africa and its Hinterland: The Role of Africa in South Africa's Economic and Political Strategy', in Suckling, op. cit., p. 97.
[2] Cited by Innes, op. cit., p. 155. The most precious of the raw materials mentioned is water. Without large inputs of imported water South Africa will, by AD 2000, have to shift her industrial base to the coast and desalinate the sea.

was this necessity — far more than any fears for South Africa's
military security — which made isolation unacceptable. The
White Establishment, so resilient in its economic recovery from
Sharpeville and its repression of rebellion, found that this same
resilience was now required externally, too. If it could not halt,
it must at least come to terms with the wave of African
nationalism spreading southwards towards the Republic.

By the mid-1960s it was already clear that Pretoria had
successfully absorbed the shock of this wave, establishing a
northern perimeter of neutral or even friendly states. The
difficult problem of independence for the former British
Protectorates in her midst was safely negotiated (the one
threatening radical spark, the Basutoland Congress Party, was
thoroughly doused), with satisfactorily conservative regimes
installed. The Republic's hold on South-West Africa was
consolidated, with even the unexpected windfall of a favourable
World Court decision. On the western and eastern flanks
Pretoria could support and rely upon an intransigent Portuguese
colonialism in Angola and Mozambique. Directly to the north
Rhodesian UDI in 1965 created a state which was both more
dependent on, and ideologically closer to, Pretoria than the
half-heartedly liberal Todd and Whitehead regimes had ever
been. Moreover, Britain's immediate refusal of military action
against the Smith regime as strategically impossible and politically unthinkable clearly left South Africa as the paramount
power in the region. In May 1963 it had been strategically
possible for Britain to airlift into Swaziland a whole battalion of
Gordon Highlanders to break the wave of African strikes then
centring on the Havelock asbestos mines,[1] where the workers

[1] The Havelock intervention threw a garish light on British interests in the
area. The strikes followed a constitutional conference in January–
February 1973, chaired by the Colonial Secretary, Duncan Sandys
(Director, Ashanti Goldfields Corporation, 1945–51) and his Minister of
State, Lord Lansdowne (the 8th Marquess). Whitehall's plan, in essence,
was to install in power a conservative coalition under King Sobhuza —
Sandys was to pass legislation retrospectively absolving the king's men
from any responsibility for the electoral offences they had committed. In
March Lansdowne visited Swaziland, returning to London in time for the
wedding at Westminster Abbey in April of HRH Princess Alexandra and
Angus Ogilvy. Both Lansdowne and Ogilvy were already linked to the
royal family — Ogilvy's father, the 12th Earl of Airlie, was then
Chamberlain to the Queen Mother, while Lansdowne, like his father before
him, had been a Lord-in-Waiting to the Queen and a member of her Body
Guard for Scotland. They also both had business links with southern
Africa — Lansdowne's father was a director of Barclays Bank, while Ogilvy

were demanding a quintupling of their wage to £1 a day. The Gordons were still there in April 1965, standing by in case of trouble in the Basutoland independence elections. (These passed off happily — the conservative Chief Jonathan won, touring the constituencies in a South African helicopter.) Just seven months later, at UDI, British military action in the region had become 'strategically impossible'. The point was not lost on Pretoria — Britain would deploy troops in the area, even in her own colonies, only with the Republic's tacit approval. When, in 1967, the first ZAPU—ANC guerrillas made their appearance in Rhodesia they were met by South African troops, and Pretoria warned that it would not tolerate such 'outside interference' in Rhodesia. Britain, under whose jurisdiction the colony legally still lay, said nothing. The heirs of Kruger could now send their own Jameson raiders into the land of Cecil Rhodes with impunity.

With this northern perimeter secured, Pretoria was able to proceed towards a limited rapprochement with some of the independent states lying beyond it. Malawi was the easiest and most complete catch. Its leader, Hastings Banda, maintained a friendly neutrality with the Republic from independence on for reasons of transparent and acknowledged economic self-interest. Banda's open complicity with Pretoria and Lisbon

---

was a director of Lonrho and, indeed, via his directorships in the Drayton group had a direct interest in the Havelock mines. Sandys was not, like Lansdowne and Ogilvy, an aristocrat (though he was Churchill's son-in-law), but he shared their Scottish extraction and old Etonian background. The despatch of the (suitably Scottish) Gordons required the agreement of two further old Etonian Scots to be found among the guests at Ogilvy's wedding, Harold Macmillan (Prime Minister) and Lord Home (Foreign Secretary). A non-Etonian among the guests was 'Tiny' Rowland, whom Ogilvy had recruited to the Lonrho board and who, immediately after Swazi independence, secured King Sobhuza's signature to a contract for a further asbestos mine near Havelock. Ogilvy and Princess Alexandra arrived in Swaziland a year later on a royal visit to celebrate the first anniversary of independence. King Sobhuza made them warmly welcome, (which was just as well, since the planned next stage of the royal tour, to Mauritius, had to be cancelled due to the planned mass demonstrations against the couple, who were seen as representatives of Lonrho).

The circle was complete in 1971 when Rowland recruited Sandys too to the Lonrho board — on terms which led the Prime Minister, Mr Heath, to castigate the 'unacceptable face of capitalism'. Ogilvy finally resigned from Lonrho's board in 1976 after being publicly criticised in the report of the official enquiry set afoot by Heath. The Gordons, this time, remained at barracks.

produced a major showdown within Malawi, the more radical
leaders, Chiume, Chisiza and Chipembere leading an open
insurrection against his leadership in October 1965. It was a
critical moment for South Africa. Banda's defeat would have
doomed all notions of detente with Pretoria in the minds of
African leaders further to the north. But the insurrection was
crushed. Banda assumed the presidency in 1966 and in 1967
signed a trade agreement with South Africa. Pretoria's influence
and economic presence in Malawi grew apace.

Zambia presented an altogether more ambitious target. With
Banda's defection Kaunda enjoyed a unique status as the most
'legitimate' African nationalist leader existing on the critical
interface with the White South. His long perorations against
white racism drew the applause of an admiring international
audience which pointed to the high price of principles such as
these. Foreign investors noted thankfully at the same time that
the strange brew of 'Christian humanism' enunciated by
Kaunda provided a comprehensive escape-route from the sort of
realpolitik which might have disturbed the region's delicate
balance. And just as Banda made his position clear in 1967, so
did Kaunda with the Lusaka Manifesto, spelling out his
abjuration of violence as a means to solving the southern
African conflict. This enunciation of Christian principle in a
wicked world may not have faced up to the brute realities of the
situation — which are essentially about economic and military
power — but Kaunda's status helped this document get adopted
as official OAU policy.

Kaunda's position was certainly always a difficult one, but it
was also not quite what it seemed. Openly he offered a generous
welcome to southern African liberation movements — with the
crucial proviso that he would not tolerate actual guerrilla bases
on Zambian territory. But secretly he was involved in a variety
of informal contacts with Pretoria, including a protracted
correspondence with Vorster himself. The history of these
contacts, stretching back almost to Zambian independence, was,
to Kaunda's fury, published by Vorster in 1971. The fact was
(and is), of course, that Zambia has much to fear and as much,
potentially, to gain, from South Africa's military and economic
power. Above all, Zambia's copper-based and South Africa's
gold-based economies are crucially integrated via the giant
Anglo-American corporation which provides a continuing nexus
of power, interest and communication between Lusaka and
Pretoria, and also provides, for both, connection into a major
informal network of international financial and political con-

tacts.[1] In sum, Zambia would not consent to be on the same terms with Pretoria as Malawi. Kaunda's position in Africa and further afield depended on this *not* being the case. Pretoria, elliptically, had an interest in bolstering his position while it enabled him to secure OAU agreement to documents such as the Lusaka Manifesto. But at least Zambia did not — and could not afford to — provide the Republic with a wholly intractable and hostile neighbour.

As Pretoria gazed further north from Zambia the picture in the early 1960s looked bleak, however. The earliest, most glamorous, and diplomatically most active African leaders, the Nkrumahs, Tourés and Ben Bellas, were also the most radical. They made the pan-africanist running, they were beyond Pretoria's reach, and they were utterly intransigent in their hostility to the White South. Briefly the terrible prospect had loomed of their numbers being reinforced much closer to home by a Congo (Zaire) under Lumumba, but the latter's timely assassination removed the threat, and the country settled down gradually under Mobutu to become a byword for reaction, brutality and American influence. Nonetheless, the outlook for Pretoria was hardly bright, particularly since it was quickly apparent that a common front over the southern African issue provided almost the only basis for uniting the motley, divided and often conservative ranks of African leaders.

By the late 1960s, however, even this tide had visibly turned in Pretoria's favour. Throughout the continent radicals suffered a high casualty rate. Lumumba (of the Congo), Ben Bella

[1] Colin Legum's account of the (abortive) Zambian initiative over Rhodesia in August 1974 sketches the following network: Vernon Mwaanga (Zambian Foreign Minister) travelled to Geneva to obtain the support of James Callaghan (British Foreign Secretary) for an initiative also involving Tanzania and Botswana; went on to Washington as one of the select few African foreign ministers to have private talks with Kissinger at that date. Meanwhile Kaunda talked to Vorster via two intermediaries, Harry Oppenheimer (Chairman, Anglo-American) and Zac de Beer (Anglo-American representative in Lusaka); Vorster's intermediary in reply was Gen. Hendrik van den Bergh (head of BOSS — the Bureau of State Security). Negotiations were continued by sending Mark Chona, Kaunda's personal envoy, to talk with Vorster in Cape Town. (*Southern Africa: The Secret Diplomacy of Detente. South Africa at the Crossroads*, London, 1975, p. 7.) Kaunda's willingness to rely upon two white South African businessmen as *his* negotiators is not the least remarkable aspect of this diplomatic spider's web, though Kaunda's wish to gain State Department clearance and backing for an initiative in no way involving the USA is equally instructive.

(Algeria), Nkrumah (Ghana), and Modibo Keita (Mali) all disappeared as did, at secondary level, Chipembere (Malawi), Mamadou Dia (Senegal), Bakary Djibo (Niger), Babu (Zanzibar), Odinga (Kenya) and, somewhat later, Kapwepwe (Zambia).[1] Nasser, the continent's senior radical, was never to recover his position after the shattering 1967 Israeli war. The remaining radicals — Touré (Guinea), Massemba-Débat and, later, Ngouabi (Congo-Brazzaville) and Nyerere (Tanzania) — were left vulnerable, isolated in general and from one another, and presiding over small, poor, and impotent states. The African elder statesmen still surviving from the independence era, Senghor (Senegal), Houphouet-Boigny (Ivory Coast) and Kenyatta (Kenya), were all ageing conservatives whose stance now seemed confirmed by the prevailing rightward wind. Their ranks were strengthened by the emergence of Busia in Ghana, Gowon in Nigeria and a host of Francophone military leaders, mostly nondescript conservatives when they were not byzantine reactionaries such as Bokassa of the Central African Empire.[2]

South Africa took the opportunity presented by this conjuncture to move, at first stealthily and informally, from 1970 quite openly, beyond its northern *cordon sanitaire*. The Republic was in a strong position. It merely wanted friendship, it said, and was willing to be lavish in its generosity. Pretoria was not slow to perceive that so parlous was the economic situation of many of the northern states that even relatively little largesse could command considerable leverage. Busia was bankrupt; Banda was poor; Senghor could not pay his civil servants; Kenyatta seemed simply conservative and greedy. The lynchpin, however, was Houphouet-Boigny of the Ivory Coast. The Ivory Coast was affluent, dynamic and important, and it commanded under its economic and political sway the whole group of Entente states (the Voltaic Republic, Niger, Togo and Benin (formerly Dahomey)). It was the heart of the French implantation in Africa. Houphouet himself was a militant anti-communist and had the entire confidence of the Elysée and, within it, of Jacques Foccart, whose political and intelligence network overlapped with Pretoria's own. Houphouet and his habitual lieutenants, President Bongo of Gabon and President Tsiranana of Malagasy, were, to say the least, highly susceptible to the suggestions they received from

[1] Of these, three were shot dead, one died in exile, one is still in exile, one died in jail, and the rest are still (1977) in detention.
[2] See Introduction, p. 11.

Paris, Houphouet had led the Ivory Coast since 1945 and served in Cabinets of the Fourth Republic — including the Mollet government which had launched the Suez expedition. Despite, or possibly even because of such experience, together with his shrewdness and sophistication, Houphouet was a man of commanding stature and wide influence in Africa's politics. Pretoria's special relationship with Paris here again proved invaluable, for the access to Houphouet lay through Paris, and Houphouet could provide the diplomatic bridge to independent Africa which Pretoria so fervently desired.

Houphouet, for his part, was dominated by his apprehension of Nigeria. The Ivory Coast was the only state in West Africa whose influence equalled that of Nigeria. The French, seeing Nigeria as merely a British stalking horse, backed the Ivory Coast as hard as they could. In the long run the sheer facts of Nigeria's oil revenue, physical size and larger population made this a rivalry Houphouet could not hope to win. Houphouet and the French had supported Biafran secession to this end in the hope of weakening his foe, if not by Biafran success at least by the protracted and debilitating war required to end it. The end of the war left Houphouet casting around for some new lever. His gaze, focused and guided by Paris, fell upon South Africa.

Vorster did not stage a public launching of the detente policy until he was confident that it would achieve some success and that he could overcome any internal opposition to it within Nationalist ranks. It quickly did achieve success. Indeed, once news of the first cautious contacts had been made public it seemed possible that a veritable bandwagon might develop. Houphouet had emancipated South Africa from her status as a political untouchable and not a few African presidents hastened to ensure that their countries should not be left behind in the queue for Pretoria's largesse. Already South African tourists and businessmen had begun flocking into Malagasy, Mauritius and the Seychelles, bringing a boom in hotel and casino development to these East African islands. The statesmanlike rehetoric of 'dialogue' grew in volume. Pretoria seemed poised to roll back the tide of African nationalism in a manner that would make the efforts of a Dulles or a Metternich appear almost parochial by comparison. South Africa's fiercer critics were appalled by the prospect; practicians of *realpolitik* were impressed.

The View from Washington

Metternich's biographer, Dr Kissinger, had hardly taken up his position as special adviser to President Nixon when he asked

the National Security Council (NSC) to prepare a comprehensive review of US policy towards southern Africa. Nixon had
squeezed in on a minority vote at the election and was quite
crucially indebted to southern conservatives, most notably
Strom Thurmond of South Carolina. Despite this support the
third party candidacy of George Wallace had very nearly cost
Nixon the election. With his eyes fixed firmly on re-election in
1972, Nixon adopted from the outset a 'southern strategy' — of
consolidating and expanding his support among southern
conservatives. His reference of the southern Africa question to
the NSC within three months of taking office reflected this
urgency, for conservatives such as Thurmond had long
expressed deep dislike of US policy in this area. Rhodesia and
South Africa were, in their eyes, their white, anti-communist
kith and kin; it was grotesque that the US should operate
sanctions and an arms embargo against these bastions of the
Free World. If Nixon was disposed from the first to appease
such pressures, he received strong support from Kissinger, and
not merely because the latter was bent on squeezing out William
Rogers, the State Department Secretary, by winning the favour
of his new employer. Kissinger was a notable spokesman for
realpolitik, strongly of the opinion that the proper object of US
policy was the foreign policy of other states, not their internal
social arrangements. South Africa was a perfect case in point.

The NSC presented its views by outlining five possible
options for the US. Nixon, on Kissinger's strong advice, opted
for the second of these, to 'maintain public opposition to racial
repression but relax political isolation and economic restrictions
on the white states'.[1] This policy was based on the blunt
premise that

> The whites are here to stay and the only way that
> constructive change can come about is through them. There
> is no hope for the blacks to gain the political rights they seek
> through violence, which will only lead to chaos and increased
> opportunities for the communists.[2]

[1] NSC Interdepartmental Group for Africa, *Study in Response to NSC
Study Memorandum 39: Southern Africa* (Aug. 15, 1969). The entire
study is usefully reproduced in Spokesman Books, *The Kissinger Study of
Southern Africa* (London, 1975) which includes an interesting introduction by B. Cohen and M. A. El-Khawas.
[2] This involved writing off the chances of the FRELIMO and MPLA
guerrillas. After their victory Kissinger reacted with fury against the CIA,
from whom this erroneous estimate had come. Publicly Kissinger took the
line that he had never been much involved in African affairs, attempting to

Kissinger's attitude to independent Africa reinforced Nixon's predispositions: it was poor, dependent, laughably irresponsible and violent, and, in general not worthy of much consideration. When, in 1969, Kissinger's aides attempted to engage his sympathies for Biafra, they were caustically dismissed. His reply then — 'Do you really think that there's a Nobel Prize in Biafra?' — revealed a cast of mind which some were surprised to find capturing the hearts of the Nobel judges four years later.

As Kissinger's ascendancy in Washington increased, so US policy towards the White South softened noticeably. A major test of Kissinger's strength came over the Byrd Amendment, by which the US was to break UN sanctions against Rhodesia and recommence the importation of its chrome. The State Department made no secret of its opposition to the Amendment, which was the brainchild of the two most powerful southern conservatives on Capitol Hill, Senators Harry Byrd (Virginia) and Strom Thurmond. Despite State Department pleading Nixon took Kissinger's line. The President made no comment on the Amendment, exerted no pressure against it in Congress and refused to veto it when it passed.

The Kissinger line was heavily reinforced by a State Department report[1] which underlined the crucial importance to the US of southern African minerals. In 1969 the region as a whole[2] had provided 69% of the world's gold production, 64% of its gem and industrial diamonds, 57% of its cobalt, 32% of its chromite, 29% of its vanadium, 28% of its platinum, 31% of its vermiculite, 28% of its antimony, 22% of its copper, 14% of its manganese, 10% of its beryllium and 17% of 'Free World' uranium. In almost every case the proportions were tending to rise. US interests, Kissinger argued, lay with the White South in every sense — not only for raw materials, but in terms of global strategy: in a future war Soviet submarines off the Cape would be able to deny the West critical supplies of war materials. US

---

evade responsibility for the Angolan débâcle later on by claiming to have been involved above all with Vietnam. This was untrue. Not only had he strongly urged Option Two on Nixon in his Memorandum of 2 January 1970 (damagingly leaked to the press in 1974), but he fought a major battle against Rogers and the State Department in an attempt to stop them from closing the US consulate in Salisbury. See also B. Oudes, 'The United States' Year in Africa' in *African Contemporary Record 1974—5*, op. cit.
[1] African Affairs Advisory Council, *Africa's Resources* (Aug. 1971).
[2] That is, South Africa, Namibia, Rhodesia, Lesotho, Botswana, Swaziland, Angola, Mozambique, Zambia, Zaire, and Malagasy. South Africa produced the lion's share in almost every case.

investment and trade with South Africa was large and growing. Its companies there were, moreover, perfectly placed to take advantage of South Africa's 'forward' policy. With their capital base secure in the White South, US firms could take advantage of Pretoria's detente with the north and expand their markets throughout Africa.

Nixon was disposed to agree, not only for domestic political reasons but because he too, prided himself on a sense of brutal *realpolitik* and was quick to recognise and promote kindred spirits. The spirit of the White House in these years was best expressed in the famous dictum of another aide, Charles Colson: 'If you've got them by the balls, their minds and hearts will follow.' Kissinger's star rose in such an environment and, as it did, US policy towards southern Africa hardened visibly. In Nixon's February 1970 'State of the World' message he had contented himself with the statement that 'the 1960s have shown us — Africa and her friends also — that the racial problem in the southern half of the continent will not be solved quickly'. In the corresponding message of a year later Nixon's line had hardened:

> The United States believes that the outside world can and should use its contacts with southern Africa to promote and speed change. We do not therefore believe that the isolation of the white regimes serves African interests, or our own, or that of ultimate justice.'[1]

After this green light, US support for the White South became increasingly overt. In March 1971 the US Export—Import Bank altered its policy to allow long-term loans to South Africa, an offer promptly accepted by Pretoria. IBM and ITT supplied computers and other electronic equipment to the South African Defence Department. Between 1967 and 1972 the US sold 1376 aeroplanes of various types to South Africa, including ten giant C-130 troop-carriers.[2] In 1972 NATO

[1] Cited in R. First, J. Steele, and C. Gurney, *The South African Connection* (London, 1972), pp. 128—9. Britain had not, at this point, endorsed Pretoria's detente policies, but a few months later Sir Alec Douglas-Home, the Foreign Secretary, urged the wisdom of 'dialogue' on the unlikely ears of President Amin of Uganda.

[2] When a 1974 court order forced the release of Nixon's list of 1972 campaign contributors it also emerged that the CREEP chairman, Maurice Stans, had taken $12,500 from Flying Tiger airlines in return for his signature on the export licence to Rhodesia (in defiance of sanctions) of 'Tango Romeo'. This turned out, on investigation, to be not a dance record, but a DC-8.

secretly requested SACLANT (Supreme Allied Command in the Atlantic) to devise plans for the protection of the Cape route — plans which necessarily involved Pretoria.

Even more striking was the alteration in the US attitude towards Portugal. In 1971 the US agreed to extend $436 million in aid and loans to Lisbon in exchange for US use of the Azores base. This was four times the total of all such US loans to Portugal since 1946. Officially the US maintained its arms embargo on Portugal but it now revised the 'guidelines' relating to dual purpose civilian equipment so generously that Portugal was able to take delivery of transport planes, Bell helicopters and Rockwell photo-reconnaissance aircraft. US exports of herbicides to Portugal suddenly sextupled in one year. These made their way to Mozambique where Lisbon had begun to resort to the aerial defoliation tactics employed by the USAF in Vietnam. The number of Portuguese military personnel seconded for US training similarly rose sharply from 1969 on.[1]

It was in Angola, however, that all these strands were most closely knit together. The Nixon years witnessed a veritable explosion of US capital into the territory. Most notably there was Cabinda Gulf Oil, with $209 million invested by 1972 in the rich Angolan oil-fields, and expanding rapidly into other forms of mineral exploitation. Gulf was followed by a whole host of other American companies who were granted prospecting rights. In 1969 three New York diamond firms were granted concessions in southern Angola and the Rockefeller group was simultaneously allowed prospecting rights for phosphates. Other major US concerns to move in between 1969 and 1972 were Bethlehem Steel, the Riverwood Corporation (rock asphalt) and the Great Lakes Carbon Corporation (copper).

What gave a special interest to Angola, however, was that it was rapidly transformed into a tripartite consortium of French, American and South African capital. France was represented by ELF—Total (which had actually had more oil concessions (32) than any other company), Geoterme (copper), Pechiney

---

[1] This move also represented something of a triumph for the CIA, which had thrown in its lot with Kissinger against the State Department, and particularly for the Roosevelt cousins, Archibald and Kermit (both grandsons of Theodore Roosevelt). Archibald was the CIA's Africa desk chief throughout this period. Kermit, who had been a CIA official in Tehran during the overthrow of Mossadegh, had left to join Cabinda Gulf in the early 1960s, leaving them in 1964 to become the Washington representative for the Portuguese government's intelligence and propaganda agency until 1974. Kermit's son, Jonathan, was employed by his uncle Archibald as a CIA agent in Kinshasa (Zaire), resigning only to join his father's Washington operation. Oudes, op. cit., pp. A91—3.

(bauxite), Cefremet (phosphates), and the Rallet Bank, among a host of others. South Africa was represented by the Federal Maybou Bank, the General Mining and Finance Corporation, De Beers, Inexcafé (coffee), Johannesburg Consolidated Investments and a variety of other interests, including oil prospectors.[1] While considerable British and other Western interests were also represented, there was no doubt that the three senior partners were France, South Africa and the USA — quite frequently to be found fused in joint operations. Thus the Angolan economy of the late 1960s and early 1970s came to symbolise more perfectly than any other the rich complexity of the political and economic relationships entwining the southern African region. It was, moreover, a model of a sort, for it represented the full-blown vision of South African expansion. It was, in a sense, 'detente in action'. To be sure, the model when operated further to the north would require a different protective colouring and certain adaptations to the local environment. Some black faces at the management table, perhaps even a 51% share in companies for the independent government, and above all no Portuguese around to dictate terms and antagonise the local population by herding them into strategic hamlets or dropping defoliant on them and their crops. Such overt colonialism was a nuisance and the senior partners would be more than happy to urge their respective governments to vote against it at the UN. They would sponsor African cultural festivals, commission soulful enquiries into negritude, endow university chairs in race relations. . . . It would all be worth it.

It was, however, only a dream. For, apart from a somewhat less dramatic replication of this model in Mozambique, South Africa was unable to achieve this degree of penetration anywhere else. Pretoria's main successes, as we have seen, came in Francophone Africa. There was hotel and tourist development in Mauritius and Malagasy, with not a few South African goods finding their way there for re-stamping with the local trademarks and re-export to black Africa. There were some indirect South African holdings in Kenya, including a Rothmans branch headed by Joseph Murumbi, who had resigned as Vice President and Foreign Minister to take up the post. South African goods found their way in some measure into Senegal, the Ivory Coast

---

[1] For further information see J. Bonaldi, 'Angola: the economic interests', *Race and Class*, Vol. XVII, Spring 1976, No. 4.

and Zaire. But overall the results were extremely disappointing and the White Establishment achieved nothing like the northward surge of trade and investment it had hoped for. It was Pretoria's only real failure in the golden sixties and it was more significant than many of its successes. There were several reasons for this failure. Most obviously, despite all the talk of detente, African political sensibilities remained extremely delicate. Even Houphouet always maintained that the success of 'dialogue' depended on visible, if gradual, reform in South Africa. It was a conditional commitment, even if no time limit was attached. And, despite occasional (and sensational) hints by Vorster and others, there was no sign of any relaxation of apartheid in South Africa. Also, while the conservative African states might allow themselves the fruits of a little under-the-counter trade with Pretoria, the prospect of South African firms, manned by white South Africans, setting up shop in their main cities remained politically inconceivable. For the radical African states such as Guinea, Algeria and Somalia had stood fast against detente with Pretoria and condemned it from the first as the purest treachery. This threw conservative states on to the defensive. Much more damaging, however, was the fact that the Nigerian government, though led by the conservative General Gowon, awoke to the fact that the new alliance between Vorster and Houphouet was obliquely directed against themselves. Accordingly, Nigeria swung its enormous diplomatic weight, ponderously but definitely, on to the radicals' side against detente. This was a major setback for Pretoria. Not only was Africa's largest and fastest-growing market to remain closed to her, but the detente bandwagon slowed noticeably. South Africa was paying the price, indirectly, for Houphouet's support of Biafra. In the end Gabon — whose own oil wealth made her invulnerable to Nigerian influence — was the only new state to announce publicly that it was trading with South Africa.

There was a second, and equally obvious, major reason for Pretoria's failure. The Western powers might lend their support to detente but this did not mean the Western companies welcomed the idea of a determined and cut-throat new competitor in African markets, particularly since a South African presence might have the effect of attracting opprobrium against Western multinationals in general.

There was, in this respect, a quite crucial difference between France and the other Western powers. The US and Britain, via their huge stake in South Africa, would be amongst the chief beneficiaries of South African commercial expansion northwards.

The Germans had even more reason to feel enthusiasm for such a *Nordpolitik*, having both no captive markets elsewhere in Africa to worry about and a rapidly expanding base in South Africa. When the Afrikaans financier, Anton Rupert, decided to set up a new development bank, EDESA (Economic Development for Equatorial and Southern Africa), he was able to marshall an impressive array of British, American, but above all, German support for it. EDESA brought together Rupert's own Rothmans group and Anglo-American with Barclays Bank (UK); IBM and Universal Leaf (US); the Swiss Banking Company, and the Luxembourg Credit Bank; and Daimler Benz, Bosch, and the Deutsche Dresdner Bank from Germany. EDESA was headquartered in Zurich to the convenience, no doubt, of its president, Professor Karl Schiller, Helmut Schmidt's predecessor as Minister of Economic Affairs in Willy Brandt's SPD government. The absence of French concerns from the list above was not accidental.

France's stake in the White South was, as we have seen, small. It stood to gain little from the success of Pretoria's forward policy; indeed, it stood to see its captive African markets flooded by goods produced by British and American firms headquartered in Johannesburg. France remained extremely jealous of its continuing neo-colonial hold over Francophone Africa, as the mass expulsion of US officials from Malagasy in 1971 showed yet again.[1] Paris, accordingly, was happy enough to continue its balancing game against the Anglo-Saxons by encouraging Houphouet into political dialogue with Pretoria. But it had no intention of sacrificing major French interests in order to allow South Africa — let alone the perfidious Anglo-Saxons — to reap the real (economic) benefits which Pretoria always intended as the main point of dialogue and detente.

A critical moment came in 1972 with the overthrow of the Tsiranana regime in Malagasy amidst a welter of bitter recrimin-

---

[1] The U.S. Ambassador, Anthony Marshall, and John Hasey, his CIA station chief were among those expelled. Marshall, a former CIA operative himself, had secured his diplomatic post with generous political contributions to Nixon (including $48,500 to CREEP in 1972). Hasey had fought with the Free French and had been the CIA liaison man with De Gaulle in the 1950s. All of this was perfectly well known by Paris and the Tsiranana regime in Malagasy, but Marshall incurred the wrath of the local French business community by attracting a competing wave of American investors into the island. Local French intelligence agents obligingly put together a dossier suggesting that Hasey and Marshall were plotting Tsiranana's overthrow, which was handed to the president. Tsiranana angrily threw the Americans out, though admitting the falsity of the accusations against them only a few months later. See Oudes, op. cit., pp. A91—2.

ation from young radicals over the island's ties with South
Africa. The new, radical regime which emerged under General
Ramanantsoa immediately severed all links with Pretoria,
embarked on socialist policies, and became enthusiastically
involved with Russia, China and North Korea. The regime
decided to break its economic and political ties with France,
left the Franc zone and denied its Diego Suarez base to the
French and other Western navies. By 1974 over 7000 of the
23,000 Frenchmen in Malagasy before the coup had left. The
Malagasy coup was an utter disaster for Pretoria, and not merely
because her tourists, like the French navy, had now to be
redirected to Mauritius. One of her most important bridgeheads
had gone, and gone in a way which constituted a terrible
warning to other African conservatives. (Already there were signs
that the government of Sir Seewoosagur Ramgoolam in
Mauritius was coming under strong left-wing pressure for its
links with Pretoria.) It was rapidly becoming clear that the
internal political consequences for an African state of full
detente with Pretoria might be dire indeed.

The coup also left Paris feeling bitter and the other Western
countries wry. If the price for favouring Pretoria's detente was
seeing safely conservative states gravitate by process of reaction
towards the socialist bloc, then the game was hardly worth
playing. Diplomatically the forces of African conservatism
collapsed after the Malagasy coup. Detente had been voted
down by the OAU in 1971 — but the coup killed it. Diplomatic
and commercial contact continued between Pretoria and the
conservative states, but the ranks of the latter ceased to expand.
All impetus had gone.

The Malagasy coup was a violent and dramatic defeat for
South African expansion. Perhaps even more important was the
quieter and more gradual defeat Pretoria suffered in Zambia.
Zambia was the lynch-pin of central Africa, the gateway to the
continent and one of the continent's richest markets. Two-thirds
of Zambia's imports had come from South Africa before
independence (1964) and Lusaka had been the earliest and most
lavish recipient of Pretoria's overtures. But, steadfastly and with
considerable self-sacrifice, Zambia had turned her face from the
south. This mighty and sustained effort to re-orient her trade
toward the north was most tellingly symbolised by the
(Chinese-built) Tan-Zam railway, a work of such protean
proportions that, like the Union-Pacific, it had passed into
legend long before it was finished. The great dream of
commercial expansion northward from the Cape, dreamt now
by Pretoria as once by Cecil Rhodes, was to be reversed by a

project whose grandeur and scale perhaps Rhodes alone could truly have appreciated. By the early 1970s, with the line's completion still to take full effect, Zambia was buying less than 20% of her imports from South Africa. The dream was further off than ever.

The origins of Pretoria's detente policy lay in the need to satisfy the market-hungry needs of a dynamic and expanding South African capitalism. Whatever the political rhetoric, the final judgment on the success or failure of detente would be found in the Republic's trade statistics. Pretoria, knowing this, and knowing that publicity might embarrass her trade partners and thus prove counter-productive, shrouded all such figures in the greatest secrecy. Moreover, after Rhodesian UDI in 1965 Pretoria altered the classification of her gross export figures to Africa so as to include goods re-exported to Rhodesia in defiance of sanctions. After 1965 Pretoria ceased to publish any figures at all detailing exports to individual African countries — including the all-important Rhodesian figures. The gross figures are laid out below.

Table 2. South Africa's Exports to Africa as percent-age of total Exports (excluding gold) 1947—72

1947—54	20.9	1964	11.9*
1955	19.3	1965	13.9*
1956	19.3	1966	16.3*
1957	19.2	1967	16.7*
1958	18.8	1968	16.5*
1959	18.6	1969	16.7*
1960	17.6	1970	17.1*
1961	15.2	1971	18.6*
1962	12.6	1972	14.9*
1963	11.7	* includes re-exports	

Source: Suckling *et al.*, op. cit., pp. 192—4.

The pattern to emerge from these figures is revealing enough. South Africa's exports to Africa fell regularly but slightly until 1959; fell sharply in the next four years as the states to the north became independent; and then rose again under the impact of Rhodesian UDI, though never recapturing the levels achieved in the mid-1950s. The figures were, in fact, even worse than they at first appeared. Even before UDI the lion's share (70—80%) of all South African exports to Africa had gone to Rhodesia, while exports to independent Africa had fallen steadily (19.5% in 1959, 17.4% in 1963, 12.7% in 1965). After

UDI Rhodesia's share of Pretoria's African trade rose steeply, not merely because of the re-exports which confuse our table above, but because South Africa stepped in to fill the gap left by UN sanctions against Rhodesia. Sanctions were, it is true, raggedly applied — in 1966, the first year of sanctions, West German exports to Rhodesia actually *rose* by 3%, while the USA's fell by 33% and Britain's by 85%. Nonetheless, the net effect, especially over time, was very considerable indeed: the gaps left for South Africa to fill almost certainly amounted to over 80% of all Rhodesian imports. At the same time South Africa's trade with the Portuguese colonies was increasing rapidly (her exports to Mozambique rose by over 50% between 1961 and 1965). If one adds in the fact that many of the so-called 're-exports' to Rhodesia were simply goods in transit to Rhodesia through the South African transport network and were not, in any real sense, exports — one begins to get some idea of how badly South Africa failed in its attempt at commercial expansion into black Africa. In the last pre-UDI year of 1964 Rhodesia and Mozambique together accounted for 85% of all Pretoria's exports to Africa. By the early 1970s this proportion was quite certainly higher. The briefest of calculations from the figures we have is sufficient to show that by the early 1970s no more than 3%, and quite possibly less than 2%, of South Africa's total (world) exports were going to black Africa, her 'natural market'.

The failure of South African expansion was of critical importance. By the early 1970s the Republic's effort at detente had been sufficiently energetic to create a split in the ruling Nationalist party, but South Africa was not much less isolated than she had been a decade before. More serious still were the economic implications of this defeat. South Africa needed to grow and needed military security. These aims she could only achieve by the large-scale import of advanced technology from the West. Through the 1960s these imports rocketed: from R1,821 million in 1963 to R4,114 million in 1971. At the same time South African exports (excluding gold) rose from R1,286 million to R2,178 million. The gap between the two figures was widening alarmingly and so rapidly that even the inflows of foreign capital could not bridge it. It was a matter of desperate urgency to the whole White Establishment that the gap *should* be bridged, for the alternative could only be an economic crisis of enormous proportions. Even the Republic's military security would be threatened, for how to afford huge imports of arms in the face of a trade gap where imports were already running at twice the level of exports and accelerating away from them? It was absolutely essential that South Africa expand her exports, above all to her natural market, black Africa. By 1972 it was clear that in this most critical direction South Africa had comprehensively failed.

Attempts at trade boycotts of South Africa in the West had been a dismal failure, but the African trade boycott, despite all the gaps in it, had backed the Republic into a desperate corner. How was she to escape from it? The answer came down to one word: gold.

4 South Africa's Salvation: The War over Gold

After the great rise in world oil prices of 1973—4 it became common practice in political and financial circles to perform a peculiar conjuring trick with trade statistics. A country was said to have two sorts of deficit (or, more rarely, surplus). There was the 'non-oil deficit' — used as the significant indicator figure for all practical purposes — and its poor relation, the 'oil deficit'. It was a considerable sleight of hand since, at the end of the day, the figure which really counted was clearly the one which was inclusive of the vital oil. Undoubtedly this habit is rooted, deep down, in a vague but pervasive belief that some simple mineral, merely raised out of the soil of the happy country in which it lies, should not be allowed to 'count'. Count, that is, in terms of international trade against such works of human ingenuity and labour as cars, televisions and jet planes. But, of course, count it does.

This sleight of hand had been practised on South African exports for decades before it was applied to the oil trade. South Africa sold 'exports excluding gold' — and gold. The description was equally as misleading as when the same conjuring trick is performed on the economies of the OPEC states. For while there are many of them, South Africa was and is *the* gold-based economy of the world. She has long produced three-quarters of the world's gold. The whole world that is, not the 'Free World', for the USSR is the only other significant producer. Moreover, while oil may be an almost invisible part of a producer-country's economy (it takes only a few men to work the pipeline pumps and a few more to collect the cheques), gold is the overwhelmingly visible, nay tangible, fact of South African life. Her greatest city, Johannesburg, is, in every sense, built on it. Her largest company, Anglo-American, owes its position to its ownership of two-fifths of the mines; the mining operations are vast and employ some 700,000 people. Of the economically active workforce in 1960 one in every seven men and one in every twelve women (of all races) worked in mining. It is, above all, the dominant fact of life for urban African men, In 1960, of all such men who had jobs, more than one in every three worked in the mining sector.[1]

The contribution of gold exports to South Africa's overall trade position is a critical one. In 1946 gold accounted for over 56% of all exports by value, and in 1962 the figure was still 38%. If gold exports were excluded South Africa ran a huge and perpetual deficit which, even in a good year, was nowhere near met by inflows of foreign capital. Moreover, although gold was in the unique position of having an immovable price, the absolute contribution to the economy of gold grew continuously. In 1946 gold output was worth R203 million; in 1960 R530 million; in 1967 R775 million — although it was fetching the same $35 an ounce throughout. This soaring production in the face of a static price was achieved by a variety of means: by ever-increasing capital investment in new equipment and techniques; by a system of average production costs;[2] and by holding down the wages of African miners to levels miserable even by the standards of other African workers.[3]

The fact that the gold price was fixed was a source of great grievance to South African mine-owners and politicians alike. What other commodity had had its price fixed in 1934 and held static ever since? Their gold was really 'worth' more, even if one merely allowed for inflation. The price of South Africa's imports had trebled between 1934 and 1960, after all. If the world insisted on preserving such an unfairly low gold price it would, in the end, kill South Africa's golden goose.

The trouble was that the gold price had nothing to do with economics. The price was fixed by Franklin Roosevelt's Gold Reserve Act of 1934 which had committed the US Treasury and Federal Reserve to exchange $35 for an ounce of the metal. This in no sense represented an economic 'floor-price', for the figure of $35 had been fixed entirely by whim. Roosevelt, encouraged by his advisers, George Warren and Frank Pearson,

[1] A majority of whom were in gold mining. My calculations are based on D. H. Houghton, *The South African Economy* (Cape Town, 1964), Table 2, p. 222.

[2] The government compels mining companies to calculate an average production cost for all mines. This has the effect of keeping otherwise uneconomic mines in operation, thus sustaining total production and employment.

[3] In 1960 the average annual earnings of non-whites in mining were R142; of non-whites in manufacturing and construction R371 and R365 respectively. The position was reversed for whites for whom the comparable figures were R2238, R1938 and R1907 respectively. Houghton, op. cit., Table 19, p. 238.

had, in 1933, embarked on a campaign to drive up the price of
gold in the mistaken belief that it would result in a general rise
in prices and thus provide incentive for an expansion of
production to lift America out of depression. Roosevelt took
some pleasure in personally dictating the price levels up to
which gold was to be driven each day (by the US government's
offering that price for it). Typically, he fixed the price each
morning over breakfast by random amounts — once, for
example, deciding it should rise 21 cents in the day because,
being three times seven, it seemed a lucky number.[1] Having
taken the price up from $20.67 to $35 the President lost faith
in this panacea and the latter price was frozen. He had, like
governments of our own day, been poorly advised by moneta-
rists, but had realised it more quickly, having no pretence to
economic knowledge of his own. The $35 price level rested on
political fiat, and the South African economy rested on that. If
there was any 'real' gold price beneath this it was what jewellers
would pay for it, which meant, on the whole, what pretty
women or their consorts were willing to pay. If there was any
'real' economic purpose for which the black miners of
Johannesburg dug the gold (for about R1 a week in 1934) it
was this.

   Behind this political fiat lay, of course, the awesome
economic power of the USA. If the US Treasury would pay $35
an ounce for gold, so would all the world's central banks. The
international financial system rested, in the last analysis, on the
strength of the American colossus; its rules were theirs. The $35
price was accordingly accepted as the stable bedrock of the
world financial order, one which persisted quite happily
through the Bretton Woods Agreements and the setting up of
the International Monetary Fund (IMF). Theoretically, the IMF
was supposed to replace the old gold standard by a complex
system of deposits and guarantees. In fact the US Treasury
exercised a dominant control over the IMF and the Treasury
continued to offer $35 for every ounce of gold. The world's
currencies were pegged against the dollar, the dollar was pegged
against gold, and the bankers of the world gratefully accepted
the enduring stability this provided. South Africa could plead
for a higher gold price (i.e. for the devaluation of the dollar),
but against such an unacceptable change stood arrayed the
whole might of the US. Only a decisive challenge to America's

[1] J. K. Galbraith, *Money. Whence it came, where it went* (London, 1976)
pp. 223—4.

economic hegemony could produce such a revolution in the
international financial system.

Gradually just such a challenge developed. For the post-war
economies of the EEC and Japan regularly grew at much faster
rates than did that of the US. The enormous American
predominance was gradually eroded. In 1953 the US had
accounted for 52% of the whole capitalist world's industrial
output; by 1970 the figure was 40.5%. This was a large, though
not an enormous, fall. More significant was the growing
commercial and financial strength of the other great capitalist
states. In 1953 the UK, EEC and Japan combined accounted for
30.7% of 'Free World' exports, the US for 21%; by 1970 the
figures were 46% and 15.5%. Even more dramatically, while the
US held 43% of entire 'Free World' gold and foreign reserves in
1953, in 1970 it held only 8.3%. In the same period the
combined UK, EEC and Japanese holdings went from 18% to
51.7%.[1] The increasingly competitive position vis-à-vis the US
of the other great capitalist powers began, inevitably, to
undermine the stability of the international financial order, for
this order rested on an American predominance which was
becoming less and less real. And once the stability of this order
was threatened the question of the gold price crept ineluctably
back towards the centre of the stage. If America was weakening,
the dollar would weaken and gold would tend to rise in price.
The prospect was alarming for almost everyone, and in a
pre-emptive move in 1961 the EEC countries, Switzerland, the
UK and the New York Federal Reserve set up the world gold
pool with the aim of selective market intervention to maintain
the $35 level.

Meanwhile the US exploited the strength of the dollar to run
large and perpetual deficits in its balance of trade with the rest
of the world. By the early 1960s an increasingly self-confident
and assertive European capitalism began to object strenuously,
pointing out that this deficit was being used to maintain an
American army in Europe, buy up European companies, suck
up European goods, and set Europe awash amidst an inflationary flood of dollars. Had any European country run such
deficits its currency would, of course, have suffered recurrent
devaluations. Because such a fate was unimaginable for the
dollar the US could act thus with impunity and, indeed, could
pay for its military and economic dominance with debts which
were never actually redeemed. De Gaulle decided to force the
US to reform its ways by the simple expedient of changing his

[1] E. Mandel, *Late Capitalism* (London, 1975) pp. 335—6.

dollars into gold at every opportunity, telling the Americans that the only solution if they did not like this haemorrhage of gold (and they didn't) was a devaluation of the dollar against gold. Although De Gaulle thus incurred the particular wrath of Washington he was merely the most assertive spokesman for a European capitalism which was beginning to think increasingly in terms of resistance to the *défi Americain*. Italy, for example, quietly followed the French example and began to hold an increasing proportion of her reserves in gold. This process gradually brought pressure on the gold pool which, from 1966, became a large net seller of gold (effectively, at a loss). The French promptly quit the pool in June 1967, leaving the USA carrying 59% of the pool's burden. This set the scene for an era of international financial turbulence which is not yet over. The French had nailed their flag to gold and the war against the dollar could now begin. Pretoria could only pray, silently, for a French victory.

Anyone who has played roulette may appreciate Pretoria's position. One player, bolder than the rest, had had the temerity to mount a sustained attempt to break the bank. Pretoria quietly placed her side-bets on this player (France) and even provided her with a reserve of gambling chips (the gold shipments for the Mirages). But she had no control over gambling strategy — De Gaulle chose the numbers on the wheel. Moreover, Pretoria was interested in winning her bets but had no real desire to see the bank broken. If the Americans lost, well and good (the gold price would rise), but if the bank was actually broken, an irate Washington management might step in, order the players out of the casino and change the rules (by demonetising gold) before the game could be re-started. It might even decide that the business of casino management was over-rated, and close down. This would be a complete disaster, but it seemed a remote prospect. In any case, the deadly game was now on, whether Pretoria liked it or not. And no gambler could possibly stay away from such a game — the stakes were so high and the tables were red-hot. Moreover, it escaped no-one's attention that the bank had foolishly become involved in another game (the Vietnam war) in a back-room. The opposition there had seemed paltry but it was very determined and was gradually bleeding the bank of funds at just the time when its whole strength was required to withstand the bank-breaking coup being attempted in the main casino. The Vietcong were, in effect, a critical ally for Paris and Pretoria, and the French had waited, before launching their main assault, until the bank had become hopelessly bogged down in this back-room game. By

1967 the Vietnam war was pushing the US into ever-larger deficits and French reserves stood at a peak. In June 1967, after years of skirmishing, the moment had come for an open war over gold.

In November 1967 the weakest of the front-line troops, the British pound, collapsed and a tremendous speculative rush for gold developed. The dollar was clearly weak, for the US had, at this point, run a trade deficit for 17 of the previous 18 years. American gold losses were huge as pressure increased against the dollar. From $575 million in 1966 losses soared to $1,175 million in 1967. By the end of 1967 US reserves were down to $12,909 million — of which $1,000 million were actually IMF holdings on deposit and a further $10,000 million were ear-marked by US law to provide 25% cover for the currency, a law the Administration tried desperately to get a fractious Congress to repeal. Thus cover was now down to 27.1% and the US had only $1,909 million left with which to support the $35 level. French reserves now topped $6,100 million. The faster the US sold it, the quicker the gold made its way across the Atlantic. In February 1968 a further huge gold buying rush started amidst rumours that South Africa was planning to move its gold sales from London to Zurich to take advantage of the speculative (high) prices there. The gold pool met in crisis and produced the Washington Agreement. The $35 level would be kept for the purpose of all international monetary transactions but the gold pool would no longer sell gold on demand. A 'second tier' free market in gold was now to be allowed for other buyers. By this stage, of course, Washington was determined to preserve the $35 level simply to ensure that the French would not be rewarded for their speculative attack on the dollar.

This was the breakthrough South Africa had so long desired. She now placed her first open side-bet. While announcing that she would honour her commitments to sell gold to the IMF she immediately switched her other sales from London to Zurich, an aggressive move and one almost certainly co-ordinated with Paris. The Zurich gold market, until this point very much a side-show to the principal world bullion market in London, had always been 'free' in the sense that its prices were usually rather above the prevailing London 'official' level. South Africa had hitherto foregone the extra profit to be derived from selling in Zurich for fear of incurring charges of attempted destabilisation of the world financial system. France had for long encouraged

Pretoria towards such a move, seeing it as essential to a really aggressive campaign against the dollar. It would, too, transfer the world bullion market to Europe and out of the hands of the Anglo-Saxon enemy. In the event Pretoria had not dared risk Washington's wrath until the February 1968 Agreement provided at least a shaky public rationale for such a move. Although the rumours which preceded the move had clearly been an act of psychological warfare, they could (perhaps accurately) be blamed on Paris. South Africa, for her part, had no wish to annoy the Americans more than was absolutely necessary. She nailed her colours to the mast now not for political reasons but because she anticipated a bonanza.

It did not occur, in good part because the US, having now abolished the 25% cover rule, was determined to keep the free market price down. For, as was almost immediately apparent, the Washington Agreement really meant the end of gold as a true international currency, for no central bank in practice would transfer gold to any other at $35 for fear that this would be quietly sold at higher prices on the free market. So the free market price settled at around $43.50. The fact that the world had lurched towards the demonetisation of gold as well as towards a higher price for it had dawned fully on Pretoria by July 1968 when a badly rattled Finance Minister, Dr Diederichs ('Mr Gold'), launched a bitter attack on all the gold pool countries, alleging that they were trying to 'discredit and reduce' the monetary role of gold. The IMF had been refusing to buy South African gold, forcing her to dispose of it in the free market, thus driving the price down. The two-tier system was, he announced, an abomination. South Africa was too strong to be forced to sell and would simply freeze gold sales and play the market as it suited her. South Africa thus clambered quite openly on to the French side (as Paris had always told her she would have to). Having lost her first side-bet, she doubled-up her stake in approved casino fashion.

It was, as it turned out, only a threat. For all Diederichs' bluster, South Africa continued, for the moment, to supply the market with what it wanted. South Africa was facing balance of payments problems enough at this time without cutting off her own nose to spite her face. The incoming Nixon administration was no respecter of those who barked but didn't bite and Pretoria was soon punished for its empty truculence.

The US and IMF inexorably forced the price down — by December 1969 all the way to $35 and even below. Diederichs had to come to Canossa, obtaining an IMF promise to buy gold in return for a South African promise to sell gold only to obtain

needed foreign exchange, and not to speculate. This effectively
provided South Africa with a (humiliating) floor price of $35.
Thereafter the free market price hovered around $37 and,
despite the commodity price boom affecting other materials,
was only $45 in mid-1971.

Paris and Pretoria were left to contemplate their almost
complete defeat. They had gone to the brink — and stopped.
When the chips had been down Pretoria had lost its nerve at the
idea of challenging the US head on.

If Washington were pushed hard enough she might, in her
fury, tear up the rules and demonetise gold. To do this, though
she — not Paris and Pretoria — might have to take the
responsibility for subverting the world's financial system. And
she would have to feel strong enough to do it — would have to
feel confident that the dollar was strong enough to carry the
strain of replacing gold. It was here that the Vietnamese, slowly
bleeding America dry in the back-room game, were so
important. Indeed, it was quite probably they who were the real
cause of the February 1968 Washington Agreement. In January
1968, they had launched the great Tet Offensive, briefly
occupying Hué and even the US Embassy in Saigon. Tet had
made it quite certain that the US would have to pour more and
more troops and money into the war to 'save' it, with enormous
consequences for the US balance of payments. President
Johnson's morale and public standing had alike evaporated with
Tet. One set of enemies, on one front, at a time seems to have
been Johnson's conclusion as he sought, with the Washington
Agreement, to call at least a truce in the gold war with France.
It saw out the rest of his presidency, which was what mattered
to Johnson. Pretoria had lacked the nerve and determination of
the back-room gamblers — and joined the long list of those who
had lost at poker to Lyndon Johnson.

An uneasy truce continued while political leaders were changed.
Nixon took office and sped off immediately to Paris (March
1969) where De Gaulle was exposed to the full blast of the
President's unique oratorical style, finding himself praised for
his 'epic leadership rarely equalled in world history' and
described, with a certain literal truth, as 'a giant among men'.
The May Events, a run on the Franc, and De Gaulle's
resignation all contributed to leave things hanging. It was only
with Pompidou's election as the new French President that
events began to move towards a new and shattering conclusion.
Pompidou, a former Rothschilds banker, shared his former

master's belief in the gospel of gold as preached by De Gaulle's favourite economist, Jacques Rueff, a veritable prophet of Ozymandias. Pompidou was, moreover, determined to assert his own stature and independence to show he required no less respect than De Gaulle.

The critical move was probably made in the Middle East. France was quick to realise that the oil-rich states would be unable to accept for ever Israel's shattering victory in the 1967 War. With a not atypical ruthlessness the Elysée decided to change sides, announcing that France was to sell 100 Mirages to Libya and simultaneously refusing to supply any more to Israel — not even the 50 for which Israel had already paid. This volte-face was a deeply impressive demonstration to France's allies — and Pretoria in particular — that her friendship needed to be continuously earned. The move also infuriated American public opinion, particularly the influential Jewish lobby. In March 1970 Pompidou took up Nixon's unwise invitation that he visit the US. The visit was a total diplomatic disaster. Landing in Chicago, Pompidou was met by 10,000 hostile demonstrators whom Mayor Daley's police allowed close enough to spit upon the French President and his wife. Pompidou was mortally incensed, accusing Daley (correctly[1]) of complicity in what he termed a 'stain on the forehead of America'. The honour of France had been dragged through the dust and Pompidou had been used as De Gaulle never had been. Only with the greatest difficulty was he dissuaded from flying home immediately. Nixon attempted to make amends but dared not condemn the powerful pro-Israeli lobby. The visit deteriorated to its end.[2] Pompidou was by no means convinced that it was beyond the power of an American president to control his

---

[1] Daley, who boycotted the visit himself, was nothing if not famous for his control of the police, as their and his behaviour during the 1968 Democratic Convention in Chicago had demonstrated. When Nixon commented of the Chicago demonstration that 'a few citizens who have acted in a discourteous and disrespectful manner do not represent the American people', Daley issued a statement that 'Nothing occurred in Chicago during the visit of President Pompidou for which anyone is required to apologise. My own feeling is that compliments are due to those who turned out to demonstrate and for the orderly manner in which they exercised their rights. . .' Nixon did not comment. Pompidou gave his own bitter account: 'We rubbed elbows and they were able to shout insults into my face and the face of my wife.'

[2] In New York Pompidou refused to meet the leaders of the American Jewish community. Governor Rockefeller and Mayor Lindsay both boycotted the visit. Nixon's motives for encouraging a visit which, in the circumstances of the time, could only be disastrous, remain obscure.

mayors, police and citizenry if he really wanted to, and left with the smouldering suspicion that he had been the victim of a deliberately planned humiliation. After all, there were anti-apartheid groups in Paris, but they were not allowed to mar Vorster's visit a few months later.

It was from about this point on that the gold war began to re-kindle. Vorster's visit to Paris may well have been the turning point. South Africa and France had both been humiliated by the US and had had time to reflect on the reasons for their defeat on the gold markets. The French had not changed their attitude to gold — they continued to trade in their dollars for it at every opportunity. But now, fatefully, South Africa moved. A higher gold price was becoming a more and more urgent necessity as her attempted trade drive into Africa faltered. And she needed to be re-assured of the security of French arms supplies after the awful example of Israel. The elements of a deal existed — particularly if the French would extend loans to Pretoria to cover her through a new period of gold warfare. As we have seen, French-backed loans to the Pretoria government and para-statals *did* increase at this point. Equally, the deal for the sale of French nuclear power stations to South Africa, revealed much later, may have been arranged then too.

Whatever the reasons, from about this point South Africa began to make the move which she alone *could* make and which Paris had so long and ardently desired: she began to manipulate the gold market against Washington. De Gaulle had long before realised that South Africa, alone of all countries in the world, had this power. If Pretoria would use the weapon which the control of three-quarters of the world's gold supply gave her, then he was fairly bound to win his long struggle against the financial *défi Americain*. It was this, above all else, which had provided the underlying rationale for the Paris—Pretoria alliance. If one day Pretoria could be induced to use this weapon, all the slings and arrows which Paris had attracted for supplying South Africa with arms would be as nothing. All that Pretoria had to do to exercise an ultimately inexorable pressure on the gold price was to restrict the supply of gold to the market.

This she now began to do, gingerly at first and then by larger and larger amounts. In 1970 she still supplied over 32 million ounces to the market. By 1974 she had cut the supply by over 23%, to 24.5 million ounces. She pleaded, of course, that the productivity of her gold mines was diminishing and that this was a 'natural' constriction of supply. This was technically true in the sense that the Witwatersrand mines were having to burrow deeper and deeper into the earth for the metal. But the fact remained that her gold output had been on a steadily rising trend until then. Indeed, between 1959 and 1967 it had risen year by year quite steadily — by 54% over the whole period. From 1970 on Pretoria discovered a major 'natural' restriction on output, and somehow managed to discover it in a period where the rising gold price was making it economic to reopen large numbers of low-grade but not unproductive mines. Odder still, the restrictions on output got worse, not better, as the gold price climbed. . . .

It was a simple but staggeringly audacious strategy. Men had dreamt before of the ultimate market coup, 'cornering gold'. The last such attempt had taken place exactly a hundred years before in 1869 when the New York financier, Jay Gould, and his agent, Jim Fiske, had realised that the secret of such an operation lay not in open market dealings but in somehow managing to restrict governmental supplies of gold to the market. Gould and Fiske had sought to do this by bribery of officials and, most importantly, by 'buying' President Grant's brother-in-law who, it was hoped, would either buy or persuade the President.[1] Grant wasn't bought and the coup collapsed ignominiously. But Pretoria could go one better than Gould and Fiske — it could control the supply because it had the mines themselves. In the end, though, Pretoria faced the same problem that Gould and Fiske had — whether the US government would stand for such effrontery.

The pressure began to tell quite quickly, especially as another US deficit (of $2014 million) began to pile up in 1971. Speculation against the dollar and into gold mounted again. This time (August 1971) the US played rough — suspending the convertibility of the dollar against gold and slapping on a 10% import surcharge aimed, successfully, at the yen.[2] The $35 level, though maintained, was now entirely notional since the US was effectively off the gold standard. All other currencies pegged against the dollar floated up against it. John Connally, the Treasury Secretary, when asked why the US had not simply devalued the dollar in terms of gold, was typically blunt. He was

---

[1] J. K. Galbraith, op. cit., p. 115.
[2] A truly Nixonian stroke. The fact was not lost on the Japanese that the measures coincided to the day with the anniversary of their surrender to the US in 1945. Hubris followed, three years later, when Nixon had to resign on the anniversary of Nagasaki.

not, he said, going to reward those who had brought down the whole structure by building up their gold reserves (i.e. France). In any case, the US government 'recognised that gold had to be demonetised in the future international monetary structure, and certainly did not want to do anything to re-emphasise the importance of gold in the system'. Words to make Pretoria shiver. In December 1971 a new order was ushered in with the Smithsonian Agreement. The official gold price was raised to $38, the import surcharge dropped, and in return a new world alignment of currencies favourable to the dollar was extracted from the finance ministers of the major powers.

With this new stabilisation of currency alignments the US could at last afford to let the free market gold price rise without having to worry about the dollar. In any case another massive payments deficit was building up ($6439 million in 1972) and it would become expensive to keep speculators at bay as the world inflationary boom developed. So, for the first time, the gold price broke free in June 1972 to a $60—70 level — the US intervening to prevent it ever breaching $70. Even this brought US reserves down to a low of $10,000 million by the end of 1972 and the news of the final 1972 payments deficit produced another huge speculative run against the dollar in early 1973. So in February 1973 the dollar was devalued by another 10%. George Schultz, the new Treasury Secretary, was careful to emphasise that the devaluation was in terms not of gold but of IMF Special Drawing Rights (SDRs) which were thus posited as the new international currency to replace gold. In terms of gold equivalent this put the dollar at $42.22 per ounce.

This was the point when prudent gamblers would have retired from the game. Paris and Pretoria had hoped simply to base the existing world financial system on a much higher gold price. In this they had failed, but they had still doubled their stake (from the official $35 to the free market $70). Even achieving this much had shaken the system to its foundations. The US was regaining strength. Her Vietnam involvement was ended by the close of 1972 and that year's deficit was actually turned round into a $1.3 billion trade surplus in 1973, an almost unheard-of event. If Paris and Pretoria pressed on they would either lose or, if they won, they might bring down the entire world financial system. They pressed on. If anything they went for 'over-kill' — in the single year 1973—4 South Africa reduced her gold supply to the market by no less than 11.2%. This was far more than enough. Drawn by the scent of a kill, other gamblers had begun to crowd to the tables and a speculative mania took over.

Despite its new elements of strength, the US had lost control — not only of the gold market but of the world economic order as a whole. In the late 1960s all the major capitalist economies had fallen into step and in 1971 a great synchronised world boom began. The result was a world shortage of raw materials, a commodity price explosion, and rapidly increasing world inflation. In 1973 this inflation really took off. While the average inflation rate for the OECD (i.e. industrialised) countries had averaged 3.7% in the 1961—71 period, this rose to 4.7% in 1972 and 7.7% in 1973. For the year ending January 1974 it was no less than 11%. The result was a generalised flight away from all forms of money into gold. Under these circumstances it simply became too expensive for the US to hold down the free market price any longer. They let it go. By February 1973 it had bounded up to $95.

An entirely new factor now began to play a part — Watergate. Rumblings of the affair, generated mainly by the *Washington Post* reporters, Woodward and Bernstein, had already begun to disturb the markets slightly, but on 19 April, 1973 the *Post* delivered its bombshell, flatly naming John Mitchell and John Dean as responsible for a deliberate cover-up. The *Post* clearly now had hard evidence implicating major figures inside the White House in the affair. On 30 April the White House fired Dean, while the Attorney General, Richard Kleindienst, and the two top presidential advisers, John Erlichman and H. R. Haldeman, all resigned. From that moment on until Nixon's eventual resignation (8 August 1974) the executive branch of the US government was effectively paralysed. Abroad, confidence evaporated in Nixon's ability to give firm direction to the government; at home Congress would do nothing for the President; inside the White House (as the tape-recorder was ultimately to disclose) the scene increasingly resembled Al Capone's famous hide-out in Cicero, as the President, utterly distracted, sought by desperate means to shore up his crumbling position.

Watergate was the best news Johannesburg had had in years. By June gold had reached $127 before falling back to $95. De Gaulle had not lived to see his triumph but the new golden age of South Africa was undeniably due to the General's sustained gold-ramp of the 1960s. In October 1973 the Arab—Israeli war brought the last great commodity, oil, into play and there was a fresh gold stampede. When the gold pool met, in November 1973, it was to admit defeat and to accept the American resolution that it dissolve itself. South Africa tore up the 1969 agreement with the IMF in the confident belief that she would never need the $35 floor price again.

By January 1974 the gold price had reached $130, by February $160, as the Watergate news got worse (for Nixon). If the US had lost control, so had France. The world boom, faltering by summer 1973, had been killed completely by the oil price rise. A new world depression set in amidst still climbing inflation. The US was no longer underpinning the stability of the world financial system and the resulting chaos was general. In seven months (July 1973 to February 1974) the French lost a whole one-third (F17 billion) of their gold reserves built up so determinedly over the years, and Paris had to let the Franc float (downwards) in order to staunch the flow. The situation was even worse in Italy; so bad, indeed, that in June 1974 the Group of Ten Finance Ministers, with Washington's consent,[1] agreed that any country which so wished (i.e. Italy) could use its gold reserves, *valued at the free market price*, as collateral for loans. Italy immediately pledged one-fifth of its gold, valued at $155 an ounce, as collateral for a $2 billion loan from the Germans. This was the breach in the dam that the French had so long sought, for it virtually established the free market price as the only price. In December 1974 President Giscard d'Estaing, meeting with President Ford in Martinique, secured a joint communique spelling out the logical extension of this move: 'it would be appropriate for any government which wished to do so to adopt current market prices as the basis of valuation for its gold holdings'.

It was the ratification of a famous victory for France — even if her reserves to be revalued upwards were badly depleted. Meanwhile, the gold price continued to sail up, reaching the undreamt-of height of $197.50 by the end of 1974. 'Market analysts' (and speculators) explained earnestly that gold was not a commodity like any other. There was no reason to believe that a price rise would lead to a fall in demand, for the whole point of buying gold was its 'eternal value' which made it the perfect hedge against inflation. It could go on up — through $200, to $300, perhaps $400. There was no upper limit, no ceiling which might not be breached.

---

[1] The move may have been made by the US Treasury and State Department on their own initiative. Nixon was by now near his last gasp and giving scant attention to such affairs. (When aides tried desperately to interest him in the fate of the Italian lira his reply, as the White House tapes all too faithfully record, was 'Fuck the Italian lira'.) The Treasury is unlikely to have agreed to such a move save under the most extreme pressure from the State Department, mortally worried that the crushing defeat of the Italian Christian Democrats in the May 1974 divorce referendum might bring the Communists to power.

For South Africa the gold war opened up a whole new Promised Land. The value of her gold output rose from R775 million in 1967 (the last full year under the *ancien regime* of $35 an ounce) to R847 million in 1969, R922 million in 1971, R1161 million in 1972, R1770 million in 1973 and R2560 million in 1974. Her reserves soared. The Rand was upwardly revalued to $1.49. Every $10 on the average annual price of gold meant an increase of 1% in her GNP.[1] These fabulous figures were achieved despite a falling gold output, indeed, as we have seen, largely because of it.

But victory in the gold war brought gains greater than money. If, as expected, gold maintained its 1974 heights then the failure of South Africa's drive for African markets hardly mattered. The trade deficit, even allowing for the huge rise in the oil price, was clearly a thing of the past in such circumstances. Gold would make South Africa much less vulnerable to fluctuations in the level of foreign investment. It would insulate her from the world recession — while other economies slumped in 1974, South Africa's grew at a real rate of 8%. It would buy arms, it would buy self-sufficiency, it would buy detente — or, if that could not be bought, it would more than cover the cost of isolation. The cliché references to a 'golden future' had to be taken seriously. Pretoria's planners made plain their confidence in such a future by announcing massive expansions in expenditure on the para-statals.[2] Defence expenditure rose 40% in 1974 over the (record) 1973 level and Pretoria confidently announced that it had been decided to fulfil the ten-year Defence Plan in five years.

Confident talk of a golden future provided altogether too simple an assessment, however. Through the booming 1960s South Africa had become even more highly integrated into a world economic system — trade now accounted for well over half of her GNP. In particular she had become involved in major new relationships with the expanding power of the EEC bloc. She had participated in the headlong prosperity of European capitalism and had found herself siding with it in its growing resistance to the *défi Americain*. This resistance had, at first, taken the beneficent form of a competitive struggle for growth. Gradually it had become a bitter struggle of opposition to American hegemony over the world financial system, a struggle in which the gold price had been the symbolic battlefield. South

[1] 'South Africa' in C. Legum (ed.) *Africa Contemporary Record, 1974—5*, p. B475.
[2] See pp. 203—4.

Africa, as we have seen, had happily ridden these trends, luxuriating in the climate of growth and emerging a major winner in the gold war too. She had, though, been riding a tiger. Growing involvement with the EEC bloc also meant growing vulnerability to it. Growth had brought accelerating inflation. It had, too, brought a commodity boom which had ended in the oil crisis. Most important of all, if the US had been displaced from its former position of control, what now underpinned the world economic order? To what rock could one cling with the world sliding into a chaotic period of depression, inflation and radical political change?

It was a pertinent question, for the period 1971—3 was to face South Africa's White Establishment with a growing series of crises. Although these crises were to have important internal repercussions with a momentum all of their own inside South Africa, they were all essentially generated outside South Africa. The world inflation of 1971—3 helped touch off a wave of African strikes, creating a new and assertive mood amongst South Africa's blacks. Changes within the EEC brought about both an alarming alteration in South Africa's relationship with Britain and the collapse of the Portuguese regime. The commodity boom ended with the oil crisis, which was to have major repercussions for both Pretoria's foreign relations and her economy.

Finally, the collapse of the world boom at the end of 1973 ushered the world into a deep depression which was to have important consequences for South Africa not merely because the depression was to hit her too, but because it also helped usher in a new international economic order, pregnant with new threats to South Africa's position. It is to an examination of these crises that we now turn.

5 The Crisis of the Early 1970s

The breakthrough in the gold war had come with the Washington Agreement of 1968. Nonetheless, as we have seen, it was some time before this breach in America's defences could be widened enough for the gold price really to 'take off'. Only in June 1972 did the price break free from a level around $40 to one around $65, and only with the oil crisis of late 1973 did it become established safely above $100. It was not a moment too soon — indeed the ruthlessness of South Africa's tactics in this period (above all the huge cut in gold output of 1973–4) reflected in good part Pretoria's sheer desperation. For the Republic was faced with a new wave of internal unrest, a rapidly deteriorating economic situation, and the dire consequences of changes in the structure of the EEC.

Black Workers and the Economic Conjuncture of 1971–3

Faced with a rocketing import bill, Pretoria had, as we have seen, placed her hopes heavily on a trade drive into Africa. By 1971 the failure of this drive had begun to have alarming results: while the Republic's exports were R211 million less than the planners had projected, imports were R781 million more.[1] If gold wasn't counted, South Africa had a trade gap of R1352 million in 1971; even when the sharply increased value of gold exports was taken into account, this left a gap of R430 million. The inflow of foreign capital reached an all-time record level in 1971. Even allowing for this, a sizeable deficit remained. Should foreign investment fall (and it did) — or should the gold price fall — South Africa's situation would be nothing less than

---

[1] D. Innes, 'The Role of Foreign Trade. . .', in Suckling, op. cit., p. 134. Apart from the disappointment of African trade hopes, the problem derived from the much higher prices of South Africa's high-technology imports as against her mainly raw material exports. The result was a steep deterioration in the terms of trade (excluding gold): taking 1963 = 100 on this index, the terms had fallen from 109 in 1957 to 93 in 1970, 91 in 1971 and 86 in 1972. Even if one includes gold the fall is from 105 in 1957 to 95 in 1971.

desperate. As it was she was forced into a devaluation of the
Rand in December 1971.

These alarming trade figures coincided with a sharp slow-
down in the growth rate. While GDP had grown at a real average
rate of 6.2% per annum in 1963—71, this slowed to around 4%
in 1971—3. Such a rate would have been thoroughly acceptable
to many countries, but it was hardly satisfactory in South
Africa, where a population growth rate of around 3% per
annum meant that an economic growth rate of less than about
3.3% would actually produce a decline in real per capita
incomes. For South Africa a rapid growth rate was not a luxury;
it was essential to political and social stability.

The final element was inflation. Through the 1960s this had
averaged about 3.3% per annum, but now the mounting wave of
world inflation began to hit South Africa. Taking 1970 = 100,
the consumer price index had risen to 141.5 by August 1974.
For food — the key item in the budgets of African workers —
the increase in the same period was much steeper, to 156.4.[1]
The golden sixties were over. Truth to tell, they had never been
very golden for African workers anyway. Black—white
inequalities increased sharply as the whites appropriated the
lion's share of the benefits of increased national affluence. In
April 1969 the Johannesburg *Financial Mail* estimated that on
average the ratio between per capita shares of GDP was better
than 14.5:1 in favour of the whites.[2] At the end of 1970 the
(white) Association of Chambers of Commerce estimated that a
Johannesburg black family of five needed an income of R73.64
a month to maintain a minimum living standard. This businessman's estimate was questioned by academics who suggested that
the true poverty line lay 50% above such a figure. Yet in March
1971 average earnings for black workers in the (relatively
privileged) manufacturing sector were less than R57 a month.[3]
In the mining sector workers were much worse paid — indeed,
black workers in gold mining achieved no increase in their real
wages in the whole period 1911—71. Such a picture of
immovable — or, at least, unmoving — misery and inequality
amidst a sea of affluence was virtually without parallel in the
Western world.

This situation rested to an important degree on black feelings

---

[1] 'South Africa' in C. Legum (ed.) *Africa Contemporary Record, 1974—75*,
p. B483.
[2] *Financial Mail*, 18 April, 1969, cited in R. First *et al.*, op. cit.,
p. 53 — my calculations.
[3] First *et al.*, op. cit., pp. 46—7.

of resignation and hopelessness. The era of Sharpeville had left Africans in very much the state of the nineteenth-century English agricultural labourer described by Thorold Rogers:

> ... scattered and incapable of combined action with his fellows, bowed down by centuries of oppression, hard usage and hard words, with every social force against him, the landlords in league with the farmers and the clergymen in league with both, the latter constantly preaching resignation, the two former constantly enforcing it, he has lived through evil times.[1]

It was, though, a resignation which in turn rested on the known likelihood of repression. Trade unions and strikes by blacks were forbidden by law and the law was backed up by the full power of the state's police and military machine. No black worker could be in any doubt as to the likely consequences of defying this power. At least, there seemed no doubt until December 1971 when Ovambo workers in Namibia staged an intransigent and prolonged strike. The Ovambos were, it is true, 'sheltered' to some extent by the continuous UN scrutiny of Pretoria's actions there. But what gradually sank in amongst their counterparts in South Africa was simply the fact that black workers had defied Pretoria and got away with it.

As inflation mounted at an accelerating rate in 1972 black wages fell further and further behind. In October the dam broke and a great wave of strikes began, centred on workers in the manufacturing sector in and around Durban. Soon there were 60,000 on strike. This was, of course, entirely illegal, but the police made no attempt to enforce the law, though they maintained a strong and intimidating presence. As it was there were a number of violent incidents and it was clear that any attempt to confront the strikers head-on could only produce a major explosion. The strikes ended in February 1973 with the

---

[1] J. E. Thorold Rogers, *Six Centuries of Work and Wages* (1903), p. 509, cited in R. Hilton, *Bond Men Made Free. Medieval Peasant Movements and the English Rising of 1381* (London, 1977) p. 232. The reference to the clergy is not entirely apposite to South Africa where a minority of clerics, particularly among the Catholics, have made a determined stand against apartheid and racial inequality. On the other hand, if one seeks examples of wage freezes elsewhere in the world to parallel the South African case, it is the Catholic Church which holds the record: at the accession of John XXIII the gardeners of the Vatican palace had not had a wage increase in this century. The parable of the labourers in the vineyard can seldom have been so closely, even religiously, followed.

workers winning increases of 15—18%. In March, however, a
fresh strike wave began, again centred on Durban but quickly
spreading round Natal and into the Transvaal. The government
laid the blame on 'agitators', and several hundred arrests were
made. Nonetheless, when the strikers returned to work in
mid-April they had won substantial raises and even certain
legislative concessions.[1] Around South Africa employers
hastened to give pay increases to pre-empt trouble — between
March 1972 and December 1973 Anglo-American increased
basic monthly wages for black miners by 70%, for example.
Nonetheless, the next wave of unrest came in the mines. In
September 1973 at the Western Deep Levels mine at
Carletonville (near Johannesburg) police opened fire on an angry
crowd of black miners protesting at the rejection of their pay
demands. Five of the 12 who died were migrants from Lesotho,
whose government quickly announced that it was suspending all
recruitment in Lesotho for workers for Western Deep. In
January 1974 a further strike wave broke around Durban, with
some 10,000 textile workers coming out. In March they were
joined by workers at British Leyland's Durban plant. It was
reported that more than 20,000 blacks around Durban had now
joined (illegal) trade unions. The police moved in more quickly
this time, arresting some 250 'troublemakers'.

By this stage strikes by black workers had ceased to be
exceptional events, despite the fact that before 1972 nothing
like them had been seen for at least a generation. The new black
working class forged in the boom of the sixties had come of age
and the long quietus since Sharpeville had been rudely
shattered. Time and again strikers had defied the law, government, police and employers and had won not insignificant
concessions. A new and assertive mood had broken surface
among urban blacks which would not easily be quenched or
denied. Faced by thousands of angry and determined Zulu
workers, not only had the police had second thoughts but so
had the KwaZulu Bantustan leader Chief Buthelezi, who had
hastened to give moral support to the Durban strikers. The new
mood was visible, too, in the growth of a 'black consciousness'

[1] Strikes were legalised — under conditions so limited as to be virtually
impossible to fulfill; black workers were given the right to elect
representatives to liaison committees with employers; and urban representative councils were set up for blacks, creating a major, if mainly
theoretical breach (the councils were effectively impotent) with apartheid
doctrine which viewed urban blacks as mere temporary sojourners in
'white' towns.

movement amongst black students grouped in the (all-black) South African Students' Organisation (SASO). The level of social tension between black and white had increased and the calm which returned in the wake of the strikes was incomplete and fragile.

None of this was lost on foreign investors. To be sure, the strikes had not posed the threat which Sharpeville had, but they raised questions as to the Republic's future political stability all the same. The result was a sharp fall in the inflow of foreign funds (down 35% in 1972 over 1971). The strikers had the government cornered — not in the factory yards, but in the world money markets. If strikes went on, investor confidence would remain depressed: if the government stopped them bloodily in their tracks investor confidence would vanish altogether. Gold was the way out and, as we have seen, gold supplies to the market were cut with a new ruthlessness by no less than 11.2% in the following year. It worked — South Africa ran a huge overall surplus of R503 million in 1973 as the gold price rocketed — and the government was saved from the economic consequences of unrest.

At least as significant as the sheer fact of the strikes had, however, been the fact of repression. Sweeping waves of arrests had, in every case, followed the strikes. The legal concessions granted amounted to virtually nothing in practice. The wage increases won were quickly eroded by further inflation. Finding their black labour more expensive white employers attempted to reduce their work-forces and demanded a *quid pro quo* of higher productivity from the rest. Above all, the workers had failed to win either the right to unionise or, in practical terms, the right to strike. The strikes produced no coherent new African organisation; many of those who might have led it were in jail and some strikers had been shot dead. The strikers had not managed to find means of autonomous political expression, and had had to settle for being politically expropriated by Buthelezi. The White Establishment had been jolted more sharply than at any time since Sharpeville, but it had been equal to the challenge. The new mood persisted but the efficacy of repression suggested strongly that industrial action held limited possibilities for the frustrated urban blacks. It pretty well guaranteed that the next wave, when it came, would be more formless, more violent and more difficult to come to terms with. The seeds of Soweto had been sown.

The Fateful Consequences of Georges Pompidou

(a) Britain

A key feature of the 1960s, we have seen, lay in South Africa's successful attempt to lessen her old semi-colonial dependence on Britain. In the 1947—54 period a full 35% of all her imports had come from Britain, and 24.3% from the US with no other single country accounting for more than 3%. By 1972 the UK provided only 23% of her imports and the US 18%; Germany (16%) and Japan (11%) had, to Pretoria's satisfaction, emerged to diversify and broaden the base of South African dependence. Motivation for this drive could, of course, be found easily enough in the anti-imperial traditions of Afrikaner nationalism. But there was a much more down-to-earth reason too. If Macmillan had dropped a bombshell when he rose to give his 'winds of change' speech in Cape Town in 1960, it was a minor one compared to that which he delivered eighteen months later when he rose in the Commons to announce that Britain was applying for EEC membership. Nothing concentrated Pretoria's mind so wonderfully as this, for it was clear that the success of the British application could have dire consequences for South Africa. Even after her exit from the Commonwealth in 1961 South African trade with Britain had continued to enjoy the beneficent cover of the Commonwealth preference system. Now this lynchpin of South African commerce was threatened and her loss of Commonwealth status made it much less likely that Britain would achieve for her the 'special terms' she hoped to negotiate for her other former colonies. This was something Pretoria had not really allowed for. Britain had been seen as the staid and stable metropole which one admired or railed against according to one's predisposition. Suddenly, this fixed star was fixed no more and an entirely new sense of urgency began to infect South Africa's drive for commercial diversification.

The trouble was — as not a few other ex-colonies were discovering at the same time — that long-established trade relations of a neo-colonial kind are not easily or quickly altered. Above all, South Africa needed time. Anything which could delay, let alone halt, Britain's EEC entry would bring blessed relief indeed. Thus Pretoria's overwhelming dislike of the British Labour party quickly took on a more ambivalent tone as the party, particularly its left wing, adopted a stance hostile to EEC membership. Perhaps Harold Wilson and Michael Foot would save Pretoria yet. . . . In the event Pretoria found the ally she needed in the Elysée. In 1963 De Gaulle flatly rejected the

British bid for EEC membership and in 1967 he did it again. Not for the first or last time France came to South Africa's rescue.

Pretoria, as we have seen, used her reprieve well in diversifying her intake of high-technology goods. But her exports were a different matter. Even by 1972 Britain was still taking no less than 31% of all her exports and in certain key sectors her dependence was even greater — in that year, for example, Britain took 72% of her canned fruit and 43% of her fresh fruit exports. With Britain out of the EEC less than 5% of South Africa's exports to her were subject to customs duties; on the terms under which Britain was eventually to enter, this figure would rise to 53%. Mr S. L. Muller, Pretoria's Minister for Economic Affairs at the time, calculated dolefully that South Africa would thereby lose around 11% of her total export earnings.[1] The brunt of such a disaster would, moreover, fall most particularly on the Afrikaans farming community, the bedrock of the government's electoral base. Despite a full decade of determined effort the fact remained that Pretoria was still desperately exposed by her dependence on British markets. It was all very well trying to diversify, but the fact was that British consumers had a taste for South African goods which others obstinately refused to develop — Britain, for example, imported more tinned fruit than all the other EEC countries put together. There could be no easy escape from imponderables like that.

While De Gaulle remained in office it seemed tolerably certain that South Africa's reprieve would last. But in 1969 a new French president, Georges Pompidou, was elected. It was a fateful moment. However accommodating of Pretoria's interests Pompidou might prove in other respects, it rapidly became evident that he did not share his predecessor's rooted objection to British EEC entry. Pretoria's (silent) prayers might be with the anti-marketeers of the Labour left, but Pompidou was clearly the pivot. By 1971 it was certain that Britain would indeed join. By the terms of the Heath—Pompidou agreement the full rigour of the EEC tariff system would finally be clamped around the British market by the end of 1977. A vast new trading bloc would then emerge — for others would be swept in on Britain's coat-tails — to South Africa's grievous disadvantage. Indeed, its formation would largely nullify South Africa's attempts to diversify her export markets, for her

[1] I am, again, indebted in this section to D. Innes, 'The Role of Foreign Trade...' op. cit., esp. pp. 140—7.

dependence on the European market as a whole (the EFTA and
EEC blocs together) had been increasing, not diminishing. In
1947—54 this market had taken 50.2% of all her exports; by
1963—70 it was taking 55.2%. Perhaps even more alarming was
the fact that Britain's entry would also sweep into association
with the EEC most of independent Anglophone Africa. Since
the Francophone states were already thus associated, this would
mean that virtually the entire African continent *except* South
Africa would have a special relationship with the EEC. South
Africa could, of course, plead in Brussels for similar treatment
but this massive African presence would be there too, arguing
forcibly against her. And with EEC access to the raw materials
of the rest of the continent thus increased, South Africa's
bargaining points in Brussels would be commensurately weaker.
South Africa's hopes for increased African trade would also be
still further reduced — the EEC could provide black Africa with
manufactured goods a-plenty and EEC manufacturers would
have preferential terms to help them. As disasters go, it was
fairly complete.

There was not a great deal Pretoria could do. She could try to
develop markets elsewhere — but she had been trying to do this
for years without notable success. Great hopes were held of
Japan, but the Japanese record for buying large quantities of
other countries' manufactured goods was hardly very encouraging. Perhaps the most promising prospect lay in trying to vault
indirectly into the EEC market by developing special trade and
investment relationships with associated third-party states.
Mauritius was the main hope here — in 1971 its government
announced that it would issue permits for re-packing and
re-exporting goods free of all tax, customs and port duties. But
attendant upon this strategy were severe political difficulties,
which might grow. If none of these strategies worked, or
worked only partially, South Africa would simply have to pull
in her belt very sharply, put her faith in a permanently high
gold price, and keep pleading with Brussels.

(b) Portugal

These dangers lay ahead in the medium term — Britain would
not be fully in the EEC until the end of 1977. Long before that,
however, the expansion of the EEC bloc was to have dire and
immediate consequences for the stability of the northern buffer
which South Africa had so carefully constructed around her
borders. In this buffer the black states — Malawi, Lesotho
Botswana and Swaziland — were merely 'in-filling' between the
two great flanks provided by Angola and Mozambique. These

territories in turn could only remain part of the White South as long as Portuguese colonialism remained in control of them. By saying 'Yes' where De Gaulle had said 'No' President Pompidou indirectly, and doubtless unintentionally, had deprived South Africa of something more important than Commonwealth preference. For, as soon became clear, Portuguese colonialism could not survive British entry to the EEC.

Essentially Portugal had been able to exercise colonial sway in Africa until 1974 because she had kept out of the Second World War. Entry on either side would have resulted in her being over-run by the other and losing her colonies, either immediately, or after the war when she would have been too weak to resist. It was no accident that she should have stood to one side of the European conflict, for the Salazar regime was keen to distance itself from the whole wave of European (democratic) develop-ment. The appeal of Africa was precisely that it allowed Portugal to pretend not to be a part of Europe. After 1945 the US used her economic strength to coax her European allies into disgorging their colonies. The Dutch, the British, the French and the Belgians all needed American support for their currencies, Marshall aid for their ravaged economies, and the American umbrella of defence and goodwill too much to resist these pressures indefinitely. Portugal could and did resist. Salazar had amassed enormous gold reserves and the world's most stable currency. It was not Salazar who particularly needed or wanted the Americans. It was they who wanted Portugal. NATO could afford Spanish, but not Portuguese, non-membership. She commanded the mid-Atlantic and the central approaches to the whole of Europe, and her island possessions — Cape Verde, Sao Tomé, the Azores — enjoyed situations of great strategic importance. Moreover, Portugal's island possessions, as also Timor, Goa, and Macao, raised little political heat, while her only significant colonies — Angola and Mozambique — were remote parts of an anyway delicate region in which the USA wanted stability and South African goodwill. So though the State Department might express polite dis-approval of Portuguese colonialism, it made no serious effort to force her into line with the other decolonising powers. Meanwhile the Salazar regime proceeded with an extraordinarily ambitious programme of colonisation (by 1974 there were some 350,000 settlers in Angola, 200,000 in Mozambique) with the idea of binding these 'overseas provinces' tightly to her bosom, a self-sufficient, self-encapsulated zone of imperial preference, allowing Portugal an escape route from a Europe in which she felt alien and uncomfortable.

It simply couldn't work. Portugal was too weak economically. If she, or her colonies, were to grow at the desired rate she
simply had to allow foreign investors in behind the imperial
walls.[1] More significant still was the formation of the EEC in
1957. Portugal was part of Europe and could not prevent the
rays of this mighty and ever-growing economic sun from beating
in through her doors, windows and roof. Her economy
depended more on EEC trade and tourists with each passing
year. Her people were sucked bodily into the EEC economy. By
1973 there were 1.5 million Portuguese (one-sixth of her
population) living and working abroad, mainly in France and
West Germany. Despite her best efforts the proportion of her
trade done with her colonies declined steadily, from 34% in
1960 to 25% in 1969. She sought escape by joining the
loosely-structured EFTA, but even this was a major compromise
of her non-European orientation. She could not join the EEC
without sacrificing what was left of imperial protection, nor
without a fearful shock to her unproductive agriculture and her
weak industrial base.

The result was that in the 1960s Portugal under Salazar began
to bleed to death; indeed, it could be said that the ageing
dictator, as life drained out of him, settled on the same fate for
his entire realm. Between 1960 and 1970 the population of the
rural interior fell by as much as a third as migrants left for the
EEC, to the colonies as settlers, and to the colonies as soldiers
to protect the settlers. During the 1950s and 1960s Portugal's
population, uniquely in Europe, actually fell. Portugal clung to
Africa more and more desperately, asserting her anaemia into a
principle, a mission; a dying man insisting on his right to be a
blood donor.

This policy could not last. It was simultaneously threatened
from two directions. In the colonies the rise of the liberation
movements — FRELIMO in Mozambique, MPLA in Angola, and
the PAIGC in Guinea-Bissau — taxed her strength more and
more; to win they had, ultimately, only to survive, for their
opponent couldn't. A more immediate threat was that
Britain — still her major trading partner — would join the EEC.
If this occurred Portugal would simply have to join too and
accept her European fate. When De Gaulle vetoed British entry
in 1963 Lisbon withdrew her application with a sigh of relief;
his veto, in effect, extended Portugal's colonial life by a decade.
When Britain applied again in 1970 Dr Patricio (Portugal's

---

[1] This occurred only after 1962 when the colonial investments laws were
liberalised. For the effects on Angola, see pp. 59—60.

Foreign Minister) pointed out the country's dilemma. The EEC
and EFTA blocs between them accounted for 72% of Portugal's
exports and 69% of her imports. She could not afford to stay
out. On the other hand she could not afford to go in — her
economy would be simply overwhelmed. If the British were
bracing themselves for the 'cold shower' of EEC membership,
Portugal knew that she would drown. So Dr Patricio announced
that, while Portugal could not afford full membership, she
would negotiate for 'an appropriate formula'. All hope vanished
when Pompidou assented to British entry for 1 January, 1973
(along with Denmark, Ireland and Norway). By the end of April
1972 protracted negotiations had secured special arrangements
for only 38% of Portugal's total exports and 53% of her
imports. Dr Xavier Pintado, the Secretary of State for
Commerce, pointed out in desperation that

> unless these conditions are changed, more than a quarter of
> our exports destined for the enlarged Community will be
> subject to restrictions, and tariff barriers will again be erected
> in relation to about 40% of our exports to the existing
> members of EFTA who are joining the Common Market
> where these barriers have been eliminated.

Worse still, Portugal had only until 1980 to abolish all tariffs on
EEC imports (they would have to be reduced by 60% by 1
January 1978). She pleaded desperately but unsuccessfully for
time, for further concessions, for some possible let-out. The
new arrangements came into force on 1 January, 1973, which
meant that the really severe effects of tariff reductions would
begin to be felt by 1975—6. It was clear from the outset that
Portugal could only survive if quite massive aid could be
provided to bolster her industry and agriculture against this
coming wave. But no foreign donor was in sight, and the
Portuguese state was wholly committed financially to the
efforts of funding the colonial wars.

Thus the writing was in the wall for Portuguese colonialism
from 1971 on. The fate of the Portuguese bourgeoisie was clear
then: it was to be fastened to the iron clock of the EEC, and it
simply could not survive unless it could bring the colonial wars
to a speedy end. Consciousness of this imperative spread deeply
and quickly among Lisbon's elites. It was hardly a new feeling
among radicals and the war-weary, but it now gained ground
amongst all shades of conservative and reactionary opinion —
even military conservatives like Spinola who had fought the
wars happily for a decade. Hence the increasingly desperate

search for 'solutions' to end the wars. Perhaps the wars could be
ended summarily by desperate acts of cloak-and-dagger daring
(the invasion of Conakry in November 1970, the assassination
of Cabral in 1972)? Or perhaps by throwing every ounce of
force into a great sweep against the liberated areas (the Tete
province campaign of 1970—1 in Mozambique)? And, when it
became clear that neither of these tactics had substantially
disposed of the liberation movements, perhaps, after all, the
'solution' could be found in 'reforms'? Thus Caetano's 1971
measures — bold indeed in the context of his factional struggles
with the Salazarist die-hards, for Caetano spoke of the
possibility of the 'overseas provinces' one day becoming
'autonomous states'. None of these 'solutions' remotely
answered to the situation. In the end it was merely a race
against time, with one desperate 'solution' following pell-mell
on another. The conclusion was hardly in doubt: Portugal
would decolonise. If Caetano could not do it, someone else
would have to. In the Portuguese context this 'someone else'
would necessarily have to be found among the military. And so
he was. The final *coup de grâce* was given by the wave of world
inflation, lapping into Portugal as it had with such dire effects
already in South Africa. If the Salazar regime had had one
saving grace it had been a strong currency and stable prices.
Now these too were gone.

By April 1974, however, the pressure had been allowed to
build to a point where there could be no easy or orderly
transition to the Centrist—Catholic coalition which European
analogy suggested as the most natural and appropriate reflection
of Portuguese social forces. Instead, a great radical effervescence
had to work itself out over two years before such a regime
could settle comfortably into place, decolonisation happening,
raggedly, en route. The conservatives and intransigents of
Lisbon had fought one another, while both were squeezed by an
unlikely alliance of the liberation movements on one side and
the EEC Commissioners on the other. Salazar had always known
that Portugal could not choose both Africa *and* Europe, and so
chose Africa. His successors had the choice of Europe forced
upon them and tried desperately to choose both. Salazar had
been quite right and, for all their contortions, his successors
quickly found that they had chosen Europe alone. This,
together with the sheer turmoil surrounding their own accession
to power, gave them problems enough, making the fate of the
African colonies seem little more than a distraction. There the
PAIGC, MPLA and FRELIMO stood waiting to inherit the
fruits of their own long, patient, and determined struggles.

President Pompidou, the indirect and unwitting author of their triumph, did not live to see it, for he died just three weeks before the Lisbon coup of April 1974.

For the White Establishment of southern Africa it was an unequivocal disaster, by far the greatest of the several which the 1970s had brought flooding in. The regimes likely to assume power in Angola and Mozambique were those of the radical guerrilla movements, committed for many years past to carrying the armed struggle further south, against Rhodesia, and against South Africa itself. Meanwhile, the whole of Pretoria's northern buffer stood ready to collapse. For Pretoria the only question was to what lengths she would go to stop, divert or accommodate herself to this disaster. But, from April 1974 on it was clearly the problem of Humpty-Dumpty: no amount of effort could put all the pieces back together again.

Yom Kippur, Oil, and the Afro-Arab Front

The oil crisis — that is to say, the dramatic rise in the oil price and the long-term threat to oil supplies — emerged from the Yom Kippur (Arab—Israeli) war of October 1973. In fact the fundamental precondition of the price-rise, so damaging to all non-oil producers, lay not in the war but in the gradual erosion of American self-sufficiency in oil through the 1960s. While the USA had an oil surplus — or was even self-sufficient — there could be no basis for an oil cartel. The whole Western world, including South Africa, had been shielded from the oil power of the OPEC states by the richness of the Texan reserves. By 1973 this shield had for some years ceased to exist, but it was not without importance that the last pretence of it was so brutally ripped away in an Arab—Israeli war.

The oil crisis was, of course, a crisis for the whole world, but its incidence on South Africa took a highly specific form. The sheer increase in price — 'the' problem for the rest of the world — was almost the least significant aspect of the crisis for South Africa. True, South Africa had no oil of her own and the new price cost her an immediate R700 million a year — with more to follow — on her balance of payments; and the imposition of petrol-saving constraints was a shock to a car-based white South African society. But only 23.4% of South Africa's gross energy needs were supplied from oil, the rest coming from coal, of which she has some of the world's largest (and most cheaply mined) reserves. Pretoria had, moreover, made good use of its golden decade. SASOL, the oil-from-coal para-statal, had been built up by dint of huge state subsidies to provide 8—10% of the country's oil needs, and within a year of the crisis the government announced that it would build a second SASOL plant with ten times the capacity of the first. South Africa had, moreover, been one of the very few countries in the world which had actually prepared for the eventuality of an oil boycott. Oil had been stockpiled in disused gold mines — enough of it for the country to withstand a two-year total blockade.[1] Finally, the oil price-rise, as we have seen, had an almost immediate self-cancelling effect, for the crisis thus produced helped send the gold price spiralling up. That rise was, of course, already 'mortgaged' by the need to compensate for failures in African trade and the fall in foreign investment, but even so it helped, initially at least, to cushion South Africa from the body blow of its hugely increased import bill.

The Yom Kippur war of 1973 had provided a more immediate blow, however. Despite overtly cool relationships between the two states, South Africa had always felt strong affinities with Israel as another ethnically defined Western state threatened by a surrounding sea of third world nationalism.[2] The realisation that Israel would quite probably lose any future war to the Arabs, and had almost lost this one, was a considerable psychological shock. South Africans had always made a tacit assumption that Western military superiority was in part founded upon an intrinsic human superiority, soldier to soldier. Surely this was why mere handfuls of Western mercenaries had achieved such striking and repeated success in African wars? The formidable performance of the Syrian and Egyptian armies threw grave doubts on to these assumptions. The fighting itself had provided a dramatic demonstration of the potency of

---

[1] It is worth pointing out that the doubtless enormous expense of these and other contingency schemes had never been entered into calculations of the Defence Budget which had always been much larger than it seemed (even though it accounted visibly for over one-fifth of *all* public expenditure). The (huge) police budget is also accounted separately from that for Defence.

[2] The fact that Israelis cited the Old Testament in order to explain their unwillingness to be mingled with the Arabs could not but evoke deep echoes in Biblically-minded Afrikaners. Dr Verwoerd had drawn the parallel quite directly in 1961, noting how the Jews 'took Israel from the Arabs after Arabs had lived there for thousands of years. In that I agree with them. Israel, like South Africa, is an apartheid state.' In the same year Verwoerd had warned the South African Jewish community that 'it had not gone unnoticed' that so many of them were supporting the Progressive Party, while it was a not uncommon taunt by Nationalist MPs against the Progressives' lone MP, Mrs Suzman, that 'Karl Marx was also a Jew' (like her). The happy co-existence of Afrikaner anti-semitism and pro-Zionism exactly inverts the official Arab position of anti-Zionism and a denial of anti-semitism. There seems little doubt which Tel-Aviv prefers.

one-man, hand-held missiles against Israeli Mirages, Alouettes, and Centurions, which were, of course, also the basic weaponry of the South African armed forces. What havoc might not ensue if guerrillas began appearing in the Caprivi Strip (for example) armed with the same surface missilery? The idea was not far-fetched. In March 1973 the PAIGC guerrillas in Guinea-Bissau had begun to make successful use of SAMs (surface-to-air missiles) against Portuguese aircraft in Guinea-Bissau. It is only about once in every generation that a weapon is developed which can, on its own, decisively alter a state of military balance. The tank had been one such. SAMs, it now seemed, were another, largely negating the normal airpower and armour advantages enjoyed by counter-insurgency forces against guerrillas.

The war and the oil crisis also had a major and deleterious impact on South Africa's international position, deepening the Republic's isolation in two separate ways. First, the Algiers Arab Summit of November 1973 decreed an oil boycott against South Africa and Portugal. This move apparently represented a major coup for the African States which, for a decade and more, had unsuccessfully sought to gain Arab support for their campaign against apartheid and Portuguese colonialism. They had, it seemed, at last achieved their object at a single stroke by capitalising on a wave of emotional Third World feeling against the West.

In fact the Arabs had their own reasons for action against South Africa. Despite Pretoria's formal declaration of neutrality in the Yom Kippur War, Israel's public denunciations of apartheid and the diplomatic coolness between the two states notwithstanding, it had gradually become clear that this was a mere front which more and more thinly disguised the existence of a de facto Pretoria–Tel-Aviv axis, stretching back at least to 1967. In 1967 Pretoria had relaxed its foreign exchange controls specifically in order to allow some R21.5 million to flow out to Israel from the South African Jewish community and the South African blood transfusion service loaned blood to Israel.[1] More significantly, it gradually became known that South African army officers had been present as observers during the June war, and in 1968 the Chief of Staff of the Israeli Air Force, General Mordechai Hod, visited the South African staff college to explain in detail the aerial lessons of the war. These clearly sank in at a high level, for P. W. Botha,

[1] I am much indebted in the following section to P. Hellyer, *Israel and South Africa. Development of Relations 1967–1974* (London, 1975).

Pretoria's Minister of Defence, publicly warned Zambia in 1968 that acting as a base for guerrilla movements could lead to air-strikes against her analogous to the Israeli reprisal raids against Palestinian guerrilla bases. Meanwhile, the hitherto negligible trade between the two countries began to expand. The year 1969 brought to South Africa a number of leading Israeli visitors, including the former premier, David Ben Gurion, and the former intelligence chief, Haim Herzog, who was known still to be an influential actor in the Israeli military establishment. From 1970 on reports began to appear of a trade in arms between the two countries, South Africa showing interest in light Israeli planes (including the Arava fighter), Israel a reciprocal interest in a South African monster (65 ton) tank as a substitute for the Chieftain which she was having difficulty in acquiring from Britain. In 1971 came more such reports — that South Africa was manufacturing the famous Israeli Uzi machine gun (via an elaborate licensing system leading through Belgium); that Israel had replaced three South African Air Force jets which had crashed into Table Mountain; and, most electrifying of all, that the Israeli espionage service had obtained blueprints of the French Mirage fighter and made them available to Pretoria. In 1972 and 1973 there was intensified diplomatic traffic. Among the Israeli dignitaries to visit South Africa in this period was the Chief Rabbi, Shlomo Goren. The Rabbi, who displayed an interest in military affairs perhaps unusual in a man of God, held meetings with the Defence Minister, P. W. Botha, the Commandant-General of the armed forces, Admiral H. H. Bierman, and sundry other defence chiefs. Visitors in the other direction included Pretoria's Interior Minister, Connie Mulder, and General Van den Bergh, the head of BOSS. Van den Bergh's visit clearly gave the seal of approval to the new relationship from the most powerful man in South Africa's entire military—security complex. Van den Bergh, despite a previously outstanding reputation for anti-semitism,[1] returned flushed with Zionist enthusiasm to tell South Africa that 'as long as Israel exists we have a hope'.

The Arab Summit at Algiers in November 1973 was doubtless well aware of this growing evidence of South African—Israeli

---

[1] In 1971, the author met a leading official of KANU, the Kenyan single party, who had been on a private 'goodwill' visit to South Africa where he had, inter alia, been entertained by the head of BOSS. The General had bemused his guest by going through the Johannesburg telephone directory with him, pointing out with indignation the plethora of large Jewish business enterprises listed therein.

military co-operation, and is unlikely to have been much impressed by Pretoria's formal declaration of neutrality. During the Yom Kippur war both Vorster and P. W. Botha had spoken of their sympathy for Israel in her struggle against 'communistic militarism, which also poses a threat to us'. Over R20 million reached Israel from South African donations during the war, as did several thousand South African Jews to reinforce the Israeli armed forces and medical teams.[1] Most damaging of all were reports that Pretoria had flown several SAAF Mirages (via the Portuguese Atlantic islands) to reinforce the Israelis, one of which the Egyptians claimed to have shot down on the Suez front. The Portuguese had attracted Arab ire on their own account. For Lisbon had repaid Nixon's favours by making the Azores base quite openly available to US planes flying crucial arms reinforcements to Israel in the midst of the war.

Thus it was the Arabs who were the bidders at Algiers, not the Africans. They were infuriated at the behaviour of Portugal and South Africa, with whom they would probably have broken off diplomatic relations whatever the Africans had done. As it was they were able to use this as a bargaining counter to gain the additional prize of African support against Israel, thus forging an alliance which had eluded their pursuit for many years.

Israel had expended great energy to prevent such an alliance. She had maintained a large-scale diplomatic and aid presence throughout black Africa. This effort, it was later revealed, had been financed by the CIA, to whom the Israeli presence was decidedly useful, posing for Africans the image of a technically impressive model of development which took an uncommitted 'third way' between the super-power blocs — but which was, in fact covertly and implicitly pro-Western. These efforts were now undermined in a single great wave of oil — and by a straightforward deal at Algiers: the Arabs bought African solidarity against Israel by guaranteeing their support against South Africa. The Israeli diplomatic presence in Africa abruptly collapsed.

In 1967 a handful of the more radical African states had broken off diplomatic relations with Israel, but their example was now followed by 27 others in the space of a few weeks. Simultaneously, the African front against South Africa became an Afro—Arab front. South Africa was, in the event, able to gain

---

[1] These included, notably, Dr Barry Kaplan, a member of Christiaan Barnard's heart transplant team, and Dr C. L. Kowalsky, who was captured by the Syrians on Mt Hermon.

access to oil supplies from non-Arab countries (principally Iran), but her sources of possible supply were, at a stroke, greatly narrowed. The international coalition against her was now greatly strengthened, for it now included the mighty presence of Saudi Arabia as well as all the other Gulf kingdoms. Even if Pretoria could get by without them for her oil, there was no gainsaying the fact that these states were the new arbiters of the world energy market and had voices which were listened to with rapt attention in every capital in the world. Moreover, although Pretoria had in the past always sneered at the threat of the oil-boycott weapon being used against her, she could not but be alarmed at the clear efficacy of that weapon now. Once it had been invoked and used in 1973, and then only half-heartedly — even supplies to Holland (black-listed by the Arabs for her open pro-Israel stand) were not seriously interrupted — it became clear how powerful a weapon it was. For, in fear of that weapon and with quite disturbing speed, several major pro-Western powers, most obviously Japan, hurriedly slid on to the diplomatic fence, or even simply vaulted right over it to the Arab side. If Japan — the second economic power in the world after the USA — could be made to dance to Arabian music, then what did this portend for South Africa? What if the Arab states went further and refused their oil to all those countries who dealt with Pretoria? South Africa had been playing with fire in cultivating an Israeli alliance after 1967 but it took the Yom Kippur war to show just how great the risks might be.

Related to this latter consideration was the second major effect of the oil crisis on South Africa's isolation, the weakening of the protective umbrella held over her by the Western powers. For the West had to take prudent account not only of the formidable strength of the Afro—Arab alliance against Pretoria, but of the fact that the crisis had endowed the African states themselves with a wholly new economic and strategic importance. The rise in the oil price meant that overnight new riches were bestowed on the oil-producing states of Africa — Libya, Algeria, Gabon, Nigeria and Angola. The result was a major shift in power and influence, particularly since three of these states had 'radical' regimes and Nigeria, for its part, was keen to assert a powerful and authentic (i.e. anti-South African) African voice. The major Western powers, until 1973, could not but be conscious of the fact that South Africa was a trading giant. More than half of all British trade with Africa, for example, was conducted with South Africa alone, and the same was true for the other major trading powers. Even in the British case this rapidly ceased to be true. Oil and its attendant effects for general economic expansion now made it certain that with every passing year the relative gap in trading terms would widen against South Africa. A single statistic threw the new situation into sharp relief: in 1978 Nigeria's GNP, swollen by oil revenues, would reach $32 billion, making her economy, not South Africa's, the largest on the African continent. The Western powers could not be oblivious to such a major economic shift, nor of the need to manifest a new regard for African political sensibilities. The British, with the largest stake in both black Africa and the White South, provided the most sensitive weathervane. When a majority Labour government took power in Britain in October 1974 one of its first acts was to retire the Royal Navy from use of the Simonstown base. In the context of British politics this was viewed as a triumph for the Labour left, which it only very partially was. The Foreign Office had had little difficulty resisting clamour against Simonstown throughout the whole period of the 1964—70 Labour government; that it now simply ceased to hold its line was a reflection of the power not of the Labour left, but of the post-1973 Afro—Arab bloc. In fact the Foreign Office had already shown its new colours in September by displaying a quite unwonted — and public — zeal in castigating Jordan for selling British arms to South Africa and Rhodesia.[1] The British had been quick to scent and catch the new prevailing wind but it was clearly only a matter of time before the other Western powers turned their sails about too. Such a move was even more threatening to Pretoria than the formation of an Afro—Arab front against her. For by 1974 the international political and economic order which had prevailed since 1945 was visibly breaking up. In the new and uncertain situation thus created South Africa, shaken by internal unrest, threatened by the collapse of Portuguese colonialism and menaced by the OPC powers, needed all the friends she had.

---

[1] The Foreign Office's first announcement — that it was investigating reports that 100 Hawker Hunters, 50 Centurion tanks, and the Tigercat missile system, originally sold to Jordan, had been sold on to South Africa and Rhodesia — drew fierce denials from Jordan. After a few weeks the FO announced that these items had indeed all gone to South Africa. The Jordanians now admitted that this was true of at least the tanks and missiles, gratuitously adding that it was untrue to suggest that Jordanian technicians had gone to instruct the purchasers in their use. Until then no-one had suggested it. . . .

6 A New International Economic Order?

The oil crisis was not merely a crisis for South Africa but for the world. The great world boom of 1971—3 had, before the crisis, already begun to judder and slow under the combined impact of record inflation, raw material shortages and industrial capacity bottlenecks, but the oil crisis provided the *coup de grâce*. As 1973 ended the Western industrialised world began to nose-dive, like a stricken ship, into the deepest depression it had known since the 1930s. Not surprisingly, the oil crisis and the Arabs were widely depicted as the villains of the piece; the long beneficent upswing of the post-war world economy had, it seemed to many, been killed off somewhere in the Mitla Pass or the Golan Heights. In fact, as we have seen, this was a superficial and misleading view. Throughout the 1960s the international economic order inaugurated at Bretton Woods had come under steadily increasing stress. The old order had essentially been one of American economic hegemony, an order based on the final power and certainty of the US dollar. With America letting her own blood in Vietnam and rival powers growing stronger every year, this dollar hegemony had become weaker and weaker, a fact reflected in the increasing instability of the world financial system. None of the various attempts to patch up the old order could work for long; the house was falling down and even the most ingenious building extensions to it did not compensate for its basic structural weaknesses. In a sense the old system ended in a blaze of glory, with a great, final, concerted and giddy boom.

It was only with the crash that the world began, dimly, to recognise that the day of the old system was over, that a wholly new and uncertain epoch had begun. As this fact was grasped there was mounting discussion of the 'new international economic order', usually envisaged as a world in which the primary producers of the Third World either had established or were about to establish an entirely new position of strength in relation to the industrialised world. This view was fallacious, not merely because there was no other commodity which provided the bargaining power that oil did, but because it was

102

altogether too simple a picture of a complex and confused reality. South Africa, we have seen, was peculiarly vulnerable to changes in the international order. Not only did the crises which brought an end to her boom period of the sixties all have their origins in the world beyond, but gold, on which so many of her hopes rested, lay at the disputed centre of the international financial system. If we are to assess the position of South Africa in the post-1973 world it is necessary to explore the main contours of the new 'order'.

The first and most obvious feature of the new situation was that there was no 'order' to it at all. There was, rather, a confused and unstable multi-polar world. The US had lost control not only economically but also politically. The combination of inflation and recession produced a wave of political instability which helped bring the demise of governments and regimes among the more fragile states of the 'Free World' — not only in Vietnam, Cambodia and Laos, but in Thailand, Pakistan, Bangladesh, Lebanon, Ethiopia, Greece and Portugal. Others — in Italy and Spain for example — trembled on the brink. Revolutionary regimes came to power in Portuguese Africa; and in several other states — Benin, Jamaica and Guyana,[1] for example — already radical governments moved sharply further left. Many of the casualties were conservative American-backed regimes, secure enough in the heyday of American supremacy, but now no longer so. Many more such regimes — Brazil, Zaire, Mexico and the Philippines were among the more obvious examples, but there were literally scores of others — were kept afloat only by dint of enormous and often uncollectable loans. These loans, mainly of American provenance, were the chief lever by which the US sought to retain control of the chaos which threatened. It was an impressive demonstration of Western, especially American, determination to hold the political line in the Third World at a time when there were problems enough at home. But the stability it bought was only partial and the price was considerable.

At the same time the OPEC nations emerged as a powerful array of states all willing and able to take up and maintain highly independent positions, without necessary reference to the State Department view of the world. It was, as often as not, their money, recycled through the financial centres of the West,

---

[1] Guyana, once a watchword for American determination to prevent left-wing governments coming to power in Latin America, applied for associated membership of Comecon (the Communist economic community) early in 1977.

which provided the funds for the life-saving loans. Nonetheless,
the money they lent to the Western banks continued to
constitute a real claim on Western resources. If, for example,
Chase Manhattan borrowed from Kuwait in order to lend to
Zaire which then defaulted, it was Chase Manhattan that
suffered, not Kuwait.

There had been no OPEC bloc to complicate the picture in
the 1930s Depression, and neither had there been a strong
Communist bloc. Indirectly it was this bloc which was
responsible for the rise of OPEC, for there could be no doubt
that in an earlier period the West would have simply dealt with
the oil price rise by sending in gunboats. The might of the Soviet
bloc had stood interposed against such a solution since at least
1956. In 1973 Kissinger railed furiously against OPEC and
refused, at first, to rule out resort to military action, but the
Soviet bloc stood firm and Kissinger's bluster merely served to
underline American impotence. The OPEC states immediately
began to arm themselves to the teeth with weapons which
America, making the best of a bad job, sold them.

The OPEC states were, of course, untouched by the
recession. They boomed and grew at unprecedented rates, while
the industrialised West stagnated or even registered negative
growth. This, indeed, was the distinguishing characteristic of the
1970s depression. In the 1930s there had been a Depression in
the whole world (save the USSR). In the 1970s there was a
Depression in the Western capitalist world — which had shrunk
to be only half the world. The communist states, like the OPEC
states, continued to grow steadily in strength. The relative
effect was quite dramatic. After 1973 the Western states
experienced several years of effectively nil growth, while the
Communist states grew by 15—25% and added a commensurate
margin to their military strength. The significance of this shift
was not widely noted in the West at first. There was, for
example, little comment on the fact that East Germany had
surpassed Britain in per capita GNP. As the 1970s progressed
there was, however, increasing Western unease at growing
Communist military strength and, accordingly, an increasing
American urgency for progress in the Strategic Arms Limitation
Talks (SALT). The most visible outward symbol of this shift
was the new strength of the Soviet Navy on the world's seas,
and an increased Soviet capacity to affect events in far-flung
corners of the world — Angola being perhaps the clearest
example. In the US this turn of events provoked ferocious
criticism of the policy of 'detente' — criticism which tended to
assume a failure of will rather than ability. American politicians,

like their British counterparts before them, found it difficult to admit the facts of relative imperial decline to a public long fed on the rhetoric of 'greatness'.

More serious than this for the Western economy, however, was the loss of American leadership. If the Great Depression of the 1930s had had a single cause it was to be found in the vacuum created by the inability of the British to provide a continuing bedrock for the international economic order and the unwillingness, and perhaps inability, of the USA to take their place.[1] A crisis of such magnitude could only be tackled if one state of sufficient economic strength was willing to keep its market open, provide a secure 'basic' currency, be a leader of last resort, provide discount facilities and keep long-term capital flowing. In the 1930s no such state or stable combination of states could be found. The British had lost the ability to play this role by 1918 and the USA perhaps could not, and certainly did not, consent to play it until 1945. The consequences had been a post-war recession, a giddy boom ended by the crash of 1929—31 and a protracted depression from which the world was rescued only by war. Now, in the 1970s, a similar vacuum threatened to appear at the base of the international economic and financial order. Each of the major capitalist states — Japan, Germany and the US — urged the others to lead the Western World out of recession by reflating *their* economies, but none would accept the burden which such leadership would impose. The result was, of course, stagnation at a depressed level, just as it had been in the 1930s. Ironically, it was the Communist states which offered a major element of stability for the capitalist world by their willingness to borrow heavily and expand their imports of Western goods, thus maintaining production and demand in the West at appreciably higher levels than would otherwise have obtained.

However, while the post-1973 world depression witnessed an indubitable weakening of the USA's overall strength, it para-doxically increased it in relation to the other major capitalist powers. Under the favourable circumstances of universal boom the relative strengths of the European, Japanese and American economies had been to some extent disguised. Under the weight of depression these relative strengths re-emerged very sharply indeed. Thus in the wake of 1973 the Italian and British economies rapidly neared a point of collapse, leading them to

[1] In this interpretation I am following, of course, that of C. P. Kindleberger, *The World in Depression, 1929—1939* (London, 1973).

scurry, cap in hand, into the debtors' queue at the IMF in Washington. France was only marginally better off. The Japanese, humiliated by Nixon's 1971 measures and conscious of their dependence on foreign markets and raw materials, made it clear that no challenge to Washington would come from them. The Germans, rendered the more anxious by the transparent weakness of the EEC bloc, huddled as closely as ever under the American military umbrella. The worse the crisis got the stronger the resolve of the second-tier capitalist states became to seek shelter under the tall walls of Fortress America. De Gaulle, at a peculiarly favourable conjuncture, had had the quixotic nerve to mount an essentially political challenge to American economic and financial hegemony. After 1973 it soon became clear that there was neither any prospect nor any real basis for a further such challenge. If the Western world *was* to escape from depression it was tolerably certain that only the USA had even the potential strength to lead the way out (by reflating her economy first and hard). No other state could do it, and the formation of a combination of states able to perform such a function seemed most unlikely. Thus while the roots of the depression lay in the relative weakness of the American economy vis-à-vis her rivals, a striking result of the depression was to increase American strength and leverage over these rivals.

Moreover, it gradually dawned that the oil crisis had immensely reinforced America's position. Not only was it her companies who were dominant within the Arab world, but she was, after all, an oil-rich country. Even if she *was* as much as 40% import-dependent for her oil, Japan, Germany and other Western states were virtually 100% dependent. She had enormous potential reserves in shale and tar-sands deposits. She was still the world's granary to an important extent — a fact emphasised by the vast Russian purchases of grain. The Vietnamese drain on US resources was over — a fact which, together with the oil crisis, greatly strengthened the dollar. The US payments deficit vanished — in 1973 she actually had a trade surplus of $1680 million. US relations (and trade prospects) with Russia *and* China were good. She could even turn purposively to bringing a peace settlement to the Middle East, dispose of the Chilean 'threat' and successfully warn Italy away from a Communist government.

None of these developments boded at all well for South Africa. The depression could only bring her woe, as it did to others.

The 'new wave' of radical regimes in Africa and Asia increased the number of her enemies. The rising strength of the Communist bloc was a straightforward threat and cause for alarm, as was the rise of the OPEC states. The plunge into indebtedness of so many countries could only mean that, should Pretoria too need to raise loans, she would have to bear with political discrimination against her in the debtors' queue. Finally, the resurgence of American power relative to the other great capitalist states had alarming implications for Pretoria. South Africa's economic fortunes in general, and her fortunes on the gold market in particular, had, as we have seen, been directly but inversely related to the financial strength of the USA within the international economic order. When Washington was on the defensive against a (Gaullist) European capitalism, South Africa benefited. When the combination of a world speculative mania and a unique crisis of American executive government led the USA to lose control of the situation in 1973—4, Dr Diederichs was able to end his Ministerial career as a sort of vindicated modern Midas. (He did, indeed, become President.) As the overwhelming financial strength of the USA began to re-assert itself, so the picture clouded.

That the new elements of American strength were not immediately apparent was due to essentially political factors. Until August 1974 the US government was 'artificially' paralysed by the accident of Watergate. Thereafter the main objective of the new Ford administration was the pursuit of a common front with the major European states against the OPEC bloc, in order to force the oil price down again. This aggressive policy was the brainchild of Dr Kissinger and William Simon, the New York broker who had become Secretary for Energy in December 1973 and then Secretary for the Treasury in April 1974 as Nixon's last major appointee. Simon and Kissinger were both tough, ruthless conservatives; they both perceived the central importance of international economic questions to US foreign policy — and so, naturally, quarrelled bitterly on occasion.[1] Together — or even singly — they dominated Gerald Ford and, in the two and a half years which followed, made themselves the leading arbiters of the world's political economy, fully exploiting America's dominant position

[1] It was to become a proud boast in the early days of the Carter administration that 'there is now a state of detente between the Treasury and the State Department'.

in the international agencies to which the depression had lent a
new significance.[1]

Simon had watched with dismay the rise and rise of the gold
price, a veritable index of America's economic weakness and
thus a sort of inverted virility symbol for US Treasury
Secretaries. Moreover, the Treasury was still smarting from the
humiliation of the great Russian raid on the Chicago grain
markets, when the Soviet Union had bought up enormous
supplies of American wheat at bargain prices to compensate for
poor harvests at home. The Russians were clearly going to pay
their debts by selling off gold — and the higher the gold price,
the cheaper the already cheap grain they had bought effectively
became. This could not be allowed, and Simon was determined
to bring it down. The State Department fought and won the
battle to make him stay his hand. About 80% of the world's
official gold stocks, they pointed out, were held by just six
countries — the US, Germany, France, Switzerland, Italy,
Holland and Belgium (in that order). Any US action to depress
the price of gold would thus have an extremely deleterious
effect on the notional value of the EEC bloc's gold. While this
provided Simon with much of the appeal of his plan (it would
punish the Europeans for their gold ramp and prevent them
making ill-gotten gains at America's expense), Kissinger knew
that such an action would destroy any possibility of a common
EEC—US front against OPEC. The Europeans were, from the
start, deeply resistant to the idea of such a front, knowing full
well that they, as 100% oil-importers, would suffer most from
any OPEC retaliatory action. There was, in any case, the
prospect of lucrative third-party relationships with the OPEC
states which, in French eyes at least, might provide a useful
extra counterweight against American economic strength. The
French were, as always, the key to the situation and Simon's
plans had to wait upon President Ford's summit meeting in
Martinique in December 1974 with the new French president,

---

[1] The most important of these was, of course, the IMF. Simon had little
difficulty in imposing himself almost entirely on the IMF and the World
Bank. Both have their headquarters in Washington, where the US Treasury
looms over them. It is much bigger than them, has more money and has
more and better personnel. The US provides the lion's share of funds for
both, and thus has dominant voting rights within them. There is a strong
tendency for IMF and Treasury staff to be virtually interchangeable, and
even non-US staff tend to be selected partly on grounds of their
congeniality to the US viewpoint.

Giscard d'Estaing. It quickly transpired that Giscard was no more inclined to fall into line with American plans than his two predecessors had been. The meeting ended amicably, but within days of Giscard's return to Paris Simon struck, announcing that the US Treasury would break its 42-year rule and allow private citizens to buy gold, starting with a sale of 2.22 million ounces (62 tons) from US stocks. France responded immediately by declaring its faith in a high gold price and officially valuing the nation's reserves at the free market price. With so many private French citizens holding gold it was of no little political importance to Paris to be seen to be keeping the price up.

By releasing large new supplies of gold into the market — and making it clear that there was a great deal more where that had come from — Simon began to pull the price down. From a level of almost $200 an ounce at the end of 1974 it fell sharply to $165 in March 1975. After an initial rush to buy, American private citizens realised they were witnessing a classic bear squeeze (operated by a man who had become a master of the art on Wall Street) and interest in the sale evaporated. Ultimately only 38 of the 62 tons could be sold. Meanwhile gold-holders began to disgorge their stocks on to the market in order to cash in before the price slid further — the Russians sold off 149 tons, for example. In three months the value of the EEC's reserve had fallen by a sixth, thanks to Simon who quickly became the man most hated by gold speculators the world over.

Even worse was to follow. In August 1975, the IMF (under American tutelage) decided on a series of tough policies to reduce the role of gold. The official (dollar) price for gold was declared abolished; the IMF resolved that it would no longer use or accept gold in any of its transactions; the IMF and the Group of Ten (the major industrialised countries of the West) agreed not to increase their gold holdings; the IMF resolved to begin disposing of its own gold holdings by (a) handing back one-sixth of these holdings forthwith to member states, and (b) by auctioning off a further one-sixth of its reserves (i.e. 25 million ounces) over a two-year period.

This was extremely rough medicine, and the gold price plummetted immediately to under $140. There could be no doubting Simon's hard-line determination now, particularly since the US used the occasion of the UN special session of Development and International Co-operation in September to ram through its gold sales proposal, emphasising that the proceeds from the IMF gold sales would be used to make soft loans to developing countries — a carrot on the end of the stick.[1]

Here was a necessary sop for the West — and particularly the USA — which was coming under increasing pressure from the poorest countries, the hardest hit of all by the Depression. The poor countries wanted two things: the cancellation, or at least the relief, of their massive debts, and a permanent alteration in their favour of their terms of trade with the West. The French, seeking to open a new, flanking alliance with the developing world vis-à-vis the USA, encouraged the setting up of the so-called North—South dialogue in Paris as an alternative to the common front against OPEC advocated by Washington. From the developing-country bloc (the South — seven OPEC and twelve non-OPEC states) came much heady talk of the need for a 'new international economic order' of the type they desired. Such talk was irrelevant unless the OPEC states were willing to put their bargaining power at the disposal of the developing world in general, but it had a nuisance value, particularly to the Americans, the putative leaders of the Western bloc. Washington was furious that the French should, by their initiative, have set the poor countries snapping embarrassingly at its heels, and did not hide its exasperation.[2]

The main American thrust had doubtless been directed against the Europeans and the Russians, but it had produced a major disaster for South Africa. With her gold crutch knocked out from under her she slid rapidly into a deep recession. All Pretoria could do was to restrict gold output even further — by the end of 1975 it had been cut no less than 36% since 1970. But even this was not enough to do more than stabilise the price at around $135. Every $10 off the gold price meant a loss of R200 million a year to her.

The result was a South African payments deficit which

---

[1] The proposal was contained in a speech, jointly authored by Simon and Kissinger, which was a classic of its kind, inveighing against 'the exercise of brute economic power to gain unilateral advantage'. This was not, as might have been thought, autocritique, but an attack upon the 'arbitrary, monopolistic' OPEC states. Third World criticisms of the 'imperialist rapacity' of US multinationals was turned aside with the argument that these 'transnational enterprises have been powerful instruments of modernisation ... the controversy over their role and conduct [was] in itself an obstacle to economic development'.

[2] Mr Jacob Myerson, a US delegate at the UN special session cited above expressed the American contribution to the North—South dialogue thus: 'The US cannot and does not accept any implication that the world is now embarked on the establishment of something called "the new international economic order".'

multiplied *six-fold* in the single year 1974 to 1975 (to R1700 million). In June 1975 the Rand was devalued from $1.49 to $1.42. Three months later it was devalued again — to $1.15. Senator Horwood, the new Finance Minister, visited Switzerland in September 1975 to make a bitter 'no surrender' speech in which he expressed 'unalterable confidence' in the future of gold. It was, he said, 'completely incorrect to imagine that gold is being demonetised'. The trouble was that 'certain institutions and certain countries have gone out of their way to interfere with the free functioning of the market'. The devaluation of the Rand had been forced on his government by this 'artificial situation' — that is, the need to restore the price of gold to its Rand price at the August 1975 level, thus helping a number of marginal (high-cost) gold mines to remain in operation.

Despite Horwood's 'unalterable confidence', the market was unimpressed and by January 1976 the price had fallen below $130. At this point, however, Pretoria had scant thought for the ways in which this disaster had come about, or even for the gold price at all. For by January 1976 all eyes in South Africa were fixed upon but a single object — the advance of Cuban troops towards the Namibian border. There the South African army waited, while Pretoria frantically debated the risks involved in trying to prevent the collapse of her entire northern buffer. Beside this, all the crises of the 1970s paled. The thing which Pretoria had so long predicted, but so little really believed, had come to pass. A Communist army was marching through Angola towards her.

7 The New Politics of Detente, the Great Powers - and Rhodesia

The Lisbon coup of 25 April 1974 undermined, almost at a stroke, South Africa's 'northern buffer' strategy of the previous decade. General Spinola, the new Portuguese head of government, had, as military commander and Governor of Guinea-Bissau, gradually come to the conclusion that Portugal could not win its colonial wars save by an 'anti-reactionary social revolution', rather on the lines once attempted by the French army in Algeria — an attempt to steal the thunder of the guerrilla movements with radical concessions offered by a mailed fist. But this, he realised, was impossible without a democratic revolution in Portugal itself. By September 1973 the general, having suffered a series of shattering military reverses at the hands of the PAIGC in Guinea, resigned his posts and returned home. Coming to power seven months later, he attempted to put the plan into effect, calling on the guerrilla movements to cease fire pending (unspecified) Portuguese concessions. The guerrillas refused and Spinola's strategy was dead. For the Portuguese army had had enough; the mailed fist no longer existed — in July the Armed Forces Movement took power in Portugal with a programme calling for outright African independence as the only means to ending the wars. Spinola had hoped at least to 'save Angola for Portugal' — and had, indeed, appointed the Salazarist General Silveiro Marques as Governor there in June — but even this, it soon transpired, was too late. By September 1974 Lisbon had recognised the independence of Guinea-Bissau and installed a FRELIMO-majority transitional government in Mozambique with an independence date set for June 1975. In January 1975 a tripartite provisional government of the three main nationalist movements[1] was installed in

[1] These were the Popular Movement for the Liberation of Angola (MPLA) led by Agostinho Neto; the National Union for the Total Independence of Angola (UNITA) led by Jonas Savimbi; and the National Front for the Liberation of Angola (FNLA) led by Holden Roberto.

112

Luanda, and Angola's independence set for November 1975. Portugal, having boasted for decades of the 'eternal' nature of her role in Africa, decolonised completely in the space of 18 months.

Pretoria's buffer strategy was now put to its severest test. The strategy had been based on two simple principles: to prevent the possibility of a state adjacent to South Africa offering sanctuary to a guerrilla movement aimed against her; and that South African support of the buffer should stop short of large-scale military involvement beyond her own borders. This latter principle could, of course, be rationalised in terms of the precept so dear to Pretoria's propagandists of 'non-interference in the domestic affairs of other countries'. But Pretoria had read the history books too; indeed, she had taken the lessons of 1905 and 1917 more closely to heart than had her opponents in the CPSA. A repressive oligarchy might be able to contain any amount of internal unrest, any number of 1905s, as long as its armed strength was intact, but once let its army become bogged down and whittled away in a foreign war and there was no limit to the challenges which might develop on the home front. . . . If the existence of a buffer was necessary to the preservation of the White Establishment, so too was restraint in its defence.

In the 1960s these two potentially contradictory principles had been compatible enough, and Pretoria was not forced to decide which of them, in the last analysis, she would choose. The temptation was strong to use her military might, as well as her economic strength, to consolidate the whole southern African region. In September 1965 (two months before UDI) a secret top-level meeting was held between Rhodesia, Portugal and South Africa at which an agreement for the common defence of the entire region against 'communism and nationalism' was reportedly drawn up. As the guerrilla war in Rhodesia developed, South Africa sent police detachments and helicopter squadrons to help Salisbury. She built up airbases in the northern Transvaal and the Caprivi strip from which her Mirages and troop-carriers could, if they wished, range over the whole of the southern African region. From 1970 on there were signs of increased Portuguese — South African military co-operation. Not only did South African troops stand guard over the Cabora Bassa hydro-electric project in Mozambique but, according to some reports, as many as six South African battalions saw service there. Other reports spoke of South African police seconded to Angola and even of reciprocal Portuguese troop support in Namibia during the Ovambo strike movement of 1971—2. Moreover, while Pretoria's BOSS collaborated closely with the intelligence networks of Salisbury and Lisbon, it also maintained an independent system of surveillance within the region — and, indeed, beyond. While Portuguese colonialism remained intact, however, Pretoria could afford this ambivalent, double-headed strategy. Only in April 1974 did she have to choose, and she chose against a forward military role: the second principle was preferred. Admiral Biermann, the Defence Forces C-in-C, made it clear in August 1974 that this decision had not been automatic. 'We were not', he said, pointedly, 'completely unprepared for the change which occurred in Lisbon.' SAAF chiefs had been electrified by the appearance of the heat-seeking SAM-7s in Guinea-Bissau in 1973, and had warned that this introduced an entirely new element into the situation. Admiral Biermann also said that a pre-emptive strike 'as used by Israel in 1967' was disallowed because South Africa was 'in no position, given the world climate today, to antagonise the world'. The options, though, had clearly been weighed.

It is not usual for the chief of a country's armed forces calmly and publicly to admit that launching unprovoked military strikes against two or more of its neighbours has been under consideration. It illustrated rather well the gravity of the crisis which now faced Pretoria. From the moment of the April coup in Lisbon, indeed, it became quite impossible to disentangle the fate of South Africa from that of the southern African region as a whole. It need not have been so. Had the British and Portuguese decolonised in Rhodesia, Angola and Mozambique in 1960 there is no reason to believe that these states would have thrown up leaders more radical than Banda, Kenyatta or, 'at worst', Kaunda. By 1974, however, it had become certain that a left-wing guerrilla regime would take over in Mozambique; probable that another such would succeed in Angola; and only too possible that a third might emerge from the mounting war in Rhodesia. Such regimes could be expected to provide a safe and vast sanctuary for guerrilla action against South Africa. Even Pretoria could not hope to stand for ever against that. The domino theory of political change so dear to American strategists in South-East Asia, much though it had been ridiculed by the Pentagon's critics, had, in the end, turned out to have a certain rough validity there. There was no reason why it should be less valid in southern Africa. No wonder, then, that Pretoria had been debating — if ultimately rejecting — the extreme measures of which Admiral Biermann spoke.

Instead Vorster met the challenge of the Lisbon coup by a dramatic heightening of the policy of detente, immediately holding out the hand of friendship to FRELIMO: 'A black Government in Mozambique holds no fears for us whatever. . . . . Whoever takes over in Mozambique has a tough task ahead of him. . . . They have my sympathy and I wish them well.' Pretoria's strategy became crystal clear in mid-1974 when the white settlers of Angola and Mozambique staged brief and bloody revolts, making it clear that they would welcome South African support. The guerrilla movements, they pointed out, had strength mainly in the north and centre of both countries. It would be simple for Pretoria to hold southern Mozambique (including Cabora Bassa) and southern Angola (including the Cunene dam), and the settlers could, with a modicum of help, hold the situation for years to come. In 1965, after all, Pretoria had gone to the aid of a white settler population in Rhodesia little larger than that in Mozambique and considerably smaller than that in Angola. When Pretoria held its hand and the revolts collapsed the writing was on the wall for the Smith regime in Salisbury: South Africa had made it plain by implication that it would prefer even moderately hostile black regimes to the alternative of a protracted military confrontation at arm's length. Given that Rhodesia's position was anyway now undermined by the new developments of 1974, this could only mean that South Africa was planning to renege on its support for white rule in Rhodesia.

This was indeed part of the bold plan visualised by Vorster. Pretoria would meet the challenge of decolonisation in Portuguese Africa not merely by welcoming the new regimes there, but by actually assisting the process of decolonisation in Rhodesia, and perhaps Namibia too. With this as a *quid pro quo* South Africa would hope to sell a single great package deal to the more conservative states to the north in which they not merely gave their blessing to the new arrangement of the region but, perhaps, even to South Africa's Bantustan policy as well. The Bantustans were now approaching the stage where a large number of them might soon accede to independence. Southern Africa would thus become a great federal patchwork of (moderate) black states and a single, smaller white state which put its capital and expertise at the disposal of the collective good. This was, of course, merely a South African version of the idealised dream of Israel-in-the-Arab-world so beloved of Zionist propaganda. The model had not worked in the Middle East, but perhaps a variant would in Southern Africa.

The problem was that such a plan could have little hope of either immediate or long-term success unless it could be legitimised by the benediction of at least some of the African

states to the north. Such an accord, we have seen, South Africa
had failed to achieve even in the period of open detente of
1970—2. Now, after the Yom Kippur war and the formation of
the Afro—Arab alliance against Pretoria, it would be even more
difficult. Which African state would be willing to risk not
merely the wrath of the OAU but now of the OPEC powers too
by assisting South Africa? Clearly, to achieve even minimal
prospects of success Pretoria would need to appear more liberal
and supple in both its domestic and external affairs than ever
before. There would have to be real, or at least symbolic,
concessions to make such an appearance credible — a major
relaxation of social apartheid in sport, for example, with a
promise of more to come. On its own, though, such a policy of
promised liberality could hardly be enough. If African leaders —
Houphouet and Senghor would again be the obvious can-
didates — were to risk their entire positions by associating
publicly with Pretoria in the greatly changed and highly charged
atmosphere of post-April 1974, something much more tangible
than the sight of black athletes competing with whites would be
required. There would, in a word, have to be fresh and strong
pressure on such leaders from Paris.

(i) The International Dimensions of Detente
President Pompidou's desire to expand the EEC had indirectly
undermined Portugal and created this disaster for Pretoria. Now
only President Giscard could help her out of it. But why should
Giscard wish to do so? The Yom Kippur war had, as we have
seen, greatly raised the cost of open assistance to South Africa.
The British decision not to sell more arms to South Africa and
to give up the Simonstown base already had the effect of
accentuating the isolation of the French as Pretoria's arms-
supplier. What possible reason could the new — and would-be
liberal — French President have for sticking his neck out further
still? The answer could be summed up in one word: Angola, or,
more precisely, Cabinda. The Quai d'Orsay had been very quick
to perceive the opportunity which might be created by the
Portuguese evacuation of Angola. As we have seen,[1] French
interests there were already considerable; given the number of
concessions granted to the French oil company, CFP, it might
well one day overtake Gulf as the major oil company there. As
the Portuguese retreated so the French, already well-established
in neighbouring Zaire, might move in to replace them. France

[1] See above, pp. 59—60.

would thus at last secure a French-influenced state of sufficient size and wealth to balance Nigeria.

Indeed, the stakes were bigger even than that. The oil crisis had, as we have seen, greatly weakened the EEC bloc vis-à-vis the USA. The whole French challenge to the *défi Americain* had been greatly weakened, might even have to be jettisoned altogether. The secret of power under the new dispensation was clearly access to cheap and plentiful supplies of oil. No less a prize than this might be plucked from the looming Angolan crisis. Most of the Angolan oil thus far discovered lay in the tiny enclave of Cabinda, entirely surrounded by Zairean territory. Perhaps, by judicious encouragement of Cabindan separatism, Paris could achieve there what it had attempted unsuccessfully in Biafra eight years before? The idea excited the French — journalists travelling with Giscard were to find that the presidential party talked of little else. The requirements of such a strategy were clear. The Cabindan separatists of FLEC (Front for the Liberation of the Enclave of Cabinda) would need to be patronised. Second, the French would need to increase their presence in Zaire and win Mobutu away from American influence. This was achieved by a variety of stratagems as 1974 proceeded.[1] And third, Paris would need the co-operation of the greatest power in the area — South Africa. In the event of a struggle for power between the Angolan nationalist movements South Africa would be in a strong position to influence the course of events. With Pretoria's help a situation of balance — or chaos — might be created in which an independent Cabinda might emerge, under the benevolent protection of Zaire, France and the Compagnie Française de Petroles. . . .

For Pretoria to play such a role she would first have to be persuaded to abandon the 'hands-off' policy she had clearly adopted by mid-1974. Playing an active role, particularly a military one, in Angola would, if it were discovered, do

---

[1] When the Belgian, Jules Chome, published his muckraking biography, *L'Ascension de Mobutu; du Sergent Joseph Désiré au General Sese Soko* (Paris, Maspero, 1974) Mobutu sought desperately to have it banned. The Belgians refused, the French complied. (The book accused Mobutu of various political murders, of having spied on his fellow Congolese for the Belgian Sûreté when a student, etc.) As the year progressed the French Embassy in Kinshasa was strengthened with the addition of military attaches. At the same time Mobutu's attitude towards the US suddenly changed. He unexpectedly launched a campaign against 'foreign exploiters'; made a sharp leftward turn in domestic policy; visited China; and expelled the US ambassador, accusing him of complicity in a coup attempt against him in late 1974. Cf. the Malagasy affair of 1971; see above p. 62.

irreparable damage to South Africa's reputation in Africa. Detente would be dead, South Africa's strategy in ruins. If Paris wished Pretoria to take such breathtaking risks as this it was no good merely pointing to the allegedly Marxist nature of the MPLA regime which might succeed without Pretoria's intervention; something else, something much bigger had to be offered. It duly was. A few weeks after Giscard's election Paris revealed that it was supplying South Africa with five Daphne submarines. France, by continuing her arms deliveries, was now sailing into the teeth of a howling political gale, but continue she did. The UN Special Political Committee now passed a resolution specifically asking France to cease her military co-operation with South Africa; Britain had ceased such co-operation the month before and France was now alone. France voted against the resolution — and announced that the first wing of Mirage F1s to be assembled under license in South Africa was to be delivered in early 1975. By this stage even the Francophone African countries most loyal to France were beginning to find their position almost intolerable, for the furore over the Mirage deal was nothing less than deafening. Even this was as nothing, however, when the news leaked out that a French consortium was tendering for the construction of nuclear plants in South Africa. Observers noted that Pretoria's programme of nuclear plant construction made it certain that she would, before long, be producing far more nuclear fuel than she could conceivably use for peaceful purposes. And Pretoria had, like Paris, always refused to sign the international treaty against the proliferation of nuclear weapons. . . .

It is, of course, impossible to specify the contents of any deal between Paris and Pretoria at this point, or to be categorical that there *was* a deal — even though the elements of one stare one rudely in the face. Giscard, after all, had hinted during his election campaign that he would ban arms sales to 'undemocratic' countries, and he was in no way bound by the agreements made by his Gaullist predecessors. It seems inconceivable, at the least, that Paris did not attempt at this point to exact a promise of South African support for French interests in Angola. The main threat to such interests, it should be seen, came from the Americans, in the shape of the entrenched and well-connected Gulf Oil Company,[1] and only

---

[1] Gulf had been convicted of making large illegal payments to the 1972 Nixon campaign. Subsequent investigation revealed that the company (the 8th largest in the US) had kept a special Bahamas-based slush fund from which political contributions around the world were made — with over

secondarily from the MPLA — Paris had not found left-wing nationalist regimes elsewhere impossible to deal with. For Paris the critical assessment of South African policy in Angola would rest on whether it sought to serve American or French interests.

Washington appears to have been conscious enough of the position and, indeed, there would seem to have been something of a competition for Pretoria's favour at this point. Just three months before the announcement of the Mirage F1 deliveries *Die Burger*, frequently Pretoria's mouthpiece in such matters, had announced that the US was defying the UN arms ban to sell South Africa helicopters and reconnaissance aircraft.[1] The report had been specifically cleared with the South African Defence Department. Presumably the point of this (unusual) publicity was to exert pressure on Paris to join in the bidding. Similarly, news of the French nuclear deal was immediately preceded by the announcement that the US was to supply Pretoria with the enriched uranium vital to its first nuclear stations. It gradually emerged, moreover, that the State Department was allowing the US General Electric Co. to tender for the nuclear plant contract (Krupps of Germany also put in a bid). If, as seems possible, Pretoria was attempting to play off Kissinger and the Quai d'Orsay against one another, the US decision at the end of December 1974 to start pushing the gold price down[2] must be interpreted, in part, as the beginning of an attempt to bring Pretoria (as well as Paris) to heel. Certainly, Kissinger gave fairly public notice at this point (November 1974) of a newly aggressive American posture in African affairs by firing his Assistant Secretary of State for African Affairs, Donald Easum, and replacing him with Nathaniel Davis. Easum

---

$4 million distributed in the US alone. Among other notable recipients were the Democratic Senate majority leader, Hugh Scott (who also acted as funds-distributor to lesser politicians), Congressman Wilbur Mills and Senator Henry 'Scoop' Jackson, the 1972 and 1976 presidential candidate. Ford's running mate in 1976, Senator Robert Dole, was cleared from similar charges after a Federal investigation had decided that William Kats, Dole's assistant, had taken Gulf's money without 'specifically' telling Dole.

[1] Announced in September 1974, this must have been either the last act of the Nixon administration or the first act of Ford's. In reality, of course, US foreign policy in this period was a matter of unhampered Kissingerian private enterprise. Kissinger's activity in this period emphasises yet again how false was the notion that he took no interest in African affairs until 1975—6.

[2] See above, p. 109.

had, apparently, annoyed Kissinger by his statement that US policy was to exert pressure on South Africa to dismantle apartheid. Davis, his successor, had been the US Ambassador to Chile who had co-ordinated Kissinger's 'de-stabilisation' programme which had brought down the Allende regime. Davis's appointment was universally viewed as representing a major softening of the US attitude towards South Africa.[1]

This had not arrived out of the blue. The collapse of Portuguese colonialism in Angola and Mozambique had come as a nasty surprise for Kissinger, whose 1970 NSC Memo had ruled out the possibility that guerrilla movements might come to power anywhere in southern Africa. Incredibly, the US had relied entirely on the Portuguese intelligence service for its information, the CIA stations in Luanda and Lourenço Marques having been closed down for economy reasons in 1969.[2] As a result the State Department had been caught flat-footed and in need of South African support and intelligence in the region. It was, doubtless, something of a godsend that Admiral Biermann, Pretoria's C-in-C, was in Washington on a public relations[3] visit only a few weeks after the Lisbon coup. Thereafter Kissinger moved rapidly, in the ways noted above, towards a closer relationship with South Africa, for he was no less conscious than the French of the major role Pretoria was bound to have in the new settlement of the region's affairs which now appeared inevitable. Given the untoward deterioration of relations with Zaire, America's normal 'base' in the area, South Africa took on a further, heightened importance. Washington's objectives were, of course, never in any doubt. There was probably no way left in which FRELIMO could be prevented from coming to power. In Angola the situation was still open enough for the US to be

---

[1] Interestingly, President Mobutu was the only African president to go so undiplomatically far as to attack the appointment publicly. Zaire's sudden outburst of anti-American radicalism sat oddly with its lonely defence of France over her arms deals with Pretoria.

[2] Oudes, op. cit., p. A92. Kissinger furiously ordered a large and immediate increase in the CIA budget for Portugal to improve matters. The increase was so large that many in Washington felt the funds must also be intended for a Chile-style 'de-stabilisation' campaign, should one become necessary, against a leftist regime in Lisbon.

[3] Pretoria had made increasing use of the Washington firm of Shannon, Collier, Hill and Edwards to arrange such visits, and of the good offices of John McGoff, a right-wing millionaire newspaper baron who was a close friend of President Ford. Shannon & Co. in turn made campaign contributions to a number of Congressmen, including Representative Thomas Morgan, chairman of the House Foreign Affairs Committee. Oudes, op. cit., p. 94.

able to hope to avoid a Soviet-backed MPLA regime assuming power there. As for Rhodesia, the US would be happy to back any South African initiative which would strengthen the chances of a stable pro-Western regime there. There was, in a word, a fairly easy and complete consonance of views between Pretoria and Washington — provided that Pretoria was not enticed into the arms of the French. Pretoria, faced with a choice between Washington and Paris, would find herself in a difficult position. An American alliance was overwhelmingly attractive in what it could offer and in its relatively straight-forward anti-communism, far more to Pretoria's taste than the Quai d'Orsay's idiosyncratic view of the world. But she could not afford not to be ambivalent — the French alone could offer her contacts with the likes of Houphouet, and they alone seemed a safe source of arms supply. Happily, in the first instance there would be no need to make such a choice. For, in the wake of the Lisbon coup, Pretoria's top priority was clearly the achievement of a settlement in Rhodesia. If the White Establishment of South Africa was to be made secure, Pretoria could no longer afford the luxury of Ian Smith.

(ii) Rhodesia: leaning on Smith, leaning on ZANU
In mid-1974 Dr Hilgard Muller, the South African Foreign Minister, set off for a series of meetings with Francophone leaders, his way smoothed by the Elysée. In September Vorster himself set off on a secret trip, during which he held talks with Senghor, Houphouet, and (probably) President Bongo of Gabon. Contact was also established with President Tolbert of Liberia, Sir Seretse Khama (Botswana), Dr Kaunda (Zambia), and with Dr Banda, who was sweetened in October 1974 by a R19 million loan to Malawi railways.

The Zambians, by the elaborate diplomatic network already noted,[1] were simultaneously in contact with Kissinger and the British Foreign Secretary, James Callaghan. Kaunda in turn widened the diplomatic net by bringing Nyerere, Khama, Mobutu, and Samora Machel, the FRELIMO leader, into consultations. The object of the talks was, centrally, Rhodesia, but Pretoria did not hesitate to make it clear that more generally a sweeping settlement of the whole region was in prospect. In June 1974 Vorster had suddenly reversed Pretoria's long-standing position on Namibia, saying that South Africa had no wish to dictate the territory's future and that this might best be left to 'the peoples' concerned.

---

[1] See above p. 53, n. 1.

The stage was set, but the danger loomed that the UN might jeopardise the entire enterprise in October 1974 by accepting the OAU resolution to expel South Africa.[1] This necessitated a public launching of the secret diplomatic effort. Vorster now risked the wrath of his party's right wing by a series of bold statements. First, he told the Cape Town Senate (and the invited diplomatic corps) that there had to be a peaceful solution: the cost of confrontation would be 'high — too high for southern Africa to pay'. The next day Pik Botha, South Africa's UN representative, delivered a remarkable speech, including the following passages:

> . . . unsavoury and reprehensible incidents between blacks and whites *do* occur in South Africa, incidents which no civilised man can defend . . . we *do* have discriminatory practices and we *do* have discriminatory laws . . . If we have that discrimination it is not because the whites in South Africa have any *herrenvolk* complex. We are not better than the black people, we are not cleverer than they are . . . *we shall do everything in our power to move away from discrimination based on race or colour* . . .

A few days later Vorster followed this speech up with his promise to black Africa: '. . . give South Africa a six months' chance by not making our road harder than it is already . . if you give South Africa a chance, you will be surprised where we will stand'.

So great was the consternation caused by these statements in Afrikaner circles that Vorster had hurriedly to declare that his statements applied only to South Africa's foreign relations, and not to the creation of a multi-racial parliament in South Africa. 'That,' he said flatly, 'will never happen.' Despite this there was a clear, even enthusiastic, desire by the black states, particularly Zambia, to take advantage of the initiative. Kaunda spoke glowingly of Vorster's 'voice of reason'. The Zambians spelt out their price publicly — the decolonisation of Rhodesia and Namibia. These were the 'minimum . . . which could open the way to peace'. It was clear that Pretoria was willing to pay such a price: the elements of a deal now existed. The stage was set for the first (October—November 1974) round of Rhodesian talks.

---

[1] South Africa was saved by the vetoes of France, the US and the UK. Perhaps as many as a third of the OAU bloc sponsoring the motion must have been simultaneously in at least indirect diplomatic contact with Pretoria.

This season of goodwill did not extend to the two parties at the centre, between whom the talks had actually to take place — the Smith regime and the Rhodesian (Zimbabwe) nationalists (released by Smith under pressure from Vorster at this point). As the talks neared, Pretoria's pressure on Smith increased — Rhodesian exports in transit through the South African railway system began to pile up due to 'congestion' and Vorster promised publicly to withdraw the South African police detachment from Rhodesia once 'terrorism' had ended. Smith, who had been told by his own police and army chiefs that the long-term outlook in the guerrilla war was bleak, dared not protest publicly.[1] The Zimbabwe nationalists, particularly the ZANU radicals, came to the conference table equally reluctantly and under strong pressure. Mugabe, the ZANU leader released from Smith's jail at Vorster's behest, hotly denied that he had ever wanted to negotiate, and asserted that he had been 'forced' to do so by Kaunda, Khama, Nyerere and Machel. The talks broke up after only a few days, with each side blaming the other. It was a fateful moment, signalling the failure of Pretoria's ambitious response to the Lisbon coup. Vorster would never be as strong again. As the talks failed (December 1974) the gold price peaked and began to fall; South Africa began to slide fast into depression; all the policy's momentum and originality was lost; and, in South Africa, domestic criticism of Vorster began to mount. He had trounced his right-wing opposition in the April 1974 elections, thus giving him a free hand for a few months, and enabling him to climb daringly far out on a limb, both in his public statements and in his pressure on Rhodesia. The failure of the talks saw him retreating hurriedly on to the defensive against a growing groundswell of dissidence from the Right, both inside and outside his party.

Vorster was clearly stunned by the failure and, while insisting that he would not interfere in Rhodesia, declared that further negotiation would have to take place: 'The alternative is too ghastly to contemplate.' The same desperation was shared in Zambia. For although the collapse of Portuguese colonialism had been greeted with euphoria in Lusaka, it rapidly became clear that developments in Angola and Mozambique, together with the mounting war in Rhodesia, represented a major threat

---

[1] The Rhodesian attitude was, however, no secret. The Rhodesian Front chairman, Desmond Frost, said after the talks: 'Let's be honest. This was something the South Africans started. It wasn't something, as far as I know, that we started.'

to the delicately balanced Kaunda regime. Things were bad
enough already. The Zambian national plan had envisaged an
annual growth rate of 7.4%[1] but in 1973 the actual rate
achieved had been 0.3% and even in 1974, aided by an all-time
record copper price of £1400 a ton, the rate had been only 1%.
Given population growth and increasing social inequalities, this
had meant a steep fall in per capita incomes for most Zambians.
The closure of the Rhodesian border in 1973 had led to the
increasing suffocation of Zambia's commercial links with the
outside world, as imports and exports alike piled up in East
African ports quite unable to deal with such quantities of
goods. On top of this had come a quite calamitous fall in the
copper price — down to £600 by September 1974 and £532 by
December. In line with the other CIPEC states (Peru, Chile and
Zaire) Zambia had cut copper production by 10%, but it hadn't
helped.

Kaunda had reacted by introducing an official one-party
regime, which led to a much greater concentration of personal
power in his hands but this in no way allayed the growing wave of
internal dissent. Neither right nor left could take Kaunda's
Christian moralism seriously for all that the Philosophy of
Humanism was now espoused as official party doctrine.
Radicals gossiped bitterly about the president's illegitimate
children, the advancement of his girl-friend, the wonderfully
named Petronella Kawandami, into high political office, his
ownership of French Riviera property, a hotel in Switzerland
and his shareholdings in private foreign companies. All of this,
they felt, cast a certain doubt on the president's socialist faith,
quite apart from the continuing importance in Zambian affairs
of such mighty concerns as Lonrho and Anglo-American.
Conservatives, for their part, were aghast at the damaging
consequences of yet further confrontation with the White
South, viewed with alarm the radicalism of FRELIMO and
MPLA to east and west, and wished to push Kaunda into the
speediest possible detente with Pretoria. On the Copperbelt
Kaunda's former henchman, Simon Kapwepwe, was building a
threatening base amongst the powerful mineworkers and the
Bemba people. In the deteriorating economic climate there was
a clear worsening of tribal hostilities and growing manifestations
of resentment against white expatriates. At the end of 1974
there was a muffled attempt at a coup which saw the Chief of
Police commit suicide and Kaunda purge the whole upper rank

---

[1] 'Zambia' in *ACR, 1974—75*, op. cit., pp. B326—43.

of the police force. Kaunda's long balancing act looked in greater danger than ever.

This balancing act had all taken place in the context of Zambia's position on the edge of Pretoria's northern buffer, in an environment of *limited* confrontation with the White South. Lusaka's position as a major political capital and Kaunda's status as a courageous progressive alike depended on this precise context. Zambia would support guerrilla movements — but refuse to provide them with sanctuary. Kaunda would rail aggressively against the white racism of the South, but would also earn plaudits in the West for his Gandhian pacifism — would even dream, like Kissinger, of a Nobel Peace Prize.[1] He was now thoroughly upstaged by the radicals of FRELIMO and MPLA. They would quite certainly give sanctuary to the Rhodesian guerrillas, and so Zambia too might have to, thus getting drawn into a bloody confrontation with Salisbury, or even with Pretoria. The prestige, the balance, the context — perhaps even the life — of the Kaunda regime would be lost.

Pushed by these political exigencies, by his own con-servatives, and by the West and its business interests, Kaunda had reacted to the Portuguese coup by turning towards a 'conservative detente' just as Pretoria was adopting a policy of 'liberal detente'. Straight after the coup he had renewed links with Dr Banda, warmly welcoming the Malawian leader to Lusaka. Banda's claim that he and Kaunda had 'far more in common than many people realise' he was now happy to accept, though not long before he would have regarded it as an insult. In the next month he was host to the equally conservative President Tolbert of Liberia, one of Pretoria's key contacts in West Africa. When Sekou Touré sent a Guinean party to Lusaka in August 1974 to urge Kaunda to support the Neto faction of the MPLA, thē delegation left the next day without having seen the president at all. Meanwhile Kaunda began to lend his support to the UNITA leader, Jonas Savimbi,[2] and to the conservative Chipenda faction of the MPLA against the Neto radicals.[3] When Zambia celebrated its tenth in-

---

[1] Branches of UNIP, Kaunda's ruling party, which do not normally act without the president's approval, frequently distribute large numbers of nomination forms for the Peace Prize, exhorting a write-in vote from Kaunda's admirers.
[2] See below pp. 133—4 for an explanation of these divisions.
[3] Zambian security forces protected Chipenda from the wrath of the Neto wing, and he was allowed to set up offices in Lusaka, authoring bitterly anti-Neto tirades in the Zambian press. Officially Zambia continued to support the MPLA.

dependence anniversary in October 1974 there were two South
African envoys among the guests. Sir Roy Welensky, once
Kaunda's hated Rhodesian opponent, was invited too, but
arrived only in January 1975 when he drew warm and
favourable comparisons between Zambia and contemporary
Brazil. . . .

The failure of the October 1974 talks on Rhodesia had thus
been as great a disappointment to Kaunda as they had to
Vorster. In both Lusaka and Pretoria it seemed absurd that a
handful of ZANU radicals and Smith's relatively puny regime
should prevent the Rhodesian settlement which both Lusaka
and Pretoria wanted so badly. Accordingly, Kaunda increased
his pressure on ZANU while Vorster increased his on Smith.
From about April 1974 (the time of the Lisbon coup) a new
moderate ZANU faction, with clear Zambian support, had
begun to make headway against the radicals who sheltered
under the centrist leadership of the ZANU chairman, Herbert
Chitepo. The moderates were led by Sanyanga, a Lonrho
company secretary and close personal friend and former
classmate of Mark Chona, Kaunda's right-hand man and
personal envoy to Vorster. Sanyanga became the ZANU district
chairman in Lusaka in 1974 and was able, with the help of the
apparently substantial funds at his disposal, to establish links
with a dissident faction of the ZANLA guerrilla army. On the
day the October 1974 Rhodesia talks had begun these dissidents
attacked a ZANU camp at Chifomba where four of the leading
ZANU radicals, including Josiah Tongogara, the ZANLA military chief, were present. The radicals escaped and their
attackers were arrested and handed over to the Zambian
security forces, who promptly announced that their prisoners
had escaped custody. Sanyanga went into hiding; the Rhodesia
talks failed; and ZANU, to Lusaka's embarrassment, moved to
the left, with Chitepo taking an intransigent stand at their head.

On 17 March, 1975 Chitepo was killed, under extremely
suspicious circumstances, when his car was blown up by a
plastic bomb planted inside it.[1] Six days later the Zambian

---

[1] Chitepo, who had twice earlier requested Zambian police protection for
fear of his life, had parked his car on the previous evening in the grounds
of Kaunda's State House where he had gone to confer with the president,
other nationalists leaders, and a visiting South African envoy. Chitepo left
the meeting after a fierce altercation during which he had refused to hand
over the ZANLA army to a joint military command with Nkomo and
Muzorewa. He was returning to State House the next day when the
explosion took place. The Zambian police at first attempted to explain the
event as the result of a guerrilla land mine run over by the car. There was,

police swooped on ZANU militants in mourning at Chitepo's house, arresting about 100 of them, including a number of the radicals. In the next few days the Zambians rounded up and jailed over 1,350 ZANU militants, though Tongogara and a number of the other radicals escaped to Mozambique, accusing Lusaka of responsibility for Chitepo's murder. Virtually only the Sanyanga faction was left untouched by the police raids, and it was to this faction that Lusaka now lent its open support. From Mozambique Tongogara and his associates claimed they had been victims of a frame-up masterminded by Lonrho and State House in Lusaka. The truth of these accusations and counter-accusations could not be known but it was, at least, clear that the ZANU radicals would not torpedo the next round of Rhodesian talks.

Vorster's recoil from the failure of the October 1974 talks did not last for long, and in February 1975 he was off to gather fresh African support, secretly visiting President Tolbert in Liberia. In the same month he began to exert fresh pressure on Smith, withdrawing South African police from their border duties on the Zambezi. In theory they had been there to prevent guerrilla infiltration from Rhodesia into South Africa; in fact they had been there to close off the border to Zimbabwe guerrillas needing to retreat from Rhodesian forces. At the same time the 2,000 South African police inside Rhodesia were withdrawn from anti-guerrilla activities — despite the mounting tempo of the war. By July, when it was clear that a further round of talks over Rhodesia was in prospect, Van der Byl, the Rhodesian Minister, revealing the withdrawal, complained angrily that the move had strained Rhodesian forces and made black Rhodesians 'more arrogant'. This more or less open play for white South African sympathy was quickly answered by Jimmy Kruger, Pretoria's Minister of Justice, who announced that only 200 SAPs were left in Rhodesia and that these too were being withdrawn. South Africa, he added, did not wish to become involved in an 'internal struggle between Rhodesians'. Van der Byl fulminated publicly at this. Nonetheless, the pressure was sufficient for another round of talks to begin.

---

though, no crater in the road to support such a theory and the damage to the car was wholly inconsistent with it. Rather, it seemed probable that a bomb had been placed in the car's boot either outside Chitepo's (guarded) house or in the grounds of State House.

On 25 August Vorster and Kaunda met at Victoria Falls[1] to chair a meeting attended by Smith and the black nationalist leaders. These latter were divided but Nkomo, in particular, showed signs of willingness to do a deal. Vorster returned to Cape Town where he spoke with some optimism of the talks' prospects. Smith immediately returned to Rhodesia and announced the 'failure' of the talks. Vorster declined all comment. It seemed fairly clear that, if the first round of talks had failed because Kaunda had failed to 'control' the Zimbabwe nationalists, this time they had failed because Vorster's pressure on Smith was still not enough. But how much further could Vorster go? He was already a long way out on a limb with his conservative critics at home, who accused him of 'betraying the white man in Africa'. The Smith regime was more than conscious of this gallery and had begun to play to it over Vorster's head.

Having sabotaged the talks, Smith proceeded to fire off warning shots against the possibility of any further such initiatives. In a broadcast interview on South African television he stated bluntly that Vorster's withdrawal of the SAP had been 'wrong'; negotiations had been made difficult because the Zimbabwe nationalists 'believed that the South African government was pressurising us to come to an agreement with them'. In thinly disguised code Smith added that Salisbury—Pretoria relations were 'under some strain . . . mainly as a result of the campaign against us by the press media in South Africa . . . which has made the average Rhodesian believe that the South Africans are prepared to ditch Rhodesia'. Smith was, in effect, daring Vorster to go any further. It was, indeed, difficult to see how Vorster could go further in the face of a South African domestic situation which was deteriorating fast, politically and economically. Pretoria's energetic and determined push towards a liberal detente had petered out. Precisely with the failure of the Victoria Falls talks (August 1975), she moved fatefully towards armed confrontation in Angola.

---

[1] This was, officially at least, the first time the two men had met. Vorster apparently regaled Kaunda with jokes such as that about Van der Merwe (the legendary South African equivalent of the Australian Barry McKenzie) returning from working on the Zambian mines to tell President Diederichs that 'where I've been they've got a black man to do your job'. Kaunda was extremely sensitive about the meeting and the series of events leading up to it. When the London *Guardian* reported that Vorster had offered him a huge interest-free loan to tide Zambia over its troubles, Kaunda sued and won a retraction. The same sensitivity seems to have been responsible for the ferocious Zambian police action against white university lecturers in Lusaka who had shown an (academic) interest in analysing the strange fish swimming in the same murky water of detente.

8 Mozambique, Angola - and the Search for New Alignments

Pretoria's policy of detente after April 1974 had two major objectives: the achievement of a Rhodesian settlement, and the establishment of the friendliest possible relations with whatever new black governments might emerge in Mozambique and Angola. In Mozambique there was never much question but that FRELIMO would be that government and, as we have seen, Pretoria from the outset put aside all earlier hostilities to the guerrilla party in an attempt to win its friendship. Despite FRELIMO's bitter heritage of hostility to the White South, despite her powerful Soviet and Chinese backers, and despite Mozambique's quite open and large-scale support of the Zimbabwe guerrillas operating against Rhodesia, Pretoria was able to achieve, at least temporarily, a quite remarkable accommodation with the new regime of Samora Machel. So successful was this policy that it was even able to survive the utter disaster of South African armed intervention in Angola. For Angola was quite a different story.

(i) Mozambique
The thought of a revolutionary guerrilla regime taking power in Mozambique was, to most South Africans, more incongruous and alarming than anything that might happen in Angola. Angola was far, far away across the vast wastes of the Kalahari Desert and the Okavango Swamp. Geographically Moscow is rather nearer London, after all, than Luanda is to Cape Town. Few South Africans had been to Angola or knew much about it. But Lourenço Marques was only a few hundred miles from both Cape Town and Durban: every year thousands of South Africans had gone there on holiday for decades past. LM Radio provided South African teenagers with the steady diet of slickly disc-jockeyed pop music that Radio Luxembourg provided to their British counterparts. LM meant Beatles' records after they were banned by the SABC; it meant adverts for Coca Cola, games on the beach, family holidays; by air just a forty minute hop from two of South Africa's main urban centres. It was no

small shock when LM was rechristened 'Maputo', when the glib
DJs and the Rolling Stones were suddenly replaced over the air
waves by African voices delivering vulgar marxist tirades against
imperialism and neo-colonialism. . . . Mozambique was, moreover, integrated with South Africa in a way that Angola simply
wasn't. The bulk of the lucrative traffic through Maputo derived
from South African trade; the Cabora Bassa hydro-electric
scheme was to be an integral part of the South African power
grid (it would not be remotely viable otherwise); and around
100,000 Mozambique migrants came every year to work on the
Rand mines. This migratory flow provided more than employment for Maputo — it provided over R100 million a year in
gold.[1]

None of this was lost on FRELIMO, even before it had come
fully to power.[2] In September 1974 Samora Machel promised
that the new Mozambique would become 'a base for revolutionary change in Africa', but Joaquim Chissano (the Foreign
Minister-to-be) added that this meant a 'revolutionary base in
ideas'. Economic links with South Africa would not be cut, nor
would Mozambique offer sanctuary to guerrillas against South
Africa: 'We do not pretend to be the saviours of the world. We
will not be saviours or reformers of South Africa. That belongs
to the people of South Africa.'

After independence (June 1975) the FRELIMO Deputy
President, Marcelino dos Santos, made it clear that the
recruitment of workers for the Rand mines would not cease: 'In
principle we are against recruiting workers for the South
African mines because this gives support to colonialism and
imperialism. However we must also be realistic. We cannot
assume our full responsibility to South Africa in a month or
even a year.'

In fact by September 1975 the South African Chamber of
Mines reported that the flow of Mozambiquan workers was
'very good, if not better than normal' — there were 107,000 of
them in South Africa by December, a record — handily com-
pensating for the reduced flow of migrants from other sources.[3]

---

[1] In terms of the Mozambique Convention the South African government
had paid the Portuguese part of the migrants' wages directly in gold valued
at the official (formerly $35 per oz.) price, but specifically allowed them
to sell it at free market prices. The rising gold price thus brought a major
windfall to the Portuguese — and later to FRELIMO, under whom the
arrangement continued.
[2] In this section I am indebted to Wendy de Beer, *Mozambique and South
Africa* (unpublished MA thesis in International Politics (Africa), S.O.A.S.,
University of London, 1976).
[3] See below, p. 160.

With the complete economic chaos wrought in Mozambique by the revolutionary change-over, a wave of nationalisations, FRELIMO army revolt, Rhodesian border raids far across the border, and the exodus of almost all the country's technical and skilled (Portuguese) personnel, the fact was that Maputo needed Pretoria more than ever before.

Pretoria strained every muscle to help. When major problems of congestion occurred on the Mozambiquan rail and harbour network thanks to the exodus of trained personnel the General Manager of South African Railways, Kobus Loubser, visited Maputo in February 1975. He met FRELIMO officials who gratefully accepted his loan of S.A.R. locomotives, rolling stock, spares, and signalling equipment and his sending of a team of S.A.R. technical experts to help. To be sure, South Africa needed Maputo's port capacity for her commerce — Mozambique could, for example, have greatly embarrassed her had she cut off the flow of supplies to the south during Pretoria's military incursion into Angola. Even then the traffic — quite possibly including supplies of military use — continued to flow. When further congestion caused major problems in mid-1976 Pretoria made it clear that she was keen to continue using the port of Maputo 'both in the sense that it is convenient and well equipped, and because it is diplomatically desirable to do so'. Indeed, South African businessmen were put under strong government pressure to use the Maputo facilities and in July 1976 Loubser, the S.A.R. chief, escorted a party of businessmen there to impress the port's virtues upon them.

Pretoria's efforts to woo Mozambique centred on this railway diplomacy but did not stop there. On several occasions after 1974 Pretoria made gifts of emergency food supplies to Mozambique and offered aid in the wake of a coal-mining disaster in 1976. Most dramatic of all was an incident in March 1976 when FRELIMO troops crossed into South Africa in hot pursuit of Portuguese soldiers active in a continuing OAS-style campaign against the new independent government. The FRELIMO soldiers, though arrested, were handed back to thier government, Pretoria announcing that she was confident that their incursion had been a mere mistake caused by a broken border fence. This sweetly reasonable attitude was, doubtless, bitterly viewed in Salisbury, whose traffic through Mozambique was sharply terminated by the FRELIMO government — a government with which Rhodesia was, effectively, at war over its harbouring of Zimbabwe guerrillas. It was indeed, on Mozambique's western border with the White South that the situation was at its most Kafkaesque. On the south bank of the

Limpopo FRELIMO was faced with the energetic friendliness of
the Transvaal, on the northern bank by armoured cars and
Hawker Hunters hurtling in with guns ablaze.... But, somehow — because both countries wanted it to — the compromise
held.

(ii) Angola

Mozambique offered a model of Pretoria's determination, under
even the most difficult and trying conditions, to maintain
friendly relations with the new black regimes born of the
Lisbon coup. Angola presented a different and, on the whole,
an easier matter.

To be sure, there was the worrying complication of possible
Angolan support for SWAPO guerrillas operating into Namibia.
The problem was hardly insuperable, though. Namibia, after all,
is essentially a desert almost the size of Nigeria but with about
1% of Nigeria's population. SWAPO's activity was largely
confined to the Caprivi Strip, separated from South Africa by
the vast emptiness of Botswana, and to the Ovambo peoples of
Nambia's extreme northern edge. A smooth and speedy
decolonisation of Namibia might succeed in devolving power to
the territory's conservative and staunchly Christian traditional
elites. Even with an eventual SWAPO regime Namibia would
present a much smaller 'threat' than the FRELIMO regime
in Mozambique already did. The prospect of such change was
certainly disturbing, particularly when Namibia's great mineral
wealth was taken into consideration, but a little reflection
showed there was not much to be alarmed about.

As for Angola itself, South Africa, as we have seen, had not
inconsiderable economic interests there. But they were hardly
crucial to her — it was Gulf, not Pretoria, who had the oil — and
it might be possible, if detente fulfilled the expectations held of
it, to reach some accommodation with the new regime over them.
Pretoria could hardly welcome the possibility that the MPLA
might succeed in taking power in Angola, but the MPLA was, as
a movement, almost indistinguishable from FRELIMO after all.
Pretoria and the South African press had quickly been able to
stop referring to FRELIMO as 'terrorists' and start calling them
'nationalists'; they could do the same easily enough with the
MPLA. Above all, Angola was, mercifully, so very far
away.... South Africa, in a word, had no very pressing reason
to get involved there and every reason for not doing so. It was,
anyway, by no means clear that the MPLA *would* take over.
There, ironically, was the rub. In Mozambique the position had
been fairly well cut and dried: the new government would be a

FRELIMO government, and that had simply to be accepted by the great powers and Pretoria alike. In Angola the position was altogether less certain and France, the US and Russia all had their favourites It was going to be a tug-of-war, probably a bloody one. South Africa would do extremely well to stay out of it, if only her Western friends would let her. . . .

The Angolan nationalist movements had a chequered history. After the Luanda rebellion of 1961 Holden Roberto (he is named after an American Protestant missionary), the leader of the oldest movement, the UPA (later GRAE, later FNLA),[1] had fled to the safety of Zaire, where he had been educated. Formerly a close friend of Nkrumah and Lumumba, his fortunes now became inseparably entwined with Mobutu, whose brother-in-law he became. The complexion of his movement-in-exile changed. Mobutu had been brought to power largely through the efforts of the CIA and was the major recipient and conduit for CIA funds in the whole of southern and central Africa.[2] Roberto, too, became a major recipient of such funds which enabled him, inter alia, to become the owner of a string of taxi firms and gambling casinos in Kinshasa. He was also able to back his luck with funds from Peking, which saw him as a balance against the Russian-backed MPLA. By 1975 Roberto was a gaily dressed veteran of Kinshasa night life as well as of the exile movement, entirely dependent on his external backers.

[1] The UPA (Union of the Peoples of Angola) became a full member of the OAU as GRAE (the Government of the Republic of Angola in Exile) and also changed its name to the more militant-sounding National Front for the Liberation of Angola (FNLA).

[2] The CIA's involvement in Zaire has been so long, so large, and so byzantine that it is a worthy subject for a book on its own. In 1975 the US Senate Committee of Frank Church concluded that Allen Dulles, the CIA Director, had taken Eisenhower's expression of concern about Lumumba in 1960 as authority to assassinate him. Thereafter the CIA became so deeply involved that by 1964 its (Cuban exile) pilots were actually flying regular bombing missions in the country. Mobutu was recruited by the long-time CIA agent, Lawrence R. Devlin, who became head of the CIA's Clandestine Services Africa division under Nixon before retiring to a lucrative business career in Kinshasa. Among his employees was Howard Hunt, whose career was to reach a spectacular peak with the Watergate burglary (Hunt's duties were the planting of articles in the Zairean press). Devlin was the key link man between Mobutu and Kissinger in 1975, making numerous trips to Washington. See V. Marchetti and J. Marks, *The CIA and the Cult of Intelligence* (London, 1976) and B. Oudes, 'The United States' Year in Africa: Postscript to the Nixon Years', *ACR, 1975—76*, pp. 119—20.

The MPLA, founded in 1957 and with considerable support
from Angolan intellectuals, had disputed the OAU's recognition
of the FNLA throughout the 1960s. It had been expelled from
Zaire in 1963 and, since 1965, had been established in Lusaka
and Dar-es-Salaam. UNITA had been formed in 1966 by Jonas
Savimbi, a doctor in law from Lausanne and, like Roberto, a
strong Christian (though, for 'political reasons' a polygamist).
He had split from Roberto in 1964 over the latter's receipt of
Chinese funds, and had launched a guerrilla campaign from
Zambia which, however, had expelled him in 1967 after his
forces had attacked the Benguela railway on which Zambia
relied for its exports of copper.

The MPLA had, through the 1960s, gradually established
itself as the most significant movement on the ground in
Angola — in 1969 it was able to host an OAU mission for ten
days, travelling through 100 miles of 'liberated' Angola. The
mission reported back that 'the MPLA was the only force
fighting effectively in Angola'. This led the OAU to relegate
Roberto's GRAE back to the status of nationalist movement,
on equal terms with MPLA (UNITA was disregarded altogether). As a result FNLA guerrillas staged a major rebellion
in early 1972, repressed with customary ferocity by Mobutu,
who jailed over 1000 of them. Roberto now sought a
reconciliation with the MPLA, within whose ranks his offer
created grave dissension. On the one hand, the MPLA favoured
armed struggle, Roberto negotiation with the Portuguese; on the
other hand the MPLA desperately wanted access via Zaire to the
central and western districts of Angola, and Mobutu would not
allow them this unless they came to terms with Roberto. They
decided to do so — and split.

The Russians, who had backed the MPLA throughout the
1960s with a (modest) supply of arms, perceiving the leadership
struggle, put their money on Daniel Chipenda. Chipenda was a
man of parts — a former inside forward for the Benfica football
club *and* a holder of the 1970 Lenin Centenary Prize. (He was
also, according to Neto's later accusations, a bank-robber, a
diamond-smuggler and a drunkard). When it became clear to the
Russians that Chipenda would lose, they summoned Neto to
Moscow, where Soviet intelligence revealed to him an assassination plot against him mounted by Chipenda. On Neto's
return to Angola in early 1973 Chipenda, who had gained
strong support from Kaunda, split away with his Easter
Rebellion Group in the Mbunda zone, neighbouring on Zambia.
In May 1974 a leftist faction, the Active Rebellion Group, split
away too, fulminating (from Brazzaville) against the anti-

democratic ways of Agostinho Neto who, partly by virtue of these splits, had become the MPLA's dominant figure. Neto, a doctor and also a considerable poet,[1] had spent years in Portuguese jails as a result of his activities in the Portuguese left-wing underground. A taciturn figure, lacking the flamboyant appeal of Holden or Savimbi, Neto came to be regarded as 'Moscow's man'. This was somewhat ironic given that one of Neto's major difficulties was that he was badly short of arms precisely because the Russians had cut off supplies to his wing of the movement in 1972—3 as part of their campaign in support of Chipenda (whom they had continued to supply). Only in March 1974 did the Russians begin to replenish Neto with arms. He was very much their second-choice candidate, and even at this stage Soviet support for him was probably chiefly motivated by the need to balance the Chinese aid (including military instructors) being provided to Roberto in Zaire.

In 1972 the MPLA had, without much question, been the dominant nationalist force in Angola — Roberto had not set foot in the country since 1961 and UNITA had almost entirely disappeared under the weight of a Portuguese military campaign in 1972. By the time of the Lisbon coup, however, the complex machinations noted above had greatly clouded the picture. Although the Neto faction gradually asserted its leadership over the whole MPLA organisation, the party had been weakened by the split. During the summer of 1974 its position was somewhat strengthened by the resumed flow of Soviet weapons into its stockpile and, more significantly, by the fact that the population of Luanda spontaneously and massively rallied to its cause. Control of the capital, the communications nerve-centre, was a considerable prize. Nonetheless, the MPLA had been deprived of the dominance which had earlier suggested that it might play the happy role which fell to FRELIMO in Mozambique, that of the unifying nationalist movement and natural inheritor of power. As it was it faced considerable competition. During 1974 Savimbi's UNITA hurriedly resurfaced, gaining strong support from the mainly right-wing

---

[1] In 1961, protesting against the imprisonment of 'this distinguished poet', C. Day Lewis, Doris Lessing, Iris Murdoch, Angus Wilson and John Osborne wrote to *The Times* of London arguing, with unintentional understatement, that 'the importance of Agostinho Neto in Portuguese-speaking Africa is comparable with that of Léopold Senghor in French-speaking Africa'.

Portuguese settlers, as well as from Zambia and, to a lesser
extent, from Mobutu. It had, though, only a few hundred
guerrillas to its name, against the MPLA's 6000, and while
UNITA had significant support among the Ovimbundu peoples
of southern Angola, the MPLA had a strong base amongst the
Mbunda peoples of the centre and east and amongst the
educated Angolan élite across the country, particularly in the
capital. Luanda had once been counted FNLA territory, but
what support Roberto's movement still had was now concentrated in the north. The FNLA was, in fact, less popular than
either UNITA or MPLA, but potentially stronger in military
terms than both, for thanks to its backers it had some 15,000
well-armed and amply funded regular troops waiting in Zaire.
Should this army prove insufficient (as it did), it could always
be beefed up (as soon it was) with Zairean regulars and white
mercenaries. UNITA, too, had no aversion to the use of
mercenaries, the initial recruitment trail probably leading
through Lusaka. There was, finally, FLEC, the tiny separatist
movement for the Cabinda enclave, which owed what significance it had mainly to its external backers, France — and
Zaire.

   Mobutu had never been entirely content to back a single
(FNLA) horse, and had long cast covetous eyes on the Cabinda
enclave. The enclave was too small (with a total population of
70,000) to make sense as a state on its own; whatever its formal
status it was bound to depend in fact on either Angola or Zaire.
Mobutu's appetite had hardly been diminished by Zaire's
growing economic difficulties. It was not just that his country
had been despoiled by its president's brutal, corrupt and
extravagant administration (though it had). The fall in the
copper price had hit Zaire as hard as it had hit Zambia, and the
damage was compounded by the difficulties of exporting the
copper at all through the war-torn railway network to
the south. Zaire had resisted the effects of world depression
and dearer oil by exploiting its own importance and the
favour of its American backers to run up truly prodigious
debts, which Mobutu could not possibly repay. To the growing
alarm of the American banking community, particularly Chase
Manhattan who were most heavily involved, it was becoming
clear that Zaire was not merely bankrupt, but bankrupt on a
scale quite beyond the dreams of mortal debtors. The bankers
could hardly feel very heartened when, with the storm gathering
over neighbouring Angola in late 1974, Mobutu decided to
emulate the example of the Philippines (another bankrupt

American protectorate) and lash out several million dollars to stage the Ali—Foreman world heavyweight fight.[1]

Zaire was FLEC's most obvious backer but, as we have suggested already, the French took a healthy interest too. ELF, the French oil company, was strongly entrenched just up the coast in Gabon, and was prospecting offshore all the way down to Angola, while the Quai d'Orsay maintained a strong official presence not only in Gabon and Congo-Brazzaville, but also in Zaire. Mobutu, like Vorster, was a good customer for the Alouette and the Mirage — planes for which the American bankers were, again, indirectly footing the bill.

Such was the muddled and complex scene in late 1974. The events which were to follow, and were to culminate in the triumph of the MPLA, with Cuban help, in early 1976, remain the subject of violent controversy, much of which hinges on simple chronology. It is perhaps best, then, to lay out such a chronology, which begins on p. 138.[2]

This calendar of events rewards careful study. Several themes or phases emerge.

(i) Fairly clearly, in the period July—September 1974 Spinola was engaged in a holding action to 'save Angola' or, at least, Cabinda's oil, for Portugal, doubtless with the aid of the more right-wing government he was hoping to place in power in Lisbon. Chipenda lent himself opportunistically to this move, unavailingly, for none of the three nationalist movements could envisage losing the vital enclave.

(ii) Cabinda's oil was also a major stumbling block for the

---

[1] It is to be hoped that Chase Manhattan's shareholders enjoyed the fight, for it was they, in effect, who were paying for it. Further poignancy was added to the situation by the fact that Chase's president, David Rockefeller, had been encouraged to extend the loans by the US government in which, of course, his brother Nelson was Vice-President.
[2] My principal source has been C. Legum and T. Hodges, *After Angola. The War over Southern Africa* (London, 1976), supplemented by a variety of press reports, particularly the series of articles by Robert Moss in the *Sunday Telegraph* (London), Jan. 30 — Feb. 20, 1977, press reports of the official South African account, and similar reports of Gabriel Garcia-Marquez's articles in *Proceso* (Mexico) in Jan. 1977. Garcia-Marquez clearly writes as a surrogate for the Cubans, Moss for western intelligence services. Details contradicting other accounts I have noted by bracketting the source from which they are taken.

CHRONOLOGY

1974

MAY

MPLA—FNLA rapprochement; they denounce Savimbi as agent of Spinolists; publish Savimbi correspondence of 1972 proving UNITA—Portuguese military collaboration against MPLA.

JULY

27   Spinola recognises right to Angolan independence.

28   MPLA—FNLA sign Bukavu unity pact.

AUGUST

5—8   Portuguese settlers riot in Luanda in support of UNITA, against MPLA and FNLA. Formation of settler private armies.

9   Spinola announces decolonisation to take three years; ethnic representation in new state with special position for whites; calls for cease-fire from MPLA, FNLA.

10   MPLA, FNLA refuse to cease fire.

SEPTEMBER

(Spinola now attempting to reach agreement with UNITA, FNLA and Chipenda.)

1   Chipenda holds talks with FLEC; announces recognition of right to Cabindan independence.

3   Three MPLA factions sign Brazzaville reconciliation agreement; immediately disregarded.

14   Spinola meets Mobutu in Cape Verde Islands; discusses Cabinda question, support for FLEC, FNLA.

16   Spinola announces he is taking personal charge of Angolan de-colonisation.

28   Attempted Lisbon coup; Spinola implicated, forced to resign. Portuguese settler groups in Luanda also implicated — arrest of their leaders.

OCTOBER

(Lisbon signs cease-fire agreement with MPLA, FNLA, UNITA.)

15   Chipenda announces Brazzaville Agreement dead; break with MPLA now irreparable.

African strikes, riots, rural unrest against settlers; MPLA, FNLA, UNITA appeal without effect for cessation.

NOVEMBER

1—7   Riots and fighting in Cabinda between FLEC and MPLA; FLEC favoured by local Portuguese commander.

Portuguese troops at Belizi mutiny, march on Cabinda with MPLA, put down FLEC, arrest local commander and officers.

French. But, as Moss rather unconsciously puts it,[1] 'in many ways the French were more adventurous than any other Western power'. The French intelligence service, SDECE, maintained a large and continuous presence throughout the war. Moss mentions that when Pretoria withdrew its instructors from the UNITA forces at the end, it was SDECE 'mercenaries' who took over, and that Portuguese agents in league with the SDECE were responsible for blowing up several Cuban ships. But the spirit of adventure clearly existed at a higher, diplomatic level too. It seems only too possible that France played some role in the November 1974 FLEC rebellion — it was actually French-led, and the FLEC rebels fled to Brazzaville where (as in Libreville, Kinshasa and Pointe-Noire) the French maintained a strong presence. With the failure of this initial FLEC rebellion, if not before, it became clear to Paris that stronger allies were needed.

In February 1975 no less a person than the French President, we may see, took a hand. Paris may, at this stage, have attempted to gain influence (partially via Mobutu) with FNLA (by giving cash and encouraging the integration into FNLA of Chipenda, a known friend of Cabindan autonomy) and with UNITA (by providing early and vital diplomatic support for Savimbi from such French clients as Senegal, Ivory Coast and Cameroun). France would also appear to be responsible for the first South African involvement in the affair, arranging for Savimbi to make contact with South Africa in what Moss, perhaps protecting SDECE informants, refers to coyly as 'a European capital' — but which was almost certainly Paris. The French interest is also readily apparent in the recognition by Gabon (another Quai d'Orsay surrogate) of FLEC/Cabindan autonomy in June 1975, and in the double declaration of Cabindan independence by the two FLEC groups in July–August 1975, the first of them based quite bare-facedly in Paris, the second on the almost equally friendly soil of Zaire, Mobutu

[1] Moss writes as an extreme cold-warrior — his previous works include *Chile's Marxist Experiment* and *The Collapse of Democracy*, providing the rationale for extreme right-wing military government in Chile and Britain, respectively. As his *Sunday Telegraph* biographical sketch puts it, 'He has personal experience of political warfare in many countries. . . .'. A disadvantage of Moss's political lenses is that they discriminate only between 'the West' and 'the Communists', leaving him blithely unaware not only of shades in between, but of divisions within these camps. His articles on Angola were extensively used by South Africa as propaganda material, just as his book on Chile was disseminated free by the Chilean government for its propaganda purposes.

Chronology cont.

10   FLEC rebellion led by French mercenary, Jean Kay; put down by Portuguese; FLEC leaders flee to Brazzaville.
25   UNITA—FNLA pact signed in Kinshasa.

DECEMBER
18   UNITA—MPLA pact signed.

     MPLA officers sent to USSR for training. [Moss]

1975

JANUARY
5   UNITA, FNLA, MPLA sign Mombassa unity agreement; Chipenda and FLEC excluded from common front.
10   Algarve Agreement. Portuguese agree 11 November 1975 as independence date with Transitional Government of MPLA, FNLA, UNITA to take office on 31 January.

     MPLA, FNLA, UNITA, Portuguese all agree that 'Cabinda is an integral and inalienable part' of Angola.

     US cash aid now flowing to UNITA, FNLA — $300,000 from CIA ($6 million given by June). FNLA flooding money and troops in — buy up newspapers, TV station. FNLA troops, heavily armed, arriving in motorised columns.

     (Kissinger appeals to USSR that both Great Powers stay uninvolved in Angola.)

     Mobutu appeals to Kissinger for aid, citing fears of possible Angolan developments and Zaire coup rumours.

     Kissinger asks Congress for programme of military aid to Zaire.

FEBRUARY
     President Giscard d'Estaing visits Zaire, discusses Cabinda question with Mobutu who signals FNLA opposition to Cabinda separatism.

     Le Monde reports France giving aid to FNLA.
13   MPLA attack on Chipenda group in Luanda. Chipenda joins FNLA.

     Build-up of FNLA financial and armed strength continues. FNLA in receipt of arms from China, Romania, N. Korea; cash from US and Zaire. FNLA leaders urge Roberto to declare war on MPLA; Roberto orders delay.

MARCH
     MPLA—FNLA fighting breaks out in Luanda.

     Savimbi appeals for peace, national unity. Gains support of Ivory Coast, Senegal, Cameroun, Zambia.

     Savimbi makes secret trip to 'European Capital' [Moss], meets senior South African BOSS officer, requests aid. Apparently refused.

having declared his colours in May. Paris's hope, almost certainly, was that by maintaining an active presence throughout in Angola, and attempting to back almost every horse in sight, French governmental and commercial interests might somehow succeed in riding an eventual winner. Such hopes rested heavily, of course, on the defeat of the MPLA. Once the MPLA had won, however, France greatly annoyed her EEC partners in February 1976 by bolting to recognise the new Angolan regime a week before the date she had agreed with her European colleagues shortly before. *Faute de mieux*, even the MPLA might be worth cultivating. . .

(iii) If the French were the first in the field to back their favourites, the Americans were only a little slower. The best source on American involvement in Angola, the Pike Report,[1] records that Kissinger received a request from Mobutu during the 'winter' of 1974 to send aid to the FNLA and responded almost immediately with the Forty Committee's[2] funds — an action which, the Pike Committee suggested, 'may have panicked the Soviets into arming their MPLA clients'.[3] This aid went to the FNLA only — UNITA only began receiving US funds in 'mid-summer'. In order to do this Kissinger had to over-rule the desperate pleadings of the State Department's African experts. These latter believed that there was no chance of an outright military defeat being inflicted on the MPLA. Presumably at Kissinger's behest National Security Council aides removed the African experts' recommendation in favour of diplomatic rather than military efforts from their report to the NSC in April 1975 so that President Ford and other NSC members were presented only with the alternatives of doing nothing and giving large-scale aid. The NSC may not have known what they were agreeing to — not only had the Forty Committee already gone ahead, but the Pike Report suggests

[1] That is the Report of the US House of Representatives Select Committee on Intelligence, chaired by Congressman Otis Pike. See Spokesman Books, *CIA. The Pike Report* (Nottingham, 1977). Pike did not endear himself to the intelligence Establishment with his Report and quoted Michael Rogovin, the CIA's Special Counsel, as saying, 'Pike will pay for this, you wait and see . . . We will destroy him for this.' Ibid., p. 7.
[2] The Forty Committee is the inter-departmental panel which clears all projects of the CIA's Clandestine Services branch. According to Marchetti and Marks, op. cit., pp. 355—63, the Committee invariably rubber-stamps what is put before it. The Chairman of the Committee under Nixon and Ford was Kissinger.
[3] *CIA. The Pike Report*, p. 199.

Chronology cont.

Savimbi states 'Economic co-operation with South Africa is only realism'. Through Kaunda obtains interview with Nyerere, who suggests asking China for aid. Savimbi flies to Peking, obtains promise of large arms consignment to be shipped through Dar-es-Salaam.

25   First consignment of Russian and Yugoslav arms for MPLA arrives in Brazzaville.

28   Transitional Government set up.

APRIL
Collapse of Transitional Government. Fierce fighting between FNLA and MPLA in Luanda — 20,000 dead.

14   Savimbi meets South African envoy in Lusaka, requests cash and arms. Rejected by South Africa on account of Savimbi's refusal of alliance with FNLA.

15   Chipenda becomes Vice-President of FNLA.

Portuguese authorities prevent Yugoslav cargo of arms for MPLA from being unloaded at Luanda: 230 Cuban instructors with MPLA at this stage. [Moss]

Kaunda visits Washington, tells President Ford that Zambia, Botswana and Tanzania are supporting UNITA.

MAY
Neto visits Brazzaville for discussions with Cuban envoy about possible Cuban assistance to MPLA. [Garcia-Marquez]

20   Mobutu announces support for FLEC, now based in Kinshasa: 'Cabinda is not Angola: it is separated by Zaire'.

Savimbi flies to African capitals in search of further support in his personal Learjet, flown by pilots loaned by Lonrho. Savimbi also in receipt of aid from diamond company, Tanganyika Concessions ('Tanks').

JUNE
4   Violence breaks out in Luanda between MPLA and UNITA. Complete collapse into camps after this point: MPLA *v.* UNITA/FNLA.

Ghana and Nigeria now backing UNITA.

US now sending arms to UNITA/FNLA; hitherto only cash. Financial aid also stepped up. $6 million given up to this point; a further $25 million given by November.

21   MPLA, UNITA, FNLA sign Nakuru peace pact under OAU auspices; immediately disregarded.

22   Gabon recognises FLEC and right to Cabindan independence.

that the accounting procedures used by the CIA managed to at least halve the real value of the aid being given. There seems little doubt that Kissinger and the CIA had decided on a policy of flat-out support for the FNLA and simply forced or fiddled their policy through. The Pike Committee pressed William Colby, the Director of the CIA, to explain this intriguing preference for the FNLA, but Colby replied that actually there was little to choose between the FNLA and its two rivals: 'They are all independents. They are all for black Africa. They are all for some fuzzy kind of social system, you know, without really much articulation [*sic*], but some sort of let's not be exploited by the capitalist nations.'[1]

Covert American aid began to flow in significant quantities to the FNLA from January 1975 on. As the well-armed, thoroughly trained and numerically superior FNLA forces streamed down towards Luanda in early 1975, it seemed that Roberto's strategy of the previous decade had been vindicated. He had kept back the bulk of his troops, waited for the Portuguese to collapse, and was now swooping in to take control of the capital — always the critical objective. Since Roberto had the arms and men he needed, US aid was restricted to cash with which to smooth and reinforce this take-over bid (buying up the press, TV etc.) What stood in the way was primarily the very large degree of popular support the MPLA had picked up in and around Luanda in 1974.

(iv) The strength of this FNLA bid, backed as it was by the US and Zaire (with the French perhaps also taking out a side-bet), alarmed Savimbi, who sought support from every quarter. The French, who viewed the FNLA as too bound to the US, quickly seized on this new prospect by March 1975, but Savimbi was also able to gain critical Zambian support. In part this may have been because Savimbi advertised himself as the peace candidate (he had to, having few troops), but the Zambians (and Lonrho) were doubtless also influenced by the fact the UNITA's support in southern Angola gave it immense leverage over the future of the crucial Benguela railway. They were, too, looking for the best anti-MPLA candidate they could find — Kaunda's earlier support for Chipenda had made it clear enough that Zambia would prevent the Neto faction coming to power if at all

---

[1] Ibid, p. 218. Congressman Aspin queried Colby why the Chinese were also backing FNLA, producing the following exchange: Colby: 'Because, the Soviets are backing the MPLA is the simplest answer.' Aspin: 'It sounds like that is why we are doing it.' Colby: 'It is.'

Chronology cont.

JULY
   MPLA—UNITA fighting continues — UNITA/FNLA alliance formed.

   Savimbi confers with South African envoy in Kinshasa. South Africa agrees to provide arms.

   Roberto authorises Chipenda (Mobutu concurring) to go to Namibia to see Gen. Van den Bergh, chief of BOSS, to request South African help. Savimbi, on hearing news, much alarmed.

9   Outbreak of full civil war. MPLA, armed with Soviet-bloc weapons smuggled in during April—June, launches attacks against FNLA in Luanda region. FNLA driven out of Luanda and MPLA take over capital and most of central Angola. FNLA driven back into northwest corner.

13 US 'Forty Committee' send aid to UNITA/FNLA — $60 million.

   Kissinger lobbies Congress in support of $89 million military aid programme to Zaire (for FNLA). Congress resistant.

13 17,000 FNLA troops, reinforced by Zairean regulars, mercenaries etc., mass in Zaire; placed on full alert from 13 July.

14 South African troops cross Namibian border into Angola. Resisted by UNITA and MPLA forces. South African troops victorious; attack SWAPO bases; take up position to protect Cunene dam.

20 Roberto announces start of FNLA march on Luanda. He and Chipenda rule out all possibility of compromise and declare fight to the finish against MPLA.

26 FLEC breakaway group in Paris announces formation of provisional revolutionary government of independent Cabinda.

26 Col. Otelo de Carvalho on visit to Havana; Fidel Castro requests that he ask Lisbon government's agreement to Cuba sending aid to MPLA. Request 'a dead letter'. [Garcia-Marquez]

   FNLA claim that 50 Cubans have already arrived in Brazzaville to help unload Russian arms.

   Nyerere refuses to trans-ship Chinese arms (now arrived at Dar-es-Salaam) to Savimbi: has no wish to encourage war.

   OAU Summit at Kampala, Amin as Chairman. Amin collaborating closely with Mobutu. OAU calls for unity of UNITA, MPLA, FNLA; opposes all foreign intervention; opposes Cabindan separatism.

AUGUST
   MPLA holding off FNLA advance on Luanda in fierce fighting. MPLA now in control of 12 out of 16 provincial capitals, including all key ports — Luanda, Lobito, Benguela and Mocamedes.

possible. In mid-April Kaunda cleared his position with the US — which, doubtless, had no objection to any reinforcement of the anti-MPLA forces.

Paris may also have fancied that the southern nature of Savimbi's support would make it easier to come to terms with him over Cabinda (in the far north) than with Roberto, who enjoyed whatever support he had in the north. Savimbi's military weakness, moreover, made him an attractive candidate to *all* external backers, for it made their bargaining position with him commensurately stronger.

(v) The threat from the FNLA also alarmed the MPLA and their Soviet backers. The latter now had reason to regret their hold-up of arms to Neto in 1972–3, and sought to repair their 'error' by fresh arms shipments, but it was not until 25 March 1975 that their first major consignment arrived in Brazzaville, whence they could be smuggled in time to the MPLA in Luanda through the good offices of Marien Ngouabi, the left wing Congolese President.

(vi) Quite possibly as a result of this shipment, or the known imminence of its arrival, there was a major and bloody show-down in Luanda in early April. Surprisingly, perhaps, the FNLA were unable to expel the MPLA from the capital. The resulting stand-off led the MPLA to seek Cuban help and the Russians to increase their arms supplies. By July these developments had produced a bipolarisation into MPLA and FNLA/UNITA camps, a diverse alliance of Western and conservative African interests solidifying behind the latter.

(vii) The great revelation of April–June 1975 had been how formidable a force a combination of popular support, long years of guerrilla struggle, and Soviet arms had made the MPLA.[1] Equally, it had become clear that no amount of money and arms was going to transform the badly disciplined and rapacious FNLA army into a force capable of certain victory over the MPLA. Those who backed the anti-MPLA forces had, by June,

---

[1] *Pace* Moss, it is exceedingly unlikely that the Cubans were involved at this stage. Even the FNLA and UNITA, never slow to espy Cubans, did not claim they were present until early August. Moss's account, moreover, has the MPLA requesting Communist troop support for the first time in late August, and only being referred to the Cubans by Moscow then. His reports of 430 Cubans with the MPLA by mid-August are, simply, incredible.

Chronology cont.

1   FLEC (main group), based in Kinshasa, issue declaration of Cabindan independence.

     Further wave of South African troops cross into southern Angola, but remain in Cunene region.

3   Savimbi's jet shot at by MPLA troops; he claims assassination attempt.

7—9 President Giscard d'Estaing visits Zaire for discussions with Mobutu. Announces that henceforth France will not supply air or land weapons to South Africa, but will honour orders already placed.

     UNITA claims to have seen Cubans engaged in fighting on MPLA side.

16   200 more Cuban instructors join the 230 already in Angola. [Moss]

     MPLA claim that US arms now being air-lifted into Angola by C-130 aircraft direct from USAF bases in West Germany.

21   UNITA formally declares war on MPLA.

     MPLA Defence Minister, Iko Carreira, visits Moscow, asks for Russian troop support. Russians refuse, suggest he tries Cubans. Meets Cubans, advises them South Africans soon to intervene on large scale. [Moss]

     Savimbi meets South African general in Namibia. South Africa to provide UNITA with military instructors. 6,000 UNITA troops rapidly trained.

SEPTEMBER

     US financial and military aid to anti-MPLA forces now admitted officially for first time.

     FNLA advance on Luanda still bogged down.

21   Team of South African military instructors arrive in Silva Porto (central Angola) to train UNITA troops — reinforced by 120 Zairean regular troops with six armoured cars. South African objective to help hold Nova Lisboa (Huambo), Angola's second city, for UNITA at all costs. South African 'Foxbat' column sent to hold line 30 km north of Huambo. MPLA advancing south, while still holding centre and north.

     Gulf Oil Company (Cabinda) pays quarterly payment of $116 million to Angolan government directly into MPLA account.

OCTOBER

     MPLA now within sight of overall victory but massive reinforcements of arms for FNLA still arriving, plus Zairean troops.

7   MPLA clash with UNITA and South African military instructors near Silva Porto. Instructors urgently request reinforcements, Large shipment of equipment flown in by C-130s.

to face the fact that they needed a major reinforcement in fighting *manpower*.

The MPLA stood poised to expel the FNLA from Luanda (which, in early July, they duly did) and extend their control over the rest of the country (which, again, in the course of July they did). If they were to be stopped the FNLA would not be enough, and UNITA had never been a serious military force. The same thought occurred, with a certain comic effect, to both Roberto and Savimbi simultaneously. There was only one real possibility — South Africa.

(viii) In early July South Africa agreed (with Chipenda) to intervene. On 14 July she did so, reached the Cunene — and stopped. Given all we have said of Pretoria's desire for non-involvement, the move appears incomprehensible. But Pretoria was being pushed hard, by both France and the US. An obvious first point is that Pretoria would not have intervened simply because asked to do so by Chipenda. She had already turned Savimbi down twice at least (in March and April), and was hardly likely to have risked her entire detente policy on the request of the erratic Chipenda. Pretoria, when approached to intervene by Washington or Paris, would doubtless have stipulated that she hear the request directly as well from those she was intervening to help. Equally certainly, those backing UNITA (the French, Kaunda) and FNLA (the US) would have had little difficulty in ensuring this took place. Pretoria was later to hint darkly of 'guarantees from a Great Power which were not honoured', as she was also to claim that African heads of state had pleaded with her to intervene. In this Pretoria is fairly certainly telling the truth, for she would have been foolish indeed to intervene without very considerable inducements. The French, of course, had very straightforward inducements to offer: in June 1975 Paris suddenly announced that she had agreed to sell four Agosta submarines to South Africa.

The US must, however, have been offering superior inducements for the events of July bear all the hallmarks of Pretoria—Washington coordination. On the day before Pretoria's first incursion Roberto put his troops on full alert to march on Luanda, and Kissinger, using the CIA Forty Committee, began to pour in funds on an unprecedented scale. Kissinger also stepped up pressure on Congress for aid at this point. South Africa was clearly to move into the south just as Roberto, understandably brim-full with confidence in his declarations of imminent victory, which only foreknowledge of Pretoria's impending intervention could provide, swept down from the north.

Chronology cont.

      More South African troops moved across border into Angola.

9   Order given by Pretoria for formation of 'Zulu' column.

10   Chipenda, together with 1,000 FNLA troops, meets on Angolan/ Namibian border with South African army, joins forces.

      Formation of 'Zulu' column — South African troops plus UNITA plus Chipenda's FNLA troops.

14   Operation 'Zulu' begins. Column advances northward across border into Angola. [Moss]

19   Neto warns of massive imperialist invasion of Angola now in progress. Mentions Chipenda—South African talks.

23   South Africans launch Operation 'Zulu', driving up Angolan coast, thus fulfilling agreement with Chipenda. [Official South African version]

23   China withdraws instructors from FNLA camps in Zaire, citing OAU Kampala Summit opposition to foreign involvement as reason.

24   US State Department asks Congress to vote $79 million in aid to Zaire/FNLA. CIA already airlifting massive supplies into Zaire in C-141s.

      SDECE (French intelligence) report 12 Mig-21s being uncrated for assembly in Pointe-Noire (Congo). Cuban supplies also stepped up.

26   'Zulu' column takes Sa da Bandeira from MPLA.

28   'Zulu' column takes Mocamedes from MPLA.

      FNLA attack on Cabinda repulsed by MPLA.

NOVEMBER

3   Lobito falls to 'Zulu' column.

4   'Zulu' column attacks Benguela; strongly resisted by MPLA forces.

5   'Zulu' column takes Benguela.

5   Central Committee of Cuban Communist Party, meeting in Havana, decides to send troops to Angola in 'Operation Carlota': informs USSR of decision [Garcia-Marquez].

6   Roberto marching towards Luanda with 800 FNLA troops, 130 Portuguese troops led by Salazarist secret police, PIDE—DGS officers, 3 battalions of Zairean regulars, and accompanied by US and South African advisers. [Moss]

8   Nigeria denounces Soviet intervention in Angola.

10   Savimbi flies to Pretoria to see Vorster; tells him that he (Savimbi), Kaunda, and other conservative African heads of state all wish that South African forces should stay on in Angola after Independence (11 November) in order to bolster anti-MPLA forces at least until

(ix) South Africa's troops stopped at the Cunene River, however, with Pretoria claiming that her intervention was solely motivated by a desire to protect the dam installations there. This does not ring true. There was no fighting going on near the dam — the battlefield lay in the north. Secondly, Pretoria had not acted to protect the much more important Cabora Bassa scheme in Mozambique — had, indeed, withdrawn her troops protecting it after April 1974. Thirdly, had she wished to send troops to Cunene, she could have done it at any point after April 1974. She scrupulously desisted for 15 months — and then sent them just as the FNLA offensive in the north was about to begin. It was a movement clearly co-ordinated with the FNLA and only a Great Power could have persuaded Pretoria to it. The hand of Henry Kissinger is, in a word, fairly clearly indicated. *Any* South African presence in Angola — even right down on the Cunene — was a major threat to the MPLA, and might well force them to divert southwards troops desperately needed to withstand the FNLA in the north. If this occurred, then the American-backed FNLA would take the capital, the MPLA might well fold up, and Pretoria might be asked to do no more.

(x) Pretoria may well have advised Paris of her intentions, but the French must have been infuriated by this emergence of a Pretoria—Washington axis. To be sure, the (French-backed) Cabindan independence movements attempted to cash in on the fighting in the north by two UDIs at this point. Neither got further than Paris or Kinshasa respectively: South Africa could not help *them* from the remoteness of Cunene. The French, moreover, had clearly hoped that Pretoria would lend its support to UNITA. This she had refused to do: even in July she only promised Savimbi arms, not troops. At the same time she was coordinating her troop movements directly with the 'American' FNLA. UNITA clearly did not even know that the South African incursion was about to take place — indeed, UNITA forces actually attempted to resist it. If a South African incursion was to be any use to Paris it had to be coordinated with UNITA and it had to go a long way further north to be of any help to the Cabindans.

This, at least, seems the only rational interpretation of Giscard's remarkable announcement in Zaire in early August that henceforth France would sell neither land nor air weapons to Pretoria. This was Paris's ultimate bargaining counter and the French president chose to make a special visit to the borders of southern Africa to play it. Giscard had, after all, conferred with

Chronology cont.

OAU meeting on 9 December, and thus to procure OAU vote for tripartite FNLA—UNITA—MPLA government and prevent MPLA victory.

Vorster also under strong US pressure to same effect; also receiving pleas to same effect from conservative African leaders via BOSS agents in liaison with them.

Vorster agrees that South African forces will stay on.

10 Roberto's FNLA—Zairean army marching on Luanda runs into ambush by MPLA (plus Cubans?); virtually destroyed by fire from 'Stalin organs', troops flee.

11 Independence Day. MPLA declares People's Republic of Angola in Luanda; UNITA declares Social Democratic Republic in Huambo; FNLA declares Democratic Republic in Ambriz. MPLA government immediately recognised by Soviet bloc and radical African states (30 countries in all).

11 'Zulu' column ordered by Pretoria to procede to Novo Redondo, Quibala and Porto Amboim (just short of Luanda).

12 'Zulu' column takes heavy casualties at hands of MPLA outside Novo Redondo.

14 'Zulu' takes Novo Redondo. Its commander, 'Rommel', now facing strong opposition, radios Pretoria saying he is unable to procede without reinforcement and requests paratroop company to be dropped behind enemy lines. Request refused. 'Rommel' then suggests that he retreat to Lobito rather than remain in exposed position. Request refused; told he must stay put and await further instructions.

16—19 Central African Foreign Ministers' conference in Libreville (Gabon). Cameroun, Chad, Rwanda, Sao Tomé and Principé, Zaire, Central African Republic and Gabon all condemn 'foreign intervention in Angola, wherever it comes from'.

17 Further FNLA attack towards Luanda repelled by MPLA.

26 'Zulu' commander, 'Rommel', recalled by Pretoria, though column apparently remains in Novo Redondo.

MPLA puts four captured South African prisoners on show at press conference.

27 Nigeria reverses previous stand: recognises MPLA government, citing South African intervention as crucial factor in its decision.

OAU meeting on Angola now postponed from 9 December to 18 December.

27 First three ships of Cuban troops arrive at Luanda (despite

Mobutu in February and had met with central Africa's foreign ministers in Bangui (Central African Republic) as recently as March 1975. Another trip to Zaire at this juncture was a clear *coup de théâtre*. France had braved Afro—Arab wrath over arms-supplies to Pretoria as recently as June 1975 — yet less than three months later came this dramatic reversal of French policy of over a decade. Pique it must have been, but also perhaps an indication to Pretoria of how hard she must needs work to repair the damage. It is also possible, of course, that Paris had threatened to cut off arms supplies if Pretoria did *not* help her over Cabinda, and was now carrying out her threat.

(xi) In fact Roberto's confident crusade towards Luanda quickly bogged down. By the end of August it had become clear that victory for the anti-MPLA forces would depend on South Africa taking on a larger role. Nonetheless, Pretoria clearly had to be dragged in by stages. Only at the end of August did she agree to direct military co-operation with Savimbi, flinging in her instructors in an attempt to provide him with an army (and, perhaps, to mollify Paris). Only in late September did she go further, sending small-scale military aid to protect the UNITA capital, Huambo. Only when this force came under severe threat on 7 October did she reinforce it. Only after that did she agree to launch a full-scale attack in the shape of the 'Zulu' column. And, finally, when she did intervene it was with the express and limited objective of preventing a complete MPLA victory before 11 November (Independence).

(xii) By this time it was almost too late. By 19 October the MPLA knew of the 'Zulu' thrust and fairly soon thereafter must have called for Cuban help. The precise dating of the Cuban arrival is, of course, problematic. Moss, naturally, wishes to insist that the 'Zulu' column was meeting Cuban resistance all the way, but does not offer a shred of evidence ('Although no Cubans were actually sighted during the fighting around Mocamedes the precision firing was the clue to their presence' etc). The first clear clue to a Cuban presence offered by Moss comes with the destruction of Roberto's army on 10 November by the dreaded 'Stalin organs' (Soviet 40-barrel rocket launchers) which, presumably, only the Cubans could operate. This would, in fact, give us a date which tallies roughly with other accounts. Moss wishes to claim that there were some 1,500 Cubans in Angola by 18—20 October and 'at least 4,000' by 11 November. Garcia-Marquez claims that by 20 November there were only 650 Cubans in Angola, with instructions to hold on

Chronology cont.

harassment by US Navy). 3,000 troops, tanks, other heavy equipment disembarked. [Garcia-Marquez]

DECEMBER

MPLA starts major offensive against FNLA in north.

5   MPLA takes Caxito from FNLA.

5   Tanzania recognises MPLA government.

(by) 17 Under US pressure Barbados refuses further air staging facilities to Cubans en route to Angola. Cubans also decide not to continue using facilities in Cape Verde Islands for fear of Western retaliation against Islands. Request use of Guyana air-lift facilities; Guyana government agrees but Texaco—Guyana refuses to supply fuel for planes. US Ambassador to Guyana threatens Guyana government with US aerial bombardment of airport if Cubans use it. Guyana refuses to give way, but Cubans respond by fitting four extra fuel tanks to each plane and flying direct across Atlantic. [Garcia-Marquez]

OAU meeting postponed again from 18 December to 9 January 1976.

US aerial surveillance reveals presence in Angola of ten Mig-17s and twelve Mig-21s.

18   US Senate votes to impose total ban on further US aid to UNITA, FNLA

'Zulu' column takes heavy losses around Quibala.

20   Savimbi flies to see Vorster, having sought and obtained Kaunda's agreement to such an initiative after Pretoria had informed Savimbi that it was about to withdraw its forces. Savimbi pleads for continued South African presence; Vorster agrees that troops will stay a little longer, but will soon have to withdraw.

Gulf Oil Co. pays $125 million quarterly payment into 'suspense' account under orders from US State Dept.

Continual diplomatic activity between Pretoria and other African capitals, especially Lusaka; continual pleas from conservative states that South Africa should stay on longer in Angola.

Britain, France warn South Africa that they will be unable to support her at UN Security Council debate on Angola in early January 1976.

31   Kaunda changes position: suggests South African forces leave Angola by or during OAU meeting on 9 January, now postponed to 11 January.

1976

JANUARY

5   MPLA captures FNLA airbase at Negage and city of Uige.

until reinforcements arrived. The US State Department, which was more likely to exaggerate than minimise the Cuban presence, suggested a figure of only 1,500—3,000 for mid-November. Moss also undercuts his own estimate by asserting that South African—UNITA—FNLA forces enjoyed 'a clear military superiority' before Independence Day, 'but their advantage was rapidly eroded after November 11'. Independence Day could hardly have been such a turning point if there had really been as many as 4,000 Cuban troops there by then. But Moss is certainly right in asserting that soon thereafter the weight of Soviet arms and Cuban troops began to tell very quickly and heavily.

(xiii) Independence Day was a turning point in another way. South Africa had, by this stage, become caught up in what Moss depicts as a general Western coalition to stop the MPLA:

> Before the end of the conflict, most Western nations — America, Britain, France, West Germany, Italy, Spain and Israel — had contributed their mite to the anti-Soviet forces in Angola .... Intelligence officers from all these countries met — sometimes at remote airstrips — to compare their inventories, and to check that they were not duplicating arms supplies.[1]

But South Africa was far more deeply involved than the rest. According to Moss, by early November Pretoria not only had two columns of troops in the south with UNITA (the 'Zulu' and 'Foxbat' forces) but had military advisers with Roberto's forces right up in the north as well. As Independence Day neared Pretoria came under overwhelming pressure to stay on longer — and gave way. Thereafter Pretoria appears to have become almost paralysed by indecision, with the folly of reversing her previous firm commitment to withdraw by 11 November becoming increasingly clear. By 14 November her troops were stuck at Novo Redondo and could not proceed without heavy reinforcements. Ahead of them lay in wait not merely the hardened troops of the MPLA, determined to defend Luanda at all costs, but a rapidly growing number of Cubans. The Cubans were, moreover, amassing an arsenal of heavy mortars, armoured vehicles, tanks, the fearsome 'Stalin organs' and, most alarming of all, Mig-17s and Mig-21s. What if these took to the air to strafe and rocket Pretoria's tiny forces? The only way to

[1] Moss, op. cit., 6 Feb. 1977.

Chronology cont.

11   OAU Summit. Machel (Mozambique) proposes recognition of MPLA
      government. Strongly opposed by Senghor and Khama (Botswana),
      who argue for recognition of coalition government of national unity.
      Nigeria takes strong stand in favour of MPLA, attacking South
      African and US attempts to pressure African states. Complete
      deadlock: 23—23 vote.

12   MPLA captures Ambriz, former FNLA seat of government.

22   South Africa decides to withdraw troops.

24   MPLA captures Novo Redondo.

FEBRUARY

4   South Africa announces that all its troops withdrawn to within 50
      km. of Namibian border, staying in Angola only to protect Cunene
      Dam installations.

8   MPLA takes Huambo, former UNITA capital.

11   25 out of 46 OAU members now recognise MPLA government;
      People's Republic of Angola accepted into OAU as 47th member.
      Zaire protests at 'illegal' decision; Zambia refuses to recognise
      Angola.

MARCH

25   South African troops withdrawn across Namibian border from
      Cunene area.

APRIL

1   MPLA troops and Cubans complete defeat of UNITA and reach
      Namibian border.

---

prevent annihilation would be to commit the S.A.A.F.
Mirages.[1] If Pretoria took up the challenge presented by the
Cubans she would have to commit her entire armed forces to
battle several thousand miles away in unfamiliar territory
against possibly superior armaments, all in the face of violent
international denunciation. It would be the complete nightmare
which, we have seen, it had been the great cardinal principle of
South African policy to avoid. From 14 November on there was
really only one thing Pretoria could do: withdraw. To be sure,
the pressure on her to stay in Angola, from Lusaka, Kinshasa,

---

[1] At least one African leader thought about the Mirages too. According to
Moss, Mobutu 'implored the South Africans to bomb northern MPLA
positions'.

and numerous other African capitals, was very great, but it could hardly have weighed very heavily with Pretoria in the light of the appalling consequences of staying. None of these African leaders, after all, had even gone so far as to defend South Africa in public, for all their pleading with her in private. Indeed, when the MPLA produced its South African prisoners these African leaders joined in the expressions of horror which this dramatic evidence occasioned across the African continent. It was difficult to grant much weight or even respect for men such as these. Far more important, however, was the enormous pressure emanating from Washington for South Africa to stay on. For almost two further months this pressure was strong enough to balance Pretoria's equally desperate desire to get out.

Henry Kissinger had, until 1975, been riding high. A true heir to Metternich, he had led a largely successful crusade on a world scale against 'disorder' and social revolution. He had quite shamelessly bullied Israel into peace with an Egypt which rapidly became a grateful client state. He had successfully destabilised Chile, and Salvador Allende had not even lived to tell the tale, let alone make more trouble. He had survived the Watergate holocaust with only minor scratches (he had, it was discovered, been 'bugging' his own State Department employees). The Nobel Committee had taken the hint and given him its Peace Prize. But there was the rub. The Vietnamese negotiator, Le Duc Tho, had declined the Prize on the grounds that peace had not really been achieved in his unhappy country. Nor had it, and as time wore on Le Duc Tho's decision had looked better and better, Kissinger's own prize an increasingly sick joke. For the American *imperium* had begun to decay and Kissinger, unluckily, had to preside over the process. An early portent had come in Bangladesh, whose birth Kissinger had fought bitterly to prevent, fulminating furiously but impotently against India, the midwife of the new state. Much worse was to come, for in early 1975 the whole Indochinese garment, sewn together with such blood and toil, began to unravel and come apart at the seams. Kissinger was torn between his futile attempts to beg and cajole a resistant Congress to intervene and a more elemental desire to hide, isolating himself from public view and the need to comment. In the almost 30 years since the Chinese revolution the US had not suffered a Communist success anywhere in the world, saving the 'accident' of Cuba. Now there

had been three together, in Vietnam, Cambodia and Laos. The
CIA, the State Department and its Secretary of State had not
had much experience of being on the losing side; it was not
surprising that they made such poor losers.

And now there was Angola. Had Kissinger realised that
Vietnam was liable to collapse in early 1975 he might, perhaps,
have respected his own appeal to the Russians that the Great
Powers should keep out of Angola. Instead the US had begun to
intervene, covertly but quite heavily, from January 1975 on. By
the end of the year it was clear that these efforts had merely
pushed a left-wing nationalist regime into the arms of the
Communist powers who were, moreover, going to win. It simply
could not be allowed to happen. The South Africans *must* stay
on after 11 November, at least until the OAU had time to meet
and impose a coalition government on Angola.

Meanwhile. crude and desperate measures were applied.
Gulf, who had begun to accommodate themselves not unsuccessfully with the MPLA regime,[1] were ordered, to their
great indignation, to risk their own future by braving the
regime's displeasure and denying them their tax and royalties
payment in December. Against the radical African states
Kissinger's ire knew no bounds. Guinea, Algeria, Somalia, the
Congo (Brazzaville) and the former Portuguese colonies had all
actually appealed to Castro to send his troops, and all of them
offered or actually provided utterly crucial air and sea staging
facilities for the Communist side, resisting Washington's fury to
do so. Until this point US policy had tended to treat the
African radicals indulgently as wild and wayward children; now
they became the object of Washington's open and bitter
hostility — none more than Marien Ngouabi, the Congolese
president, whose decision to allow the Cubans disembarkation
and trans-shipment bases at Brazzaville and Pointe Noire were
vital to the success of Cuban intervention.[2] According to
Garcia-Marquez the Caribbean countries offering similar staging
rights were threatened with nothing less than aerial bombardment. It is not known what pressures were applied to the
African radicals, but they may even have been of the same

---

[1] According to Legum (Legum and Hodges, op. cit., p. 12) Diamang, the
multinational diamond corporation, also reached an early and friendly
agreement with MPLA. The company is one of Harry Oppenheimer's
Anglo-American subsidiaries.
[2] President Ngouabi was assassinated on 18 March 1977 by a mysterious
'suicide commando'. See below, p. 285.

order. It is known, though, that Kissinger toyed with the idea of a naval blockade to prevent the ships carrying Cuban troops and equipment from getting through to Angola. Such ideas vanished when the Soviet Navy, displaying its new range and might, provided powerful escorts for the ships across the Atlantic. Meanwhile Kissinger applied the crudest of pressures to the African heads of state as they dithered and postponed the crucial OAU meeting, attempting simply to order them into line. This last tactic backfired disastrously by infuriating a number of African leaders, most particularly General Murtala Mohammed of Nigeria. When the OAU did meet Mohammed bitterly attacked the hapless President Ford (whose signature Kissinger had obtained) for having

> ... taken it upon himself to instruct African Heads of State and Government, by a circular letter, to insist on the withdrawal of Soviet and Cuban advisers from Angola as a precondition for the withdrawal of South African and other military adventurers. This constitutes a most intolerable presumption and a flagrant insult on the intelligence of African rulers.[1]

The 'other military adventurers' were, of course, the mainly British, American, Rhodesian and Portuguese mercenaries who fought alongside the South African, UNITA and FNLA troops. There seems to have been a last desperate bid to fill the gap left by the withdrawing South Africans by an accelerated recruitment of such mercenaries in January 1976. Philip Agee, the former CIA agent, interviewed a number of such mercenaries and reported three separate sources tracing back disbursements of money to the recruits from officials of the US Embassy in London (whom he named).[2] The accusation, thinly veiled, was that the mercenaries had represented Kissinger's desperate last throw, all else having failed. When Agee was placed under a British deportation order late in 1976 *Le Monde* argued persuasively that he and his compatriot (and fellow-deportee), Mark Hosenball, were the victims of a final act of vengeance for their revelations concerning the CIA's wide-ranging operations in southern Africa, and particularly the agency's strong reciprocal relationship with its South African

---

[1] Cited in Legum and Hodges, op. cit., p. 30.
[2] *Oui*, December 1976.

counterpart, BOSS.[1] If there is any truth in these allegations it
lends a certain point — and piquancy — to the decision by Sean
McBride (UN Commissioner for Namibia) and Morton Halperin
(formerly US Assistant Secretary of Defence and aide to
Kissinger himself), to testify to the British government's
deportation tribunal on Agee and Hosenball's behalf.

Despite all these desperate machinations, it was simply no
good. In early 1976 the efforts of the mercenaries collapsed in
murderous farce. The *coup de grâce* to Kissinger's last-ditch
efforts came in two instalments. First, on 18 December the US
Senate flatly refused to listen to the Secretary of State's almost
hysterical pleading and voted down all further US aid to the
anti-MPLA forces. Three weeks later the OAU Summit, whose
continual postponement and re-postponement must have been
the purest agony for Pretoria, met — and split down the middle.
Once Nigeria had opted decisively for the MPLA there was an
inevitable rush to its side by a number of smaller African
states. The same bloc of Nigeria, her clients, and the radicals
which had defeated 'dialogue' with Pretoria in 1971 now again
frustrated her. This left the issue to be settled by *force majeure*
in Angola, which it duly and quickly was. By February 1976
the MPLA regime took its place in the OAU. For Pretoria — and
for Kissinger — the denouement was complete. Kissinger reacted
as he had over the Vietnamese debacle, hiding himself away. As

---

[1] *Le Monde*, 24 Nov. 1976. Among the Agee—Hosenball revelations
which, according to *Le Monde*, so infuriated the US (and thus, indirectly,
the British) government were details of an RAF electronic base in
Botswana used for monitoring the signals of the Zimbabwe guerrilla
movements; of BOSS—CIA collaboration to promote the Herero chief,
Clemens Kapuuo, as the conservative head of an independent Namibian
(puppet) state through the South African-financed Madison Avenue firm,
Psychom; BOSS—CIA collaboration in a fresh campaign to support UNITA
against the MPLA government in Angola; details of the US AID project for
the study of 'the problems of transition to majority rule in southern
Africa' (in fact, they alleged, a straightforward espionage operation);
details of US National Security Council and NATO agreements on military
collaboration with South Africa leading to joint manoeuvres between the
South African and French fleets in March 1974; secret electronic
surveillance use of the Simonstown base by the NATO powers; and a
variety of other such contacts. *Le Monde*'s argument was that Agee and
Hosenball had greatly embarrassed Kissinger in the eyes of leaders such as
Nyerere; that London was the pivotal centre of BOSS—CIA—M15 joint
operations; and that Kissinger was determined to 'clean up' the London
network (by getting Agee and Hosenball out of the way) before Carter
took office. In this way the new chief of the CIA London office, Ed
Proctor, named by Kissinger as one of his last acts in September 1976,
would be guaranteed a clear field.

Moss puts it, 'Dr Kissinger — who was a hawk on Angola but was extremely nervous of Press and Congressional efforts to expose American connections with South Africa — had taken steps to isolate himself from direct contacts with the South Africans.'[1] He also sulked, vetoing Angola's admission to the UN, just as he had vetoed Vietnam's.[2] It was, in its way, a telling gesture — about Kissinger. Vetoing their admission did not make the governments of these states cease to exist, but the wish was clearly there. Their very existence mocked and affronted the Secretary of State — who, he was determined to show, was never lightly mocked. For Pretoria, however, the situation was too grave for such antics.

The Angolan adventure had, for Pretoria, been an entire and appalling catastrophe. Pretoria's enemies rejoiced at the sight of white South African soldiers as defeated prisoners of an African army; they took this as evidence that South Africa had been thirsting for battle and had been roundly defeated. This was extremely unfair on several counts. Pretoria had never wanted to go into Angola; she had been pushed, pulled and cajoled into the war. Once in she had limited her commitment — there were never more than 2,000 South African troops there. She had never deployed her air force, her navy or even the bulk of her army. Once in, she had wanted to get out as quickly as possible. Still, the sight of the prisoners hurt white South African eyes too. The smell of defeat *did* hang in the air; fearsome tales of Soviet might (particularly the 'Stalin organs', which caught the horrified imagination of the South African public) spread, demoralising white opinion. It was a dramatic and thought-provoking sight for black South Africans as well. . . . . The MPLA hung on to the prisoners: at the time of writing (April 1977) they have them still.

There were more tangible aspects to the disaster. Above all, South African intervention had merely had the result of

---

[1] Moss, op. cit., Feb. 13, 1977.
[2] The vote on Angola's entry to the UN in June 1975 was enlivened not merely by the US veto but by China's policy of absenting herself from the debate. China had withdrawn her support from the FNLA in October 1975, just as South Africa launched into full-scale intervention, but Peking had always insisted that her decision was simply in accordance with the Kampala Summit appeal to foreign powers to keep out. The Kampala Summit had been in July, however, and China did not leave then. . . . Her attitude at the UN was, in fact, a clear admission that China too had been defeated in Angola.

bringing about a large Communist presence not far from her borders. The war and South African intervention in it had merely served to discredit Angolan conservatives such as Savimbi (who might otherwise have played a moderating role in the Angolan government). It had strengthened the most radical elements within the MPLA and assured South Africa of the continuing hostility of that regime. There was no hope now in Angola for the rapprochement policy which had shown positive results in Mozambique. Havana, and perhaps Moscow, now had in southern Africa a regime which would cling to their skirts in fear and suspicion of South Africa, which might provide them with a base for further operations throughout the region — for they could not but be encouraged by their triumph. This new challenge South Africa would have to meet on her own, for the war had only served to heighten her international isolation — and to emphasise that her Western friends would, in the last analysis, let her down. Betrayal was not too strong a word for the treatment she had received — from the US in particular — and feelings in Pretoria were correspondingly bitter.

The consequences for the southern African region as a whole were no less dire. The northern buffer, and with it the policy of detente, lay in ruins. Relations with Mozambique had hardly been helped by the Angolan affair — it was Samora Machel who led the pro-MPLA forces at the OAU Summit in January 1976, with a bitter attack on South African intervention against his sister movement. But the events of 1974–6 had a more general effect too on the small states of the region. Once they had accommodated themselves to the reality of South African power; now they began to accommodate to a wholly new set of realities. In 1974, seizing upon an air-crash in which 74 Malawian migrant workers in South Africa had been killed, Banda ended all recruitment of Malawian labour to the Rand mines. Gradually Lesotho and Botswana followed suit, and by early 1976 the number of workers recruited in Mozambique began to decline too. It was an extremely serious development — the mines were progressively starved of labour — but more significant was the fact that these states were cutting off their most important single economic link with South Africa, despite the very considerable cost to themselves.[1] All the minor states of

---

[1] About 75% of South Africa's 400,000 black mine workers had been migrants up to this point. The cost to Malawi (for example) of the ban on recruitment may be judged from the fact that in 1973 Malawian migrant workers in South Africa made up almost 30% of *all* Malawians in paid employment.

the region — even Malawi — hastened to form friendly links with the FRELIMO government. Banda began to woo not merely Zambia but Tanzania as well. In late 1974 Botswana established diplomatic relations with Peking, having expelled the Taiwan embassy. In May 1975 Lesotho not merely followed suit but invited the Chinese to help in building a larger airport at Maseru in order to lessen the country's dependence on Jan Smuts airport (Johannesburg). In November 1975 a member of the left-wing Basotho Congress Party was brought into the Cabinet[1] — in Lesotho terms a large swing to the left. Relations between Pretoria and all these former clients cooled perceptibly. By late 1976 Lesotho was sending delegates to an anti-apartheid conference held in . . . Havana. The effects of the sea-change caused by the Lisbon coup and Angola were visible even further afield. Sir Seewoosagur Ramgoolam of Mauritius suddenly discovered a wholly new and critical attitude towards South Africa. Seeking to allay OAU criticism of his island's close economic links with Pretoria he offered to host the July 1976 OAU Heads of State meeting, and temporarily closed the island to all South African visitors (hitherto 75% of the Mauritian tourist trade). All traces of the South African connection were expunged from hotels. At the meeting itself Sir Seewoosagur condemned Pretoria for the Soweto deaths — 'victims of oppression and racialism'; accused Pretoria of being an accomplice to the Israelis' raid on Entebbe; and broke off diplomatic relations with Israel. South African tourists, no longer welcome in Malagasy, were no longer secure in Mauritius either.[2] And even the last tourist bastion in the Indian Ocean — the Seychelles — suddenly discovered that it no longer wished to be a colony; that it was African; and would like to join the OAU.

Tourism was hardly Pretoria's chief worry, though it had been a major indicator of the success of detente policies. But

---

[1] See p. 51 above for the efforts once made by Pretoria to keep the BCP out of power.

[2] The Mauritian election of December 1976 made it certain that there would be no full resumption of South African links with the island. Sir Seewoosagur's Labour Party lost half its seats while Paul Berenger's far-left Mauritian Militant Movement, which had hitherto been unrepresented in parliament, now won 34 out of the 70 seats. The MMM had campaigned fiercely against the South African connection and against the presence of the giant US base at Diego Garcia, the former Mauritian island 1,500 miles to the north-east. Sir Seewoosagur managed to cling on to power with a one-seat coalition majority, but his long dominance of Mauritian politics was clearly almost over. He is 76.

even detente itself now began to look like a luxury. The Angolan crisis had the effect of making the Rhodesian situation more critical than ever — South Africa could not afford another Angola there. But the war in Angola had also made the Rhodesian problem more difficult — frightening the white Rhodesians, providing an enormous boost for the Zimbabwe guerrillas, and making conservative opinion in South Africa more dubious than ever of the merits of sacrificing white rule in the last remaining northern outpost.

Finally, a less noticed but utterly critical consequence of the Angolan imbroglio was the falling out with France and the resulting ban on future purchase of land and air weapons from that quarter. This was nothing less than a complete disaster, and it was difficult to see how it might be repaired. Moreover, if there were already Mig-21s in Angola, how long before there were Mig-23s and Mig-25s too? Pretoria's Mirages would be far outmatched by them. She needed supplies of sophisticated modern weaponry now as never before — and now her sole supplier was lost to her.

There should, perhaps, have been at least one benefit for South Africa from the Angolan debacle, and that was the better and closer relationship with the conservative African states which had at least in part formed unofficially during the war. But even this she was deprived of, with the partial exception of Zaire. For if Pretoria had annoyed France, then her relations with French Africa were bound to deteriorate too. This was made clear to Pretoria immediately after Giscard's arms-ban in August 1975, when, in September, a junior minister from the Ivory Coast arrived. The invitation had been made to Houphouet himself. His envoy, moreover, seemed little inclined to make a good impression on his hosts — announcing loudly that segregation was 'poison'; that Pretoria had little hope of further detente if she did not reform further (by, for example, giving her Africans and Indians the vote). The visit was not a success. French ambitions in Angola had been rudely thwarted and the displeasure of Paris, if the arms ban did not make it evident enough, would now be communicated by underlings from Abidjan.

Pretoria did not even gain much advantage with Kaunda. Angola had been a disaster for him too, but it was not long before Zambia, inevitably, began to adapt herself to the new realities of the situation. Kaunda soon began to wax more militant over Rhodesia, to talk tearfully of the need to fight there. By the end of 1976 Zambia had recognised the MPLA government, expelled UNITA from Lusaka and banned the organisation. In early 1976 Kaunda had railed against the Soviet and Cuban presence in Angola as a fearsome 'tiger and its cubs', and denied the sovereignty of the Angolan regime. A year later he had apparently discovered that there are no tigers in Africa. In early 1977 it was announced that Kaunda was to play host to Fidel Castro and President Podgorny of the USSR — and would, shortly after, pay a state visit to his brother president, Agostinho Neto.

Podgorny duly came but Castro apparently decided against playing a role in this new act of Kaunda's political contortionism. Lusaka prepared itself excitedly for the Cuban premier's visit; flags flapped, red carpet was unrolled and Zambian dignitaries waited at the airport — only to hear that Castro had flown straight on to Luanda, pleading pressure of (diplomatic) business.

(iii) *The Search for New Alignments*
The crises of 1973—6 served greatly to deepen South Africa's international isolation. An Afro—Arab front had formed against her; her tenuous contacts with conservative Africa were weakened; her clients and allies in her northern buffer fell away; Britain had cancelled the Simonstown agreement; France had cut off arms supplies; and towards Washington Pretoria could, after Angola, feel only bitterness. Meanwhile she sought, with a flexibility born of desperation, new friends and allies.

Even by the time of the Yom Kippur war, South Africa had, as we have seen, established not insubstantial links with Israel, for all the latter's public disapproval of apartheid.[1] The war, and the emergence of the Afro—Arab front, led to a rapid and quite open consolidation of this alliance. In part this was merely a matter of making public what had earlier been dissembled, but there was also a strong sense in which it was a second-best alliance which both states needed. Israel had lost the favours of Africa; she might as well enjoy the full benefits of a South African alliance. Pretoria, for her part, was now the object of an Arab oil boycott and had nothing further to lose by an open alliance with Israel. Both states were isolated and (they felt) badly treated by the Great Powers; they would pool their resources.

In a sense, of course, this was nothing new, for the entire Israeli economy and state has long depended on South Africa in one respect. Easily the most important industry in Israel is the

[1] See above, pp. 96—100.

production of polished gem diamonds. It employs some 15,000 Israelis and provides 40—50% of Israel's total exports by value.[1] Most of the finished diamonds go to the US and constitute a key economic link between Israel and America. The diamonds — or 85% of them — come from Southern Africa and Namibia. This quite fundamental link between the two countries had, of course, always been disguised by the CSO mechanism.[2]

After 1973 Israel abruptly ceased to vote against South Africa at the UN, and commercial, cultural and military links between the two states began to expand at a rapid rate. By 1975 trade between the two countries, around R3 million in 1968, had passed the R100 million mark and was still growing fast. Essentially the relationship appeared to be based on an energy-for-guns swap. South Africa agreed to provide Israel with a million tons of coal a year by 1979, promised her uranium supplies and may also have agreed to give Israel privileged access to South African coal gasification know-how — a field in which SASOL is very easily the world leader. Pretoria also agreed to help Israel in a host of projects, including the construction of a railway in the Negev which, the *Rand Daily Mail* hinted heavily, 'will under certain circumstances be advantageous to South Africa as well as Israel'.[3] In return South Africa had, by late 1976, placed orders for six Reshef 420-ton gunboats, equipped with sea-to-sea Gabriel missiles, and purchased quantities of military electronic fencing equipment for use 'primarily in population movement control and in counter-insurgency', presumably on the Namibian and Mozambique borders.[4] But, inevitably in the wake of the French arms ban,

---

[1] In 1975 the industry's exports were $548.5 million, in 1976 $711.8 million
[2] The Central Selling Organisation, run by the South African (and world) diamond monopoly, De Beers, is based in London and virtually all world diamond sales are channelled through it.
[3] Cited in article by R. Manning, *African Development*, Dec. 1976. The Negev railway will allow the bulk shipment of goods from the port of Elat at the head of the Gulf of Aqaba to the Mediteranean ports of Israel. If South Africa is to use Israel as a trojan horse via which to export her goods into the EEC without tariff penalty she will need to make large-scale use of these facilities.
[4] In August 1976 the SWAPO leader, Sam Nujoma, claimed that Israeli soldiers in South African uniform had been participating in counter-insurgency activities in Namibia. Ovambo villagers had, he claimed, found that these soldiers spoke only Hebrew amongst themselves and had no knowledge of Afrikaans. In July 1976 the Israeli newspaper, *Yediot Aharanot*, reported the ex-Israeli army soldiers were being recruited by mercenary agencies to fight in Rhodesia. The Israeli army is, of course, the acknowledged world leader in counter-insurgency desert warfare.

most speculation surrounded the possible acquisition by Pretoria of the Kfir fighter, a Mach 2.2 aircraft closely modelled on the Mirage V. It would clearly be most advantageous to South Africa, which already had service and assembly facilities for earlier Mirage versions, to purchase the Kfir. In April 1976 Vorster headed a strong South African delegation to Israel, and held high-level talks with Israeli ministers and defence chiefs. Both Vorster and his hosts were, however, emphatic in their denials that there was any possibility that South Africa might buy the Kfir, denials which sat oddly with the fact that the visitors had spent much time touring Israeli aircraft factories, including the Kfir production line itself. The problem was that the Kfir uses General Electric J-79 engines supplied by the US, and the State Department was, inevitably, sensitive on the subject of third-party deals by Israel, particularly a deal which would make the US a party to breaking the UN arms embargo against South Africa.

There was also a very definite strategic point to the new alliance with Israel. The whole of the eastern seaboard of Africa had, by the mid-1970s, become a patchwork of left-wing regimes. At the head of the Persian Gulf stood the People's Democratic Republic of Yemen whose capital, Aden, offered the Red navy a major potential base. Opposite the PDRY sat the equally left-wing Somali Democratic Republic, in 1974 the first African country to receive visits not only from President Podgorny but also from Admiral Gorchkov, the commander-in-chief of the Red Navy. The Ethiopian military regime was similarly of left-wing hue, while the whole of the Eritrean coast was in the hands of left-wing Eritrean guerrilla movements. Further down the coast came the left-wing regimes of Tanzania, Mozambique and Malagasy. Even the unclassifiable Amin regime in Uganda was heavily dependent on the Soviet Union for its arms supplies.

Neither South Africa nor Israel could take any comfort from the thought that almost the entire eastern side of Africa was now in the hands of regimes whose hostility to Tel Aviv was surpassed only by their hostility to Pretoria. If, however, a countervailing Israeli—South African alliance was to carry any weight it had to bring in the only remaining conservative regime on the coast, Kenya. Kenya had earlier been one of the leaders of the 'dialogue' cause with Pretoria; the cause had failed, but unofficial links continued. Kenya had also broken off relations with Israel in the general African diplomatic rupture of 1974, but Nairobi—Tel Aviv relations remained close, with a heavy commercial and diplomatic traffic continuing between the two countries on an informal level. Kenya, for her part, was at odds with almost all the left-wing regimes around her. It was a natural alliance for her too.

This emergent Pretoria—Nairobi—Tel Aviv triangle had, of course, to remain a discreet one, surfacing only partially in July 1976 during the Israeli raid on Entebbe airport to recover hostages held there by Palestinian terrorists. The Israeli Hercules aircraft which carried the raiders were, of course, operating at the very limits of their range. For the raid to be conceivable at all they had to have advance arrangements for stop-over and refueling facilities in Kenya and, fairly certainly, contingency plans to fly on from there to South Africa. Had the raiders failed to destroy the Ugandan Migs stationed on the ground at Entebbe the Hercules would have been far out of range of Israeli air support. Their only hope would have been to head southwards where they would almost immediately have come within range of the S.A.A.F. Mirages based in the Caprivi strip which, doubtless, would have been able to see off any pursuing Ugandan Migs in short order. As it was the intrepid Israelis succeeded in destroying or immobilising virtually the entire Ugandan air force while simultaneously freeing the hostages they had principally come for, so none of these contingency plans had to come into play.

Such plans quite certainly must have existed. Stevenson mentions how the raiders, faced with refueling difficulties at Entebbe (the Hercules had only 90 minutes fuel left on landing), had to 'choose from several alternative plans'.[1] He also records an Israeli soldier telling a South African doctor among the rescued hostages 'Look, doctor — you've got the chance to return home to South Africa from here.'[2] Ofer notes that shortly before the raid a camouflaged Israeli Hercules was observed stationed at Maseru airport (Lesotho) and suggests that its (ultimately unnecessary) purpose was as an 'intelligence' plane or even a reserve to carry reinforcements of (Israeli?/South African?) commandos to Entebbe if required.[3]

Understandably, Nairobi, Tel Aviv and Pretoria kept a tight-lipped silence over the question of the advance collaboration which must, undoubtedly, have taken place between the three capitals. George Githii, editor of the Nairobi *Daily Nation*, which had scooped the world press with the news of the raid, was later the subject of a dawn visit by the Kenyan commissioner of police in person, ordering him to discontinue the

---

[1] W. Stevenson, *90 Minutes at Entebbe* (New York, 1976), p. 121.
[2] Ibid., p. 106.
[3] Y. Ofer, *Operation Thunder: The Entebbe Raid* (London, 1976), p. 39.

newspaper's serialised story of the raid. Continuation of the story would be regarded as 'a danger to Kenyan security'. On the same day (15 October 1976) it was announced in Jerusalem that Warner Brothers had cancelled plans to make a film about the raid after learning that it 'would receive no new information about the action'.[1] By then, however, it was too late — other film companies were clearly determined to go ahead with similar projects. Making the best of a bad job the Israelis apparently decided that, if there was to be further publicity about the raid, it would be *their* publicity.[2] Ultimately not one but three films were made and, with not atypical panache, the Israelis invited President Amin to attend the premiere of the 20th Century Fox version in Jerusalem. This was too much even for the Ugandan president who was led to wonder 'whether someone was just pulling his leg'.[3]

It was, perhaps, fairly predictable that the Yom Kippur war would see a consolidation and increase in the links between South Africa and Israel. Somewhat more surprising, at least at first glance, was the relationship between Iran and South Africa which the war and the oil crisis also accentuated. In fact, as with Israel, it was in good part a case of the war accentuating and making overt a relationship which already existed. For the National Iran Oil Company had taken a 17.5% share in the South African state oil refinery, NATREF, at the start of its operations (1971), and had signed partnership agreements guaranteeing the project supplies of crude oil. When the Yom Kippur war forced the Shah to choose sides he showed no hesitation, immediately announcing that Iran would not be party to the Arab oil boycott against South Africa.

Iran quickly became Pretoria's major oil-supplier, providing a third or more of all South Africa's oil imports. It became clear, however, that more than just oil was involved in the new relationship, for the two countries enthusiastically set about

[1] *The Times* (London), 16 Oct. 1976.
[2] The two books cited above are the only available accounts. Stevenson is a former British intelligence officer and member of the secret Intrepid organisation which 'helped to establish the state of Israel'. He has, since 1945, been intimately associated with the Israeli military-intelligence community, and is the author of *Zanek!: A Chronicle of the Israeli Air Force.* Interestingly, he also saw service in Kenya against Mau Mau. Ofer was for 20 years deputy editor of the Israel Air Force magazine and was, he claims, able 'to have access to sources that were not released to other journalists'. It would appear that Israeli Intelligence has, in its generosity, provided the world with not one but two official accounts of the raid.
[3] *The Times* (London), 31 Dec. 1976.

expanding their trade and diplomatic links. The basis of the
relationship was, in fact, a strategic one. Pretoria was, of course,
only too delighted to offer her assistance in the lucrative
business of assisting the Shah's programme for the accelerated
industrialisation of Iran. But there was quite a queue of other
developed countries ready to play their part in furthering the
Shah's economic objectives. The more important fact was that
the Shah had major ambitions in the Indian Ocean. Iran had
already become the major military power in central Asia and
the Persian Gulf. The Shah's troops had seized the Tumb Islands
(in 1971) and intervened in Oman (in 1973) to assist the Sultan
there against the left-wing Dhofari rebels, the Shah announcing
that he was willing, if invited, to intervene against radical
movements anywhere in the Arabian peninsula.

Now, his revenues swollen from the oil price rise, the Shah
was looking further afield. The Chah Bahar air and naval base
would, when complete, be the largest operated by *any* power in
the Indian Ocean, where the Shah believes the future of Iran
lies. As the Shah gazed out over that ocean it was clear enough
that if he was to succeed in his stated aim of undermining the
super-powers' dominance of the region he would need to form
links with its other medium powers. Australia was obviously
one such (the Shah visited Canberra in September 1974) — and
South Africa another. There was not a little irony in the
situation: the father of the Shah (and of modern Iran), Reza
Shah, had died in Johannesburg, whither he was exiled during
the Second World War by the British for his pro-German
attitudes. Now Reza Shah's son was to seek his place in the sun
with the help of South Africa, whose leader, Vorster, had been
imprisoned in wartime Johannesburg for *his* pro-German attitudes.

Pretoria looked further afield too. In April 1974 President
Stroessner of Paraguay had visited South Africa and signed a
number of economic agreements with her. In August 1975
Vorster returned the compliment, bearing with him loans to
finance Paraguayan orders for South African goods. He also
made a private visit to President Bordaberry of Uruguay. If
South Africa's manufactured exports were blocked in Africa,
perhaps she might find outlets in Latin America?

The Angolan débâcle prompted an even bolder thought.
South Africa was looking for a powerful counter to the growing
Soviet presence in the region and was also eager for relations
with less-developed countries with markets large enough to
absorb the manufactured goods Africa wouldn't take. There was
one country obvious before all others: Communist China. In

1971 Vorster had referred to 'the Chinese bridgehead' as 'the greatest single threat in Africa at present', but if Peking could support the FNLA in Angola could that any longer be true? Peking was easily the most important external aid source for the FRELIMO regime in Mozambique — perhaps a relationship with Peking could help defuse tensions there too? Within South Africa China had always lent its support to the PAC, led by Robert Sobukwe, as against the (pro-Moscow) ANC—CPSA alliance. Perhaps it would be worth resurrecting Sobukwe, for all that he had been the leader of the demonstrations which led to Sharpeville. Mandela, the ANC leader, was still incarcerated on Robben Island, while Sobukwe had now been freed from the dreaded island and allowed to live, banned and restricted of course, in Kimberley. Chief Buthelezi, the KwaZulu Bantustan leader, had clearly begun to think along not dissimilar lines, for early in 1975 he announced that he wished to appoint Sobukwe to his cabinet. Buthelezi saw Vorster at this time and discussed the problem of Sobukwe and Mandela. Reporting back, Buthelezi said that while Vorster had made it clear that Mandela would stay where he was, he had taken a notably softer line on Sobukwe:

> ... the PM said that Mr Sobukwe did not fall into the above-mentioned (hopeless) category. In other words he was not a communist, even though he had other problems. He said that his case was reviewed from time to time. On being asked by me on whether he would not initiate a special review of Mr Sobukwe's case, at his special instance, the PM said he would do so...[1]

Sobukwe might be a useful counter with Peking — and even with Washington. In late 1974 the American tennis player, Arthur Ashe, was allowed to visit him along with Martin Luther King's former aide, Andrew Young. Young, who was to become President Carter's UN Ambassador in early 1977, had become the guardian of Sobukwe's two eldest children, and sang Sobukwe's praises, comparing him to Martin Luther King and Jomo Kenyatta (*sic*). Sobukwe's treatment was further relaxed to the point where, by early 1977, he was effectively giving press interviews despite his banning order.[2]

[1] 'South Africa', in *ACR 1974—5*, op. cit., p. B435.
[2] For example, the thinly disguised interview ('If he could give interviews Sobukwe would emphasise his view that...' etc.) given to Jim Hoagland in his article in the *Guardian* (London), 26 Jan. 1977, on which I have drawn above.

Sobukwe was only a symbol, a pawn, but the stakes were high. Jan Marais, the Afrikaner millionaire-head of the Trust Bank and pillar of the Nationalist Establishment, announced that 'I would vote with both hands for good ties with Red China', while Connie Mulder, the Information and Interior Minister, began to punctuate his routine denunciations of Communism with the qualification 'I mean Moscow by that, not Peking'. As the northern buffer states slithered to the left in 1975—6, Pretoria may well have encouraged them to establish diplomatic relations with Peking (none of them dared establish relations with Moscow). It might, after all, be useful to have Chinese embassies in Botswana and Lesotho to talk to.

These were, of course, largely pipe-dreams, castles in the air. It was as much a measure of Pretoria's desperation at her growing isolation as anything else which led her to go looking for friends in Latin America, the Middle East and China. It did not require much thought to see that such new alliances could be of only limited utility. Israel, after all, was a much smaller country than South Africa; was very far away; and, to put it mildly, had some problems of her own. The same applied *a fortiori* to the embattled military dictatorships of Paraguay and Uraguay. Iran was a considerable power, certainly, and would be a greater one; but it was difficult to see the Shah's ambitions extending as far as military intervention on South Africa's side in a future conflict. He had bitten off quite enough in Oman, and was getting out of *there* by early 1977. He would sell South Africa oil, and that was enough to be grateful for. As for China, which country in the world could place much rational weight on Chinese foreign policy after its ludicrous twists and turns of the previous decade? Perhaps Hua Kuo-Feng would be a bit saner than Mao, but in any case he was clearly going to have problems enough of his own and had no real (naval) means of making Peking's weight felt in the Indian Ocean. Even if any of these new friends had the capacity to help South Africa any further it was far from clear that they would feel they *needed* to. And only that would be good enough. There wasn't really any substitute for the alliance with the Western Great Powers on which South Africa had traditionally based her hopes. In any case, the more Pretoria sought to escape into these new third-party relationships the more she was brought up against the fact that these, too, were merely functions of her relationships with the Western Great Powers. She would not get far with the Latin Americans, after all, without US approval. Similarly, a large part of the appeal for Pretoria in the relationship with Israel was the hope that Israel might offer her the sort of backdoor into the EEC that Mauritius had once promised. For by the association agreement of May 1975, the EEC had agreed that from 1 July 1977 it would accept all Israeli imports without tariff duty. There were possibilities here for a massive export and re-export business through Israel — but on such a scale that the EEC powers would have to agree to it, implicitly at least. A similar possibility existed via Iran. But the Shah had repeatedly asked for a special trading agreement with the EEC and had been offered mere technical co-operation agreements which he indignantly rejected. Pretoria could fervently wish him all success in his efforts, but only Paris, London or Bonn could actually make the decision. It was the same with arms. Vorster could go to inspect the Kfir production line, but he would remain a child gazing without hope into the shop window while Israel continued to depend on the US for its J-79 engines. The Shah had no less than 600 American Phantoms and F-5s, and was ordering the even more advanced F-14 Tomcat. Similarly, Israel was, by the 1980s, going to have an air force bigger and stronger than that of any west European power, and was taking delivery not only of the Tomcat but of the F-15 Eagle and even the super-advanced F-16 and the Grumman E-2C Hawkeye. But neither Tehran nor Tel Aviv could sell any of these craft on to Pretoria without jeopardising their (much more important) relationships with Washington. It all came back to Paris and Washington in the end. Pretoria had, after Angola, many good reasons to resent both Giscard and Kissinger, but it was with them she was going to have to deal. If there was one reason why she had gone into Angola it was because she wanted an alliance with these powers, particularly the US, more than almost anything else. For all that they had led her into disaster in Angola and abandoned her to it, the objective of alliances with them remained as desirable as ever.

9 The Road to Soweto

The Angolan débâcle was, for South Africa's White Establishment, an appallingly comprehensive disaster. The triumph, first of FRELIMO and then of the MPLA, contributed powerfully to the new and assertive mood of the Republic's black population. The always shaky credibility of the government's Bantustan policy was dealt a shattering blow. Pretoria had hoped that she could spawn a patchwork of petty Bantu states, hand-picked traditional chiefs at their head, which would blend in not too inconspicuously with their equally conservative sister states of Lesotho, Swaziland and Botswana — all of which also had traditional chiefs at the helm. It was now painfully clear that even this doubtfully viable strategy had depended on the maintenance of the northern buffer. It was not just that the Bantustans' independence — starting with the Transkei in 1976 — would hardly survive much comparison with that of neighbours such as the new Mozambique. Worse, the collapse of the buffer exercised strong leftward pressures on the old sister states themselves, and even on the Bantustan leaders as well. It was not long before they were talking of their wish for good relations with FRELIMO. No sooner had the Transkei achieved its independence than Chief Matanzima, a man imposed by Pretoria's heavy hand on his own unwilling subjects, began to talk of allowing the banned PAC and ANC to operate freely within his territory.

Angola was, too, an economic disaster. South Africa, as we have seen, had been protected from the effects of world depression in 1974 by the soaring gold price. As the gold price fell throughout 1975 the economy faltered badly. The government's economic development programme for 1972—7 had set a target annual growth rate of 5¾%. In 1974 this had been more than fulfilled; in 1975 real GDP growth fell to 2.2% — and even this was achieved in good part thanks to a necessarily short-lived boom associated with the introduction of television. The South African economy was always inflation-prone, for its high growth rate resulted from large external capital flows; now it imported world inflation as well. Inflation was soon running well into double figures and the position was, of course, only worsened by the two Rand devaluations (of 23% altogether). The economy's dependence on foreign investors grew in direct proportion to the fall in the gold price. The confidence of these

investors — as also the local business community — was deeply
shaken by the Angolan disaster. In part the government found
itself a victim of its own propaganda. Had South Africa stayed
out of Angola and treated the MPLA regime as merely a variant
of African nationalism there was little reason to believe that its
arrival in power would have shaken confidence any more than
that of the FRELIMO regime in Mozambique had done. But
since the world had now been told that the MPLA were
Communists in all but name; since South African intervention
had brought the Cubans running to help; and given all the talk
of a Soviet naval base possibly being opened up in Lobito —
foreign investors could hardly be blamed for concluding that
the Russian bear was about to make a determined lunge in the
general direction of Johannesburg.

The ignominious South African retreat from Angola, moreover, encouraged such investors to believe that the Pretoria
government was not strong enough to withstand the threat. This
was utterly grotesque: even if the largest estimates are accepted,
there were never more than 15,000 Cuban troops in Angola
(and probably less than 11,000))— and of these the first 3,000
were departing for Havana by May 1976. Against that had stood
the armed might of possibly the greatest military power in the
southern hemisphere . . . unused. Nonetheless, the damage was
done. There was a major slump in South African shares as
foreign investors hurriedly drew back. The result was a galloping
economic crisis whose magnitude had become clear even before
Soweto added further to the panic in June 1976. By then real
GDP had actually been declining for at least six months — the
first time that the economy had registered negative growth since
before the Second World War. It was in this deteriorating
economic situation, as well as in the more direct psychological
impact of Angola, that the root cause of the violent black—
white confrontations of 1976 lay.

(i) The Whites: The importance of being Andries Treurnicht
Angola had also been a major blow to Vorster's position within
Afrikanerdom. Though the *verkrampte* extremists of the
HNP — the Herstigte Nasionale Party (Purified National
Party) — had been roundly defeated in the 1970 election, they
had not gone away. Vorster had called that election in good
part to squash the rebels and thus give himself a clear field for
the open efforts at dialogue which ensued. Vorster had won
because the strategic elites of Afrikanerdom — in the Churches
(above all), the universities, the Nationalist press, in the
Afrikaner cultural organisation and in business circles — had
preferred the proven benefits of Afrikaner solidarity and unity.

This had by no means justified any inference that the new wave of *verligte* Afrikaners were now the majority; indeed, the reverse was generally recognised to be the case. But Vorster had nudged official policy gently and guilefully towards a reformist path, never giving his party's increasingly discontented conservatives too large an issue to stand on. Finally, in 1969, their leader, Albert Hertzog, led off his followers into the HNP over the question of the government's acceptance of a New Zealand rugby team which included Maori players. For all that this move dramatised the regime's willingness to relax apartheid under external pressures, it had been the wrong time and the wrong place to pick a fight. South Africans love their sport; of all their sports they love their rugby best; they wanted the All Blacks to come; the price of temporary cameraderie with a few foreign 'natives' did not seem too high. In any case, in 1969 the economy was booming and it was Hertzog who had to bear the responsibility of creating the split. It was not, under such circumstances, too difficult to persuade even the most bitterly *swart gevaar* ('Black peril')-minded Afrikaners that they should keep a winning team and preserve team unity at all costs. And, as we have seen,[1] Vorster had taken out further insurance by campaigning in the most reactionary manner possible, leaving no room at all on his right.

Joining in the general stampede for Afrikaner unity behind Vorster had been many, very many, who had much more than a sneaking sympathy for the *verkramptes*, who felt that Hertzog's combination of rigid Calvinism and unadulterated white supremacy did indeed represent the true and traditional way of Afrikanerdom and, moreover, that such straightforward *baaskap* was, in the last analysis, the white man's best guarantee of survival. But such spirits were stilled by the sight of such notorious *verkramptes* as Piet Meyer[2] and Koot Vorster[3]

[1] See above, p. 45.
[2] A former head of the Broederbond and chairman of the South African Broadcasting Corporation, whose predelictions are perhaps best summarised by the fact that his son bears the unusual name of 'Izan'. Which, Meyer unblushingly explains, is 'Nazi' spelt backwards.
[3] Dr Vorster was for many years head of the largest of the Dutch Reformed Churches, the Nederduitse Gereformeerde Kerk, to which some 42% of all South African whites and almost a million non-whites belong. Dr Vorster used this enormously powerful position to preach a holy war against Communists for whom, he claimed, he had an unerring nose. Among the tell-tale signs of such affiliation, according to Vorster, were a liking for certain kinds of popular music, readership of *Time* magazine, and the wearing of red ties. He is an elder brother of the Prime Minister, the latter being the 13th child of the family.

remaining in line with the Nationalist leadership. This, indeed, was the premier's tactic — and his weakness: the overwhelming majority of the *verkramptes* stayed on inside the Nationalist party where they gave continuing vent to their views, while (crucially) accepting Vorster's continuing leadership. Vorster carefully refrained from identifying himself with the *verligte* faction and maintained the balance, insisting that while differences of emphasis might exist, there was a fundamental unity of views within the government's ranks. This was, of course, essentially true, for the *verligtes* were, in the main, concerned with modernising white supremacy, not surrendering it.

Though routed in 1970, the HNP remained a persistent, worrying presence with an importance belied by its tiny size. It knew that it had many followers and near-followers amongst the influential leadership of the Dutch Reformed Churches, and it had already effectively taken over the Broederbond, the secret society which had, until the 1960s, lain at the very centre of Afrikaner power. It was extremely confident of its own principles and of the fact that, at grass roots, probably the large majority of Afrikaners shared them. It knew, too, that it had a vast reservoir of potential strength still within the Nationalist party and that the history of Afrikaner nationalism is one of recurrent splits in which the weight of Afrikanerdom had always swung in the end behind the 'true' (i.e. more extreme) faction. History was on its side. Vorster and the Nationalist establishment knew this too; large sections of Afrikanerdom teetered on the *verkrampte* brink; they had to be continually reassured; the government needed to achieve success and affluence. If once it faltered or failed the position of the *verkramptes* was such that any decisive movement towards them was likely to be an avalanche. What was at stake, after all, was not just the fortunes of a political party but the Afrikaner nation. To most Afrikaners a nation, and especially their own, does not *have* principles — rather, it is defined by them, indeed, almost consists of them. Thus to most Afrikaners Smuts ceased to be an Afrikaner *because* he collaborated with the English-speakers. As Dr G. Scholtz, an editor in the 1960s of the leading Afrikaans newspaper, *Die Transvaler*, put it, a nation 'is a spiritual entity. If you don't subscribe to its principles, you belong to another group'.[1] This was not a figure of speech: when Dr Geyser, a leading Dutch Reformed Church theologian,

---

[1] Cited in J. Hoagland, *South Africa. Civilisations in Conflict* (London 1972) p. 42.

spoke ill of apartheid in the early 1960s, his church made him
the object of a show-trial for heresy.

It was this context of pure Calvinist idealism, too, which
made the HNP a threat. Hertzog claimed to speak not merely
for the interest of the Afrikaner nation, but for its soul. In the
late 1960s many Afrikaners conceded half-guiltily that he
probably did speak for the nation's soul, but not, in a period of
headlong affluence, for their interests. The HNP inveighed
bitterly against this new tide of 'materialism', exemplified, of
course, by the new class of Afrikaner bankers, industrialists and
agri-businessmen. It found its natural audience among the (more
numerous) Afrikaner blue-collar workers, small farmers and
lower middle class. While the great boom continued the bitter
accusations of the HNP against the treachery of the Afrikaner
establishment (and from the first it attacked BOSS as a possible
instrument of its own suppression[1]) fell on half-deaf ears, for
the effects of affluence trickled down to the lowliest poor
white. If, however, the boom should collapse, heightening poor
white fears of black competition in the labour market and their
suspicions of government softness in the face of the *swart
gevaar*, then the HNP might suddenly find it a much easier
matter to convince the Afrikaner nation that its soul and its
interests alike resided in the toughest possible policies of white
supremacy both internally and abroad.

If the 1970 election had been called so that 'dialogue' could
begin, the 1974 election was called essentially so that 'detente'
could begin. Dialogue had been a failure, to the relief of the
verkramptes. With the first rumblings of unrest in Lisbon
Vorster called a snap election for April 1974. If the much
bolder policy of 'detente' was to be viable he had first to secure
his flank on the right. The gambit worked — the HNP was
trounced again (though its percentage of the vote stayed
rock-steady at 3.6). Vorster now proceeded, as we have seen,
with a first and then a second attempt to bring about a
Rhodesian 'settlement'. White public opinion was deeply
ambivalent in its attitude to such projects. On the one hand the
urgency of disposing of the Rhodesian incubus was widely
recognised; on the other, there was a deep unease and dislike of
the idea that South Africa was betraying its promises and, with
them, the white man's position in southern Africa.

Vorster's dramatic failure in both of these attempts did little

---

[1] BOSS is directly responsible to the prime minister and is thus beyond the
control of the old Broederbond network to which, traditionally, most of
the Cabinet belong.

good for his standing, creating a growing sense of frustration and, with it, an increasing groundswell of criticism of the whole strategy of detente. As the economy began to slow noticeably in 1975, *verkrampte* pressures visibly increased. In June 1975 two key by-elections in safe Nationalist seats in the Transvaal saw the HNP take an unprecedented quarter of the vote. Voter turnout had, moreover, been extremely low, suggesting that many more voters had been severely cross-pressured by conflicting loyalties. This was a clear warning-signal for Vorster, particularly since Smith, perceiving the situation from Salisbury, now began to appeal more or less openly for *verkrampte* support.[1] Vorster could not envisage exerting further pressure on Rhodesia after this without taking terrible political risks. The Angolan adventure followed, kept secret from the South African public until 22 December — two months after the launching of the fateful 'Zulu' column. Only weeks later Pretoria announced its withdrawal and the full magnitude of the débâcle became clear. Having exerted fairly massive pressure on Smith to surrender white rule in Rhodesia, the government was now running away from 'black Communists', its tail between its legs, leaving white South African prisoners behind. At the same time the economy began to go into reverse. It was a scenario tailor-made for the *verkramptes*. Ahead, Vorster knew, now lay the even greater necessity for fresh attempts at a Rhodesian settlement and, perhaps, for Namibian de-colonisation too. Ahead, too, lay rapidly deepening economic gloom. He could not possibly negotiate all these rocks without seeking, somehow, to protect his flank from the *verkrampte* threat. It was at this point (January 1976) that he re-shuffled his Cabinet. The most dramatic appointment, though, was outside the Cabinet; that of Dr Andries Treurnicht.

Of all the *verkramptes* within the Nationalist party, Treurnicht was the most renowned. He had stamped the platteland giving doctrinaire extremist speeches which left little to choose between himself and Hertzog, the HNP leader. The whole emphasis of Treurnicht's position lay in criticism of the government's deviation from the true path of Verwoerdian Afrikaner exclusivism. Many Nationalists believed that if there were a fresh election for the leadership of the (dominant) Transvaal Nationalist party Treurnicht would swamp the present holder of the post, Connie Mulder. Treurnicht was, in

[1] See above, pp. 127–8.

fact, an almost open threat to Vorster. Taking him into the
government was a desperate gambit. While the move might do
much to allay *verkrampte* suspicions, it also gave a considerable
hostage to fortune. For if Treurnicht were to resign on a matter
of principle a really major *verkrampte* rebellion might begin.
Clearly, such a man had to be kept out of the inner councils of
the Cabinet itself and given a job which, however important,
had no direct connection with such sensitive areas as 'detente'
or the economy. Instead, Treurnicht was made Deputy Minister
of Bantu Education. His sacked predecessor, the *verligte* Punt
Janson, had been for some time involved in a departmental
battle over the question of the use of Afrikaans as a teaching
medium in the African schools of the southern Transvaal.
Repeated attempts to enforce a full 50% Afrikaans medium
instruction on the schools had met with heated resistance from
African parents, teachers and pupils. Janson had talked and
occasionally acted tough but the situation remained dead-
locked. Vorster may well have been pleased to have consigned
the dangerous Treurnicht to such apparently arcane concerns as
these. Treurnicht, for his part, made his own position clear
quickly enough. Asked in parliament how many African
headmasters had asked for some relaxation of the '50%
Afrikaans medium' rule, he replied: 'I do not deem the requested
information of such importance to instruct my department to
undertake this time-consuming task' (of counting them).
Treurnicht determined to show that no Afrikaner nationalist
was more zealous than he in the advancement of the precious
taal (language) and that he fully deserved his reputation for steely
ruthlessness. African children would have to learn their maths and
history in Afrikaans even if virtually none of their teachers in
these subjects were themselves proficient in the language. The
principle was more important than whether they liked it or not.
They didn't like it, and in the Johannesburg African township
of Soweto the black pupils of Orlando West Junior Secondary
School decided they would resist. On 17 May they came out on
strike against the ruling. Treurnicht showed no sign of relenting.
Vorster may not have noticed: on 5 June it was announced that
he was to meet the mighty Kissinger himself — the diplomacy of
Rhodesian settlement was nearing a climactic breakthrough. On
14 June Leonard Mosala, a Soweto urban councillor, warned
that if the Afrikaans medium ruling was not relaxed
immediately 'it will lead to another Sharpeville'. Two days later
the shooting started. In terms of the number of casualties, it
soon became clear, Mosala had been decidedly optimistic.

(ii) The Blacks: Bantustans, proletarians and the migrant worker who came to stay

A constant theme of liberal criticism of the apartheid system so doughtily defended by Vorster and Treurnicht alike was that, in some ideal or absolute sense, it stood in contradiction to the free play of market forces and thus inhibited the development of South African capitalism. It was a peculiar argument in one sense, for the root and basis of apartheid — the migratory labour system — has been fundamental to the development of South African capitalism and stretches right back to the opening of the mines and even before, to the rise of the great Cape vineyards and Natal sugar planatations. The Nationalists, when they took power in 1948, took over a ready-made system which they renamed, extended and systematised with an entirely Teutonic thoroughness and determination. And, as we have seen, despite the growing tide of liberal criticism, South African capitalism flourished as never before.

The rationale for apartheid, and by extension the Bantustan system, was articulated in its classic form by the Transvaal Local Government Commission of 1922:

> If the native is to be regarded as a permanent element in municipal areas there can be no justification for basing his exclusion from the franchise on grounds of colour. The native should be allowed to enter the urban areas when he is willing to minister to the needs of the white man, and should depart therefrom when he ceases so to minister.

The Nationalist government filled out this basic rationale by planning the creation of a series of black 'homelands' or Bantustans where, so the theory ran, blacks would enjoy separate citizenship rights so that no inequity stemmed from their dispossession of such rights in the 'white areas'. Taking as a basis the native reserve areas laid down in the 1936 Land Act, the government set about consolidating 12.9% of the country into black ethnic areas. No special areas were set aside for the Indians or Coloureds. To tidy up this picture the government carried through a drastic programme of population transfer, uprooting and resettling over 3 million non-whites between 1960 and 1970. In part the process resembled the American solution to the 'Indian problem' in the nineteenth century — the herding of an indigenous population into tiny pockets of rural obscurity in areas which had been systematically under-developed by the development of capitalist industry and agriculture elsewhere. But the British and Boer colonists were much less numerous and less thorough than their North American counterparts, and had had as a result neither the means nor the incentive to carry through such thorough-going programmes of extermination against the indigenous peoples they found in their way.[1] From the outset the white economy needed and used the blacks — by 1976 71% of South Africa's 9.7 million workers were black — and so a simple 'Indian reservation' solution was not appropriate. Thus a good deal of the resettlement simply involved the 'clearing-up' of haphazard patterns of shanty settlement in white areas and the creation of townships not too many miles further away from which non-whites would still be well-placed to 'minister to the needs of the white man'. As for the 'homelands', something of the same rationale applied to them — the KwaZulu Bantustan abutting on to the industrial complex centering on Durban, the Transkei feeding its labour to East London and Port Elizabeth, and so on. But, it was also presumed, blacks would be happy in their homelands in their 'traditional' roles as peasants and small farmers. Here the African could be his own separate self, enjoying his own national rights, identity, and the benefits of rule by 'his' traditional tribal chiefs. Here, indeed, he would repair when he decided to cease ministering to the needs of the white economy. Or when the white economy decided it could dispense with his services, for permission to reside even temporarily in the white areas would depend on his having employment there. His situation would thus be analogous to the migrant worker of Western Europe, enjoying the high wages of France, Germany or Switzerland until either he decided to return to his village in Portugal, Algeria or Italy, there to 'cash in' his earnings in a higher social and economic status, or until the host economies decided to shunt him back there whether he liked it or not.

There, however, was the rub. The European migrants quickly became essential to their host economies, had in any case been

---

[1] The Reservation policy was, of course, in part an extension of the extermination campaign. As J. Russell Harty put it: 'The White man banished the Indian to lands where no white man could possibly survive. The Indian fooled him. He survived.' In any case the US cavalry continued its random extermination campaign against reservation Indians — most notoriously, of course, in 1890 when it bombarded Pine Ridge reservation with cannon in the 'battle' of Wounded Knee. In southern Africa only the Germans, in South West Africa, showed quite such determination, reducing the Herero tribe in 1904 from 80,000 to 15,000. In 1970 there were still only 49,000 Hereros.

driven by economic necessity from their impoverished homes, and within a decade showed every sign of settling permanently where they worked. In South Africa the whole process had been going on for at least a century, not just a decade. By 1974, according to official estimates, about half of all blacks (8.5 million), as well as all the 700,000 Indians and 2.3 million Coloureds, lived and worked in the areas allotted to the 4.2 million whites, areas which included all the mines, cities, ports, industry and the best agricultural land. The heart of the matter lay in the great white cities, and most particularly in the single great urban sprawl of the Rand. In this conurbation,[1] almost four times the size of its nearest rival, Cape Town, whites, according to the 1970 census, accounted for 36% of the population, Coloureds and Asians 7%, and Africans 57%. And this was the main white area — a full one third of all whites lived there. It was, nonetheless, predominantly black. Unsurprisingly, the prolonged South African boom had given birth to a large, mature, black working class, permanently thronging the white cities where, in theory, they were but temporary and rightless sojourners. For this was the whole point of the apartheid system: to insist against the tide that this large black proletariat should still be called, be treated as, and indeed, actually *be* migrants. The mines, of course, endeavoured to go the whole hog and recruit from outside the country — in 1973, 'foreign' Africans reached a peak of 78% of the mining labour force. To its 'own' Africans the government applied a series of draconian laws to enforce their migrant status; no black could remain in a white urban area for more than 72 hours unless he could prove he had been born there, had no criminal record and has been continuously employed there for at least a decade. Only those Africans filling these strict, and strictly applied criteria, had the right to have their families living with them. For all others migrancy was enforced at every point — by rigid work permit and pass laws (on average there are 1,400 convictions a day for infringements of these regulations), by the enforced deprivation of family life in the urban area, and by the sheer physical and architectural facts of hostels and compounds built for single migrants only.

The Bantustans are a key part of the system not only in theory but also in fact. For the government's policy has been to keep the number of Africans in urban areas to the minimum required by actual economic needs. There is no black

[1] That is, Johannesburg, the east and west Rand, Pretoria, the Free State goldfields and the Vaal Triangle.

unemployment register and a 'migrant' black without a job belongs only in his 'homeland'. This system has the additional advantage of making black unemployment by definition non-existent: only blacks who work in the towns may reside in or near them; the rest are (by definition) in their homelands where, it is presumed, they will dig the earth rather than starve. Verwoerd was fascinated by the conceptual beauty of the system, and was wont to deliver long theological expositions of all the principles and ideals which it enshrined. Vorster was somewhat blunter: 'The fact of the matter is this: we need them (the blacks) because they work for us. . . but the fact that they work for us can never. . . entitle them to claim political rights.' Verwoerd's perorations saw the apex of apartheid in the picture of the African enjoying his separate identity in the happiness of his homeland, ruled by a traditional chief: apartheid was the distilled essence of the Reservation theory, consumed neat in large and heady draughts. In fact the system finds its real apex and purest form in the urban compounds,[1] the real home of thousands of black women and perhaps a million black men. The compounds range from the relatively small (30—50 men), run by schools, for example, to the great mine compounds, housing 10,000 men or more. It is to these latter that the migrant repairs from the bowels of the earth, to rooms usually unadorned by tables, chairs or electric light. They are the dormitories in which as many as 24 workers may sleep, in double-decker concrete bunks. Defecating is also normally a communal activity, with lavatories allowing place for as many as 20 men to sit side by side. Homosexuality is, perforce, the norm, though not a few of the migrants find solace with female prostitutes, and almost all find solace in drink. The system is richly productive of drunkenness, all forms of violence, venereal disease and, of course, the disintegration of the familial relationships the men have left behind. It is on men such as these that the South African economy ultimately rests; it is they who dig the diamonds, uranium, copper and platinum. The world gold market and thus, in part, the world's monetary system rests on them too, for it is they who dig the gold, as also the coal to provide electricity for the gold mines. They are the unsung (and poorly paid) heroes of every Anglo-American

---

[1] The compound, a peculiar form of 'total society' (in Goffman's terms), is a genus of social organisation which has only recently begun to receive proper sociological attention. See, above all, C. van Onselen, *Chibaro. African Mine Labour in Southern Rhodesia, 1900—1933* (London, 1976), a truly exceptional work.

report, every De Beers balance sheet; it is the fruits of their labours which have, over the years, filled the vaults of Fort Knox, bought racehorses for the Oppenheimer family, endowed Rhodes Scholarships, and provided Elizabeth Taylor with her jewellery.

Through Oppenheimer, moreover, their labours finance the Progressives — an act of some magnanimity since even the PRP's (liberal) policies would deny them the vote. In the end, of course, the list is almost too long to be counted, for the labours of these men pay for almost everything — for the police, for the Mirages, for apartheid itself. The affluence and strength of white South Africa is their monument. A monument is only too often what they need, for the mining industry has a staggering accident rate — in the low-production year of 1974, for example, mining accidents cost 529 dead and 23,155 injured. While they live, however, the miners are proof that apartheid is not entirely inconsistent with a thriving capitalism.

For all their prodigies of achievement the miners have normally been rural illiterates from Malawi, Lesotho or Mozambique; for mining employment has, when possible, been shunned by South African blacks, amongst whom it has a somewhat unattractive reputation. This has not meant, of course, that they have thereby escaped from migrant status. According to a 1976 estimate (by the Natal University economist, Mrs Jill Natrass) male migrants constitute no less than 60% of all economically active blacks in the white areas and roughly one black worker in three is a migrant. The government's policy has been successful inasmuch as the number of migrants has been increasing more rapidly than the number of economically active Africans. Of the perhaps 2 million migrant workers, some 400,000 come from outside South Africa and over a quarter of a million are women. Even for those workers who are not strictly migrants but who live in townships or homelands abutting on to white industrial areas, the necessity for arduous journeys to work means that they share many of the disadvantages of the migrant's condition in practice. It is not by any means uncommon for workers to rise at 4 a.m. and return home at midnight from long and dangerous work and journeys in rickety and overcrowded buses and trains: a timetable allowing little latitude for the pleasures of family life. The workers are sucked remorselessly in by the white economy, which extracts their labour power and then spits them out sufficiently far to ensure that the inhabitants of the white suburbs may sleep easy at night. The government's plan, of course, is to generalise the condition of migrancy to the

majority of black workers. In 1964 government labour offices
were established in each homeland at which all Africans seeking
work must register. They will not be allowed to leave the
homelands until the labour office has obtained labour contracts
for them, and even then cannot work in white areas for longer
than 12 months at a time. They will, while away there, live in
the great hostel complexes now being built (no more houses for
African families are to be built — only hostels). At the end of
12 months they will return to their homelands, visiting their
wives and children for a few months of enforced unemployment
while awaiting their next contract. For the homelands are only
in part reservations. They are also 'a chain of labour reservoirs
where people are held in a state of compulsory unemployment
until the white economy wants them'.[1] It is assumed that such
workers will fill only unskilled or at most semi-skilled jobs,
leaving the skilled jobs which Africans *are* allowed to perform
under the job reservation system to the blacks born in the urban
areas and living in the great townships on the edge of the white
areas.

   To the burden of migrancy is, of course, added the mundane
fact of inequality. In 1973 the 17% of the population who are
white took 68.2% of all wage and salary payments; the 9% of
Coloureds received 7.9%, the 3% Asians 2.8% and the 71% who
are black received 21.1%.[2] Simple deduction from these figures
suggests that the average overall white : black income differen-
tial is slightly over 13½ : 1, though of course the differentials
for the ownership of wealth, as opposed to income, would be
astronomically higher. Such global figures, of course, hide the
extremely unequal distributions of social and economic advantage *within* the various ethnic groups. The major political
divisions within the white group (NP, HNP *v.* UP, PRP) still
reflect the weight not only of the Boer War but of decades of
snobbery, mockery and social discrimination founded in the
privileged position of English-speakers vis-à-vis poor white
Afrikaners. Within the Asian community there is a small elite of
super-rich merchants and entrepreneurs. Most significantly there
is the great and growing divide between the nascent African
labour aristocracy and middle class, allowed to live permanently
in the urban townships, and the homeland or foreign migrants
allowed more sparing access to the white centres of power and
wealth, punctuated by long periods of unemployment and

---

[1] *Rand Daily Mail*, 18 Aug. 1973.
[2] The *Economist*, 1 Jan. 1977.

possible starvation when they are consigned forcibly back to the rural areas between jobs. While English—Afrikaans inequalities are slowly being erased by the brute use of state power on the Afrikaner's behalf, the whole force of government policy is to increase and sharpen the division between these two components of the African labour force. As the black population grows and the labour reservoirs of the homelands (occupying only 12.9% of the land, after all) fill to bursting with would-be migrants desperate for work, an already present but certainly growing threat is posed to the urban Africans in settled employment. The forces pushing migrants to the towns could easily become so great as to lead to a *de facto* swamping of the townships with starving migrants eager to undercut the relatively privileged position of the urban Africans at every point. This has in fact already happened to a significant extent. Urban Africans have, in this sense, a direct interest in the strict maintenance of influx control via the pass laws, and even in the construction of strong Bantustan authorities able to keep the would-be migrants under firm control — for, of course, the essential function of the Bantustans is to hand over the repression of blacks to blacks. It is, however, far from certain that any amount of pass laws, government labour offices or Bantustan chiefs, even though endowed with their own police force and petty armies, could long control the situation if this moment of truth were reached.

By the early 1970s Pretoria had recognised that this moment of truth might indeed come. As Vorster put it bluntly in 1971, 'unemployment is a greater danger to South African than terrorism'. In theory, of course, the answer was easy. As the Deputy Minister for Bantu Administration put it in the same year, 'the removal of superfluous Bantu from the white homelands is not dependent on the development of any Bantu homelands'. That is, the Bantustans would simply be used as dumping grounds for the unemployed, irrespective of whether this meant mass starvation or not. But a mass shovelling out of paupers would be extremely dangerous too. The unemployed might become guerrillas (as in the Pondo revolt of the 1960s). They would swamp the fragile economies of the Bantustans and there would be strong resistance to such dumping, not only by the peasantry settled there, but by the Bantustan chiefs. For dumping on a large scale would be bound to endanger the political stability of the Bantustans, and if the government persisted at all long in such a course it would destroy whatever political viability these painfully constructed artefacts had achieved. On the other hand, if the unemployed were simply

allowed to stay in the townships in mounting numbers a violent
and threatening shambles would soon result.

Although black unemployment did not exist in the statistics,
it was a real enough fact. The 1970 census recorded 283,000
Africans as unemployed, but it also showed there to be a
further 253,000 men and 2.22 million women adults who were
'not economically active'.[1] Given the low level of African
incomes it was hardly realistic to imagine that this inactivity
was voluntary. In addition there were further unknown
numbers in semi- or under-employment in the homelands.
Despite much talk of 'developing the homelands', it was quite
inconceivable that sufficient job opportunities could be created
there. In the most advanced homeland, the Transkei, it was
calculated that by the mid-1970s something like 15,000 young
black men entered the labour market every year, while only
about 4,500 jobs a year were being created there. Thus the
number of Transkeians working as migrants outside their
homeland rose from 174,000 in 1969 to 303,000 in 1975. By
1971, indeed, there were six times as many Transkeians working
as migrants outside the Transkei as there were in the 'homeland'
itself. And the pressure towards migrancy was increasing all the
time.

It was, of course, distinctly useful to the system that a
reserve army of African labour of some size should be
maintained in order to prevent African workers from exploiting
their implicit labour power. But with the African population
growing fast the much greater danger was that black unemployment would escalate out of all political control. Foreseeing this
dread possibility, the government bequeathed to the first
independent Bantustan, the Transkei, a considerable repressive
apparatus — the new state inherited a 13-year-old state of
emergency, all the draconian South African security laws, a
white-officered army, laws against trade unions and so on. At
the same time the Minister of Bantu Administration warned of
fearsome discrimination against those Africans who did not play
the homeland-migrant labour-reservoir game according to the
desired rules:

Preferential treatment will be given in employment contracts,
housing, hospitalisation and in general terms to Africans who
live in white areas but who seek a healthy relationship with

---

[1] Calculations made by Prof. J. L. Sadie of Stellenbosch University, cited
in 'South Africa', *ACR 1974—75*, p. B455.

their Homelands. They will get preferential treatment over persons who seek to hide their Homeland relationship.[1]

The terrible dilemmas posed by the possibility of African unemployment getting out of control could be held at bay provided — and only provided — the South African economy grew fast enough. With the potential black labour force increasing by rather over 200,000 a year by the early 1970s, that is an annual growth rate of 2.8—3.0%, it was generally reckoned that an overall economic growth rate of about 3.3% would at least keep the number of black unemployed steady. But growth was not a luxury; it was an absolute imperative.

The South African economy more than satisfied this imperative in the 1960s — indeed, economic growth was such that African non-farm employment grew at an annual average rate of 3.8% through the decade. Even though African farm employment shrank, this meant that every year the pool of African unemployed, far from growing, actually shrank too. Africans were, of course, poorly paid and they hated their migrant status. They had rioted against the pass laws at Sharpeville, they broke the laws all the time, and they staged riots when bus or railway crashes brought home again the full potential costs of their migrant condition of life. But the jobs were there and this fact, combined with the known costs of political or social protest, was enough to ensure their quiescence. By the early 1970s the African job market may actually have become relatively tight. As we have discussed,[2] this situation, combined with high inflation and a growing black consciousness both of their labour power and of the sheer economic inequalities under which they laboured in a land of plenty, triggered major African industrial unrest from 1972 on. The strikes led to quite large increases, temporarily at least, in African real wages. The spiral of inflation ensured a continuing incidence of strikes — by the end of 1974 there had been over 300 illegal strikes since the start of the wave in 1972. But as unemployment mounted the scale of industrial action fell sharply; in 1974 only half as many man-hours were lost due to strikes as in 1973 and in 1975 the number fell to under a tenth of the 1973 total.

The strike wave, however, had had more than just economic effects. If anything, indeed, the short-term and partial satisfaction of economic demands merely lifted the threshold of workers' resentment to focus on their wider condition of life.

[1] Speech by M. C. Botha, House of Assembly, 28 April 1976.
[2] See above, pp. 85—7.

This was perhaps particularly the case in the mines where the whole battery-hen migrant system began to break down. Despite the concession of large wage increases and strongly repressive measures against 'malcontents', the 12 deaths in the Carletonville 'massacre' of September 1973 were only the first of around 200 in the next three years. The mining compounds were increasingly engulfed in a wave of diffuse violence and unrest, wildcat strikes and 'tribal fighting'. Already by the end of 1974 80 miners had died and many more had been injured in such incidents. On January 1975 a major series of mining strikes broke out in a number of Transvaal and OFS mines. Nine died this time, with 37 injured. In March 1975 'tribal' violence broke out at the Glencoe and Holbane collieries in Natal, resulting in 32 deaths. Further violence also erupted at Carletonville, leading to the death of two more black miners. The same pattern of sporadic, 'small-scale', but pervasive unrest continued through into 1976.

By 1975 the mining sector was, indeed, in a critical state. Profit margins were coming under increasing pressure due to the falling gold price. Wage costs had soared. Since 1973 the numbers of foreign workers — on whom the industry depended for three-quarters of its labour — had been drying up rapidly. The continuing exodus of Malawian workers was parallelled in 1975 by the loss of some 15,000 workers from Lesotho; the numbers from Mozambique and Botswana were also in decline. The industry seemed virtually incapable of replacing these workers with South African blacks (whose numbers also fell in 1973—4) with their deep-seated and increasing resistance to participation in the industry at all. In 1975 the Chamber of Mines began to recruit Rhodesian blacks, but it was not expected that more than 10,000 workers could be found from this source. The industry — and particularly Anglo-American — had to face up to the necessity of recruiting several hundred thousand South African blacks in the year to come. Even given black unemployment levels, this would be difficult. All else apart, wages were still lower than in most secondary industry, despite the recent increases. Anglos, at least, recognised that the only way out lay in quite dramatic changes which would produce a permanent, familially settled, home-grown labour aristocracy. There was nothing intrinsically impossible about such schemes, but they would mean driving a coach and horses through a variety of apartheid doctrines; they would still need to overcome layers of African mistrust which has mounted and accumulated over generations; higher wages and improved safety would considerably raise operating costs already under pressure; these latter changes would probably have to be accompanied by a long-term programme of heavy capital investment at a point when the whole future of the gold market lay in doubt; and, of course, the creation of a black mine-labour aristocracy would be deeply unpopular with the other white employers of labour upon whom the government depends for its political support. The mining industry was, in a word, the point at which all the major contradictions affecting South Africa most densely intersected and interacted.

The malaise went far wider than just the mining industry, however. African spokesmen of even the most establishment hue stressed over and over again that Africans were at, or beyond, the end of their last point of endurance. This was, they emphasised, particularly true of a rising younger generation of Africans, among whom the impression made by the white collapse in Mozambique and Angola had made its deepest mark. All but two of the Bantustan leaders, conservatives though they were, made it clear that they would simply refuse to accept the independence they were offered, aghast at the prospect of operating from the start a massive and unstable system of repression against their own people. A white social worker, Melville Edelstein, carried out a survey of black high school children in the vast Soweto township,[1] and in his book *What do Young Africans Think?* confirmed much of what their elders were saying of them. Edelstein found that 55% of the children regarded Afrikaners as 'the most cruel, least sympathetic people in South Africa'. He also found that 98% of the children did not wish to be taught in Afrikaans.

Soweto was, indeed, the greatest cockpit of this mounting malaise. Theoretically this vast dormitory for Johannesburg's black workers housed 600,000 people in its 100,000 'housing units'. In fact, influx control had so broken down that the real number of inhabitants was probably around 1.5 million, with hundreds of thousands of desperate job-seekers crowding anything from 6 to 25 into its little three and four-bedroom boxes of houses. Some 86% of the houses have no electricity, 97% no running hot water. There is one hospital for what is in effect one of the largest cities in Africa. The average income (of those in work) was below the poverty datum line in mid-1976. In fact

[1] An abbreviation from 'South Western Townships', Soweto groups together 26 former townships into a single sprawl of 16,000 acres.

the lumpen and unemployed proletariat and its children
forcibly redistribute much of this income by hooliganism,
protection rackets, robbery and murder. Over half the population is under 20 and a majority of all the children suffer from
malnutrition.

The township was continuously racked by a hideous crime
rate (murders passed the 1,000 mark in 1974). In early 1974 a
survey[1] revealed that many Africans living there referred to
their home town as a 'ghetto' or 'concentration camp'.
Nonetheless, the survey found, there was huge resentment that
none of the houses there could be bought or owned and that
when the male breadwinner of a family died his widow and
children were simply evicted from the house. Of those interviewed, 75% regarded Soweto as their home and two-thirds
refused altogether to regard their 'homeland' as home. 'Homelands', one respondent declared, 'are a deathbed of Africans
created by whites. They are barren. If they were fertile they
would not be allotted to the Africans.' Another declared that
'in the Homelands I visualise starvation, disease, unemployment,
drought and all that'. The mayor of Soweto, when interviewed,
warned that urban black resentment 'can no longer be
controlled'; it was difficult, he said, to find 'a so-called
moderate black man'.

This was the situation in 1974. In the same year the
Economics departments of three Afrikaans universities issued
warnings that black unemployment was rising at around
100,000 a year. Black employment opportunities were increasing at about 100,000 a year but twice this number were
annually entering the labour market (divided roughly half and
half between urban and homeland blacks).[2] Here, indeed, was
the crux. White employers and the government had conceded
real wage increases to the striking urban blacks and hoped that
this might eventually consolidate their position as an intermediate black 'privileged' class. But the cost of such rises could
only be met at the cost of profits, white jobs — or by increasing
the amount of African unemployment. Inevitably, the last
alternative was chosen. In return for the wage increases
conceded, white employers demanded higher productivity from
their black workers, thus enabling them to economise on black
labour overall. The result was increasing black unemployment.
Meanwhile, mounting inflation wiped out the wage increases
anyway.

[1] Cited in 'South Africa', op. cit., p. B457.
[2] Ibid., p. B455.

In 1975, as we have seen, the world depression began to hit South Africa and, as the gold price plummetted, the economy's growth fell. Angola worsened the situation and by 1976 the economy had gone into reverse. The Standard Bank of South Africa Review for the first half-year of 1976 commented that 'it is now evident that the downward movement of most sectors of the economy is gathering momentum'. Inflation was still running at over 11%, but wage increases for white and black alike were pegged well below such a figure. Black South Africans found themselves squeezed on all sides at once, with mounting unemployment, soaring food and transport costs, and a white working class digging in bitterly to defend job reservation to the last ditch, if necessary. Whatever slim hopes blacks may have had that economic growth would at least lead to a slow material amelioration of their position evaporated. As black unemployment increased the shock waves spread downwards, reaching black school-leavers, the group on the brink of the labour market. Young blacks still at school saw whatever expectations they might have had coming under increasing threat. This was, we have seen, in any case the group least disposed to acquiescence. The final straw came with Treurnicht's insistence that they should receive lessons in Afrikaans. It was simply too bitter. Afrikaans, as their placards of protest were to announce, was the 'oppressor's language'. But it was worse than that. English was still overwhelmingly the language of commerce and business, certainly in Johannesburg. Having to struggle with subjects in Afrikaans would add an extra handicap to such children in the bitter competition ahead in a deteriorating labour market, the more so given that their teachers in maths (a key subject specified for Afrikaans medium instruction) could seldom speak the language anyway. It was overwhelmingly clear that there was no real or educational point to the ukase being enforced by Treurnicht. It was simply a doctrinaire assertion of Afrikaans linguistic nationalism by an unbending Calvinist preacher-turned-politician. The words of Treurnicht's mentor, Verwoerd, were remembered: 'There is no place for him (the black) in the European community above the level of certain forms of labour. What is the use of teaching a Bantu child mathematics when it cannot use it in practice?'

It was simply far too much.

(iii) Soweto

On 17 May the pupils of Orlando West Junior Secondary School in Soweto walked out, saying they would not return until the Afrikaans medium rule was withdrawn. On 21 May the South

African Institute of Race Relations cabled Treurnicht express-
ing concern. Treurnicht accused the Institute of 'over-reacting'.
This was neither the first nor the last warning to be made and
dismissed. On 16 June a demonstration of some 15,000 Soweto
schoolchildren marched towards the school where the strike had
begun, there to be confronted by a line of police armed with
tear gas, batons, rifles and sub-machine guns. Firing soon started
and an unknown number of children were killed and injured
(later the police estimated the day's toll at 25 dead and 200
injured). The children fled, rioted, smashed Bantu administration offices, liquor shops and all property associated with white
authority they could lay their hands on. Melville Edelstein, who
had reported their resentments to the world (see above), was
present. He was, though, only another white man, and was
battered to death. Police reinforcements poured in, led by Col.
Theunis Swanepoel, South Africa's second most famous police-
man (after Van den Bergh), and an almost mythical figure.[1] A
considerable number of children were caught, interrogated and,
according to several reports, beaten up and tortured.
Swanepoel, however, was not the name ultimately stamped on
the Soweto events. Inasmuch as there was a personal responsibility for police tactics and actions in Soweto, it undoubtedly
belonged to Major-General David Kriel, to whom overall riot
control responsibilities were confided.

The riots spread quickly to all the other Johannesburg area
townships. The police, recoiling, attempted to cut the township
off. Alouette and Super-Frelon helicopters worked in ceaseless
shifts, dropping tear-gas and attempting to co-ordinate police
operations, but they were frequently defeated by the great pall
of smoke from burning buildings hanging over the townships.

Treurnicht, on the day after the rioting had begun, asserted
that 'it was in the Bantu's own good that he learned in
Afrikaans', but his superior, M. C. Botha, undercut him a few
days later, announcing that Afrikaans had never been compulsory anyway and that the ruling would be relaxed. The 'tragic
circumstances in Soweto were caused by misunderstanding and
confusion', he said, somewhat mysteriously. By now, however,

---

[1] Swanepoel had once headed the Special Branch interrogation teams in
the 1960s. He had developed a fearsome reputation from this role. Over
and over again tortured detainees had pointed to Swanepoel as the chief of
all their tormentors, alleging that he seemed to take a pleasure in
intervening directly to inflict punishments he could have left to his
subordinates. His fame, indeed, had spread as far as New York where he
had been denounced by name in the UN itself.

even this concession could not halt the disturbances. Rioting continued to spread throughout the townships of the Transvaal, and some of the rioters even began to appear on the edge of white suburbs or in the centre of Johannesburg itself.[1] After eight days the rioting subsided with, according to police estimates, 176 dead and several thousands injured. The police released many of those hitherto charged with rioting (though they continued to arrest leaders of black organisations).

The lull lasted almost a month. But on 27 July a wave of arson against African schools themselves began, this time not only in the Transvaal but in the Orange Free State and Natal as well. The Soweto Students' Representative Council condemned the arson and called for a return to school. Even the SRC, hitherto the leading organisation of the protest, had now lost all control, however. The police maintained heavy armoured car patrols in the townships and continued to search out and arrest suspected agitators, sometimes entering the schools to pull out suspects. On 4 August a huge and apparently spontaneous wave of violence enveloped the townships right across the Rand. At the same time the Soweto students attempted – with limited success – to discourage workers from going to Johannesburg. The now familiar pattern of stonings, burnings and police repression followed. On 11 August the rioting spread to the townships around Cape Town, and on 17 August to Port Elizabeth, with similar results. Jimmy Kruger, the Minister of Police, made the government's position crystal clear in a speech to a cheering Nationalist Party audience on 20 August: 'He (the black) knows his place, and if not I'll tell him his place. The Blacks always say "We shall overcome", but I say we shall overcome.'

On 23 August a three-day general strike was called in Soweto. On the first day the strike was almost wholly successful – though not a few workers slept overnight in their Johannesburg offices or factories, fearing above all to lose their jobs. On 24 August, after a considerable amount of advance talk about a black workers' backlash against the rioters and pickets, one actually occurred when hundreds of Zulu hostel-dwellers rampaged through Soweto. There were widespread accusations that the Zulus had been organised by the police, and one *Rand Daily Mail* reporter, hiding in Soweto during the night, claimed

---

[1] On 21 June a black appeared in John Vorster Square (central Johannesburg), shouting 'Take revenge for the children of Soweto'. A chase ensued; a wounded black was taken to central police headquarters, plunging to his death from the fourth floor minutes later.

that he had heard police units loud-hailing Zulus attacking houses 'We didn't order you to destroy West Rand (Administration Board) property. You were asked to fight people only, so you are asked to withdraw immediately.'[1] A considerable amount of circumstantial evidence pointing in the same direction accumulated, and when Chief Buthelezi visited Soweto on 27 August he emerged convinced that the police had indeed organised the backlash, providing the Zulus with transport and distributing marijuana to them.

Meanwhile in Cape Town similar unrest had begun to surface among the Coloured population. This was a startling development indeed, for the Coloureds have always occupied a social and economic position clearly superior to that of the Africans. On 23 August Coloured students held solidarity demonstrations with the Soweto strikers. Within 36 hours the police had escalated their response from tear-gas to bullets, and a new wave of agitation and repression was launched. This new development saw Vorster, largely silent till now, enter the fray:

> The enemy want to find us in a crisis and they want us to admit that we have a guilty conscience. But looking over the history of South Africa's achievements, I say we have no reason to feel guilty about anything. I want to make it clear that nowhere in the world have 4 million done so much for 18 million as in this despised South Africa.

On 30 August a small African children's demonstration took place through the centre of Cape Town. The police had clearly been taken by surprise and the demonstration ended peacefully before they arrived. Africans form only 10% of the Cape Town conurbation's population (the Coloureds form 56% and thus the bulk of the non-white working class there) and the police may not have anticipated action from that quarter. On 2 September, after an 11-year-old Coloured girl had been killed by the police, the Coloureds decided to stage their own city centre march. This was broken up by the massed assault of police riot squads, displaying a tear-gas and baton brutality which shocked white onlookers. Such tactics hardly bore much comparison with those used for three months past against Soweto blacks. The Soweto clashes had, however, been witnessed by few whites and had anyway seen the police ranged against blacks, not Coloureds, the sister-race to the whites. The next day a further

---

[1] *Rand Daily Mail*, 26 Aug. 1976. This reporter was later detained by the police.

and much more violent battle was fought in the city centre. In the afternoon police riot squads staged attacks on a series of schools, bursting gasmasked into classrooms and hurling tear-gas inside before beating up whatever children and teachers they could lay their hands on. The police action seems to have been entirely indiscriminate — not even sparing a schoolchild who was a polio victim.

After a weekend lull a similar pattern of violent confrontation continued throughout the Cape Peninsula on 6–8 September, the Coloured militants now beginning to throw petrol bombs and actually taking the initiative to attack white shops and houses. Vorster, back from his talks with Kissinger in Zurich, warned sharply that:

> There is no way of governing South Africa other than by the policy and principles of the National Party. . . . The police have contained the disorder under difficult circumstances and with a minimum of violence. . . . If it does not stop, and stop immediately, other steps will have to be taken.

Kruger, the Police Minister, spelt out the situation even more plainly: 'The day is past when people can sit at home thinking the police will protect their property. There are not enough police. . . . The task of protecting business premises is primarily that of the owners.'

The Minister advised whites that they were fully entitled to use violence to protect themselves and their property — a quite open appeal for white vigilante backing for the now over-stretched and frequently exhausted police.[1] Within days large numbers of well-armed[2] and often trigger-happy white vigilante patrols were on the streets; Afrikaans students from Stellenbosch University were reported to be going into action with FN rifles alongside the police. In fact the wave of violence in the Cape had already begun to ebb, after a particularly bloody

---

[1] The police number 35,000, with a reserve of 17,500. There is also a home guard of 75,000 'Commandos'. Riot control is, of course, a highly specialised police skill and by no means all the police force available in Johannesburg and the Cape could be used. The relative scarcity of requisite manpower was shown not merely in the widespread use of black police but also in the flying of emergency reinforcements to trouble spots.
[2] Even before the disturbances South African civilians were very heavily armed, with almost half of all adults owning a gun. The riots produced a tremendous rush for firearms, with shops frequently sold out the same day that a consignment arrived. Of the personal firearms imported about half were Russian or Czech, shipped from West Germany.

series of battles on 8 September. On 9 September Vorster announced a series of minor concessions to Coloured traders, and improved public facilities. The Cape fell back into a battered calm, punctuated only by police raids.

Meanwhile in Soweto the students sought to make further use of the strike weapon. They had learnt their lesson from the 23—25 August strike and this time were better organised, meeting with the hostel residents first to ensure that there would be support or at least neutrality from that quarter. Leaflets were run off by the tens of thousand, calling for blacks to stay off the streets and avoid confrontations. On 13 September the strike began, achieving a crippling effectiveness — something like half a million workers across the Rand supported it. The police resorted to somewhat desperate tactics in an attempt to break the strike, including house-to-house armed raids to force blacks to work or school, as well as the more routine shooting down of pickets at bus and railway stations. The strike continued on 14 September with somewhat diminished effectiveness and a rising incidence of street violence. Nonetheless, the strike still had well over 50% support by 15 September, when the strike was joined by some 200,000 Coloured workers in the Cape. Here too the police response was violent confrontation, but the strike finished with well over 50% support, despite a heavy toll of dead and injured. On 17 September Kissinger arrived in South Africa. The police reacted furiously against Soweto schoolchildren protesting against the visit (six children were shot dead, 35 seriously injured) but otherwise there was a lull, presumably so that the American Secretary of State should not be embarrassed.

On 23 September the Soweto children decided to emulate the Cape Coloureds and make their protest in the white city centre. The police were ready for them, combing the buses and trains from Soweto into Johannesburg, and breaking up the demonstration (using batons only: the lesson of Cape Town had been learnt — whites would be watching in the city centre). The city was then ruthlessly swept clean of young blacks. This last suicidal initiative towards the city centre saw the movement fall back.

What was left of the youth movement in Soweto now turned its attention to a campaign against the shebeens (illegal drinking houses) and beer halls. A number of liquor stores in Soweto and also in the Cape were burned down. The anti-liquor motif had been present throughout the movement, but only in September and October was a concerted anti-liquor campaign launched, the children asserting that their parents' generation had compromised critically with the white man's system by seeking personal release through drink, thus averting a collective confrontation with white power. On 1 November the Soweto SRC called a further five-day strike, but this failed utterly.

The police now began to attack black schools as they had in the Cape, and to launch attacks with sub-machine guns on funeral processions of their earlier victims. Further, though only partially successful, attempts were made to organise a hostel-dwellers' backlash against the children. Meanwhile the police launched a spreading wave of arrests and detentions: hundreds of leaders and suspects were rounded up, including large numbers of children. Almost every significant black organisation found its leadership behind bars — the Black Peoples' Convention, the South African Students' Organisation, the South African Students' Movement, the Black Community Programme, the Black Women's Federation, the Black Parents' Association and other individuals and bodies ranging from the Soweto SRC to journalists, church and trade union organisations were all swept into the net. Estimates of the total arrests ranged up to and above 6,000.

Sporadic violence and shooting continued through into December, but the movement had by then largely petered out. Hundreds — perhaps thousands — of students had fled to the rural areas, to Botswana, to Swaziland or had simply gone underground. The police refused to give any figures for the number of deaths resulting from the disturbances, but the *Rand Daily Mail* was able to identify 499 individuals who had died. Unofficial estimates ranged well over the 1,000 mark, with perhaps ten or twenty times as many again injured.

Soweto — the single word came to represent the whole of the disturbances, though they had swept the Cape, Port Elizabeth and beyond — was not a repetition of Sharpeville, and not merely because the casualty figures were much higher. At the time of Sharpeville national African organisations had existed but failed signally to direct or control the local explosions of riot and demonstration. The mass action of the period had been fairly primitive in form, with much local excitement and confusion engendered by a wave of (purely) African protest which was both nation-wide and socially undifferentiated. Still, there were leaders of a sort outside jail and, as we have seen,[1]

---

[1] See above, p. 19.

the largest African demonstration was willing to listen to
them — even though one was a white — and return home. The
Soweto events had no such national leadership; they were
rooted far more deeply in local communities; no leadership
which attempted to dam the flood, early on at least, would have
had much hope of being listened to; the most obviously
sympathetic white (Edelstein) was butchered on the first day;
the mass action they produced was far more sustained, despite
the ferocity of police reaction; the Coloureds participated; and
there was a clear pattern of socially differentiated response
visible within the disturbances.

On 16 June the events *did* have a resemblance to Sharpeville.
Despite well-advertised and bitterly felt black resentment
against a major grievance, the police were taken by surprise and
over-reacted, killing 25 immediately and sending in the dreaded
Swanepoel. They then drew back (relatively speaking), the
authorities quickly gave way on the immediate grievance
(Afrikaans-medium instruction) and after eight days, although
there were now 176 dead, peace returned. At this stage
attitudes were still fairly inchoate; Buthelezi had publicly
criticised the Soweto students and Botha, the Minister, was
referring to the events as 'tragic'.

The wave of arson against schools which began on 27 July
marked a new phase. It is possible that 176 dead was simply too
many to forget easily, to leave unavenged. It is possible, too,
that the very victory on the Afrikaans medium issue merely
served to concentrate black minds on the greater grievances
their conditions afforded them a-plenty. Aggressive police
tactics certainly also played some part in triggering the
explosion of 4 August. In the most general sense, however, it
was clear that the events of June had been a spark into a
powder-keg; there was simply far too much highly combustible
material still lying around. It smouldered through July, and in
August it blew up. Certainly, the Soweto SRC was not in
control. They condemned the arson and the students were
ill-prepared with their strike call for 4 August — there was no
organisation or leafletting, simply individual students standing
at bus-stops and railway stations pleading (ineffectually) with
workers not to go in. The police, too, may have been nursing
their resentments through July, but the violence of their
reaction in August doubtless also derived from government
instructions. The *verkramptes* had been humiliated by the
back-down to black schoolchildren, and in any case once the
issue of language instruction had been dealt with the rioters

were (correctly) perceived as attempting nothing less than an assault on the whole apartheid system and even white rule itself.

Until August the riots appear to have involved primarily schoolchildren and the unemployed left behind in the townships when the workers had departed for the white areas during the day. The failure of the attempted strike of 4 August, and the Zulu backlash (however far it was stage-managed by the police), demonstrated a dual social division. First, and most simply, the relatively fortunate who had employment were a class with privileges to lose, while the young unemployed had nothing to lose. The single male migrant workers of the hostels were a rather different case. They too had their jobs to lose, but they were also less rooted in Soweto — they had no families there, it was not their children being killed by the police. In many ways the most wretched category of all, such hostel-dwellers (who were also often ethnically distinct groups), occupied an extremely ambivalent social position, belonging neither to the settled labour aristocracy of the employed nor to the local unemployed lumpen-proletariat. They were, apparently, available for mobilisation by either side. After the horrors of rapine and murder committed in the Zulu backlash they became somewhat more amenable to appeals to a more general black solidarity, but this always remained tenuous.

The students, we have seen, learnt this lesson quickly, and by mid-September actually helped launch the greatest strike in South African history. The relatively more privileged sections of the non-white population — the workers and, dramatically, the Coloureds — were now, three months after it had started, drawn into the protest. Events in the Cape followed their own remorseless logic of demonstration, police over-reaction, and massive confrontation. By this stage the white authorities felt their backs against the wall. The emergence of non-white protest in the heart of the white city centre (in Cape Town) was a new and wholly alarming nightmare. The police could spend all day shooting at children inside Soweto and it might not matter very much. Few whites or journalists would know, and nothing very important to the White Establishment was threatened. But large-scale strikes and incursions into the white areas were both quite different and elicited a maximum repressive response. The appeal to white vigilantes clearly threatened nothing less than straightforward racial war between whole population groups. It was a desperate throw indeed, apparently influenced by the beginnings of urban guerrilla tactics by the rioters (the petrol bomb attacks on white houses and business premises). At the same time concessions were made to the established leaders of the Coloured community. This was possible both because there was a leadership of at least some influence which was not in jail, and also because the Coloureds still enjoyed the benefits of being a guiltily acknowledged offspring of the whites. Neither consideration applied to the young blacks of Soweto, against whom a simple policy of all-out repression was followed. At the same time the government announced that it would allow urban blacks to buy 30-year leases on their township dwellings and that their urban councils would be elective — both clearly bids for the support of the most privileged sections of the townships' black population. A concession of outright ownership rights would have meant accepting that blacks belonged permanently in white areas; it was therefore impossible. But not a few *verkramptes* must have reflected somewhat uneasily that Vorster would be 91 in 2006 when the leases came up for renewal, and therefore he would (presumably) not have to negotiate the awkward next step after that.

Meanwhile the Soweto schoolchildren mounted their own suicidal incursion towards the city centre. The fact that the police were more than ready for them was a tell-tale sign that the police had by now established a reliable intelligence service inside Soweto itself. The students, too, were learning their political tactics at precocious speed, but still far too slowly. Their movement now turned inwards and occupied itself with the shebeen and liquor question inside Soweto. This might properly have been the radicals' first move, not their last.[1] Their final (and most ambitious) appeal for a strike on 1 November simply publicised their failure, for the strike was universally ignored — by their parents as well as by the hostel dwellers. The police set about the final phase of repression as if determined to show their opponents that they had reason to be grateful merely to be left alive and left alone: that they too had that much to lose, if nothing else.

Probably the most significant of the detentions and arrests made by the police in the wake of the disturbances were those of trade unionists. The authorities were well enough aware that the critical failure of the movement had lain in the only tenuous and temporary support it had gained from black workers. (That it had received any support at all in a period of high and rapidly

---

[1] Before launching its urban guerrilla campaign against the French the Algerian FLN had concentrated its energies on cleaning up the *casbah* (the native area) of prostitutes, drug addicts and all those who had 'compromised with colonialism' or seemed likely police informers.

mounting unemployment was remarkable enough.) Quite apart
from the limitations on workers' support in Soweto and the
Cape, there had been a complete lack of response in the mining
compounds (although bloody 'faction fighting' continued to
erupt there) and in the whole of Natal, where the great
strike-wave of 1972—3 had centred. Had these workers been
galvanised as well, it might not have been very important that
the rural areas and homelands were also untouched by the
protest. The trade union arrests probably reflected police and
governmental determination to keep the workers isolated from
such troubling outside influences.

The final spasm of violence of 1976 came at Christmas, and
merely emphasised these divisions. In Natal there was a fierce
outbreak of 'faction fighting' which left at least 46 dead.
Violence also flared in the Cape African townships of Nyanga
and Guguleta, again described by the police as 'faction fighting'.
In fact black students in the townships had demanded a day of
mourning for those killed in the townships earlier in the year.
This request was resisted by the migrant hostel dwellers (single
men from the Transkei), who received police support. Fierce
fighting broke out between the township militants and the
hostel dwellers, leaving 26 dead and 106 injured. In a third
township, Langa, a crowd stoned police, who fired on them,
killing two blacks. As for Soweto, Col. J. P. Visser, the local
police chief, commented that the township had had its 'most
peaceful Christmas in years'. It was only a relative judgement,
of course — over the holiday weekend Soweto had had 18
murders.

(iv) Shooting people is bad for business

If the Soweto events had as their cause the worsening plight of
the South African economy, the events themselves were a major
influence on its downward drift. Just as at Sharpeville, the
African demonstrators showed that they wielded power in the
world money markets, even if there was not much they could
do against the brute force of the police in their 'Hippo'
armoured cars. Within 48 hours of the first Soweto shootings
South African share prices fell even more sharply than in the
comparable two days after Sharpeville. Foreign investors, still
extremely wary after Angola, drew back further still. By 1977 it
was to become clear that the township riots had done particular
damage to a number of large property companies and thus to
the banks which had financed them, creating a wave of
bankruptcies and desperate bank rescues. But the crisis in
investor confidence caused by Soweto was far more general and

affected all sectors. Thus the FT Gold Index in London registered an 11% drop in two days (as against 4.5% in the two days after Sharpeville), despite the fact that the mines were untouched by the disturbances. As in 1960, however, South African financial institutions stepped in to buy the stocks being sold by foreigners, thus holding up share prices 'artificially'. By August these institutions had begun to draw in their horns too, and a further share price collapse developed. An almost perfect indicator of overseas investor confidence was provided by the Securities Rand Discount, however.[1] In the past this had not infrequently stood at 15%, but levels higher than that were unusual. In October 1975 (before Angola) it had stood at 2%; in January 1976 at 13%. As the implications of Angola (and of the falling gold price) sank in, it widened to well over 20% by April. Soweto saw it plunge immediately to 35% and by mid-August it stood at a phenomenal 42% — at which level, roughly speaking, it stuck. (In March 1977 it stood at 41%.) Moreover, it was not just a matter of foreigners shying away from South African shares — there was a clearly discernible pattern of disinvestment.[2] To be sure, there were still major net inflows of long-term foreign capital — in August 1976, for example, British Petroleum announced that it was planning to spend R375 million in South Africa in the next five years, not the ten originally scheduled. But overall such inflows were matched by short-term outflows with the result that over the year (1976) as a whole there was no net inflow of private foreign capital at all.

Taken together with the effects of the falling gold price this situation provoked a major economic crisis. As we have seen, the government had believed its own predictions that gold would stay at $200 an ounce (and had assumed continuing foreign capital inflows of at least an average R1 billion a year)

---

[1] The Securities (formerly blocked) Rand is external currency held by foreigners and used by them to invest in South African shares. The SR is a floating currency, while the Rand itself is fixed, so that the former rises or falls in terms of the latter according to demand. The discount thus reflects foreign eagerness to invest — or the reverse. Put another way, the discount represents the premium at which stocks in Johannesburg sell over the prices asked for them in London or New York. A high discount rate strongly implies the need for a devaluation of the Rand to bring the levels back into line.

[2] Thus, for example, Marks and Spencer (UK) sold off its long-standing stake in Woolworths South Africa; London shareholdings in such major concerns as South African Breweries and Barlows fell sharply; several Swiss firms (e.g. Robeco) disinvested completely; and German and US bankers disinvested from their share in Highveld, Anglo-American's steel and vanadium subsidiary.

when it announced its massive spending programme for the
para-statals and defence. On average, foreign capital inflows had
amounted to about 3% of GDP — and now this crutch was
removed at the same time that gold fell towards $100. The
result was a rocketing deficit in public expenditure (up in two
years from R400 million to R1,400 million) and a rapidly
widening trade deficit. Since the spending programmes had
anyway had strongly inflationary effects, the government
hesitated to raise money by extra taxation or by high interest
rates which could only lead to reductions in industrial investment. This situation was already badly out of hand in June — in
the year June 1975—June 1976 there had been a soaring
current account deficit of almost R2 billion. The result of this
in turn was a prodigious run on the country's gold and foreign
currency reserves. These fell by over 37% in the four months
from March 1976, and by August there was only R754 million
left. Since South Africa owed R1,352 million in short-term
liabilities she was, in a technical sense, bankrupt; the
(mortgaged) reserves were now down to only about one
month's import cover and the situation was still deteriorating.

The government desperately wished to avoid the higher
interest rates or taxation which could only serve to extinguish
any hope of industrial recovery (capital investment was already
down on 1975).[1] But this hands-off strategy could only work if
either the gold price rose sharply again or if foreign funds began
to pour back in (and preferably both). Gold went on falling;
and then Soweto removed all possibility of foreign investment.
The government was badly panicked and immediately (in July)
slapped on stiff import controls, at the same time stepping up
further its desperate attempts to borrow abroad as much as it
possibly could. Whereas in 1975 the government had accounted
for only 6% of total foreign capital imports, in the first quarter
of 1976 the proportion soared to 65% — before increasing to
effectively 100% thereafter. The situation was alarming indeed,
for the government needed $900 million in loans simply to
avoid defaulting on the interest payments on earlier foreign
loans.

Soweto, in effect, forced the government to abandon its
Micawberish attitude to recovery and simultaneously retrench
as hard as it could in every direction. Pretoria was only too conscious of the economic (unemployment) and thus political consequences of such retrenchment — as we have seen, growth was

[1] The rate of gross domestic fixed capital formation fell from 5% to 2.5%
in 1975—6.

simply an imperative for South Africa. But now there was no
alternative to sharp deflation. In July the goverment at last
began to raise interest rates, a little at first and then more and
more until by March 1977, the lucky investor could achieve a
return of no less than 22% from government-guaranteed public
corporation bonds. In October the government also announced
draconian fuel conservation measures.[1] South Africa's
petroleum imports had amounted to over R1 billion in 1975
(15% of all imports) and they simply had to be cut if the trade
deficit was to be narrowed. The government made its predica-
ment clear by declaring that it would be willing to impose
further restrictions if necessary even if only a few million Rand
a year could be saved thereby. At the same time the government
cut back on para-statal expenditure where it could — ESCOM
announced in November that it was deferring construction of
the planned R1 billion Ilanga power station, while ISCOR
announced that its plan to build a semi-processing plant at
Saldanha Bay was shelved 'until there is an improvement in
the international and South African capital markets'. This was a
blow indeed, for the R1.3 billion plant would have made a
major contribution to increased exports. The trouble was that it
was difficult to squeeze the import bill much beyond this
without coming up against the need to make cuts in the
sacrosanct defence budget (25% of the whole budget in 1976)
and in such vital projects as the R2 billion Sasol II plant,
Secunda.[2] With the 'Communist threat' greatly increased by
events in Angola and Mozambique, the government was
determined above all not to be forced to cut defence — in fact it
freely admitted that considerably more than the budgeted
amount was already being spent — but getting money for it was
not going to be easy. In July 1976 the Defence Minister, P. W.
Botha, launched new Defence Bonds, enthusing that they
provided 'an opportunity for all South Africans to make a
positive contribution to the defence of the Republic'. By
December Major-General Webster, the Director-General of
Defence Force Resources, described the public response to the
bond issue as 'lousy'.

The measures had some effect — the balance of payments
deficit began to fall quite sharply, though not enough. But the
government deficit actually continued to rise — almost entirely

[1] The measures included a 55 mph limit, weekend closing of petrol stations
and R2,000 fines or two years' jail for contraventions.
[2] See above, p. 96.

owing to the still soaring defence component. Meanwhile the
sharply deflationary effects of the measures began to bite. The
motor industry slumped to its lowest level since the war, and
more than 4,000 workers were laid off; construction was
similarly hit; business bankruptcies proliferated. As 1977 began
it was clear that it was going to be the economy's worst year
since at least the Depression, with gross fixed investment
projected to fall by 7% and private consumption expenditure by
1%. Investment in the metal and engineering industries, already
down by 20% in 1976, was expected to fall further. The
resulting unemployment was the worst South Africa had ever
experienced as an urban industrial country. By March 1977
registered unemployment (i.e. of Coloureds, Asians and
Europeans) was rising at an annual rate of 200%. For Africans
1976 had brought no new jobs at all, and estimates of black
unemployment at the end of the year were generally pitched
around the 2 million mark, and rising at 10,000–20,000 a
month. With 220,000 more Africans coming on to the labour
market every year the outlook was nothing short of disastrous.

Bad news, as ever, came in concert, not singly. To the
disasters of the falling gold price and the collapse of investors'
confidence abroad came several other major blows. The fall in
commodity prices since 1973 had hit South Africa across the
board, but generally stability at least had returned by 1975. In
the second half of 1976, however, the world sugar price
collapsed from around £200 a ton to under £120 – a body
blow to the big South African sugar producers, whose shares fell
even worse than did the industrial indices. The slide in the £
sterling in the summer and autumn of 1976 greatly worsened
the prospect for South African exports in their key market, as
the EEC tariff restrictions around the British market were
anyway beginning to take heavy effect. Canned fruit sales to
Britain, for example, had already fallen by over 25% in 1975
and the big fruit exporters had built up embarrassingly large
stocks of unsaleable goods waiting for the situation to improve.
Now, it was clear, things would get more difficult, not better;
especially as the Greek and Spanish fruit canneries were
beginning to take advantage of their EEC relationships to
squeeze out the South African fruit farmer from the market on
which he still depended for 60% of his sales. From Namibia
came the news that the anchovy catch was badly down – the
fish were breeding too soon due to some inexplicable change in
the Angola current. There seemed to be a veritable curse on the
economy.

The white business community had been badly shaken by Soweto, as had the whole White Establishment. However, the normal gentle business chorus calling for political reform (consisting mainly of the Anglo-American group and its associates) was now joined by the business community as a whole. Businessmen had not been slow to realise that the government's actions in Angola and Soweto had greatly darkened the economic climate, but as the government met the Soweto protest with little more than mere repression, business alarm grew. The declining prospects for profits and even for business survival did not discriminate between English and Afrikaans speakers, and for the first time the Afrikaner business class which had matured in the 1950s and 1960s found itself threatened, not sustained, by the Nationalist government. This new class now tended to feel that it could stand on its own — that it did not need the government any more. It unhesitatingly joined in the protests of the English-speaking business community as it became clear that the government was refusing to hold out the sort of promises of political reform which alone could reassure foreign investors and bankers. The new alliance was perhaps best symbolised by the setting up by Harry Oppenheimer (who had long financed the Progressives) and Anton Rupert (a large contributor to Nationalist funds) of the Urban Foundation, dedicated to alleviating the problems of urban Africans. It was not clear what it could achieve beyond piecemeal co-optation of urban African leaders (it was committed to keeping out of politics and the only solutions were, by definition, political). It was, though, a sign that business had suddenly begun to care very deeply about making gestures to urban blacks. South African company reports for 1976 rang with strong statements of political concern. Basil E. Hersov, chairman of the R100 million Anglovaal mining company, told his shareholders that:

> The growing feeling of crisis has surely reached the stage where private enterprise must re-examine its role in society and question to what extent the scope of its activities should be extended in order to protect the economic structures that have been built up over the years.
>
> Business interests must ask themselves, more than ever before, to what extent their particular areas of expertise can be put to use to improve effectively the environment and opportunities of the urban black population. In doing this, businesses will be weighing short-term expenditures against the longer-term rewards of helping to ensure greater possi-

bilities for stability and growth in our society. . . our Group is ready to co-operate with other businesses and government authorities in mounting practical, constructive programmes to assist in improving standards of housing, education and other amenities in the townships so as to enhance the quality of life and earning capacity of the residents.

There was widespread talk, indeed, of business 'giving a lead' to government by unilaterally offering equal pay for equal work for black and white. This amounted, in effect, to proposing to share out some of the burden of unemployment suffered by blacks on to whites, for there could be little doubt that once a truly competitive labour market was established employers would quickly find that black labour was always going to be less unionised, cheaper in practice, and less assertive — the white mine workers, after all, were campaigning strongly for a five-day week in the midst of the economic crisis. The white workers' response to such business proposals was predictably hostile.

The White Establishment was, in fact, more deeply and publicly split than ever before. The mood of the English-speaking business classes was reflected in a complete collapse of the main opposition United Party whose leader, Sir de Villiers Graaff volunteered to put his party into liquidation if a new alignment of forces could thereby be marshalled behind political reform. The party split and the PRP quickly emerged as the major opposition party. But the more important split was within Nationalist ranks, where *verligtes* and *verkramptes* faced one another in open and quite public hostility. For the first time the Afrikaans press, in the past the almost fanatically loyal handmaiden of the government, turned to criticism of its rigid attitudes.

The government was quite unused to criticism from such sources, and in October Vorster rounded angrily on the Association of Chambers of Commerce at their annual congress, telling them to stick to business and keep out of politics. 'Giving in to unreasonable requests from business organisations', he told them, 'would be adulterating the whole political process.' As for equal-pay-for-equal-work proposals, businessmen should, he warned, be on their guard against subtle attempts to persuade them to undo the whole social and economic order by doing 'something which would threaten the whole free enterprise system, the voting system, and bring an end to democratic government in this country.'

The economic alternative to political reform was massive deflation and retrenchment. As the government swung unhesitatingly towards the latter alternative after July 1976, business despondency deepened to bitterness. In November 1976 Zac de Beer, an Anglo-American director (and former PRP MP), virtually advised foreign investors to keep out:

> If I were a foreign investor looking clinically at South Africa, I would be aware of South Africa's long-term potential but would refrain from investing here until South Africa looked safe for private enterprise — which means until the obviously essential political reforms had been carried out.

*   *   *   *   *   *   *

Soweto had sprung from complex causes — from the new mood engendered by the triumph of FRELIMO and the MPLA, from the accumulation of African bitterness over the years and, finally, from the growing crisis of unemployment. Its results were entirely self-confirmatory, self-reinforcing. For blacks and Coloureds alike now had hundreds of fresh deaths, thousands of new arrests to add to their swelling score of grievances. Thousands of young blacks fled to Botswana or further afield, determined to emulate the guerrilla struggle of their hero, Samora Machel. Within South Africa the result of the killings was a fresh and savage turn in the recessionary spiral which could only take black unemployment to new heights. Vorster sat tight, apparently praying for a rise in the gold price. As his police swept in on the townships in their armoured cars, pounced on black children, and swept thousands into the drag-net, the prime minister warned of the danger to democratic government if they were prevented from pursuing their task to an efficient conclusion. Meanwhile, in the midst of the worst depression the country had seen for at least a generation, the business classes were waging an astonishing campaign for social reform, were offering desperate charity to the workers, even devising schemes to lower their profits further by increasing wages quite above and beyond any labour market pressures on them to do so. Such was the miracle wrought by the schoolchildren of Soweto.

10 Southern Africa 1976: Henry Kissinger's Last Gamble

1976 was the year of Angola and the year of Soweto. It was also the year which saw a major initiative from Washington to head off the developing crisis in southern Africa. The initiative was led and organised by a figure who has already loomed large in our narrative, Henry Kissinger. It always seemed likely that 1976 would be Kissinger's last year of power, and southern Africa witnessed his last gamble.

With Soweto South Africa was, in a sense, back at Sharpeville. But in the unfolding of the diplomacy of 1976 all the threads of post-Sharpeville development were drawn together — the collapse of the northern buffer, Pretoria's ambiguous relations with the West, particularly the US, the policy of detente, and the gold war. It is this Kissinger initiative which, with Soweto, made 1976 a climactic year in the entire evolution of the crisis of South Africa which we have traced in this book. The failure of the Kissinger initiative — for fail it did — posed in a sharper light than ever the problems it had been intended to solve. Given the importance of southern Africa to US interests, and the centrality of US power to any future South African 'solution', the diplomacy of 1976, moreover, affords us a glimpse of the future. For, whatever its outcome, the Kissinger initiative was certain not to be the last of its kind.

Henry Kissinger had, as we have seen, been caught badly off-balance by the collapse of Portuguese colonialism in southern Africa, and from April 1974 on had desperately to pluck whatever chestnuts he could from the fire. Kissinger had, by this time, been running US foreign policy for over five years, and had developed his own characteristic strategy of response to the general problems posed by the decay of the American imperium. First, and most obviously, he had come to terms with the inevitable, attempting a detente with Soviet power which at once recognised that power and sought to contain it by giving the Russians trade and other incentives not to disturb the balance thus achieved. Second, the US sought to come to terms with the new multi-polar world balance by encouraging what in any case it could not prevent, the emergence of regionally dominant (and politically conservative) medium powers which would hold the line for the 'Free World'. It might no longer be practicable for the US marines to intervene directly in Latin America, the Middle East or south-east Asia, but this would not matter so much if the same job could effectively be left to Brazil, Israel, Iran, Saudi Arabia, Pakistan, South Vietnam and a host of lesser powers, all armed to the teeth with American weapons.

Both these strategies had problems. The first, detente, was widely viewed by the American electorate as a form of retreat, a conviction which was reinforced whenever the Soviet 'side' appeared to make gains anywhere in the world. These misgivings Kissinger sought to allay by occasional overt displays of hawkishness (such as the *Mayaguez* incident in Cambodia in 1975) and by tough public warnings to the Russians to 'keep out' of areas where the US was itself intervening (as in Angola in January 1975). In the end such gestures did not amount to much, however, and the American electorate's growing disillusionment with the fruits of detente came increasingly to threaten Kissinger's policies and public standing. The problem of the second tack — the devolution of 'Free World defence' to regional powers — was that these powers were not simply client states but had interests of their own which, if pursued, could threaten the overall balance: Greece and Turkey might use their arms to fight one another (over Cyprus), Israel and Egypt might do the same, and so on.

Kissinger sought to exercise overall control by the same tactic of 'linkage' which he applied to the USSR, that is of doing deals in one area in return for pay-offs in another. The difference between dealing with the Russians and the medium powers was, however, that whatever the general decline in American world power, in relation to each of the medium powers individually US power was still quite overwhelming and could be used to guarantee that, at least at key moments, these powers were forced to behave as virtual clients. The sources of American leverage short of direct military intervention were, after all, still very great. In particular, the US could exploit its position as arms-supplier and its power of the cheque-book. Thus the irony of US policy became that it depended on American allies being squeezed, leant upon, and made to act in terms of some general Western interest rather than their own. Perhaps the most brutal exhibitions of such tactics had been seen in the case of Israel (forced, to her furious resentment, to a peace with the Arabs in the 1973 war, after US arms reinforcements to her in the midst of the war had suffered long, agonising and mysterious delays) and South Vietnam (forced to agree to a phoney cease-fire with the North Vietnamese under similar pressures). A major danger of this tactic was that the medium powers naturally hated their subjection to client status, and protested bitterly that Kissinger's main energies seemed to be concentrated on hurting America's friends, not defeating her enemies. Such protests inevitably found a ready audience among American conservatives, who disliked detente and would have much preferred to see the US lining up four-square behind her regional allies in simple-minded crusades to 'defeat Communism'. The strategy had, nonetheless, worked brilliantly in the Middle East and, after a fashion at least, in south-east Asia too, but Kissinger had always to be extremely wary, especially in election years, of his policies' domestic political vulnerability.

(i) SATO — The Impossible Dream

In southern Africa the relevant medium power for the purposes of such a strategy could only be South Africa. Pretoria had long been extremely keen that the US should formally and publicly acknowledge such a role for her, pointing out that the closure of the Suez Canal had made the Cape sea route strategically more important than ever. Almost all the West's trade with the Far East, Australia and the Middle East — including the vital oil supplies — passed along this route, with a ship of some western nation passing the Cape every four minutes on average. The West, Pretoria argued, would simply have to take account of the danger to this vital lifeline posed by growing Soviet naval power. In the event of future war the Russians might use their submarines to cut Western supplies at this bottleneck, thus strangling the West by a 'strategy of denial' of its raw materials. The only safeguard against this, so the argument ran, lay in the positioning of major Western naval forces in South Africa and the open inclusion of South Africa in a South Atlantic Treaty Organisation (SATO) analogous to NATO. From the 1960s on Pretoria had tried extremely hard to sell the SATO idea not just to the US but to the Latin American states as well.

As early as 1968 P. W. Botha, Pretoria's Defence Minister, had revealed that South Africa had taken part in a secret international conference 'at service level' with other Southern Hemisphere nations about the joint defence of sea routes. In

1969 the Foreign Minister, Hilgard Muller, had visited Brazil and Argentina for talks with defence and foreign ministers there about the possibility of a formal naval agreement linking the three countries. A series of naval liaison arrangements resulted, and from 1969 on the South African Navy began paying 'courtesy visits' to Latin American ports. The same sort of liaison was maintained with the NATO powers, particularly, of course, the Royal Navy, which until 1975 actually had its own base in Simonstown.

Pretoria's arguments had some force and were enthusiastically taken up by a large number of Western admirals, naturally eager that their governments should view future western defence in such suitably naval terms.[1] Such western admirals forcibly drew their governments' attention to the build-up of Soviet naval strength in the Indian Ocean, visible from March 1968 on, when a Soviet squadron first called at the Indian port of Madras. Thereafter Soviet vessels were an increasingly common sight in the Indian Ocean. In July 1974 the Russians obtained the use of port facilities in Berbera by the signing of a Somali–Soviet friendship treaty, as well as similar facilities at Kismayu, near Somalia's border with Kenya. They also obtained the use of international anchorages off the island of Socotra, and in the Seychelles. On the west African coast the Russians could use port facilities at Conakry (Guinea). It was, surely, only a matter of time before they acquired facilities at Diego Suarez (Malagasy) and in Ethiopia — let alone (from 1974 on) in the former Portuguese colonies. The arguments of such Western admirals became more heated as the Soviet naval build-up of the 1970s proceeded and they were given a particular fillip by the great Soviet naval exercise, Okean 1975,

[1] Admiral Arthur W. Radford, formerly chairman of the US Joint Chiefs of Staff, visited Cape Town in 1967 and told Capetonians: 'You are now at the crossroads of the world both economically and militarily.' The importance of South Africa to the western alliance was also strongly argued by the American General S. L. A. Marshall in his *South Africa: The Strategic View* (1967). On the French side South Africa's case was put with particular force by General Beaufré, a former NATO delegate and deputy head of SHAPE. His articles on the subject were, indeed, circulated as official South African propaganda by the South Africa Foundation. In Britain, where naval-mindedness is an attitude of the whole Establishment, the importance of South Africa to western defence was stressed perhaps above all by Sir Alec Douglas-Home. Sir Alec, indeed, went further than almost anyone, strongly advocating British arms sales to South Africa and a formal extension of NATO's responsibilities to the south Atlantic and the Cape route.

in which over 200 surface vessels and 100 submarines partici-
pated, with an impressive co-ordination of forces in the
Mediterranean, the Pacific, the Sea of Japan and the Philippine
Sea.

There was indeed no doubt that in Admiral Gorchkov, the
Red navy chief, Western admirals had found a man after their
own heart. In 1975 he added fuel to their arguments by
publishing his thoughts in his book, *The Sea Power of the State*,
where he wrote:

> America, being separated from Europe by the vastness of the
> Atlantic Ocean, has for hundreds of years escaped the horrors
> of war. She has grown used, thanks to the shield provided by
> her powerful navy, to being safe and enjoying impunity. But
> the situation has changed and the oceanic vastnesses are now
> the least secure in the United States's system of defence.

South Africa, for her part, joined strongly in this chorus of
alarm from Western naval chiefs, and was, of course, only too
happy to show visiting Western admirals the blips on her
Silvermine radar screens denoting Soviet submarine activity near
and around the Cape. Surely, Pretoria and this pressure group of
Western naval chiefs demanded, the case for a SATO was
becoming unanswerably strong?

These arguments made some impression on Washington —
where, of course, the ultimate power of decision on such
questions rested. The army and air force chiefs, who knew a
naval lobby when they saw one, were rather more sceptical,
pointing to the advanced age of Admiral Gorchkov (who had
been a rear admiral in 1941) and not a few of the other naval
strategists. The whole idea of Russian submarines starving the
West into submission by a strategy of protracted interdiction or
blockade was, they pointed out, absurdly nineteenth century in
its conception. The very first ship sinking, after all, would
constitute a major act of war and the nuclear bombers and
missiles would be in the air only a few minutes later. In any
case, if one wanted to stop supplies getting through one did not,
in this day and age, attempt the chancy and difficult job of
impeding a multitude of cargo vessels on the high seas: one
bombed the supply sources and disembarkation ports. It was
quite clear, they pointed out, that the Russians were intent
merely on not being subject to blockades — as they had been,
humiliatingly, during the 1962 Cuban missile crisis. A Russian
blockade simply wouldn't make sense, especially given the still
superior stength of the Western navies. What the Russians

wanted was to be able to provide just the sort of blockade-breaking naval escorts they had during the Angolan campaign. This capability they had now achieved and no amount of SATOs or extra ships could reverse that.

Moreover, army and air strategists argued, the Red Navy didn't actually have any bases outside the USSR — there was nothing remotely comparable to the US naval bases at Guantanamo (Cuba) or Diego Garcia, simply a number of ports where the Soviet Navy was allowed to call. Gorchkov was quite right; the US navy had simply had things all its own way and was now getting hysterical because this balmy period was over. Now, as for the army and air force, well they were long used to a real balance of power — even an adverse one in the case of the army. Whatever the Russians were up to, naval schemes for the South Atlantic surely had to take second or third place to bolstering up land and air forces.

As we have seen,[1] US policy under Kissinger did, from about 1970 on, move increasingly towards a de facto recognition of South Africa as a pro-western medium power in the southern African region. From at least 1972 on NATO began to move towards closer co-operation with South Africa, furnishing a good deal of the sophisticated electronic equipment for Project Advocate — a comprehensive surveillance, monitoring and communications programme conducted from Silvermine, a vast underground base encased under tons of reinforced concrete about 20 miles from Simonstown. In March 1974 the French and South Arican navies carried out joint manoeuvres. When Britain announced her withdrawal from Simonstown in October 1974, NATO Defence ministers let it be known that the defence of the Cape sea route would not be affected — it was already 'well covered' by a NATO contingency plan, in terms of which South Africa would receive naval assistance if necessary.

Secret agreements by which South Africa became a backdoor member of NATO were not at all the same thing as the SATO pact Pretoria desired. For, of course, the real prize she was after was her *open* acceptance into a western military bloc, with all that implied in terms of international recognition and the growth, or further growth, of western vested interest in the survival of the Pretoria regime. The NATO treaty, after all, spoke of the duty of its members to protect one another not only from external threat but also from 'internal subversion'. If South Africa could only entice the US into signing an analogous

[1] See above, pp. 56—9.

SATO treaty the regime's position would be immeasurably bolstered.

Thus South Africa presented Washington with the somewhat unusual sight of an important medium power which *wanted* to be a client state. Normally the more powerful a state was the more sensitive and difficult it was about allowing a super-power base facilities. But not South Africa. When Britain vacated Simonstown she immediately offered it to both Paris and Washington as a base. In June 1975 Connie Mulder, the Information Minister, visited Washington where he argued that Britain's withdrawal made a US presence in South Africa 'necessary'. Why not, he invited his American audience, take over Simonstown 'instead of creating your own bases in the area with considerable expense'.

With Pretoria willing to be as slavish as this in public, Kissinger's problem over South Africa was certainly not lack of leverage. But he could get whatever military co-operation he wanted from Pretoria without needing to dress this up in a formal SATO pact. In any case, once such a pact existed the US would be a prisoner of it and, in a sense, her leverage would be gone. The creation of a SATO including South Africa would do Washington irreparable harm in the rest of the Third world, might even trigger another oil-boycott by the Arabs. For these reasons, a SATO pact could never actually be delivered as part of any deal. It would, in fact, be the ultimate commitment and, as such, was useless for diplomatic purposes. Kissinger worked in terms of 'deals', 'pay-offs' and squeezes, not ultimate commitments. The idea of such a pact or, at least, of greater US—South African military collaboration, could be kept dangling in front of Pretoria's nose to ensure her compliance, but that was all.

Nonetheless, it was clear from April 1974 on that Kissinger was going to need South Africa. The Portuguese coup had created a major threat to the stability of the whole southern African region. If the now inevitable political restructuring of the region were not to take a turn iniquitous to the eyes of the State Department, South Africa's compliance and assistance would certainly be required. It was only too likely that Washington might need to persuade Pretoria to do a number of things she didn't want to do — intervene militarily in Angola, risk the wrath of the *verkramptes* by a forcible decolonisation of Rhodesia, get out of Nambia, perhaps even offer some symbolic relaxations of apartheid in the cause of detente. The situation was, immediately, so uncertain that there was no knowing what might be required. But one thing was certain: Kissinger would need leverage, sticks as well as carrots. It did not take very much reflection to realise that America's ability to manipulate the gold price provided the perfect weapon, particularly when allied to Washington's dominant influence in those financial milieux to which a hard-pressed Pretoria would have to go for credit and loans.

(ii) Squeezing the Golden Goose

The US had several other reasons for wanting to depress the gold price — putting the French in their place, reducing the value of Russian gold sales, and asserting the primacy of the dollar — and it is thus hardly possible to say with complete certainty either when or whether such price manipulation was conducted solely with the object of pressuring South Africa. It was this, in part, which made it such a perfect weapon, of course, for even those most vigorously assaulted by it would never be able to prove American intent to hurt them *specifically*. It was, too, a fairly well-hidden weapon, for few journalists or diplomats could be relied upon to spot connections between oscillations in the Zurich and London gold markets and moves within the diplomatic arena. A final beauty of such a scheme was that while Kissinger and Simon, the US Treasury Secretary, might not see eye to eye on other matters of foreign economic policy, they could agree easily enough on a lower gold price being desirable — and Simon would get all the 'blame' for the actual bear-squeeze operation required.

The first serious bout of US (and French) jockeying for position over southern Africa seems to have taken place in the last quarter of 1974. In August 1974 Simon piloted through the US Congress a bill making it legal for the first time since 1933 for private American citizens to hold gold.[1] In September 1974 came the news that the US was to break the UN arms embargo and supply Pretoria with helicopters and reconnaissance aircraft; in November the announcement of the French Mirage F1 deal; then the announcement of the American intention to supply

---

[1] There is, perhaps, no human species more wishful than the gold speculator and this move caused no halt at the time in the upward rise of the bull market, where Simon's action was hailed as a positive step, bringing 220 million potential new buyers into the market. In fact, of course, Simon was merely emphasising that since gold was to be demonetised there could be no objection to private citizens holding it, just as they could, if they wanted, own scrap metal. He was, moreover, creating a new gold market-place over which he would exercise control, and whose low prices could not but exercise a bearish influence on the London and Zurich markets.

Pretoria with enriched uranium fuel and of both the French and American intention to tender for Pretoria's nuclear plant contract; and then (also in November) the firing of Donald Easum as US Assistant Secretary of State for African Affairs and his replacement by the hardline Nathaniel Davis. Davis, as we have noted, had gained experience in Chile of conducting the hardest of hard squeezes on recalcitrant governments. To this one might add that in October 1974 South Africa was excluded by vote from the UN General Assembly session, and that only the votes of Britain, the US and France prevented her exclusion as a member altogether. But the US did not choose to use her influence in that month to prevent South Africa being deprived of all representation on the boards of the IMF and the World Bank, a fact of some importance for the rough bargaining over foreign loans which lay ahead.

There is, then, a great deal to indicate both a positive (carrot, not stick) Franco—US competition for influence with Pretoria in this latter part of 1974, and also the beginning of the US *squeeze* on Pretoria. For it was now that a new phase in the war of the gold price began, with the first US attempt to introduce the IMF auctions. Theoretically, of course, this decision was first to be taken by the IMF Interim Committee of bankers in August 1975. But in the Kissinger—Simon speech to the UN special session of September 1975,[1] which strongly backed the idea of such gold auctions, an interesting passage occurred in which the two US Secretaries of State 'regretted that earlier US attempts to set up a trust fund in the IMF, in *November 1974* (my emphasis), to help the poorest nations in this way had been stalled by a dispute over . . . the role of gold'. It was only when this initiative had failed that Simon began to push down the gold price with a will by means of the US Treasury gold auctions, allied to much bear-talk about the future of gold in the international monetary system.

Simon was taking on an extremely powerful coalition of forces — not just South Africa and speculators who had grown fat on a high gold price, but those countries (notably France, Italy and Switzerland) who held most of their reserves in gold. All of these countries — as also the USSR — could be expected to intervene in the market to prevent the gold price going too low. South Africa, for her part, attempted to respond by launching the new gold Kruggerrand, specifically minted in order to cater for private citizens to join in the gold speculation. (Since they were coins, Krugerrands got round the law of

[1] See above, pp. 109—10.

countries such as Britain which still forbade the private holding
of gold bullion.) Aggressively marketed by the International
Gold Corporation (Intergold), the marketing arm of the South
African Chamber of Mines, Krugerrands were the obvious
response to the opening up of the US private-buyer market, and
to the fact that the high prices of 1974 had driven jewellery
purchasers right out of the market. Since Krugerrands were, so
to speak, 'ready processed', the diversion of South African gold
output into this new outlet constituted a further restriction on
the amount of 'raw' bullion being made available to the market.
By early 1976 something like 13% of all South African gold
production was going into Krugerrands, and as the year wore on
the percentage rose towards double that figure.[1]

Simon and Kissinger had something altogether more weighty
than Krugerrands up their sleeve, however. Until this point,
Pretoria had always been able to rely on Paris fighting the gold
war for her at international level. If Simon's squeeze on the gold
price were really to develop, therefore, this French incubus had
to be moved. In July 1975 — at just the moment when, we have
suggested, Paris—Pretoria relations took an icy turn over Angola
(the French arms ban came in August) — President Giscard
appealed to the US and the other major western powers to
attend a summit meeting at Rambouillet (Paris) to discuss
monetary matters, for the French the heart of the economic
crisis. 'What the world calls the crisis of capitalism', Giscard
claimed, 'is in reality a monetary crises.' In particular, he made it
clear, France wanted to see a return to the old world of fixed
exchange rates to provide the indispensable basis of stability.
Washington strongly disagreed with this standard French line, of
course, arguing that it was inflexible exchange rates which had
brought the collapse of the old Bretton Woods system in 1971 in
the first place. It seemed, in other words, as if the old film of
Franco—American differences on this score was about to be
re-run for the umpteenth time. In November 1975, however (at
exactly the moment, as it happens, that Pretoria was coming to
the agonising realisation that her forces were stuck at Novo
Redondo), the Rambouillet conference met and a historic deal

---

[1] Krugerrands are sold by Intergold to buyers as being not merely money,
but very superior money, to be safely hoarded as an inflation hedge. The
buyers are allowed to buy them by (e.g. the US) government quite
precisely on the grounds that they are not money but useless oddities. In
fact their value commands a slight (about 3%) premium over the gold price
and goes up or down with it. By November 1976 sales had built up to the
point where 453,000 of the one-ounce coins were sold in that month,
mainly to the US market.

was struck whereby France suddenly relaxed her long championing of the cause of gold. Kissinger and Simon, meeting in secret with the French, drew up an agreement which went a very long way to conceding all that the French wanted over fixed exchange rates.

The agreement provided for a return (leaked Giscard) to 'more stable structures' and towards reducing 'erratic' fluctuations in exchange rates. Simon agreed that Western governments and central banks would maintain daily contact and, if they decided that any particular exchange fluctuation was 'erratic', they would intervene to sustain a given rate. This may have entailed an informal US promise to support the Franc if necessary. Giscard, with good reason, entertained considerable fears that the Franc would depreciate in politically disastrous fashion and, never having been the gold enthusiast that Pompidou and De Gaulle had been, would doubtless have regarded this as a handsome deal.

Having obtained this pearl of great price (and probably having struck several other bargains as well),[1] the French agreed without demur that the August 1975 IMF decision on gold auctions should go ahead. Simon was publicly jubilant.

How much reason he had became clear only at the January 1976 IMF conference at Kingston, Jamaica, held to implement the Rambouillet decisions. For the programme adopted at Kingston amounted to nothing less than an anti-gold manifesto. Even before the new IMF Articles of Agreement allowing the sales had been ratified, the Kingston conference announced that the gold auctions must go ahead 'without delay', beginning in June 1976. Kingston also announced the impending demonetisation of gold and its complete replacement by the SDR as the new international unit of value. The conference also took enabling powers for the IMF to sell off *all* the rest of its gold above and beyond what was being auctioned or handed back to IMF members. Simon spoke with happy pride — and some exaggeration — of having been the architect of an agreement comparable in importance to Bretton Woods itself.

---

[1] The French were allowed to invite Italy, their client in monetary matters, to Rambouillet, while blackballing Canada as an American client, despite the fact that the conference was for the economic giants only and that Canada accounted for a larger share of world trade than Italy. Shortly afterwards, moreover, the US agreed that the Anglo—French Concorde, the Elysée's dearest project, could land in Washington — a service inaugurated by Giscard on his diplomatic visit of May 1976. The visit was the first by a French president since Pompidou's disastrous voyage there in 1970 — whose bitter memory it was hoped thus to erase.

It was a black day for Pretoria indeed. William Simon seemed intent on nothing less than the crucifixion of the South African gold-mining industry. His first US Treasury sale (in January 1975) had brought the gold price down from $200 to $185; his second such sale (in June 1975) had reduced it to $165; the August 1975 IMF decision on gold auctions brought it down to $140; now Kingston (January 1976) brought it down to $130. And he had now somehow got the IMF and the French to agree that at some future (unspecified) time the IMF might disgorge its entire holding of gold into the market — 150 million ounces in all, or six whole years of total South African gold production.

(iii) Rhodesia — and Ronald Reagan

Thus January 1976 — the month of Kingston and also of Pretoria's withdrawal from Angola — saw a situation nicely cued up for a culminating round of Kissingerian diplomacy over southern Africa. Pretoria was retiring, bruised and embittered, her alliances in disarray. The French had decided to cut off arms supplies and had failed to support her over gold; the Americans had given her assurances of support over Angola which had not been honoured. It seems likely that these assurances had amounted to little more than vague promises about commitment to a common struggle (there was no indication of any horse-trading over the gold price). The prize Pretoria had hoped for from the affair was to find herself as an acknowledged party to an open political and military alliance with the US. In order to achieve this, Pretoria was, it seems, willing to sell her military co-operation very cheaply. For, as she could only reflect with bitterness afterwards, she had got no *quid pro quo*, symbolic or tangible, from her disastrous intervention. Naturally, in the wake of Angola Pretoria set up a renewed demand for the formation of a SATO, claiming (wildly) that the Russians would soon have a naval base in Lobito. Admiral Biermann, the head of the South African armed forces, visited Washington immediately after Pretoria's withdrawal and held a special meeting with no less than 17 US admirals as well as with a number of Congressmen. Doubtless the subject of SATO was to the fore as the Admiral attempted to 'cash' some of the gratitude Pretoria felt she had earned from Washington for her intervention. The cheque bounced. There was, it is true, renewed speculation about SATO in Latin American capitals. But the arguments in Washington against SATO were as strong as ever. In time, doubtless, the Red navy would acquire docking facilities at Lobito and probably at Maputo as well. But there was absolutely no sign of a Russian base being constructed in either port — indeed, the Red navy would have to break completely with its normal world-wide practice for this to occur. Meanwhile, Washington had no intention of throwing good money after bad. Increased US—South African naval co-operation there could be, but no SATO.[1]

Kissinger, for his part, was already setting in motion an entirely new phase of diplomatic activity. The year 1976 was, after all, election year, and Angola had been an absolute gift to all those American politicians who believed that detente was a one-sided bargain for the Russians. This damage had to be repaired by heading off the threatening situation which now loomed in both Rhodesia and Namibia. The only conceivable way to prevent the escalation of guerrilla wars in both territories was speedy decolonisation. Rhodesia was the crux of the matter — CIA reports already indicated that the war there would soon reach a critical stage where Smith could not continue to hold off the guerrillas without substantial South African help. This had to be prevented, and Smith somehow had to be made to defuse the situation by granting majority rule — no easy matter, as both the British and Vorster had recurrently found. But Vorster remained the only man able to exercise sufficient pressure on Smith to get him to climb down so totally from eleven years of UDI.

There were two problems. First, Pretoria was not in a mood for doing gratuitous favours for Washington; and second, Vorster had already gone as far as he dared in exerting pressure on Smith. Vorster was only too well aware of the gathering strength of *verkrampte* reaction created by his first two abortive attempts to make Smith come to terms. However devoutly Vorster might desire a Rhodesian settlement, with his domestic position further weakened by Angola and recession, he could not mount the truly brutal pressures on Smith which would be necessary without running very considerable domestic political risks. So if Vorster was to lean hard enough on Smith, Kissinger would first have to lean on Vorster.

There were a further two aspects to the operation. First, it

[1] In April 1976 consultations took place in Buenos Aires between the US Commander for the South Atlantic, Admiral James Sagerholm, and the Brazilian and Argentine naval authorities. In September Vice-Admiral James Johnson, the head of the South African navy, was invited to the Argentinian naval base at Puerto Belgrano in order to be present for the south Atlantic phase of Operation Unitas, in which the Argentinian, Brazilian, Venezuelan, Colombian, Uruguayan and US navies participated.

would be desirable to involve the British in at least a window-
dressing capacity. True, the recession of British power from the
southern African region was now complete, but the British were
still impaled on their 'moral responsibility' for Rhodesia. This
doctrine had a curious history. Originally forced upon the
pusillanimous Wilson government in 1965 by the colonially
conscious Labour left, it had opened up the whole red-herring
trail of sanctions. This was a sort of moral game, wonderfully attuned to the sensitivities of the liberal left. The object,
which kept the left happy and busy, was to signal virtue
by denouncing moral cheats for 'sanctions-busting'. After
eleven years the game showed every sign of running for ever.
Indeed, the full hilarity and endless dimensions of the game
were wonderfully demonstrated in April 1977, when the
Foreign Office announced — eleven and a half years after
UDI — that it was *beginning* an 'investigation' of how Rhodesia
obtained her oil. British governments had found themselves torn
between the desire to scuttle and run (1971 witnessing the last
such attempt), the rather threadbare attraction of maintaining
an alleged authority in distant climes, and the more fundamental calculation that while British 'moral responsibility'
would not be used to get rid of Smith it might one day be
needed to rescue him and other British kith and kin from
African insurrection. Beneath a great smokescreen of debate
over the constitutional position,[1] Smith too had perceived that
the notion of a continuing British responsibility was a potential
lever for getting him off the hook if necessary. For all these
reasons it would be desirable to involve the British: they would
be umbraged if left out; their politicians were always pathetic-
ally eager to cut a dash on the world stage, and they might be
useful — perhaps even as Kissinger's 'Cubans'. Accordingly,
Kissinger sought out the British Foreign Secretary, James
Callaghan, at the December 1975 meeting of NATO Ministers in

[1] Constitutional niceties had not, after all, been paid much respect in the
ignominious British retreat from Aden in 1967. Up until ten days before
the final evacuation the British had not even recognised the NLF (the
successor regime). The Rhodesians could, moreover, point to the even
older and more exact analogy of the American colonies whose UDI has
not, in recent years, greatly clouded Anglo—American relations. The Irish
example could also be cited — for several decades after Eire's independence Britain officially regarded the new state as part of the Commonwealth, while the Irish indignantly denied they were or wanted to be
members of it. In fact British politicians who chose to take their stand on
the constitutional position of Rhodesia normally did so in order to avoid
having to stand anywhere else.

Brussels. Callaghan agreed to undertake a fresh approach to Salisbury and to keep Kissinger informed.

The second flank which had to be covered was in black Africa. If a Rhodesian settlement were to work it would have to have the support of at least the neighbouring African states (who might be needed to exert pressure on the guerrillas to end the war). But it was, of course, desirable that a Rhodesian settlement should gain general African backing: a 'Transkei' solution which led to the new state being ostracised by the OAU would be unstable and of no political use to Kissinger. A major problem was the bitterly anti-American attitude of the new Nigerian regime of General Murtala Mohamed, which had come to power in July 1975, deposing the conservative General Gowon. Murtala had been a major thorn in American flesh over Angola and an utterly critical figure at the January 1976 OAU Summit; he was now loudly suspicious of US designs throughout Africa, and might well use his influence to sabotage a Rhodesian settlement. Not inconveniently, however, Murtala was assassinated on 13 February in an abortive coup aimed, apparently, at restoring Gowon.[1]

Meanwhile Kissinger let it be known that he was considering visiting Africa. Nyerere, the Tanzanian president, took the bait and wrote privately to Kissinger, strongly encouraging him to play a more active role in southern Africa.[2] This was almost better than Kissinger might have hoped for.

Meanwhile discussions were begun in Washington with the South African Ambassador, Pik Botha, and South Africa's wounded feelings assuaged somewhat by promises that the US was now intent on a major joint intiative with her, intended to head off the potentially disastrous consequences of Angola. Vorster was, in fact, extremely keen for such an initiative (and even got the newspaper millionaire, John McGoff, to carry a message from him direct to President Ford). Vorster was anxious to break out of the isolation of the post-Angola denouement: what better way than to be seen acting in statesmanlike concert with Kissinger himself? Moreover, he

---

[1] Demonstrators in Lagos blamed the coup on both Britain and the US, but the British got most of the opprobrium — their High Commissioner, Sir Martin Lequesne, being recalled in March at the request of the Nigerian government. The new Nigerian head of state, General Obasanjo, took an at least equally radical line to that pursued by Murtala.

[2] Nyerere had long stressed that only the US had the muscle (which Britain lacked) to solve the Rhodesian impasse. As he put it to reporters later in the year: 'If the United States were to say to Smith "The game is up", well, he is not so foolish as not to understand that he can't go on.'

wanted a Rhodesian settlement badly on his own account; if
Kissinger were to be involved it might be possible to divert some
of the responsibility for 'ditching the whites' in Salisbury on to
him.

Callaghan's soundings in Rhodesia consisted of sending Sir
Anthony Duff, head of the Foreign Office Africa desk, on secret
visits to Salisbury and Pretoria, followed up by a public mission
by Lord Greenhill, a former head of the diplomatic service.
The main effect of these visits was to make Salisbury realise that
something was up — and react accordingly. The Rhodesian army
announced that it had approached its South African counterpart to pledge troops and arms for Rhodesia in the event of a
major guerrilla offensive, but that the request had been flatly
refused. Smith quickly intervened with a typically heavy hint: it
was a 'wicked lie' to think that South Africa would refuse to
help her Rhodesian brethren if they had 'any problems', he
announced on 14 February. Salisbury was clearly rattled,
though. On 25 February the Rhodesian Minister of Information
launched a bitter attack on Tiny Rowland of Lonrho who was,
he asserted, waging a campaign for immediate majority rule in
Rhodesia and attempting to set the South African press against
Rhodesia.[1] Smith now turned to Callaghan and urged him to
help solve 'the constitutional crisis' over Rhodesia, and even
suggested that he set up a commission under 'three wise men' to
prepare a settlement proposal'. Smith's position was beginning
to deteriorate fast. The guerrilla war was escalating and
Rhodesian troops had begun to cross into Mozambique in 'hot
pursuit' operations — to the fury of Pretoria, which feared that
this might result in FRELIMO inviting in a Cuban military
presence. On 3 March Mozambique closed her border with
Rhodesia (60% of whose exports had been routed across it).
South Africa — with whom Mozambique's borders remained
open — announced pointedly that she would make no attempt
to retrieve Rhodesian goods blocked there.

It was by now fairly plain that — perhaps in consequence of
the busy diplomatic exchanges between Pretoria and

---

[1] Rowland had sent two Lonrho employees, Tim Curtin and Robert
Wright, to act for Nkomo in his negotiations with Smith. Simultaneously
he had set up a company to launch a newspaper for Muzorewa's ANC. The
incident appears merely to illustrate the tangled nature of Lonrho's
involvement in the area. A few months later Rowland was to accuse the
authors of the British government report criticising him of having acquired
much of their information from BOSS. This is not impossible — BOSS has
conducted a number of appraisals of business concerns, including a major
study of the Anglo-American Corporation — and BOSS—MI5 co-operation
would hardly be novel.

Washington — Vorster was operating a gradual but mounting squeeze on Smith. For Vorster's own domestic political sake the pressures had to be subtle and unobtrusive, at least at first — Smith was being set up for the proper knock-out blow later on. Senator Charles Percy, the Illinois Republican, gave the game away in late April when, emerging from an interview (as Kissinger's emissary?) with Vorster in Cape Town, he declared that Rhodesia would have to change its ways soon 'under the pressure now being exerted on it'. Meanwhile Callaghan had decided that Smith's proposals amounted to no more than deliberate stalling and, on 22 March, announced a programme for majority rule in Rhodesia within two years. On the next day (23 March), however, this developing and not unpredictable diplomatic pattern was given a considerable jolt by Ronald Reagan's victory in the North Carolina Republican primary. Reagan's challenge to Ford for the Republican nomination had seemed stalled until then. From 23 March on the race was wide open; if Reagan could win North Carolina he could win elsewhere in the South — and he was always bound to win in California (whose ex-governor he was). The emergence of this major threat to the Ford Administration had several implications for Kissinger's southern Africa strategy.

First of all, Reagan was stongly opposed to the exertion of American pressure on Rhodesia — indeed, he advocated US recognition of the Smith regime as a bulwark against communism. While the Reagan challenge remained alive it would be extremely difficult for Kissinger to lean too heavily on Smith. Second, the North Carolina result showed what political pros had recognised for some time: the South would again be the pivot of the presidential election, as it had been in 1968. Reagan's challenge to Ford was rooted solidly in white southern conservative support (his campaign could not have got off the ground without it) and one of his major strengths was that he could probably beat the presumptive Democratic nominee, Carter, in the South, which Ford probably couldn't. Until now it had seemed that one possible prize for the ending of white supremacy in Rhodesia might be small but potentially crucial Republican gains among black voters. The strength of the Reagan movement suggested that if Kissinger were not extremely careful such an advantage might be at least balanced by the disaffection of disgruntled southern whites.[1]

[1] White racism is not, of course, the dominant force that it once was in the South, but nor is it dead. During 1976, Alabama estate agents placed advertisements in Rhodesian newspapers encouraging whites there to buy property in Mississippi and Alabama 'where the White people think as you do and are of the same Anglo-Saxon background'.

Most important of all, though, was the fact that a great deal of Reagan's electoral effectiveness had come from his bitter denunciations of detente. There was no doubt now that large sections of the American electorate shared his view that the Russians were getting by far the best of this bargain. Ford was thrown entirely on to the defensive — indeed, he quickly retreated to a point where he dropped the word 'detente' from his political vocabulary altogether and seemed close to disowning the basic policy of his own Secretary of State. Kissinger, whose foreign policy successes had always been reckoned one of Nixon's major assets in 1972, thus found himself in the humiliating role of electoral albatross round his president's neck. The Reagan movement did not alter Kissinger's objectives, but it greatly increased the pressures on him to save detente's good name by heading off a further slide to the left in southern Africa. At the same time it exercised powerful new constraints over the methods and timing of such an initiative. If Reagan pulled off the unimaginable and actually defeated Ford for the GOP nomination, any Rhodesian initiative would be killed stone dead. While Reagan even remained a threat at all, Kissinger would need to be exceptionally careful; in particular any really rough treatment of the white regimes in southern Africa was right out.

With this somewhat alarming spectre of Ronald Reagan looming on his right, Kissinger set off on 24 April on an initial African trip, thinly disguised as a tour en route to the UNCTAD conference in Nairobi. His real motives he revealed more fully only on his return, in an interview to the Hearst press:

> The situation in Africa was drifting. War in southern Africa had already started. The radical elements were gaining the upper hand. The Soviet Union was appearing from the outside as a champion; the moderate regimes were coming under increasing pressures, and therefore all the moderate governments were in danger and all the Western interests were in jeopardy.

To counter this, Kissinger swept through the continent in a manner reminiscent of the famous 'Soapy' Williams tour of 1960, showering much largesse and even more promises of it to almost any African president willing to meet him.

The difference between 1960 and 1976 was that some weren't willing; indeed, the abbreviation of Kissinger's itinerary told its own story of the erosion of American influence in the Third World. Normally, of course, the tour would have started with the obligatory visit to Ethiopia. Not long before, the antique figure of Haile Selassie, the largest recipient of US aid on the continent, had presided over an Imperial Court which included among its courtiers a number of American political scientists ('constitutional advisers'). Learned articles had been written about the 'Ethiopian model of development', described a little wishfully as a permanent form — 'modernising autocracy'. The whole edifice had collapsed finally in confusion and bloodletting. Addis Ababa was now in the hands of angry young military radicals — and off the tourist list. So was Lagos. Nigeria rudely withdrew its invitation to Kissinger, arguing the 'inconvenient timing' of such a visit. Ghana quickly fell into line, cancelling the visit owing to a mysterious and suddenly contracted 'illness of the Head of State'. Kissinger asked the Mozambique president, Machel, whether he might visit Maputo; was refused; suggested Machel might in that case like to meet him in Dar-es-Salaam; Machel decided he really wouldn't like to. Visiting Angola was, of course, out of the question with the US still refusing to recognise the MPLA regime...

The Ethiopian defection made Kenya Kissinger's logical starting point. Once the jewel of British East Africa, Kenya now looked increasingly to Washington, not London. Alarmed by the presence of Mig-21s in both Somalia and Uganda, Nairobi had asked Whitehall for replacements for its own ageing Hawker Hunters, but had been told that Britain was in no position to finance supplies of new fighters. Kissinger agreed to take the Kenyans under the American military umbrella,[1] and flew on to Dar-es-Salaam. Nyerere did not want arms but principles. Kissinger duly obliged with a statement that 'we support majority rule for all the peoples of southern Africa'. On to Lusaka: given the state of the Zambian economy, money as well as principles were required here. Kissinger now spoke in favour of repeal of the Byrd Amendment. The full hilarity of this proposal apparently eluded the Zambians. As we have seen, Kissinger had, at the least, observed a benevolent neutrality towards the Amendment's passage in the first place. Moreover, if the US didn't buy its chrome from Rhodesia it would buy it from South Africa; which, given the re-export of Rhodesian goods from South Africa and the fact that Rhodesian and South

---

[1] Following in Kissinger's tracks came Donald Rumsfeld, the US Defence Secretary, to sign arms deals with Kenya and Zaire. The Kenyans were to get twelve F-4 Phantoms as part of a $75 million deal. As if to stress the American displacement of British military protection over Kenya, US navy jets from the aircraft carrier *Guam* took part in Kenya's independence celebrations in December 1976.

African chrome ore are not immediately distinguishable products, meant that in all probability the US would continue to
buy Rhodesia's chrome anyway. Perhaps more to the point,
however, Kissinger also made a promise in Lusaka to treble US
aid to central and southern Africa over the next three years.[1]
On to Zaire, where Mobutu wanted money and arms; Kissinger
agreed to both. Then off to impecunious Liberia and Senegal,
where Kissinger again promised large-scale US aid, and even
spoke grandiloquently of measures to 'roll back the desert'. This
was going a little far: after the visit local American officials
pretended they hadn't heard the statement, and had to make it
clear that there was no US plan to solve the Sahelian drought.
Finally, Kissinger flew back to Nairobi and UNCTAD, there to
face the 111 poorer countries who had signed the February
1976 Manila Declaration calling for debt relief, commodity
price guarantees and all the other components of a 'new
international economic order'. Kissinger took a strong line
against all such propositions, as if wishing to demonstrate that
the largesse he had been scattering around the African continent
was intended only for favourite sons . . .

Kissinger returned to Washington — and bad news. While he
had been away Reagan had made a sensational clean sweep of
delegates in Texas and scored smashing victories in Alabama and
Georgia, following later in May with a similar victory in
Arkansas. He had won every Southern primary, and was now
confidently predicting a victory at the Republican convention.
Such an eventuality could hardly be dismissed, and the hideous
possibility loomed that Ford might even be made a lame-duck
president not in November (which would be bad enough) but in
August. If that happened his Administration's foreign policy
would lose all credibility overnight. It might not come to
that — it would all depend on some 200 undecided delegates —
but what was apparent was that there could be no clear result
one way or the other now until the convention met in Kansas
City in mid-August.

It doubtless did not escape Kissinger's attention that Vorster
had meanwhile been active in his own behalf, making his (April
1976) visit to Israel. The sight of Vorster inspecting the Kfir
was a jolt for Paris as well as Washington. An inspired report

[1] In Zaire Kissinger had signed agreements for loans and grants totalling
$25 million, and on his return to the US sent to the Senate an $85 million
foreign aid bill for Zambia, Zaire and other southern African black states.
The Senate did not feel bound by Kissinger's bold promises in Lusaka and
Kinshasa, and cut back the aid to $50 million.

appeared in the Paris press suggesting that Vorster and the Israelis were discussing a programme for the joint construction of nuclear weapons — a story which, however wild, greatly embarrassed Vorster and his hosts who, as we have seen, were trying hard to insist that military co-operation was not involved in the visit. It would seem, though, that the net effect was what Pretoria probably desired, a rapprochement with France. For in May it was announced that South Africa was breaking off negotiations with the two other international groups tendering for the $1 billion nuclear reactor contract, and simply awarding the deal to a French consortium.[1] A few months later it was noticed that, despite the French arms ban (which applied only to future orders, not to deals already done), French arms were making their way to South Africa as never before.[2] Kissinger was doubtless little pleased at the sight of Paris and Tel Aviv bringing aid and comfort to Pretoria at a time when the US was attempting to exert pressure on her. Certainly, the State Department made no secret of its disapproval of any possible Israeli deal with Pretoria over the Kfir, and it seems likely that Giscard encountered criticism over the nuclear deal with South Africa on his visit to Washington in May.[3] Clearly, it was about time for Kissinger actually to meet Vorster. A meeting was arranged for late June, to take place in Bavaria.

Vorster needed no second bidding. The very fact of such a meeting constituted a major diplomatic breakthrough for

---

[1] The French consortium was made up of Framatome, Alsthom, Spie-Batignolles, and Framateg. The other competing groups had been the West German Krupps and a Swiss—Dutch—American consortium of Brown Boveri, General Electric and Rijn—Schelde—Verolne. The Dutch, as if embarrassed by their kinship to Afrikanerdom, have always taken a strong anti-apartheid stand (they had tried hard to dissuade the Israelis from allowing Vorster's visit) and, after a major political row, the Dutch government refused RSV the necessary export credit guarantees for the nuclear tender.

[2] French arms exports to South Africa totalled 1575 million Francs in the first seven months of 1976 alone, as against 1735 million in the whole of 1975. It is perhaps also worth noting that, doubtless to Pretoria's pleasure (see above, p. 171), Giscard told the Shah of Iran in October 1976 that France would henceforth back Iran's bid for a privileged trading agreement with the EEC.

[3] Giscard spent several days in consultation with Kissinger. Emerging into a press conference he spoke at length in justification of French nuclear deals with non-nuclear powers, declaring that he had been willing personally to veto one such sale to South Korea out of deference to strong State Department pressure. American criticism of such sales has never been hindered by the fact that US companies (as in the South African case) have been among the chief bidders for contracts.

Pretoria — not since Smuts had conferred with Truman thirty years before had there been such a high-level meeting between South Africa and the US. But there was more to it than that. South Africa's financial position was deteriorating by the week (and the Soweto troubles, which started just before the Bavaria talks, added a huge new dimension to them, as we have seen). Moreover, the first IMF gold auction had taken place on 2 June and a price of only $126 set, with a further slow price fall after the sale. As a result, Pretoria was desperately seeking foreign loans and finding them extremely hard to get. But Vorster shared Kissinger's main concern, too — the rapidly escalating guerrilla war in Rhodesia.

Since April, clashes between Rhodesian forces and FRELIMO troops on the Mozambique border had become routine, and Rhodesian jets had raided across the border on 10 June. Both BOSS and CIA reported that Smith would face a critical position by November when the rains came, creating a dense canopy of trees and grass — ideal guerrilla cover. The guerrillas in their camps inside Mozambique were only waiting for this moment to launch a major new phase of the war which the Rhodesian army would be by no means certain to contain.

The imminence of such a threat presented the possibility of quite irresistible leverage being exerted on Smith to come to terms — provided South Africa did not come to his rescue. Accordingly, Kissinger promised financial help to Vorster if the latter could guarantee that South Africa would restrict her arms supplies to Rhodesia to a minimum and refrain from bowing to pressure to send South African forces to help their white brethren to the north. Vorster could hardly have agreed to such a strategy had not Kissinger also assured him of the imminence of a major initiative towards a Rhodesian settlement, for if the war was allowed to escalate unhindered it would be virtually impossible for South Africa to keep out. A serious reversal for the Rhodesian army or, even worse, a large-scale massacre of white civilians, would generate irresistible pressures inside South Africa for intervention. Kissinger and Vorster were at one in wishing to prevent that — particularly since such a widening of the war was only too likely to bring Cuban forces into play on the other side. Such fears of a widening war were strengthened further by the angry announcement from Maputo on 26 June that two major Rhodesian forces, supported by Hunters, helicopters and artillery, had raided inside Mozambique to a depth of 55 miles. In retaliation, the Mozambique government announced, FRELIMO troops crossed the Rhodesian border and struck at the Vila Salazar military base. Salibury both denied the report of the incursion and, somewhat oddly, refused to admit that she had been the subject of a FRELIMO raid.

No sooner had Vorster returned home than he faced a visit from Smith, whose military intelligence had come to the same conclusions as Pretoria and Washington about the likelihood of a major guerrilla offensive in November. In order to stop this, Smith intimated, he would simply have to launch pre-emptive strikes at the guerrilla camps in Mozambique. Vorster refused to acquiesce in such a move, pointing to the danger of Cuban involvement. Smith returned to Salisbury and declared that it was entirely untrue that South Africa was supporting an Anglo—American plan for majority rule in Rhodesia within two years. This was a shrewd ploy: Pretoria had always been careful to speak in general terms of its desire to see a 'settlement' in Rhodesia and had insisted that the actual terms of such a settlement could be decided only by Rhodesians. Smith was banking on the fact that it would be politically impossible for Vorster openly to support majority rule in Rhodesia. Such a stance would not only break all Pretoria's public commitments to non-interference in others' internal affairs but would, of course, pose the larger question of how South Africa could favour anything less than majority rule for herself too. . . . What suited Smith, in a word, was public diplomacy, where he could play openly to the South African public gallery; what suited Vorster was the opposite — pressure which was so stealthy that it could always be denied to *be* pressure. By late July there was quite a lot of this, particularly in the form of 'rail congestion' on the South African network which was depriving Rhodesia of precious imports and even more precious export outlets. Things had got so bad by the end of July that Rhodesia's biggest citrus exporter, Hippo Valley Estates, had to dump into the ground 16,000 tonnes of grapefruit which it could not export. Pretoria's claims that the rail delays were 'technical' and unavoidable were extremely thin but, of course, impossible to disprove. In this sense the draconian deposit scheme[1] slapped on South African imports in the wake of the Soweto-induced slump was almost a godsend; it hit Rhodesian exports to South Africa very hard but it could hardly be said to be a measure aimed at Rhodesia.

On 5 August five Rhodesian soldiers were killed in a guerrilla mortar attack at Ruda, north of Umtali. This incident

---

[1] Importers had to put down 20% deposits in advance, in cash, for six months, without interest paid on the cash, for all imports ordered.

seems to have decided Smith to call Vorster's bluff, and on
8 August Rhodesian forces launched a large-scale raid against
guerrilla camps in Mozambique leaving, according to Maputo
Radio, 618 dead. This time Salisbury did not deny that her
forces 'had become involved in hot-pursuit operations'. Pretoria,
in turn, called Smith's bluff. On 9 August Hilgard Muller, the
Foreign Minister, made a strong, though still ambiguous speech
in Durban on the Rhodesian question. In the text of his speech
released at the UN, however, there was a preamble missing from
the version for home consumption which asserted that 'A
solution to the Rhodesian issue on the basis of majority rule
with adequate protection for minority rights is acceptable to
the South African government'. The unsayable had been said.
Not by Vorster, not in South Africa, and not without qualification — but it had been said. Smith's reaction was a series of
furious speeches in which he attacked the press for interpreting
Muller's speech as implying acceptance of majority rule in two
years and pointed assertions that Salisbury would not accept a
solution imposed on her by *any* outside country.

On 18 August another bombshell followed. The Turnhalle
conference, sitting since September 1975 to discuss the future
of Namibia, suddenly announced that it accepted the idea of
independence for the territory by the end of 1978. The white
delegation to the talks — the South West African branch of
Vorster's Nationalist Party — had until this point appeared quite
irreversibly opposed to such a surrender to UN pressure (the UN
had set 31 August 1976 as a deadline for free elections in
Namibia and the withdrawal of South African troops). However, it was reported, the whites had had a 'dramatic change of
heart'. The South West African issue had, of course, been of
central concern to the South African government at top level
for several decades. Vorster now attempted to disclaim any
responsibility one way or the other for this surrender of face
and past policy, adopting the (incredible) posture that Pretoria
was willing to devolve all power of decision to the local branch
officials of the Nationalist party. The concession was denounced by SWAPO, the main African nationalist organisation,
which continued to insist on direct negotiations between itself
and Vorster under UN auspices, but the greater impression was
inevitably made by the fact that Pretoria was now openly
looking to a future decolonisation process of *some* sort in
Namibia.

At the same time South African pressure on Smith continued
to tighten. By 20 August the rail congestion had created a
pile-up of £50 million of Rhodesian goods inside South Africa,

leading Salisbury businessmen to petition Smith on the urgent advisability of a settlement. The pretence that the congestion was 'technical' was wearing ever thinner, with J. G. H. Loubser, the General Manager of South African Railways, announcing that South Africa would be happy to help Zaire and Zambia move their otherwise blocked exports through South Africa. There was, he asserted, plenty of spare rail capacity to handle such freight. On 26 August came an even more dramatic move, with the withdrawal from Rhodesia of 26 of the 40 helicopters lent to Salisbury by South Africa, together with 50 South African pilots and technicians. Helicopters are, of course, essential to modern counter-insurgency warfare, and the move pulled a large rug from under the feet of the Rhodesian forces. Pretoria had never officially admitted to the presence of the pilots and technicians in Rhodesia and might have hoped that this major exercise of pressure would thus pass unnoticed. Salisbury, however, made sure the news leaked embarrassingly out. There was no pretence that Rhodesia now had replacement aircraft or crews — indeed, at the same time a helicopter training scheme in Pretoria for Rhodesian pilots was abruptly cancelled.

Vorster was now a man walking not one but two tightropes. Had either one of the South West African white leaders or Smith launched a public attack on him for exerting pressure to 'betray the white man in Africa' he might have suffered incalculable political damage.[1] Ironically, the fact that Soweto and Cape Town were also exploding in riot at this time may actually have helped in one sense, for the unrest distracted the public's attention at the same time that it rallied it instinctively behind a strong government. On the other hand the appalling

---

[1] One might ask why Smith never took the gamble of launching an tirade against South African pressures? Above all, of course, he could not afford to offend Pretoria, on whom he depended utterly; secondly, an open attack on Vorster might alienate South African opinion — whose sympathy he had to court, not demand; thirdly, Smith had been to the brink many times before and would always be slow to decide that the final moment had come — and launching such an appeal to white opinion would be a move only for the latest of last moments. But, if that moment came, then it was, by definition too late for such an appeal. If the game for white Rhodesia really *was* up, then Smith would, from that moment, have no incentive to injure Pretoria. For Smith has long been the owner of a large farm in the Cape to which, in such an event, he will retire, and an injured or vindictive Pretoria government might well act to cloud or even disallow such a retirement. Smith's own position in this respect merely symbolises what is true in greater or lesser degree for almost all Rhodesian whites. If white rule in Rhodesia ends, they will be more dependent on South Africa than ever.

political risks being taken by Vorster in foreign policy made it quite essential that the government retained a brutally uncompromising attitude to internal discontent. Vorster could hope to get away with taking a firm hand with Smith provided an equally firm hand was used against the Soweto rioters.

Pretoria might squeeze Smith, but it in turn was being almost equally painfully squeezed by Washington, the pressure reaching a maximum in August — the month when Vorster embarked on all the bold moves we have described above. It is worth departing from our narrative briefly to examine these pressures further.

(iv) The Double Squeeze

The first IMF gold auction had, we have seen, brought the gold price down to $126. At the second auction on 14 July the price had fallen lower still, to $122.05. This further fall, though slight, was enough to ram home the fact that anyone buying gold was doing so on a market which seemed only able to go down. A selling panic set in, and within days the price had touched $107. By this stage even the large number of incurable optimists among gold speculators had begun to realise how strong the bear forces in the market were. Above all was the fact that the gold price is a politically determined price and William Simon was setting it now just as FDR had before him. Simon had preached against a high gold price, and lo . . . it had fallen. He was known to believe that a price around $80 might be appropriate, and the very fact of this knowledge was enough to depress the price further without his necessarily having to do very much more than utter. From Washington came a steady flow of bearish rumour. Analysts noted that if gold were to appreciate only as other metals had done since 1968, then $50 would be the right price.

Another extremely potent force in the market were the continual rumours of a bad or even disastrous Russian grain crop. Should this transpire, of course, the Russians would have to pour gold into the market in order to buy extra grain from the US. On 8 June the US Department of Agriculture issued a lengthy report arguing that the Russian crop was likely to be at least 10 million and probably 20 million tonnes short of its 205 million tonne target, owing to a disastrous winter grain crop. Such rumours were, of course, of great political advantage to the Ford Administration — not merely because they reinforced the general picture of the superiority of American farming but, more to the point, because they kept the price of grain on the Chicago market right up, to the enormous pleasure of American farmers who were wont, unsurprisingly, to conclude that there were many advantages to having a President from a good farming area like Grand Rapids, Michigan. Commenting on the 8 June report, the *Financial Times* noted that:

> Suggestions that the Department may be putting the worst possible gloss on Russian figures in order to drive up the price of wheat for political reasons have circulated in Chicago for some time.[1]

By mid-August Washington 'observers' were so confident of the Russian grain disaster that one diplomatic correspondent could begin his story with the flat statement that:

> Russia is preparing to import at least 15 million tonnes of wheat, corn and soya beans . . . to off-set harvest losses. The expected purchases would exceed £1,400 million . . . Washington observers commented that an estimate by an American team which toured Russia several weeks ago of a harvest exceeding 195 million tonnes might now prove too optimistic.[2]

Rumours such as these had a deeply depressive effect on the gold price. Until, that is, it became clear by late October that they were entirely untrue. In fact the Soviet crop was, at 224 million tonnes, an all-time record. In mid-December (after the US presidential election) it was admitted that Washington had been well aware of the truth all along:

> American experts confirmed the probable record Soviet harvest by using satellite reconnasissance, a White House official said . . . The US satellite programme is operated on an experimental basis by the Agriculture Department . . . It uses two Landsat satellites providing basic data on wheat production . . . estimates of the 1976 Soviet winter wheat crop last summer were within 2 per cent of the actual yield.[3]

In other words, Washington had been perfectly well aware throughout the summer of the impending Russian record grain harvest, but had nonetheless disseminated rumours suggesting another Soviet harvest short-fall. In the end the truth had to

[1] *Financial Times* (London), 9 June, 1976.
[2] *Sunday Telegraph* (London), 29 August, 1976.
[3] *Financial Times* (London), 17 December, 1976.

come out — but by then the rumours had done their damage to
the gold price and held up grain prices until the very eve of the
US election.

There were other rumours too. In mid-August it was reported
that the Russians (desperate to buy grain) had tried but failed
to raise loans on the Euromarket; failure had forced down grain
futures in Chicago, leading to margin calls met by liquidation of
other speculative holdings such as those in gold. Small investors
and large alike, it was pointed out, were now escaping currency
uncertainty by pouring their 'funk money' not into gold but
into Deutschmarks and Swiss Francs. It was noted, too, that the
Indonesian government had taken strong and successful
measures to stop gold smuggling into the country, thus cutting
off another source of potential demand.[1] And so on it
went. . . . These were the classically fanciful rumours of a bear
market squeeze. Simon himself naturally attracted a great deal
of bitter hostility from gold-lovers, but in considerable measure
he could rely on the inventive imaginations of city columnists
to do his work for him. He had any number of weapons in
reserve — he could at any moment announce a resumption of
US Treasury gold sales, for example — but he had no need for
such blunt instruments.

The US did intervene directly, however, most notably on 24
August. Under strong American pressure, the IMF announced
that it was altering the rules for future gold auctions. First
instead of selling the gold at a common price reached by
averaging all the bids received in advance (the system used for
the first two auctions), the IMF would simply sell to all those
who submitted bids at or above the lowest price 'considered
acceptable'. Second, it was announced that in future the
successful bidders would lose their anonymity, for their names
would be disclosed immediately by the IMF. This was a shrewd
blow, for the Bank of International Settlements (which acts for
central banks), had been known to have been a bidder in the
first auction. It was known, too, that a number of Swiss banks
had been active at that auction, and the suspicion was widespread that the French, the South Africans, and probably the
Russians too had been bidding to keep the price up. Under the
new rules they would, of course, be able to bid again if they
wished, but only at the cost of being seen quite openly to be
bolstering the gold price artificially. The result of these rule
changes was an immediate collapse in the gold price — which
touched a bare $100 in New York on 25 August. Gold mining

[1] All of these rumours may be found (for example) on the city page of the
Daily Telegraph of 19 August, 1976. The two *Telegraph* papers in this
period are also distinguished by their bitter vituperation against Simon.

shares followed suit. Even after Angola the FT Gold Mines index had hovered just under 200; Soweto brought it down to 'only' 170; the IMF gold auctions brought it plummetting down to under 100 in early August and under 80 by late August.

The result of this collapse was a crisis of major proportions for the South African gold mining industry and thus for the whole economy. There were several aspects to the crisis. First, both the companies and the government were badly hit by the simple and very sharp fall in revenue — at a time when they could least afford it. Very crudely the fall in the price in the first eight months of the year may have cost South Africa as much as 4% of her GNP. Second, gold had earned South Africa over 40% of her total hard currency in 1975; the price fall in July—August alone negated immediately the effect of even the quite drastic measures taken in July to cut the trade imbalance. Thirdly, the price fall meant that a growing number of the more marginal mines were operating at a large loss and could keep going only with large-scale state assistance. Actual mining costs per ounce of gold varied in mid-1976 all the way from the super-profitable West Driefontein ($33 an ounce) and Randfontein ($35) to East Rand's $148, Durban Deep's $149, and West Rand Consolidated's fearsome $274. Out of the 42 gold mines operating in South Africa at the beginning of 1976, by September no less than 16 were running as a loss; of these four had effectively closed and a further four had given notice that they would have to close shortly unless there was an extraordinary reversal in the gold price.

In fact the position was considerably worse than indicated even by such figures, for several reasons. First, the production costs cited were merely running costs and made no allowance at all for future capital investment required in the mines. The biggest single 'costs' item was, of course, the relatively inflexible wage bill. From 1972 to 1976 the mine-owners had increased the wages of black mineworkers more than four-fold. There was no prospect of decreasing wages without producing riots, strikes and greater difficulties in recruiting South African blacks to replace the rapidly diminishing numbers of foreign migrants. Indeed, as we have seen, the bloody violence of the mining compounds in recent years had made the mineowners look increasingly (if wistfully) towards schemes for a more settled — and more expensive — accommodation of a permanent labour force. Secondly, even several of the apparently profitable mines found their life-expectancies dramatically shortened by the price fall, given the fact that they would soon have to move on to mine lower-grade seams. Thus the Leslie and Bracken mines (production costs per ounce of $100 and $53 respectively) announced that they were now down to three years' life-expectancy, while Winkelhaak ($53) announced that its future earnings would be severely prejudiced if the gold price fluctuated below $130. Bracken and Winkelhaak, it is worth pointing out, were jointly the sixth most profitable mines out of the whole 42. Thirdly, of course, the collapse in gold-mining share values and the chronic uncertainty about the future of the whole industry made it all but impossible to raise the capital needed for future development of the mines. Market capitalisations were now so low that they would not pay for the sinking of a single new shaft, even in mines with 'guaranteed' 30-year life-expectancies. The mining companies found increasing difficulty in raising credit to finance even such blue-chip new mines as Consolidated Gold Fields' Deelkraal and Union Corporation's Unisel, particularly since the original development costs of these new mines were inflating out of control.

In July the president of the Chamber of Mines, R. A. Plumridge, announced that if the low gold price persisted much longer 'it will seriously jeopardise primary gold production throughout the world'. This was, of course, something of an exaggeration. But it was clear enough that, quite apart from the long shadow it cast over the long-term future, the low gold price posed a dire and immediate threat to the 16 loss-making mines. True, being low-grade mines these accounted for only 10% of total South African gold production — though the government could hardly afford to sneeze at the loss of foreign exchange which their closure would entail. More to the point was the fact that they employed fully 30% of the total mine labour force of 700,000. What their closures threatened, in other words, was the discharge of over 200,000 black workers in the midst of a breakdown in the social and political order engendered by black unemployment in the first place. It was no longer true that closure would simply mean sending migrant workers back to Mozambique[1] or Malawi. The run-down in migrant numbers

---

[1] South African policy towards Mozambique was given an extra twist by the falling gold price. On the one hand Pretoria was anxious to maintain all possible ties binding Mozambique to her — including, notably, the large number of Mozambiquan migrants in the mines and the Mozambique Convention (which entailed the payment of a part of the migrants' wages in gold to the Mozambique government). On the other hand the government was under increased pressure to find jobs for South African blacks (by, inter alia, displacing foreign migrants) and to abandon the Mozambique Convention — the gold sent to Maputo was not only a major revenue loss (it was accounted for at the official $42 price) but was, of course, quickly sold into the gold market by the needy Maputo government, adding its straw to the camel's back.

from such countries was such that by 1976 South African blacks made up 45% of the mine labour force (it had been 25% in 1973) and the proportion was rising rapidly. Gold mining was so central a part of the economy, moreover, that even a slow-down in mining expansion immediately hit the engineering and equipment industries hard. In the end, of course, there was no limit to the multiplier effects of the gold crisis — the ripples spread out to touch every sector. The mining companies cut back their order books to the bone and simultaneously borrowed what they could in order to guarantee future development. The result was that smaller companies lost orders at the same time they they found themselves squeezed out of the credit market — producing an inevitable chain of bankruptcies. The golden goose still laid its golden eggs on which the economy had depended so hard and long. The calamity was, the eggs counted for less and less. It was difficult to adapt to *that*.

It seemed downright impossible if to this unwanted situation was added the fact that the diamond market was also noticeably sluggish. Diamonds are, of course, a major South African export and are marketed through the De Beers Central Selling Organisation (CSO). The diamond market had been badly hit by the world recession, and CSO sales had fallen from $1332 million in 1973 to $1254 million in 1974 and $1066 million in 1975. (Given the rate of inflation in these years, of course, this drop in money revenue of 20% actually concealed a real drop of perhaps 50%.) It was perhaps not surprising that large gem diamonds should have found few takers in the context of tighter wallets round the world in these years, but what was far more worrying was the very large drop in the demand for industrial diamonds (80% of all diamonds). The US is, of course, the largest market of all for such diamonds, and South Africa was finding that American market forces were apparently no less hostile to her diamonds than to her gold. Under such circumstances De Beers was naturally forced to freeze all its plans for the expansion and development of its South African and Namibian mines. Both this and the large drop in revenues from diamonds were major additional blows for South Africa to bear.

The South Africa economy, as we have seen, found itself struggling against a variety of adverse currents in 1976: the effects of the falling gold price in 1975, the onset of world depression, record inflation, the disastrous effects on overseas investors of Angola and then of Soweto. As the gold price fell to further and further lows in 1976 the whole economy contracted painfully, as if in the grasp of a giant invisible fist. The government sought loans abroad. The government's parlous position could be summed up in the fact that gold receipts were by September expected to be down by almost R1 billion on the year, with a similar fall in foreign investment. The government was running massive trade and budget deficits, and needed to find nearly R800 million simply to service debt repayment on previous loans; in addition, several earlier loans were due for repayment. By the end of July the government had succeeded in borrowing only R400 million abroad (it had borrowed only slightly more than that in the whole of 1975). By August Pretoria was pursuing a further syndicated loan of $500 million (R435 million) from US banks, and was actually promising to pledge gold as collateral, *valued at $80 an ounce* — a terrible admission of weakness and pessimism as to the future gold price.

The government was, moreover, discovering the horrific difference between private and public capital inflows. Private foreign investors, when they put their money into South Africa did so unconditionally — because they wanted to, because it was profitable. But public loans raised abroad were another matter altogether, and raised all sorts of political issues which, humiliatingly, had often to run the gamut of political inquiry and debate. Thus the US Senate Sub-Committee on African Affairs had announced that it would hold special hearings on the subject of the projected South African loan, with Citibank (the syndicate leader) and other banks being interrogated publicly as to the size, terms and interest rates attached to the loan. The Black Caucus in Washington would clearly have a field day; the banks would be embarrassed, under pressure to call off or at least reduce the loan, and eager to proclaim their own execration of their client's apartheid policies ... it was a horrible prospect.[1] Western governments had traditionally conducted relations with South Africa in precisely the same fashion as they (particularly the US) had once dealt with the Arab

---

[1] In Britain the same situation arose over the purchase of R10 million worth of South African Defence Bonds by Barclays Bank of South Africa, which is 63% owned by the British Barclays International. By April 1977 the resulting furore in Britain led Barclays to promise that the bonds would be sold as soon as possible and to admit that the purchase had been 'a mistake'. It was in fact a huge non-issue — South African law compels banks to hold a stated proportion of their assets in government bonds or public securities, so Barclays (the largest bank in South Africa) cannot avoid lending to the South African state under one head or another. Nonetheless, the affair hardly brought much cheer or comfort to Pretoria.

states — public disapprobation combined with effective private subsidy.[1] These two contradictory aspects were now brought within a single dimension. This had happened in the case of Western—Arab relations in 1973—4 and had been resolved by bringing the public attitudes into line with the private. The Arabs, though, had achieved this favourable result by 'winning' a war and a massive lurch into (oil-induced) wealth. South Africa had reached the same position by 'losing' a war (Angola) and a massive lurch into (gold-induced) debt. The decision might well have to go against her.

In Bavaria, of course, Vorster had sought to win Kissinger's help in this desperate situation. By the end of August it looked very much as if Kissinger had cheated on the deal. The only payoff from Washington had been the granting (in August) of a R151 million standby credit from the IMF. It was not a great deal for which to be grateful. Whatever honeyed words the Secretary of State might have had for Pretoria's financial plight, William Simon, his cabinet colleague, seemed to be waging an economic war against South Africa as relentlessly as ever. But it was worse than that. As early as 23 May the Johannesburg *Sunday Times* had commented that the government was finding 'all long-term capital markets effectively closed to them'. Graham Hatton, editor of the Johannesburg *Financial Mail*, later put it more succinctly:

In the run-up to the crucial Kissinger—Vorster—Smith meetings in Pretoria (South Africans) suddenly found the money taps of America and Europe inexplicably being turned off. Although it has never been officially confirmed, the firm belief here is that the American State Department was at work behind the scenes.[2]

South Africa, in other words, was being squeezed at both ends. Washington manipulated the gold price against her and then, when Pretoria went in search of loans, manipulated the credit

[1] Until 1973 US policy in the Middle East consisted of public support and aid for Israel combined with indirect aid channelled to the oil-rich Arab states by means of the US oil companies' pricing and tax policies. Not for the first or last time the world balance was worked out via a series of battles between US government departments — Justice (which wanted to attack the oil cartel's price-fixing and profiteering) fighting State (which wanted to leave well alone). The State Department won then, as it seems also to have done in 1976. See A. Sampson, *The Seven Sisters. The Great Oil Companies and the World they Made* (London, 1976), especially pp. 137—40.
[2] *Financial Times*, 8 March, 1977.

market against her. The more Washington squeezed Pretoria, the
more Pretoria squeezed Salisbury. It was an operation to delight
the stock exchange gambler or the good bridge player but it
brought little joy for either Vorster or Smith.

This double squeeze reached its peak in August, Vorster
walking out ever further along his tightrope as the pressure was
turned higher and higher. Not to put too fine a gloss on it, it
seems certain that Vorster was double-crossed in and after the
Bavaria meeting. He had done all that had been asked of
him — and had been rewarded with increasing, not decreasing,
pressure from Washington. But, of course, the harder
Washington squeezed, the more desperate Pretoria's position
became. And the weaker South Africa was, the more she needed
American help. Thus, the fundamental principle of leverage: the
more it was used, the greater it became. July and August 1976
must have been long months indeed in Pretoria. There was
nothing much that the government could do, although the
situation was deteriorating rapidly on all sides (Vorster went off
sight-seeing in the Kruger National Park at this point). Diplomatic contacts with Washington continued,[1] but the simple fact
was that nothing important could happen unless and until Ford
had defeated Reagan and won the Republican nomination.

The decision remained in doubt to the end. Ford had
truckled more and more defensively to the right, and entered
the convention on a thoroughly defensive note. Detente had
become a dirty word to the delegates who assembled in Kansas
City in mid-August, and the President had to accept without
demur a resolution roundly condemning Kissinger's foreign
policies. In the end, though, Ford's willingness to trim his sails,
allied to the enormous advantages of power and prestige
enjoyed by any sitting president, were just enough. In the early
hours of 19 August Ford won through.

At last Kissinger could go ahead. There was no time to
lose — the presidential election (2 November) was only ten
weeks away. A second meeting with Vorster was arranged for 4
September in Zurich. The venue was symbolic enough, for it
was on the Zurich gold market that South Africa's economic
life-blood was at that moment ebbing away.

---

[1] It is worth mentioning that in addition to the ceaseless efforts of her
ambassador in Washington, Pretoria also had two other key actors in the
detente exercise in North America in July — Connie Mulder, the Information Minister, and General Van den Bergh, head of BOSS, were
watching the Montreal Olympics in Montreal. If necessary they could,
presumably, combine diplomacy and sportsmanship.

11   Payoffs and Sequels

With the defeat of Reagan the political axis of Kissinger's strategy shifted sharply. Hitherto he had needed to look to the Administration's right flank; now he needed to look to the left. Ford had entered the election campaign with a predictable body of conservative support which increased as the disgruntled Reaganites trickled across to him, but he was still far behind Carter in the polls. To stand any chance he needed to woo centre and liberal ground and to broaden his appeal away from WASPs and the mid-West to the big-city states of the north-east and the ethnic minorities. Kissinger could contribute very materially to Ford's uphill struggle if he could bring off a major diplomatic coup before the election.

Kissinger had, of course, provided just such a service for Nixon in 1972. Nixon had been elected on a promise of ending the Vietnam War. This, after four years, he had failed to do — in fact he had invaded Cambodia and widened the war. In September 1972 the USAF B-52s had been ordered in to pound Hanoi as never before, razing the city's centre for the first time. There was no military justification for this bombing campaign, though it did claim a fearful toll in civilian casualties. The point was, rather, that Kissinger needed to convince American public opinion of his hawkish ferocity, for he was about to make a major concession to North Vietnam which he wanted to hide; to pretend, indeed, that it was the North Vietnamese who were making the concessions. On 8 October Kissinger met with the North Vietnamese representatives in Paris and agreed *that day* to end the bombing, to a cease-fire in South Vietnam and to the complete withdrawal of US troops. It was hardly surprising that agreement was so easy to reach, for the North Vietnamese would have been only too happy to accept such 'terms' at any time from 1965 on. The agreement was kept secret until 26 October, when it was announced just in time to have maximum impact for the presidential election (7 November) — time for the good news really to sink in but not long enough for too many awkward questions to arise. The added subtlety of the agreement was that the cease-fire was set for 28 January 1973 and the US withdrawal deadline for 60 days after that. In other words, American voters could both be presented with a diplomatic 'triumph' — and the fear that failure to re-elect Nixon (and, with him, Kissinger) might jeopardise the crucial developments set for just after the election. As soon as the election was over the B-52s were ordered back into the heaviest bombing campaign of the whole war — allegedly to discourage the North from moving war material into the South before the cease-fire, but in reality to remove any American suspicion that Kissinger and Nixon were acting in anything other than the most hawkishly firm and high-principled way. In fact the saturation bombing itself gave the lie to the idea that the North Vietnamese had made some hard-won and real concession; had they done so, the bombing would doubtless have encouraged them to call it off. As it was the USAF could pound away with impunity since Kissinger was secure in the knowledge that the terms he had offered to Hanoi were a bargain for them under *any* circumstances. It was Hanoi that had stuck to its guns — it had always refused all notion of a cease-fire unless it was accompanied by a complete US withdrawal. Kissinger had refused such terms for four years of ruthless warfare — and then given them away in (literally) one day. Nixon had, of course, won by a landslide as he was doubtless going to do anyway. His Administration, however, was not one to fear the possibility of 'overkill' — as Watergate, too, was to show.

Now, in 1976, Kissinger was intent on a not dissimilar diplomatic coup. At some point comfortably before the election (when there would still be time for it to influence the uneasily shifting electoral middle ground) Smith must be made — or at least *seem* to be made — to come to Canossa, to renounce white supremacist rule. This would be coup enough — the British, the Africans, the South Africans had, after all, all tried and failed to achieve this much. The myth of Kissinger's legendary efficacy would be restored; black voters and liberals would be impressed; the good name of detente would be saved; and, just possibly, American voters would be marginally swayed into giving another four years to an Administration which, though reassuringly boring and conservative, was nonetheless highly competent in its foreign policy. Smith could be brought, a barbarian chief in Kissinger's Roman triumph, to a conference to implement majority rule. Preferably (following the Vietnam (1972) model) such a conference should start, in a blaze of publicity, just before the election. But its success should be left hanging, to be concluded only when the voters had decided they could not afford to sabotage it by refusing the Administration a vote of confidence.

Nothing, of course, could have the same impact Vietnam had had in 1972, but there weren't any other Vietnams around. In order to get the maximum mileage out of Rhodesia Kissinger (and Ford) would need to play up to the full their commitment to racial justice — indeed, they would almost apologise for the regrettable necessity of having to talk to racists like Smith and Vorster in order to achieve their noble object.

This new slant was apparent immediately after the Republican convention. Before meeting Vorster in Zurich Kissinger chose to make a major address on 31 August to a mainly black student audience in Philadelphia in which he stressed his principled abhorrence of apartheid. He pointed out, with a pride he had been careful not to display while the Reagan threat had been alive, that since his Bavaria talks South Africa had come out openly for majority rule in Rhodesia, had promised to decolonise Namibia, and had invited SWAPO to join the Turnhalle talks. Ford joined in, making a proud speech on 8 September about his Administration's contribution to peace in southern Africa by its resistance to Soviet and Cuban intervention. For Kissinger soon was loud in his hawkish denunciation of the Russians who, he alleged, were attempting to torpedo all hope of peace in Rhodesia. The more deeply he prepared to plunge into southern African affairs himself, the more he threatened a Great Power confrontation if the Russians dared to do the same; it was a (normal) virtuoso Kissinger performance — the good doctor, calmly intent on bringing peace and racial justice, standing up with righteous wrath to the Russians who wished evilly to subvert this high-minded and statesman-like mission.

(i) From Zurich to Pretoria

Vorster, as we have seen, had little reason for gratitude to Kissinger as he prepared for the Zurich talks on 4—6 September. Since the Bavaria talks South Africa had had a hideous three months: in the gold market; seeking fruitlessly for foreign loans; and over Soweto. Kissinger had set up the talks for Saturday, Sunday and Monday — and then, on the previous Tuesday, in his Philadelphia speech, had made it clear that it was some sort of diplomatic leper he was going to meet in Zurich. (He had described apartheid as 'incompatible with any concept of human dignity'.) When news of the Philadelphia speech came through Vorster reacted furiously, refusing to meet at all on the Sunday since he wished 'to observe the sabbath'. Kissinger was equal to such sulks. The State Department let it be known that although South African diplomats had, until the Tuesday, collaborated fully in the arrangement of the programme for Sunday talks, it quite understood that Vorster was 'a deeply religious man'. As for the Secretary of State, well he too was a pious man and good Jewish son; he would probably use the vacant Sunday to go and visit his mother (who lives in Germany). . . . Kissinger could afford to ignore such tantrums. After all, the Secretary of State had merely to go before the Senate sub-committee hearing on the impending loan to South Africa and advise against it for Vorster to be reduced to penury. Or suggest to his colleague, William Simon, that it was time for another US Treasury gold auction. He was holding not one, but a fistful of aces.

The Zurich talks duly took place, cloaked in secrecy. (In the end talks were held on the Sunday — 'informally'.) In some respects this secrecy was more apparent than real, for there was little doubt that Kissinger's attention was fixed upon majority rule in Rhodesia and Namibian decolonisation — press observers were unanimous that only the most cursory attention was given to South African domestic issues. Press leaks on the South African side suggested variously that at least among Vorster's demands had been (a) the use of US influence to support the price of gold and industrial diamonds; (b) the use of the Simonstown base by the US navy; (c) US support to guarantee South African arms and oil supplies; and (d) the use of the US Security Council veto to protect South Africa from hostile moves at the UN. Other reports suggest that these were all items *offered* by Kissinger, not demanded by Vorster. In one sense such a list is not very useful, since there is no indication of the items on which deals were actually struck. Moreover, whether secret treaties were signed in relation to oil supplies will become clear only in the eventuality of an oil-boycott against South Africa; it is also too soon (1977) to know whether arms supplies or US navy movements were affected (though, as we have seen, the aircraft carrier *Guam* and a force of several destroyers were cruising in the Indian Ocean off the east African coast by December 1976). What does seem all but certain (as we shall see) is that a deal was done over the gold price, over foreign loans and over the US veto in the Security Council. In November 1976 the US joined Britain and France in opposing the 'Programme of Action Against Apartheid' supported by 105 members of the UN General Assembly.[1]

The talks pointed clearly towards an immediate Rhodesian settlement. During the talks Vorster announced publicly that South Africa did indeed accept the principle of majority rule in Rhodesia (removing any remaining ambiguity caused by the two versions of Muller's 9 August speech). Smith fumed in Salisbury over the iniquity of Rhodesia's future being settled over his head, and vehemently and repeatedly insisted that Kissinger would, finally, have to deal with him. As soon as Vorster returned home Smith hurried down to Cape Town to see him. He emerged clearly reassured that Vorster too was anxious that any ultimate deal should be between Washington and Salisbury. Even in Zurich Vorster had insisted that he would put no pressure on Smith. If such a stance were to remain even minimally credible in the eyes of Vorster's *verkrampte* opponents, it was obviously essential to Vorster to appear no more than a diplomatic go-between between Smith and Kissinger. Smith also made it plain yet again (11 September) that he would have no truck with majority rule which meant, he said, counting hands 'in the same way as counting sheep'.

Kissinger, meanwhile, prepared to set off on his culminating African shuttle, the objective towards which he had been building all year. He first went through at least a show of consulting all the major Western powers — he had flown to have breakfast with Giscard immediately after concluding the Zurich talks, saw Chancellor Schmidt of Germany, and held lengthy consultations with the British. The main practical point involved appears to have been the gaining of general Western support both for the initiative and for the main carrot he was to put in front of Smith: the promise of a large financial package to tide Rhodesia through the first rough waters of majority rule. Otherwise, although he exuded a smiling, even ebullient, impression of confidence, he kept his cards extremely close to his chest. His very air of confidence seems to have affronted the British Foreign Office, which bore the scars of so many abortive

[1] The Programme called for the the rupture of all diplomatic relations with Pretoria; an oil and arms boycott; the end to nuclear collaboration with her; the suspension of all loans, investments, and technical assistance; the refusal of all landing and passage rights to South African aircraft; and the closing of all ports to South African vessels. Much though Pretoria despised the UN she was, not surprisingly, alarmed by the support of two-thirds of all UN members for such proposals.

negotiations with Smith. The British, ever prone to see themselves as savant Greeks to the Americans' muscular Romans, were extremely sceptical of the whole initiative. Publicly, of course, they gave it their blessing, though they warned Kissinger, from the bitter depths of their own experience, against underestimating the endless wiles of Smith. Privately — as a series of press leaks made plain — they thought Kissinger was rushing in where angels had already mistakenly trodden.

When, a fortnight later, Smith caved in, there were complaints that, for all Kissinger's consultations, the Foreign Office had very little idea of what he was actually doing. In fact the FO, for all its vaunted experience, its be-knighted mandarins, and its old Africa hands, was hopelessly and publicly outclassed by Kissinger. In particular, the FO seems never to have realised that the Secretary of State was not going merely to dangle carrots in front of Smith. He was walking softly but he was carrying any number of very large sticks. He had every reason for confidence, in fact.

Kissinger set off for Africa with a final declaration that a peaceful solution in Rhodesia was the only alternative to the 'almost complete radicalisation of the entire continent'. He called first on Nyerere who, a week before, had played host to the 'front-line' African presidents' conference which had announced armed struggle to be the only way ahead in Rhodesia. Kissinger needed to ensure that Nyerere did not actually mean this to the point where he would disapprove of a successful peace settlement. Nyerere assured him that, dubious as he was of Kissinger's chances of success, if the US could bring majority rule to Rhodesia, well and good. Kissinger also realised that he would probably need to see Smith, and assured Nyerere that 'If you hear I have seen Smith, it is because Vorster assures me that Smith accepts this thing.' (This was, of course, untrue: if he saw Smith it would be because Vorster was unwilling to give any such commitment on his own, over Smith's head.) Kissinger flew on to Lusaka for a fairly predictable scene with Kaunda, an even more reluctant warrior. At a public rally Kaunda declared boldly that 'If your mission fails, we fight' — and then broke into tears. This was not unusual — Kaunda's political career has been marked by not a few displays of lachrymosity, in public at least. On 17 September Kissinger flew on to Pretoria.

(ii) Finessing Smith

Kissinger spent two days locked in talks with Vorster — a long time, given the fact that the two men had negotiated for

several days on end less than a fortnight before. By the evening
of 19 September Kissinger was ready for Smith — who was only
too eager to come. By this stage Kissinger was able to present
Smith with an ultimatum jointly drawn up by Vorster and
himself, though Vorster was careful not to be in at the
kill — the talks took place in the US Embassy. The ultimatum
took the form of a 5-point programme for Smith to sign.

Smith read aloud the first point: 'Rhodesia agrees to majority
rule within two years' — and commented bitterly that 'you
want me to sign my own suicide note'. It was little comfort
that the package deal provided for a large financial trust to
be set up by the Western powers to help tide them over to
majority rule. It also allowed for an interim government equally
composed of black and white, though with a black premier and
a majority of cabinet portfolios for blacks. Smith's response
was to insist that the defence and police portfolios should
remain in white hands. Kissinger promised to clear this point
with the front-line presidents but, on returning via Dar-es-
Salaam found Nyerere resistant. He cabled Smith accordingly
but then, as he left for the US, followed this with a second
cable saying that the front-line presidents accepted the 5-point
programme. This was not quite an answer: Pretoria and
Salisbury concluded that the front-line presidents agreed about
the two crucial portfolios, though in fact they had not. This still
left Smith with little option: unless he agreed, he was told,
South Africa could guarantee neither arms supplies nor oil. The
Rhodesian Minister of Finance had admitted (to Rhodesian
Front backbenchers) that the country was 'bust', without
foreign exchange, without even any money with which to
replace basic industrial equipment, let alone buy arms. Given
the fresh threats brought to bear by Kissinger, Smith was left in
no doubt that Rhodesia would last less than three months
unless he agreed to make the 5-point announcement. On 24
September he duly made the announcement over Rhodesian
television. A conference to work out the modalities of the
interim regime was to be held in Geneva, commencing on 28
October.

Smith's statement of 24 September was, predictably, a
world-wide sensation. For the first time in recorded history the
leader of an avowedly white supremacist government had stood
up publicly to announce his acceptance of (black) majority rule.
The month that followed 24 September saw a confused welter
of events. Smith made it clear that with a 50—50 black—white
split in the interim government (and no casting vote) plus the
retention of the all-important police and army powers by the

whites, there was no reason to believe that the ultimate
transition to majority rule was such an alarming perspective. If
the blacks could not make the prospect sufficiently attractive to
the whites, after all, the latter would have a 50% blocking
vote — and they would still have the guns. For precisely these
reasons the agreement was denounced by the Zimbabwe
nationalists and the front-line presidents. Smith made it clear
that in his eyes the Kissinger package was not negotiable.
Vorster agreed. Meanwhile, one of the black nationalist leaders,
Bishop Muzorewa, returned to Salisbury to a hero's welcome
from 100,000 blacks. It was a tellingly successful opening bid
for political leadership of the future Zimbabwe. It also
thoroughly alarmed the other nationalist leaders, particularly
Nkomo. Hitherto the most conservative of the African leaders
(in Smith's terms, the most 'responsible'), Nkomo lost all
appetite for elections at the sight of Muzorewa's large popular
support, and threw his lot in with the guerrillas.

Two things stood out amidst the confusion. The first of these
was the brutal force of the pressures put on Smith by Vorster.
The best account of these pressures is to be found in the
memorandum of the speech to a Rhodesian white audience on 7
October by Ted Sutton Price, a Deputy Minister in Salisbury.[1]
The memorandum is sufficiently revealing for comment upon it
to be superfluous, and it is worth complete citation:

> The Rhodesian Front do not agree that Dr. Kissinger's
> solution to Rhodesia's problems is the best.
> The communist influence in Africa is growing and America
> is worried about the saddle formed across Africa. America
> must react or lose by default. South Africa and Rhodesia are
> the plums of Africa ... raw materials, Cape sea route,
> development. America cannot support Rhodesia with a
> white minority government because of world opinion. If
> there were an acceptable government in Rhodesia, America
> would support this country with everything to combat
> communism except troops.

[1] There is no reason to doubt the authenticity of the memo, which was
released to the press in Geneva on 31 October, shortly after the conference
there had begun. Sutton Price had been among the Rhodesian Front
caucus to whom Smith reported on his talks in Pretoria. Neither Smith nor
Sutton Price made any move to deny the memo's authenticity. Pretoria
made no comment and nor, of course, did Kissinger. The text of the
memorandum above is as it appeared in the *Financial Times* (London)
1 November, 1976.

Vorster is the bad guy. The reason for the R.F. failure was because of pressure put on Rhodesia.

U.S.$60m. exports are in the pipeline rising to $100m. by December. Without these exports moving, the government could not support an agricultural crop next year.

Fifty per cent. of the Rhodesian defence bill was paid by South Africa up until June. A reply has not been given since then as to whether they would support it for a further year. There has been a delay on war items for as long as 2½ years.

The railway system is moving very few goods — reported congestion. The border was closed over the period of the Kissinger talks 1—4 days. Fuel supply down to 19.6 days. It is difficult to prove these facts as we cannot afford to antagonise South Africa by exposing her. The Prime Minister has considered appealing to the South African public over Vorster's head, but did not have enough time.

Against this background they had no alternative but to accept the Kissinger package deal.

Saying no would have meant fighting a rearguard action to Beit Bridge (the border with South Africa). They had done the responsible thing in accepting the deal.

Kissinger deal: set up an interim government and would have two years to sort out the constitution, after which majority rule. Not seen as one man one vote. America understands the problem better than the U.K.

Parliament would go into recess and not be dissolved. If the agreed constitution was not liked after two years, parliament could reject it.

At worst we would be in a better position to fight the war than at present. We would have . . . two years' trading on an open market. Revive the economy with the two billion development fund. Two years to build up arms and war materials and the armed forces. The market for recruiting into the forces would be widened.

R.F. still stands for equal opportunity for all races, civilised standards, stable government, permanent homes and maintenance of law and order. Two billion development fund set up to try to keep the whites here, on a sliding scale.

The second point to emerge is the limited nature of Kissinger's objectives. Essentially, he wanted two things: a *public* declaration by Smith in favour of majority rule, and a conference to take place just before the US presidential election. He got both. Smith's declaration had to be public. A secret commitment would have meant nothing — he could always have

reneged on it; a public commitment on the broad principle
would impress the front-line presidents more than any amount
of detail; and — of course — it would give Kissinger the diplomatic triumph he needed for the election. The details of the
agreement or 'package' were only important if differences over
them actually threatened the calling into session of the conference. This latter had to take place; it had to have a British
chairman (where would Kissinger be if he was chairing the
conference and then Ford lost the election? That would be a
thankless task for anyone — as Ivor Richard was to discover);
and it had to open with maximum publicity in the week before
2 November (the election). Kissinger intervened in the public
wrangling over what exactly his 'package' had contained only to
say that 'I think everyone is telling the truth' (which was
impossible). Otherwise he used his assistant, William Schaufele,
and the still largely uncomprehending British to maintain a
constant (and politically eye-catching) diplomatic shuttle round
Africa during October to ensure that the conference did indeed
take place.

The trust fund envisaged for Rhodesia, on which much
attention was lavished by the press, always remained extremely
vague and it seems certain that it never, in a proper sense,
existed at all. Kissinger had seen Western leaders before his tour
and later implied their agreement to participation in the $2
billion deal. But they severally let it be known that they had
made no firm commitments at all towards such a fund. The
Japanese made it indignantly clear that they had no intention of
contributing to it. The British said they could clearly not be
expected to find any money — after all, they were begging the
IMF for loans at the time. The French and Germans said
nothing and nobody could dream of asking the Italians. By late
September State Department officials still found it 'impossible
to calculate the total sum involved'; it was hinted that it might
exist as a possible source of credit only, to be drawn on only in
emergency; that Australia and Canada might make money
available (news which must have startled Canberra and Ottawa,
capitals which had not been on Kissinger's shuttle route); and,
finally, that 'much of it might come from private investment
sources'. Fairly clearly private investors were conjured up at this
point only in order to avoid admitting that governments, at
least, were refusing to foot the bill. How businessmen were to
make a profit out of providing charity to affluent Rhodesian
whites remained unexplained. It had been the same in 1972 —
Kissinger had attempted to buy permanent compliance from the
North Vietnamese with promises of huge US aid whose amount

never became specific, which never materialised, was never voted by Congress (or even proposed to it) ... which, indeed, never existed. In 1976 Kissinger paid even less for Smith: he got Vorster to exert the necessary pressure, threatened Smith with the apocalypse — that all material support would be withdrawn just as the rainy season guerrilla offensive began — and offered him, in the American phrase, 'pie in the sky'. Provided Smith made his irreversible public statement, and provided he and the black nationalists came to the conference (Kissinger could afford not to consult *them* — how could they afford to stay away?), that would be enough. If Ford won, then Kissinger could descend on Geneva armed with more threats, more promises, more deals.

(iii) Namibia — and Angola

The 'secret diplomacy' of Rhodesia was carried through in a blaze of electorally useful publicity. The secret diplomacy of Namibia, however, was a good deal more secret. In Zurich Vorster had conceded a small but important piece of ground by declaring that the Turnhalle Convention was at liberty to invite SWAPO to attend its deliberations — 'I will accept it, even if I don't like it'. Asked whether he would break his commitment not to negotiate with SWAPO directly himself (as the UN wanted him to do), he implied that he too might be invited to Turnhalle and thus find himself sitting down with SWAPO. The offer posed a considerable dilemma for SWAPO. The Turnhalle talks were certainly not what the UN or SWAPO wanted. The conference was organised in terms of representation of the territory's eleven ethnic groups, with no attempt at numerical proportionality. Thus the 65,000 Hereros, for example, were represented by 44 delegates under the conservative chief Clemens Kapuuo, while the 396,000 Ovambos (who made up over 46% of the territory's total (1974) population of 852,000) had fifteen delegates. From the beginning Pretoria's tactic had been to play on the minority tribes' fear of the dominant Ovambos and to build up Kapuuo as a future Bantustan-style leader.

SWAPO's strength was that it was very much *the* Ovambo party — no-one seriously disputed its popular dominance in Ovamboland. But the movement was, by September 1976, a thing of shreds and tatters. Its (legal) internal wing, a fairly conservative body, heavily influenced by Lutheran and Anglican churchmen, was only too conscious of the overwhelming strength of white power, and was visibly tempted by the prospect of taking the opening presented to them by Vorster.

The SWAPO founder and leader-in-exile, Sam Nujoma, would have nothing to do with such compromise. There was, however, a considerable distance between Nujoma's marxist vocabulary and the strongly Christian cast of the internal SWAPO wing, and the movement held together largely out of ethnic solidarity and a common hatred of Pretoria.

Since late 1975, moreover, even the external (guerrilla) wing of SWAPO had been racked by a major split. A large section of the leadership had launched a bitter attack against Nujoma for refusing to call a party congress (the last had been in 1969). Among the allegations they wished to ventilate at such a congress were their claims that the leadership had connived in Zambian support of UNITA; that arms meant for SWAPO had been diverted by Kaunda towards UNITA; that SWAPO forces had actually been ordered to fight alongside UNITA and the invading South African columns in Angola; that the guerrilla movement was deprived of all modern arms, medicine and even food; and that the movement's leadership was riddled by corruption and inefficiency. It was certainly true that Nujoma had been in alliance with Savimbi's UNITA for several years, but at least by the later stages he had thrown his lot in with the victorious MPLA and their Cuban backers. By mid-1976 he was being received with great *éclat* by the Russians in Moscow. He alleged, grotesquely, that the dissidents were all South African agents planted in SWAPO.

The SWAPO dissidents had annoyed Kaunda as well as Nujoma. Kaunda was embarrassed not merely by their allegations regarding Zambian arms diversions but by their general hostility to his detente policies. As a further round of detente diplomacy got under way in 1976 Kaunda pounced on the SWAPO dissidents just as he had pounced on their ZANU counterparts in 1975. At the end of April 1976 — precisely as Kissinger's plane touched down in Lusaka — the Zambian police detained eleven top SWAPO leaders and a large number of lower-level militants. Their leader, Andreas Shipanga, took his case to the Zambian Supreme Court. Five days before the hearing the eleven leaders were bundled on to a plane to Tanzania where they were consigned, without charge, to the ill-reputed Ukonga jail. Meanwhile, around 1,000 SWAPO guerrillas were kept under armed Zambian guard in a prison camp. An attempted break-out by the starving prisoners in August saw Zambian soldiers fire upon them, killing several. Nujoma, meanwhile, strengthened his links with the Angolan regime and the Soviet bloc, and began to give increasingly radical and marxist speeches. Of the dissidents he declared that

they were all guilty of high treason; that there was no need for
their open trial; and that the only suitable punishment would be
death by firing squad.

This dramatic weakening of SWAPO created a major opening
for Vorster — and Kissinger. For South Africa and the US had
very much the same aims in Namibia. Despite its miniscule
population Namibia is an important country. Its long coastline
gives it a strategic position on the Atlantic; it is rich in copper,
uranium, diamonds and, quite possibly, oil. Neither Pretoria nor
Washington had the slightest wish to see such a prize fall under
a radical — let alone a Cuban-backed — regime. Both, accordingly, wished to avert such a possibility by decolonisation and
the devolution of power to a safely conservative regime. The
problem was that it would be difficult to achieve any stable or
externally respectable settlement which altogether excluded the
dominant Ovambos or their political arm, SWAPO. The
question was simply whether Kissinger could get Vorster to give
enough ground to provide a prospect sufficiently tempting to
force Nujoma — or at least SWAPO's internal wing — to collab-
orate in such a settlement.

Returning from Pretoria, Kissinger immediately held
audience with Nujoma, presumably in order to exert pressure
upon him to forsake his Soviet and Cuban backers for the more
tangible plums of a share in the administration of a future
Namibian state. Emerging from the talks Kissinger announced
that he was extremely hopeful that a conference under UN
auspices, to include both Pretoria and SWAPO, could be called
by the end of October. On 9 October he followed this up by
announcing that discussions were in progress to arrange such a
conference at a neutral venue at which South Africa, Botswana,
Angola, Zambia and SWAPO would all participate. The conference, he said, might well be convened within three weeks. Three
weeks from 9 October would be 30 October — three days
before the US presidential election.... Nothing further was
heard of this proposal, though it did at least have the merit of
defusing the UN debate on Namibia on 18 October, where the
US was under considerable (and electorally embarrassing) pressure over its defence of South Africa.

There is considerable evidence to suggest that Kissinger and
Vorster were planning something rather more ambitious than a
conference for Namibia. The UN Commissioner for Namibia,
Sean MacBride, had denounced the original Turnhalle
announcement of an independence schedule in August 1976,
and had warned openly that the US might be conniving with
Pretoria in plans to set up a puppet administration. MacBride

also commissioned a study of the South African Defence Force presence in Namibia. The report, released on 31 August, accused the 12,800 SADF soldiers then in Namibia of having forcibly removed 40,000—50,000 Africans from a long strip along the Angolan border, using torture, beatings and 'conduct amounting very closely to genocide' to achieve their ends. MacBride's warnings were lent support by two US AID (Agency for International Development) documents leaked to the press in Washington in mid-November. The two documents, one dated 21 September, the other 31 October, spelled out a massive programme of US aid and investment for Namibia; Namibia itself was envisaged as independent under a conservative, pro-Western government with a black army to be financed and trained by the US. The *Sunday Times* (London), which published a fairly full account of these documents, also drew attention to

> ... the crowd of more-or-less freelance operators who, as power approaches, are clustering around Chief Kapuuo. A motley collection of international hustlers, Park Avenue marketing men, mining entrepreneurs and New York lawyers are all busily assisting the emergence of a Kapuuo government. (*Sunday Times* (London), 21 Nov. 1976.)

The *Sunday Times* report went on to document the large 'marketing' effort being mounted in the US to project Kapuuo as a statesmanlike leader of the future Namibia.[1]

US AID, the source of the leaked documents, had a long history of involvement in rather dubious adventures at the behest of the State Department, of which it is a branch. (In Vietnam, for example, it once financed a Pepsi-Cola plant which was used as a cover for a heroin-processing factory.) There is certainly no reason to doubt the authenticity of the leaked

[1] Particularly active, according to the *Sunday Times*, was James Endycott (real name Nemeth Gyorgy) who had reportedly worked for the (CIA-funded) Radio Free Europe and was employed in Namibia by the US mining company, Gemstone Miners and, by his own admission, was also working in intelligence for an (unspecified) government. Endycott had been Kapuuo's contact man both with Arthur Burns, head of the New York law firm, Burns and Jacoby, which acted for Kapuuo, and with Jack Summers, head of Psychographic Communications Inc., which 'marketed' Kapuuo. Interestingly, both these concerns claimed to be working for Kapuuo without taking any fees. Endycott had also garnered support for Kapuuo from Alan Manus, a millionaire-speculator with a controlling share in Kaakoveld Land und Minen Gesellschaft, which has a claim to mineral rights for a whole one-sixth of Namibia (25 million acres).

Namibian documents (the State Department made no attempt
to deny it). The dating of the documents suggests that it would
be wrong to relate them to the Vorster—Kissinger meeting in
Pretoria (17—18 September) and that the initiative they envisage was probably conceived in the Zurich talks (4—6
September) or even earlier. The question left hanging is when
and how it was proposed to launch the programme.

Namibian independence (projected for December 1978)
would be too late a date: the infrastructure of the new state
would have to be ready well before then if a Kapuuo government was not to have start its life by calling in the SADF to put
down the inevitable SWAPO uprising in Ovamboland. The
documents themselves speak of a 'rush programme' and it seems
likely that early 1977 would have been the latest desirable date
if a future Kapuuo government was to have much of a chance.
Once the US presidential election was out of the way, in fact.

This picture was lent a further dimension by a fresh bombshell
delivered by the UN Commissioner, MacBride, on 10 December.
In his 31 August report MacBride had put SADF strength in
Namibia at 12,800 men. Now, however, he alleged that in the
intervening months this force had been rapidly built up to
50,000; that the troops were equipped with 'hundreds of
armoured cars', tanks, artillery and helicopters; and that this
force was poised for a fresh invasion of Angola from the Caprivi
Strip in mid-January, 1977. According to MacBride the
rationale for such an invasion would be provided by the claim
that the MPLA was aiding SWAPO guerrillas. MacBride linked
the invasion plan with the construction of three new air-bases in
Rhodesia and claimed to have evidence of Salisbury—Pretoria
collaboration in such a plan.

MacBride's charges had to be treated with the greatest
seriousness. The source was unimpeachable — MacBride was a
Nobel Peace Prize winner and not a man influenced by career
considerations (he was 73 in January 1977). Pretoria made no
effort to deny the estimate of 50,000 SADF soldiers in Namibia
and the Defence Minister, Piet Botha, issued only what *The
Times* called a 'somewhat muted denial ... there was some
surprise in diplomatic circles here (in South Africa) that Mr.
Botha failed to react more strongly'.[1] The Angolan regime, for
its part, fully backed up MacBride's story and claimed to have
evidence of its own pointing in the same direction. There was
also no doubt that three secret military airports were, from
October 1976 on, under rapid construction in Rhodesia — by

---

[1] *The Times* (London), 11 Dec. 1976

mid-October a Danish television crew had actually succeeded in filming one of them.

MacBride was due to retire from his position in December 1976 and submitted a lengthy annual report on doing so, in which he complained bitterly that his work had been increasingly blocked by the negative attitude and limitations imposed upon him by the UN Council on Namibia. Several members of the Council, he alleged — it was clear the Americans were meant — had no wish to see the UN play an active role in Namibia. The UN Council refused to publish his report. The State Department made no secret of its hostility to MacBride and its pleasure at his retirement. His successor, the UN Council decided, should enjoy only a one-year term of office (MacBride had had three years and been irremovable). MacBride had ruffled more feathers than anyone since his distinguished compatriot and UN predecessor in southern Africa, Conor Cruise O'Brien.

Several points should be made in connection with MacBride's allegations. First, it was quite inconceivable that a force of 50,000 men, particularly men armed in the way MacBride described, could be employed in fighting SWAPO. A 50,000 SADF force meant one soldier for every eight Ovambos — men, women and children included. SWAPO was a small, weak organisation; its guerrilla activities had never been more than occasional and sporadic, and had consisted mainly in the laying of mines. Moreover, as we have seen, it had been further weakened in 1976 — a good part of its leadership was under lock and key in Tanzania, and over 1,000 of its guerrilla fighters were being guarded and, as necessary, shot at, in Zambia. Everything *does* point to a planned second invasion of Angola. Secondly, it is quite certain that no such invasion could have been planned, let alone prepared so fully, save through the strong support and encouragement of the US. South Africa had gone into Angola in 1975 against her better judgment and at America's behest. It was quite inconceivable that she would launch a much bigger invasion against a fully independent state, now able to rely on 10,000 regular Cuban troops[1] and strong Soviet support, without Kissinger having not merely agreed to such an initiative but having demanded and guaranteed it. Thirdly, Rhodesia herself was in no military, logistic or even

---

[1] Most estimates suggest that Cuban forces reached a peak of 12,000–13,000 in early 1976. According to *Le Monde* (11 January, 1977) Castro and Neto agreed on a programme of troop withdrawals as early as 14 March, 1976, and the first 3,000 Cubans had already left by May 1976.

economic position to carry out an emergency construction programme for three airports which bore no relation to the war against the Zimbabwe guerrillas. She had at least to have outside help for such a project and, probably, it would have to be an outside operation altogether. Pretoria may seem the obvious outside candidate, but strong and persistent rumour inside Rhodesia had it that the CIA was the party involved in the construction of the airports.

These reports of a planned second invasion of Angola by South African forces have to be read in conjunction with developments inside Angola during 1976. As we have seen, the last South African forces withdrew into Namibia in March and by 1 April MPLA—Cuban forces (which seem to have held back in order to avoid a clash with the retreating South Africans) finally reached the Namibian border. Savimbi, the UNITA leader, had pleaded for Pretoria to stay on but was left to his own resources. Nothing more was heard of UNITA until early August, when reports from Johannesburg suddenly announced that a major UNITA offensive against MPLA forces was in progress; that UNITA now possessed an army of 15,000 troops and was winning; and that UNITA's amazing new accession of strength helped account for a remarkably high 'kill rate' recently achieved by SADF forces against SWAPO. This was astonishing news, if true. The *Daily Telegraph* commented that

> It is not clear how UNITA is managing to keep going in southern Angola but it is believed it is fighting literally on its feet led by the charismatic Dr. Savimbi. . . . Mercenary organisations are watching their performance closely and there is a strong suggestion that if UNITA can maintain its offensive a well-organised mercenary-backed offensive could get under way by September.[1]

Such reports could mean only one of two things: either Savimbi was receiving massive South African support — charisma does not feed, arm or train 15,000 troops, a force which Savimbi certainly did not have in early 1976; or the purpose of the reports was simply to build up Savimbi — who was 'in the vanguard of continuous attacks on MPLA positions' — as a heroic figure. How he could have re-asserted such military strength when he had felt helpless without South African assistance only months before and had been entirely unable to

[1] *Daily Telegraph* (London), 4 August, 1976.

offer any resistance to the advancing MPLA in March—April went unexplained.

At the same time (early August) there was a recrudescence of military activity on Angola's northern border. Mobutu and Neto had signed a pact of reconciliation in later February, and Zaire announced that it had ceased to allow FNLA or FLEC to remain in Zaire. In August, however, both FLEC and FLNA made their reappearance in Kinshasa; Mobutu again spoke in favour of the cause of Cabindan autonomy; and small FLNA incursions into Angola were reported. Relations between Zaire and Angola deteriorated dramatically, while those between Zaire and South Africa improved to the point where Pretoria not only emerged as a main provider of Kinshasa's food supplies but had administrative, technical and medical teams in the Zairean capital as well.

From September—October on, there was a constant flow of reports in the Western press describing the new UNITA effort in glowing terms and extolling Savimbi as a promising and 'anti-marxist' leader. These reports tended to originate either from South Africa or from interviews granted to newsmen by UNITA's 'Foreign Minister', Dr Jorge Sangumba, from his suite in the Intercontinental Hotel in Lusaka. Meanwhile the FNLA leader, Holden Roberto, on an 'incognito world tour', surfaced in Brussels to announce (on 22 October) that UNITA and FNLA now controlled two-thirds of Angola despite the presence of 30,000 Cuban troops, 'with more arriving daily', who were committing all manner of atrocities against civilians. In Brussels Roberto held consultations, with Major Canto é Castro, a member of the ruling Portugese military council. Roberto's atrocity theme gradually became dominant in reports and Dr J. de Wet, South Africa's Commissioner-General in Namibia, spoke out loudly against what he said was 'a full-scale massacre' in progress in Angola which had caused thousands of refugees to flee into Namibia and Zambia. The refugees were undoubtedly real enough — Pretoria flew Western newsmen to see them. It gradually emerged that MPLA forces had thrown a cordon around southern Angola in September and on 9 September had ordered a halt to the work on the Cunene hydro-electric scheme by the construction crews of the South West Africa Water Department — a major cause for alarm in Pretoria.[1] In late

---

[1] South African officials feared that the rainy season would see coffer dams and walls swept away, destroying much of the work on the half-finished R220 million project destined to provide Namibia with most of its electricity.

October UNITA had launched a sudden offensive to break the cordon and had been badly defeated. Savimbi emerged on 8 November to tell a French news agency (Roberto's Brussels interview had also been disseminated by a French agency) that he was continuing to lead his 6,000 (*sic*) troops against the MPLA, despite the ruthlessness of the Cubans who now numbered over 20,000. Both Savimbi and South African forces claimed that SWAPO had suspended all operations into Namibia in order to fight alongside the MPLA.[1] Neto, the Angolan president, admitted that his forces were engaged in 'cleaning up the last of the puppets', but stressed repeatedly that there was no intention to penetrate Namibia. There seemed no reason to doubt that bloody fighting was going on though, as *The Times* cautioned, 'there has been no independent confirmation of the reports of fighting and pillaging in southern Angola. The whole of the border area in northern Namibia is a military zone, and no journalist or other unauthorized person is allowed in without permission.' According to a number of reports (denied by Pretoria) the SADF had been directing artillery fire into Angola. (Pretoria gave no indication one way or the other as to whether it was officially supporting UNITA.) There were persistent reports, however, that a 'senior UNITA official' had arrived from Zambia on 7 November for talks with Pretoria, and on 10 November Dr Jorge Sangumba flew in to Jan Smuts straight from consultations with Mobutu in Kinshasa. Meanwhile *Die Burger* (which has close links to the South African military establishment) reported a telephone interview with 'a senior adjutant of Savimbi's' from which a strikingly optimistic picture of UNITA strength emerged. UNITA, it appeared, was in control of virtually every major southern town — Huambo, Moxico, Bie and Cuando, with footholds in Mocamedes, Benguela, Luso, Silva Porto, Serpa Pinto and several other towns. *Die Burger* printed these (incredible) claims without comment, but added hopefully that several big UNITA offensives could be expected now that the rainy season (November–April) had started. 'The world will still hear a lot about UNITA in the months that lie ahead', *Die Burger* predicted.[2]

In fact little more was heard of UNITA, and all the evidence suggests a more or less total success for the MPLA mopping-up

---

[1] Nujoma, the SWAPO leader, agreed that this was so. It is difficult to see how the SADF build-up then going on could be justified in terms of SWAPO activity if, by Pretoria's own admission, all such activity had ceased while SWAPO expended itself against UNITA.

[2] *Die Burger* (Cape Town), 8 November, 1976.

operation, which seems to have taken only a few weeks to complete. The interest of this sudden recrudescence of UNITA, FNLA and FLEC activity (FLEC guerrillas were simultaneously reported active in Cabinda) lies less in the (derisory) military threat they posed to the Luanda regime than in the intentions of their external backers — France, the US and South Africa. Without this external support UNITA, FNLA and FLEC had, between March and July, for all practical purposes ceased to exist. Their sudden re-birth strongly suggests a concerted move in a campaign to reverse the results of the 1975—6 Angolan war.

It is worth pointing out that Kissinger had, in the period following the end of that war, made it entirely plain that he did not accept its result. The US refused point-blank to recognise the new state, claiming the presence of foreign forces there meant that its independence was meaningless (an extraordinary principle which, if applied generally, would exclude from independent status every NATO state). Moreover, as we have seen, Kissinger not merely refused to vote for Angola's admission to the UN in June but actually used the US veto to prevent it. Simultaneously, he refused to accept the evidence of a partial Cuban withdrawal from Angola, provided in May by the Swedish Social Democrat leader, Olaf Palme. Instead he attempted to entice the Cubans by an offer of a normalisation of relations with the US in return for her complete withdrawal from Angola — an action which would, of course, have left the MPLA regime open to further Western intervention against it.

Angola was, after all, well worth fighting about; it was no banana republic but a vast state (slightly larger than South Africa) with prodigious mineral resources, a fertile agriculture and a strategic position. In time the combination of Soviet support and oil wealth might make it the key arbiter of central and southern African affairs. Its very existence would strengthen left-wing regimes in Congo-Brazzaville and Mozambique, and would pose a direct threat to conservative governments in Namibia, Zaire, Zambia and independent Zimbabwe. South Africa, for her part, had less to lose once her initial (1975) intervention had already alienated the Luanda regime for good. She would find the prospect of black governments in Rhodesia and Namibia much easier to bear if there were a conservative government in Angola. She might even assure her future oil supplies (from Angola) to boot; and, by such a plan, she would be able to involve the US in guaranteeing this settlement of the entire region. (Strong rumours surrounded the Kissinger—Vorster talks in Pretoria in September, to the effect that

Kissinger had offered to guarantee South Africa's frontiers after a Namibian and Rhodesian decolonisation.) The French, for their part, were no less interested in Cabindan oil than before (observers noted that the 'FLEC guerrillas' in Cabinda had found useful recruits among ELF—Gabon employees). Paris was enjoying a period of rapprochement with the US and, after the May 1976 nuclear reactor deal, with South Africa. In the event of a fresh Angolan war her help would be required, not only as a powerful influence with Mobutu, but to neutralise the Ngouabi regime in the Congo and thus prevent Cuban reinforcements from finding their way into Angola through Brazzaville for a second time. (As we have seen, Kissinger hurried straight to see Giscard from his talks with Vorster. They had been initially scheduled to take place in France.) Finally, such a plan would have an appeal for Smith, and make it easier to win his acceptance of majority rule, for Rhodesia need not feel it was being cut off to fend for itself in an unknown and threatening future. Instead she could become a lynchpin (via the three new airports) of the whole operation and end up with an implicit US alliance.[1] Rhodesian decolonisation would become a great deal less threatening if it were part of a Paris—Washington—Pretoria plan to create a great bloc of safely conservative and pro-western black regimes in west and central Africa stretching from Cameroun and the Central African Empire, through Zaire, Gabon (and a de-radicalised Congo?), a UNITA—FNLA led Angola, an Nkomo-led Zimbabwe, a Kapuuo-led Namibia, Botswana, Zambia and Malawi. Such a bloc (to which one could add Kenya in the east) would, especially if backed by South African and American economic and military muscle, leave the radical states of the eastern seaboard isolated and impotent. The Russians and Cubans would be evicted from most of Africa before they had properly got a hold. It would all hinge on overthrowing the MPLA in Luanda.

It is not difficult to see how such a plan might have worked. First, UNITA, FNLA — and even FLEC — must reappear, harrassing the Luanda regime and establishing a credible anti-

---

[1] Once the US presidential election had terminated Kissinger's tenure of office, Smith attempted to ensure that the pledge of such aid did not slip away by confiding to the press (on 19 November) that during their Pretoria talks Kissinger had told him that should a satisfactory settlement in Rhodesia fail due to African militancy, 'he (Kissinger) was absolutely convinced that he would get a great deal more sympathy from the Free World, and also tangible assistance'. Asked whether he understood such assistance to include the promise of military supplies, Smith answered a flat 'Yes'. Smith's claim was, of course, denied by the State Department.

MPLA presence, assisted by a sympathetic publicity campaign
in the western press. The MPLA regime must meanwhile be
denied legitimacy as far as possible and attention focused on its
shaky and provisional tenure of power. It would not be
recognised by the US; it would be denied recognition even by
its closest neighbour, Zambia (which might again become a base
for operations against it); it would not even be allowed into the
UN. Savimbi must be built up as an anti-communist paragon.
South Africa would assist the UNITA campaign and build up
her own forces on the border, simultaneously complaining
about MPLA atrocities and SWAPO complicity in them, and of
SWAPO border attacks, provoking the need for 'hot pursuit'.
(All of this had actually happened by late 1976.) Once a *casus
belli* had been provided — and as soon as the US presidential
election was decently behind — South African forces would
intervene with great force and speed in Angola, their armoured
columns and paratroopers seizing control of all the coastal
towns. Even if the Cubans were not wholly surprised they
would be at least at a 1:5 disadvantage. Simultaneously FNLA
and UNITA forces, stiffened as necessary with mercenaries,
would be airlifted into key locations via Rhodesia and Zaire.
The French would have to ensure that the Congo was sealed off,
using their influence (or something rougher) with Ngouabi.
With the Cubans cut off from all reinforcements it might all be
over very quickly indeed; the South Africans could retire,
having more than wiped out all stain of previous defeat and
leaving a UNITA—FNLA government in power. It would all go
to show that Neto's Angola was much the same impossibility
that Allende's Chile had been. In Namibia Nujoma would
either be displaced by SWAPO's internal leadership, or would
himself quickly rediscover the merits of the alliance with
Savimbi he had earlier discarded. In Rhodesia Smith would
begin the transition to a Kenyan-style decolonisation, in which
the loudest praises for Zimbabwe's Kenyatta — Nkomo or
Muzorewa — would come from his old opponents among the
white settlers.

A considerable dent was put in such a plan[1] by the pre-emptive
MPLA—Cuban offensive of September—October against

---

[1] No final proof can be given, of course, that such a plan existed. The
evidence is mainly circumstantial and it is fragmentary. I have thought it
worth putting forward this 'scenario' because it has the merit of fitting all
the known facts and known interests of the various parties; because it can
accommodate the evidence of MacBride and his staff — the nearest thing
to neutral experts on the spot; and because it also provides a context
which makes comprehensible the events of early 1977.

UNITA, but all hope was not dispelled. BOSS set to work in the refugee camps in northern Namibia, training and equipping a new UNITA force; *Die Burger* prepared the world to expect to hear more from UNITA; in the wider Western press a bitter campaign by cold warriors against the threat of the new Soviet imperialism gathered strength (led in Britain, for example, by propagandists such as Chalfont and Moss).[1] It might still work.

(iv) Pay-offs

(a) South Africa: The Golden Handshake   Grandiose plans for the future of Angola — in which South Africa took all the risks — were not new to Pretoria, which remembered only too well how such plans had disappointed her in the past. Such plans, moreover, were heavily conditional on the re-election of the Ford administration. Meanwhile, South Africa was being asked to exert brutal and immediate pressures on Rhodesia, with all the political risks that entailed. For this there had to be a tangible and immediate *quid pro quo*. Ironically, Pretoria had to pretend publicly that there was no such deal; it would be political dynamite for Vorster to admit that he was surrendering white rule in Rhodesia for foreign loans and a higher gold price. The HNP would excel itself with orations about famous Biblical figures who had reached terms over thirty pieces of precious metal. Instead, Vorster had returned from the Zurich talks to tell the Transvaal Nationalist Party Congress that South Africa's policies were emphatically 'not for sale' — perhaps in order to allay fears that the concessions towards multi-racial sport announced a few weeks later had been negotiated under US pressure. The pretence was almost entirely successful. When Smith made his sensational speech of 24 September accepting majority rule, the South African electorate was baffled and not a little alarmed: 'What is the *quid pro quo* for which the South African leader was negotiating? Here, there is almost total

---

[1] As we have seen (pp. 137—9), Moss's lengthy articles on the Angolan war, in which Pretoria emerges very much as the Free World's white knight in an anti-communist crusade, if not actually co-ordinated with official South African propagandists, were immediately seized upon and used by them. His articles appeared at just the point when, if MacBride's warnings were correct, a second South African invasion of Angola was due. Alun (Lord) Chalfont, an equally distinguished cold warrior and *Times* journalist, visited South Africa in October 1976 where, according to his own account, he seems to have been given access to confidential military reports. On his return to Britain he authored a series of prominent newspaper articles and was even given several hours of peak-hour television time to read a cold war gospel in very much the manner preached in Pretoria.

bewilderment in South Africa.'[1] The answer was not long in coming.

On 15 September — the second day of the Vorster–Kissinger talks in Pretoria — the third IMF gold auction took place. The result was worse than Johannesburg had feared: whereas the price fall from the first to the second auction had been just $3.95, the price now fell by a full $13. Perhaps most alarming was the fact that the IMF had gone ahead quite relentlessly with the sale despite increasingly angry noises from the USSR[2] and desperate ones from Italy.[3] Their objections had been simply swept aside. Indeed, the point was rammed home by the immediate setting of a date (27 October) for the fourth IMF gold auction — a firm slap in the face for the anti-gold forces.

Nonetheless, the gold price showed a surprising buoyancy in the days after the Kissinger–Vorster talks in Pretoria, actually rising to $115. By the end of September it stood at $120. Something had clearly happened. All the pointers from the third sale had been downwards — and yet the price was going up. Among all market analysts an honourable place must go to the London firm of James Capel and Co., for by 27 September they had, in their weekly review, spotted what the rest of the market had missed and suggested bluntly that Kissinger and Vorster had done a deal over the gold price: the US 'would allow the price to rise to such a level as would let the South African economy off the hook', Capel suggested, adding that a further advantage of such a ploy was that it could be done quietly and ostensibly in order to help the less developed nations who were to benefit from the auctions' proceeds. This, it should be seen, was a thin

---

[1] *Sunday Telegraph* (London), 26 September, 1976.

[2] The Russians, faced with the necessity of paying off their vast trade deficit with the West, were naturally appalled at the falling gold price. In June 1976 the quarterly review of the Moscow Narodny Bank in London had issued a headlong attack on US manipulation of the gold price and eulogised the virtues of gold as the only acceptable basis for the international monetary system in terms which must have been music to Pretoria's ears. In the gold market at least, Russia is South Africa's best friend.

[3] The Italians were watching the value of their gold reserves dropping week by week. In August 1976 they had pledged their gold as collateral for a $1.5 billion loan from Germany; as the price dropped they were forced to pay back $500 million. Italy managed to gain general EEC support for her opposition to the IMF sales, but it was no good. As it was, both Britain and Italy were desperately anxious to avoid giving offence to Washington just at the point when they were supplicants for massive IMF loans, and their weakness showed. The French, who in an earlier period would have been leading the gold forces, were only luke-warm to the Italian proposal — an astonishing turnaround.

cover. It had been anticipated that India, the largest and poorest IMF member, would be the principal beneficiary of the auctions. But by September 1976 India's foreign exchange reserves had trebled in one year to £1.3 billion and she was running a healthy trade surplus of around £50 million a month. Since the special trust fund from the auction proceeds was available only to poor countries with balance of payments problems, India was ineligible — and a large part of the scheme's rationale fell away.[1]

Strange rumours from Washington were affecting the market, however. It was noted that hardly had Kissinger arrived back from Pretoria than he was followed by South Africa's finance secretary, Gerald Brown, and that Brown had been closeted in lengthy and amicable discussions with William Simon, the US Treasury Secretary. A few days later, at the Manila conference of the IMF on 5 October, Simon dropped a bombshell, proposing that the IMF go over to a programme of weekly gold sales, since these would be 'less disruptive to the market'. Simon professed himself to be extremely surprised at the uproar caused by his suggestions; and in fact his weekly sales proposal never got far off the ground. What was so sensational was that Simon should appear to *care* about disrupting the market, that he should talk earnestly of the need for 'stability' in the gold market. On the same day that Simon made his proposal — and hardly coincidentally — the US Treasury published a major report by Thomas W. Wolfe, former head of the Treasury's Gold Policy Office and a renowed anti-gold hawk (he had organised the two US Treasury gold sales for Simon). The Wolfe report spoke, astonishingly, of an American responsibility to ensure the stability of the gold market — and went on to predict that the gold price could only go up. It might soon be necessary, the report predicted, for governments to sell off their bullion if they wished to keep the price from shooting up past $200.

The market was confused by this staggering turnaround, and did not react immediately. But the noises coming out of Washington were now unmistakeably pro-gold. At the 27 October auction the price climbed nearly $9 to $117.71. The slide had been halted; indeed, it had been reversed; and Simon's leading anti-gold official was talking about measures being required to stop the price rising over $200! Simon, for his part, gave expansive press interviews to announce his forthcoming return

[1] Moreover, the total proceeds of the sales — likely to be $600—700 million — are, of course, a drop in the ocean if the needs of the poor countries are taken seriously.

to his old firm, Solomon Brothers, whatever the result of the election — the private sector was the only right place for an extreme conservative Republican, he felt. It is worth quoting from one particularly interesting interview of this period:

> The Treasury Secretary is highly enthusiastic about his plan for regular weekly gold auctions by the IMF. He says the IMF's executive board is considering his 'darn good idea'. South African ministers recently told him they fully endorse his suggestion.
> Indeed, Mr. Simon seems to be getting on extremely well with these particular ministers right now, perhaps as a result of the diplomatic efforts of Dr Kissinger, and he notes that after resigning in January he plans to go to South Africa to lecture at universities there. (*The Times* (London), 18 October. 1976.)

In the face of interviews such as this even twice and thrice-bitten gold speculators gradually decided against further shyness. The gold price steadily climbed, taking the IMF auctions in its stride. Market analysts, having become accustomed to the new US attitude, quickly found all manner of reasons to support a new bull market. The suggestion put so bluntly by the acute Capel that the US 'has shown all too clearly in the last two years that she can control the gold price' was generally regarded as somewhat subversive. If the price was simply a matter of political fiat, then whither the craft of market analyst? No, the price rise was due to the gold-hungry Chinese merchants of Macao, to a massive return to the markets by the jewellery trade, to the fact that the German Social Democrats had instituted the blessing of gold fillings on the national health. . . . When news of the record Russian harvest fed through, this was taken as a further bull point (they would not need to sell gold now). When further news emerged that both the Russians and Chinese had been rushing to sell gold on a rising market (there was still a huge Soviet trade deficit, after all), this too was taken as a bull point, for the sales had failed to stop the upward trend. In fact, everything was a bull point. The new Carter Administration, when it took office, appeared to take no attitude of any kind to gold. Its economic intentions were said to be inflationary, however, so the gold price went up (the dollar would weaken). By April 1977 the price topped $150 before a warning rumble came from the US Treasury that if the price went too high there might be a need for further Treasury gold sales. The price stuck at around $150.

Meanwhile the South African request for a loan from the Citibank syndicate had had a somewhat rougher time — and the gold price rise was still far short of what would be needed to compensate for all of Pretoria's economic woes. Nonetheless, by November 1976 a $110 million credit had been arranged (South Africa had asked for far more). It was something, anyway. South Africa was hardly off the hook economically, but the lesson of the Angolan intervention of 1975 had been learnt. This time there was a real payoff.[1]

(b) America: Goodbye to Henry How far Kissinger's diplomatic breakthrough in southern Africa helped the Ford campaign is impossible to say, though help it almost certainly did. From being a lost cause the campaign gradually gathered strength to the point where the last polls predicted a virtual dead-heat. It was a quite astonishing achievement. In 1975 the hapless Ford seemed to have inherited the combination of scandal and depression which had led to the last defeat of a sitting president, Herbert Hoover. By November 1976 the comparison on commentators' lips was not with Hoover but with Harry Truman, the plain man of the plains, struggling uphill towards a surprise victory.

It was not to be. As the returns came flooding in on 3 November it gradually became clear that Carter had won, by the narrowest of margins. As expected, it was the South that had decided the election — it had been unable to resist voting for one of its own, and Carter had won every single southern state. Nonetheless, even here his margin was often wafer-thin — in Mississippi he had won by 50—49%, for example; in Louisiana by 52—46%, in Texas by 53—47%. When later analysis showed that he had won around 90% of the black vote it became clear that he had actually squeaked through on a minority of the white vote in the South. It may well have been crucial that

---

[1] These were the visible payoffs but there were probably others. Consider the case of the British South West Africa Company which owned and held mineral rights over vast tracts of Namibia. Established in 1892, the company was an awkward anomaly — a foreign company which directly held land and rights in the heart of the white-zoned areas of Namibia without any South African intermediary. South Africa had long wanted SWACO to be transferred to South African ownership but the (Conservative) Heath government in Britain had refused, since this would constitute open defiance of UN policy towards Namibia. In April 1976 the Labour government allowed Anglo-American to bid for SWACO and in November shareholders who refused to sell to Anglos were simply informed that, with British government permission, the deal had gone through anyway.

Reagan, still disgruntled from his convention defeat, had called off his promised tour of the South for Ford. Conservative southerners had preferred Ford but had been torn between their ideological preferences and the sound of Carter's Georgia accent: Reagan might well have persuaded them to forget the accent. Reagan, indeed, might well have won had he been nominated — the West and mid-West would have gone for him, as it did for Ford, and he stood well to take the South from Carter too. It would have been a happy day for other white southerners — in Africa — but it was only a lost dream.

A new president meant a new Secretary of State for Foreign Relations. It meant a new foreign policy, very probably — a policy which would have to be acceptable to the black voters who had provided Carter with his crucial margin, their votes delivered by men such as Andrew Young, Martin Luther King's former assistant. Young and his followers would be needed again in 1980, and Young was quickly given the sensitive job of US Ambassador to the UN. America was now represented in that forum by a man in whose house lived the children of Robert Sobukwe, the banned South African black leader who, in Vorster's words, was 'not a communist . . . but had other problems'. Pretoria might now have to deal with Young, not Kissinger. There could hardly have been a more dramatic change.

Even in the excitement engendered by the new Administration many Americans realised that the passing from office of Henry Kissinger was more significant that the retirement to full-time golf of Gerald Ford. Kissinger was far too polished a performer not to take it well — had he not hinted he might not stay on even if Ford won? Such hints are, of course, fundamental to the American political game. They are given; they are listened to politely; and, as was intended, they are ignored. In the end the reluctant and blushingly modest candidate is somehow prevailed upon to accept the heavy burdens of office for which, selflessly, he has declared himself devoid of all amibition. Kissinger had made his way to Washington from Harvard via his patron, Nelson Rockefeller, in whose councils he had long served. He had then given faithful service for nearly six years to Richard Nixon, Rockefeller's longtime and bitter political rival, until the rule of Nixon had collapsed in burglarious ignominy, ceding place to the staider ways of Gerald Ford. Kissinger had then had the pleasure of seeing his old patron installed alongside him — technically above him — as Vice President. Now he announced that he would be taking up a post as

international adviser to Chase Manhattan under David
Rockefeller, Nelson's brother. Henry Kissinger was going home.
Behind him he left a trail of confusion.

(v) Sequels

(a) Rhodesia The confusion was thickest at the Geneva conference on Rhodesia, with whose surreal activities this book
began. In fact what happened — or failed to happen — in
Geneva was relatively simple. Smith arrived several days early
for the conference and showed every sign of wishing to reach a
speedy conclusion by which the African delegates would be
bound hand and foot to the terms of the Salisbury version of
the Kissinger package. No such speedy progress was possible, for
the Africans were not only deeply divided amongst themselves
but at a loss as to what to do. Like Nyerere, they had assumed
that any true renunciation of majority rule would be synony-
mous with Smith's resignation. Now, they were aghast at the
prospect of planning arrangements whereby they would have to
sit in an interim government with Smith for two years, with no
certain prospect of majority rule at the end of it (if the
Salisbury version of the package was respected). Accordingly
they attempted to insist that the British head such a government and signify its intention of taking a stronger role by
sending the Foreign Secretary, Anthony Crosland, to chair the
conference in place of Richard. Smith declared this a foul.
Crosland had no intention of taking Richard's position as
'fall-guy' — and the Africans bitterly took this as evidence of
British complicity with Smith.

   Smith, realising that the talks were going nowhere and
determined not to find himself negotiating under the pressure
of a successful guerrilla offensive, decided on a massive pre-
emptive strike against the guerrilla camps in Mozambique.
Having no wish to be in Geneva when the attack took place, he
hurriedly announced his departure for Salisbury on 30 October.
The talks appeared to be at a point of complete breakdown.
Kissinger could hardly afford this with the US election just 48
hours away. Earlier he had announced in the most definitive
terms that no State Department official would be sent to the
talks until after the election. Smith's announcement of departure led to an immediate reversal and the arrival on the same day
of Schaufele, the Assistant Secretary of State for African
Affairs, to lend American weight to the talks and keep them in
session. Until Schaufele's arrival the nearest thing to an Ameri-

can presence had been President Mobutu who, at Kissinger's suggestion, had taken up residence in a Geneva villa for the duration of the conference.

In the early morning of 31 October a large Rhodesian force, complete with armoured cars and helicopter gunships, launched deep into Mozambique (as far as Cabora Bassa itself). The troops stormed into the camps (using heavy artillery in some cases) and retired after three days, leaving up to 1,000 dead in eight separate bases, They carried with them large numbers of prisoners, arms and documents. The UN Commissioner for Refugees, Prince Sadruddin Aga Khan, claimed that large numbers of women and children had been killed in the raids. While this may have been true there seems little reason to doubt Smith's claim that the guerrillas had suffered sufficient military damage to set back their campaign by many months.

The raid doubtless appalled Pretoria — a much smaller one in August had led to Muller's majority rule speech — for fear that it would draw the Cubans into Mozambique. The Durban *Sunday Tribune* carried a report of the raid in which large claims of Cuban, Russian, East German, Yugoslav and Chinese military involvement appeared. This produced the ironic result of strong demands from Salisbury that there was no evidence at all of any such Communist involvement.

The real end to the conference came on 2 November with the Carter election victory. The British soldiered on in the hope that Kissinger might still use the last months of office to play some further role, while the front-line presidents were still eager to see some sort of settlement and helped keep the Africans in Geneva. The delegates now settled down to a long and entirely pointless discussion of a possible independence date for Zimbabwe — a topic apparently chosen by Richard to keep talks going at all. Meanwhile Schaufele, his job done, slipped quietly away from the conference.

On 13—14 November the Rhodesians launched a further big raid into Mozambique. But this time they lacked the element of surprise, and their opponents' defences had been considerably strengthened. Within days of the first raid a consignment of Russian armoured cars and 'Stalin organs' had been delivered to Maputo, Tanzanian troops had moved in to lend support, and some 5,000 guerrillas had been transferred into Tanzania out of harm's way. Although the Rhodesians claimed to have killed another 100 guerrillas they also had to admit to casualties of their own, including an aircraft hit by ground fire. On 21 November Señor Raul Valdes Vivo, a member of the Cuban Communist Party's central committee, arrived in Maputo to 'strengthen links'. Smith was bringing Pretoria's nightmare to life.

Not surprisingly, Mugabe found himself under increasing pressure from the guerrillas to leave the conference, and only the strongest pressures from the front-line presidents kept him in Geneva. Fighting which left 45 dead broke out in the guerrilla camps after one group had indignantly declared themselves independent of any African leader who was sitting talking to the Rhodesians at the same time that they were being attacked by them. Mugabe's agitation grew when Sithole, the former ZANU leader, slipped away from Geneva to fish in the troubled waters of the guerrilla camps. Sithole had considerable competition — apart from a deputy sent by Mugabe,[1] Josiah Tongogara was attempting to regain control of the guerrillas from their new commander, Rex Nhongo. Nhongo held his own against all comers, and Mugabe was given reassurance by the arrival of a guerrilla delegation including both Nhongo and Tongogara. The conference wandered aimlessly on.

In early December came news which the British had been praying for — Kissinger was to visit Europe to address the NATO Foreign Ministers in Brussels. Perhaps he would perform some fresh magic to help the British off the diplomatic hook on which they were impaled in Geneva? Smith immediately announced his return to Geneva. He seems to have realised more clearly than anyone else that the conference should really have ended the day Kissinger lost office. He was certainly not going to prolong the dangerous charade in Geneva long enough for Kissinger to exert some new pressure on him to revise the original deal. Arriving in Geneva he declared that he had come 'to conclude the talks' and proposed an immediate adjournment for 'at least a month'. He would, he said, be prepared to continue the talks 'next year, even the following year'.

Smith need not have worried. Kissinger was a magician without a wand. He had not the slightest intention, whatever the pleas of the British, of endangering his diplomatic prestige by an impotent initiative amidst the shambles of Geneva. Instead he held a joint press conference with Crosland where the Foreign Secretary had the lugubrious duty of reading out a statement to the effect that the responsibility for the talks was

---

[1] Mugabe's deputy was simply denied access to the camps. Sithole asked for armed protection while visiting the camps but was told by the Maputo authorities that if he was truly the popular leader he claimed such precautions should not be necessary. Sithole decided not to put his popularity to such an acid test.

now entirely Britain's:

> Dr. Kissinger, sitting at the right hand of the Foreign
> Secretary, beamed his approval of this statement. He had the
> relaxed, relieved look of someone who has not been left
> holding the baby. Mr. Crosland, on the other hand, found it
> difficult to smile or relax, and appeared to give up the
> attempt. (*The Guardian* (London), 11 December, 1976.)

Almost immediately the conference broke up. It was clear that
Smith now regarded the deal struck in Pretoria as off. Even his
apparently irreversible statement of 24 September was now
retracted. Once Kissinger had made it clear he was not going to
intervene, Smith announced (on 13 December) that since the
original Kissinger proposals had been modified, his own
commitment to majority rule had become 'obsolete'.

It was difficult for many observers to accept that the whole
year's diplomacy had failed so utterly, and that Kissinger had
made a fool of Britain. Expectations had been raised in the
British press and not a few politicians were caught up in the
excitement of 'shuttle diplomacy'. They entirely failed to grasp
that Kissinger's magic had lain in the sticks and carrots he
wielded, not the mere drama of his blue Boeing swooping from
capital to capital. The result of this miscomprehension was a
strange extension of the rather sick joke of Geneva. The joke
took on wholly new proportions with the decision by Richard,
the conference chairman, to launch his own bout of shuttle
diplomacy. Richard earnestly announced that he would be
reconvening the conference, assured Lusaka, Pretoria and
Maputo (meaninglessly) that he had Kissinger's support — and
then laid down his proposals. The knotty problem of white
control of the army and police in a Rhodesian interim
government would be solved by getting the army and police to
swear an oath of allegiance to the British Crown. Africans could
take the oath too and, thus metaphysically united, the races
could progress peacefully towards majority rule. Only Smith
seems to have been blunt enough to tell Richard that his shuttle
was a waste of a perfectly good airline ticket. Samora Machel, a
gentler figure, was reported to be 'humourously sceptical' of the
proposals. Richard departed; Crosland died; his successor, David
Owen, launched into his own vainglorious tour. The Rhodesian
problem remained as intractable as ever.

(b) South Africa Pretoria was as quick as Salisbury to realise
the significance of the American election. It was just as well

South Africa had got an immediate *quid pro quo*, for the deals done with Kissinger over the future of southern Africa were off — or, at least, they were no longer definitely on. South Africa had her friends in Washington, to be sure, many of whom would stay in office through any change-over. But everything would still have to depend on the new Carter administration which was at best an unknown quantity.

This news burst upon an already confused political scene. Vorster had shocked even many white South Africans by the hard line he had taken at a Nationalist rally on 13 September, straight after the Zurich talks. Many had looked for some sign of relaxation in South African domestic policies greater than the minor concessions made to the non-whites in the wake of the riots. None were made. The rioters he dismissed briefly, saying that government funds for the improvement of non-white conditions would now have to be used instead to repair the wilful damage done to property. South Africa would not attempt to 'buy popularity' with the world; there could be no question of direct representation for all races in parliament; any change there was to be would have to lie within the established apartheid framework. This left little room for movement, it seemed. But on 24 September the government announced sweeping changes to allow multi-racial sport at all levels. Legislation would be permissive only — clubs might remain racially segregated; indeed, the government made it clear that it expected they would. Nonetheless, in South African terms, it was a major change. Vorster also let it be known that he would be willing to set up a multi-racial Cabinet council to enable Coloureds and Asians to advise him of their opinions. (Such a council would have no powers and was indignantly dismissed by those to whom it was offered.)

The combined effect of hard-line talk *and* concessions suggested to many that policy was at a crossroads. For all those who wished to urge the cause of reform, now was clearly the time to make their case. This group, we have seen, included virtually the whole of the business community, aghast at the twin consequences of Angola and Soweto. But other voices were also to be heard, for the entire spectrum of white opinion was in a heated and inchoate state. Contrary, perhaps, to what might be expected, internal disorder in South Africa has tended to produce a strong — if temporary — liberalising effect on white politics as voters realise with fresh alarm just how high the price may be for an immovable resistance to change. Thus the period after Sharpeville had seen the Progressives pick up considerably more votes than had been thought at all likely —

before the inevitable reaction towards complacency and the
right set in. Soweto had an even larger impact. The United Party
not merely split but its own leader of 20 years' standing, Sir de
Villiers Graaf, volunteered his own political immolation if the
cause of reform might thus be served. Opinion polls revealed
that, momentarily at least, large sections of white opinion had
broken free of their customary moorings. A poll published by
the Afrikaans Sunday paper, *Rapport*, showed 30% of whites
(though only 18% of Nationalists) willing to countenance
inter-racial marriage and 57% (46% of Nationalist supporters)
willing to abolish job reservation. Another poll, also taken in
the peculiar and highly charged atmosphere of October 1976,[1]
revealed that in two years the proportion of whites opposing an
equal (i.e. proportionately extremely unequal) division of the
country between whites and blacks had fallen from 84% to
63%. As many as 44% of whites declared themselves willing to
countenance some sort of restricted franchise for blacks. This
latter figure was astonishing, in good part because such a
franchise had always been the central plank of the Progressives'
policies — and yet the same poll found the PRP's support stuck
at 6%. Similarly, although such polls suggested wide diver-
gencies in the electorate from official Nationalist policies, they
nonetheless showed no fall-off in support for the Nationalist
party itself (around 58—60%). The other striking feature of the
surveys was the very large 'don't know' element they revealed.
During the 1974 election this group had been only about 1%;
now it was 20%.

Here, indeed, was the key. White opinion was badly shaken;
was willing to consider reforms if that was what was required to
make the troubles go away; but was clinging tight to its party
allegiances (particularly in the case of Nationalists); and, faced
with crisis and uncertainty, looked to strong government and a
strong leader as never before. This left the ball very much in
Vorster's court.

Things came to a head in the week after the American
election with the launching of a concerted campaign for reform
in the Afrikaans press — hitherto the unconditional redoubt of
Afrikaner nationalism. On 7 November Piet Cillie, editor of *Die
Burger*, made an astonishing call for full citizenship rights for all
urban blacks who, he argued, were 'for all practical purposes

---

[1] This poll, organised by the Arnold-Bergstreisser Institut (Freiburg) and
the Deutsches Institut fuer Internationale Paedagogische Forschung
(Frankfurt), was able to provide comparisons with an exactly similar poll
carried out by these two German institutes in 1974

immovable' from the white urban areas. The call for reform was taken up in *Die Transvaaler* and, indeed, in almost every single Afrikaans paper. There had been rumblings of this sort before but the campaign which gathered strength in November was quite different. For the first time names were named and Nationalist politicians found themselves subjected to explicit individual criticism in the Afrikaans press. Chief of the targets was, of course, Andries Treurnicht.

There is little to suggest that Vorster ever seriously entertained the suggestion being so forcefully pressed upon him, to side openly with the most *verligte* elements in his party and set course for radical reform. For a start, there were too many powerful *verkramptes* in his own Cabinet — not just Treurnicht, but his superior, M. C. Botha, a powerful and senior figure in the Nationalist caucus. How could Botha side with him if he took the line suggested by Cillie? As recently as August Botha had stressed (in connection with the Soweto riots) that blacks were allowed into white areas 'to sell their labour and for nothing else'. Or again, there was Jimmy Kruger, the Police and Justice Minister, who made the same point on 14 November against Cillie: blacks were no more than 'export labour, whether they are born here or not'. As for unrest, there was no substitute for 'maintaining the authority of the gun'. Vorster could hardly forget that he had staged *his* assent to power by striking such attitudes when he held Kruger's Ministry. The *verligtes* in the press urged him openly to drop such men from his Cabinet but Vorster knew that this could only cause a major split. In any case, there was every sign that the HNP was continuing to gain strength. Earlier in the year it had presented a candidate in the Johannesburg urban constituency of Alberton (hitherto its support had been confined to the platteland). The HNP had lost their deposit — but almost doubled their vote all the same. After Smith's 'surrender' speech of 24 September a group of HNP supporters had invaded the ground of Vorster's official residence in Pretoria to protest against the sell-out of the white man in Rhodesia. Vorster had been greatly embarrassed and, fearful of creating martyrs on the Right, the government had dropped all charges against the protestors — who were greeted by a large and cheering crowd as they emerged jubilantly from the court room.

Rhodesia was, in fact, very much the key issue. Vorster had taken a huge political risk in forcing Smith to the conference table. The risk had increased as Smith played skilfully to his South African audience, sticking heroically to (his version of) the Kissinger package and projecting himself as the reasonable man prepared to honour his commitments, foiled only by the unreasonable and alarming militancy of his black opponents. Within a week of the conference there had been a profound sea-change in South African white opinion towards Smith. Many obervers were emphatic that Smith's popularity in South Africa 'has probably never been higher ... with almost bewildering speed the image in South Africa of Mr. Ian Smith has changed ...'[1] This change of mood left Vorster ever more exposed and vulnerable.

As the implications of the American election result sank in, Pretoria realised that all Kissinger's bold schemes for a settlement of the southern African region were now no more than chaff in the wind. There was now nothing to be gained — and, politically, a great deal to be lost — by maintaining the pressure on Smith. On 7 November Vorster telephoned Smith to assure him that there was no question of South Africa closing its borders with Rhodesia or participating in boycotts against her. Announcing this to the press, Vorster supported Smith's version of the Kissinger package and declared that he was 'not prepared to twist Mr Smith's arm'. By 13 November Smith was telling the American newspaper magnate, William Randolph Hearst, that Rhodesia was getting fully adequate military supplies from South Africa. By early December he was proudly boasting that Rhodesia was 'militarily stronger than ever'. Before the talks Vorster had withdrawn his military support from Rhodesia; now he rushed to reinforce it. Suddenly the anxious talk in Salisbury about rail holdups and Rhodesia being 'bust' ceased. Had Smith ever had any intention of reaching an agreement in Geneva, Vorster's telephone message of 7 November had been more than enough to change his mind. The pressure was right off. After all, even if there was to be another round of negotiations over Rhodesia with the new Carter administration, it would still be best to establish the toughest possible hard-line position from which to bargain. Pretoria had got a higher gold price and a foreign loan out of the bargaining this time, but that was hardly enough to satisfy her. ... Vorster had played one ace. Now he snatched the rest of his cards up from the table and listened to see how the next round of the bidding would go.

Simultaneously he hastened to still the voices demanding domestic political reform. *Verligte* intellectuals and businessmen were all very well but they were talking nonsense. The Nationalist Party could be kept united from the Right; it

[1] *Daily Telegraph* (London), 6 November, 1976.

could not be led from the Left without a major split and that was that. Vorster rushed to Treurnicht's defence in the face of the hostile press campaign. By the end of November the Afrikaans newspaper editors found themselves under open attack from the Cabinet itself. Braam Raubenheimer, a leading minister, accused Wimpie de Klerk, the *Transvaaler* editor, of nothing less than open disloyalty to his party, in (treasonably) supporting the Progressives; and suggested he resign from his 'protected position behind a desk and move actively into politics'. This had roughly the equivalent force that an attack on the editor of *Pravda* from the CPSU Politburo would have in Russia. Nothing remotely like it had been seen before. The press stopped attacking Treurnicht — and turned to criticism of Koot Vorster, the premier's brother, who had begun to voice strong misgivings even about multi-racial sport, arguing that integration in any field was a threat to the identity of the Afrikaner.

The row bubbled on into 1977. Vorster had had enough, and proposed a draconian new press censorship law to the consternation of the whole newspaper world, Afrikaans as well as English. Having thoroughly frightened the wayward *verligtes* and bought a promise of self-censorship, Vorster dropped the bill. His tactic was clear: he would face the row out, reinforce the legendary political discipline of the Afrikaner group and maintain party unity at all costs. The *verligtes* had been calling for Treurnicht and the other *verkramptes* to be dropped from the government in a re-shuffle anticipated from November on. The *verkramptes* had insisted, conversely, that Treurnicht should be promoted to full Cabinet status. Very well, there wouldn't be a Cabinet re-shuffle at all. Vorster summed up his own mood in an unprecedentedly bleak New Year Message for 1977. The country was faced with threats from all sides: the 'weak-willed' West would give her no real support; the only thing to do was to dig in hard, militarily and politically. For by now the country was gripped in a climate of intense military preparation. In April 1977, despite the desperate need to cut public expenditure, the defence budget was increased by another huge margin (21.3%). Now was no time for reform, for South Africa was preparing for war.

(c) Southern Africa Pretoria's interest in a Rhodesian settlement had always been that if Smith simply waged a last-ditch fight for white supremacy, sooner or later South Africa would have to join him in the ditch. There had never been the slightest doubt that white South Africa could not stand passively by as black guerrilla armies swept in on Salisbury. To be sure, that

situation was still far away. But it was coming closer, and once
the slide started the end might be very quick. Already whites
were leaving Rhodesia at a net rate of 1,000 a month, and the
figures for January 1977 showed a further rise. It might all be
like South Vietnam in 1975 in the end. The South Vietnamese
had had the third biggest airforce in the world and a million
men under arms. They had looked invincible for years ahead.
But such was the lack of confidence in the permanence of the
South Vietnamese state that it took only a single clear reversal
to start a spreading wave of panic and, within three months, a
complete collapse. In just the same way, let word leak out in
Salisbury of a single major military reverse at the hands of the
guerrillas — or even a large-scale massacre of white civilians —
and the emigration figures would double, quintuple, or more. If
the rot started it couldn't be stopped. The state and army
machine would be weakened with every fresh departure. The
guerrillas would lose all concern with their own casualty rate if
they saw their chance. More reverses would follow. It was
perfectly possible that the whites might — like the South
Vietnamese — still enjoy a clear military superiority at the end,
but that would be simply irrelevant. The whole house of cards
would come crashing bloodily down. If South Africa wanted to
stop this happening she could not leave intervention to the last
minute — she would have to shore up the walls at the first sign
that they were crumbling. Once the American election put paid
to the possibility of a Rhodesian settlement, there was nothing
to do but prepare for this alternative, however 'ghastly to
contemplate' it was.

Smith's raids into Mozambique had been cunningly launched
with the Geneva conference in session so that Pretoria could not
react adversely — it would have been politically impossible to
pull the rug from under Smith's feet just as the conference got
under way. Pretoria had simply had to take it lying down. The
raids had the result she had dreaded — the widening of the war
to include the Cubans. Within weeks of the 31 October raid
there were reports of massive airlifts of Soviet arms into
Mozambique, together with 500 Cuban soldiers flown in from
Angola. Giant Soviet transport planes were to be seen wheeling
in to refuel in Lusaka, Maputo docks were now landing Russian
T-54 tanks, SAM missiles, 'Stalin organs', armoured cars and
automatic weapons alongside imports and exports from South
Africa. It was all very well to curse Smith for having brought
this about. The milk was well and truly spilt and there was no
use crying now. Smith had put Pretoria on the hook and it
might now be impossible to get off it.

In Pretoria the generals were in no doubt that they could not allow an extension of Cuban or Soviet influence or military power into Rhodesia. In late November General Neil Webster, head of the Citizen Force, declared that 'we cannot stand aside from developments in Rhodesia'. The implications were spelt out by the senior Cabinet Minister, Braum Raubenheimer:

> 'South Africa is committed militarily in South West Africa but is as yet uncommitted in Rhodesia. But the time will come when we have to decide whether we will have to fight there.'
>
> The government, he said, would have to 'rethink' its policy on Rhodesia if there was a Russian or Cuban invasion of the country. Asked by the press whether he meant there would be a direct South African military intervention in such circumstances, Raubenheimer replied, 'Yes, that is correct'.[1]

The trouble was that South Africa would have to make its decision long before things came to such a pass. In January 1977 the Johannesburg *Sunday Express* ran a series of articles in which it quoted government sources as saying that South Africa might soon need to reinforce Smith with troops — perhaps disguised as 'volunteers'. These would provide Smith with a sufficiently strong bargaining position to demand and get from his opponents a 'moderate solution' (i.e. one acceptable to Rhodesian white opinion). This left unanswered the question of what would happen if the nationalist guerrillas refused to accept such a solution.

For the moment the question could remain academic. The rainy season — the best fighting weather for the guerrillas — was drawing to a close. Moreover, the Zimbabwe guerrillas had made just about every mistake in the book. They were disunited amongst themselves; they fought in their camps; they annoyed the Mozambiquans; they had thrown to the winds the key guerrilla weapon of surprise and publicly announced a stepping up of their campaign for the period of the Geneva conference; it was they who had been thoroughly taken by surprise by Smith's raids on their camps in Mozambique, entirely predictable though they had been (they themselves had predicted them). They had not done the necessary political groundwork inside Rhodesia — where Muzorewa was still undeniably popular. They were throwing raw, untrained boys into the fight simply to keep up the appearance of attack. Their leaders had gone posturing

[1] *Daily Telegraph* (London). 4 December 1976.

and posing for cameramen in Geneva while their army bled to bits. Not for them the anonymity that a Guevara or a Mao had enjoyed before their success. It would have been quite difficult to do worse.

Nonetheless, time was on their side. They had numbers, they now had arms, they had sanctuary, they were gaining experience. By October 1977 they would be back in strength; woe betide Rhodesian forces which attempted to raid into Mozambique again — the SAMs and the 'Stalin organs' would be waiting for them, perhaps even the Mig-23s. Even if Salisbury weathered the campaign of 1977—8, there would be no stopping things going downhill now.

Pretoria could see all this too. It was now beginning to be quite important that she had made the fatal intervention in Angola, for it had broken the spell. Then she had intervened because she had been strongly encouraged, even pressured to do so. Now, for the first time, Pretoria began in her own right to ponder the wisdom of her entire previous policy of military non-intervention. To be sure, she would like to stay on good terms with Mozambique — on 26 March, 1977 the first electricity from Cabora Bassa had begun to flow into the South African power grid, adding a new complication. But if she wanted to stop the rot in the guerrilla war in Rhodesia, the only sure way was the one Smith had used — pre-emptive strikes in Mozambique; as Smith was no longer strong enough to make them, then, logically, South Africa would have to start thinking about making such a strike herself . . . Had not the Minister of Defence, Piet Botha, in his New Year message, asked his countrymen whether the time had not come 'to live dangerously and retain our self-respect'?

The same considerations also applied on the other side of the continent. It was all very well going ahead with plans for the decolonisation of Namibia and the handover to a Kapuuo government, but how could such an arrangement possibly work while SWAPO remained adamantly militant and had Angola as a sanctuary? The answer was, clearly, that South African forces would have to stay there after Namibian independence. But no African state would recognise a Namibia which began its life as host to a large South African 'army of occupation'; so Namibia could not be decolonised; and yet the pressure at the UN — even from the West — for decolonisation was getting stronger and stronger. Of course, the impasse would be a great deal less severe if only there wasn't an MPLA regime in Angola, or if it could somehow be overthrown.

As we have suggested, there are quite strong reasons to believe that had Kissinger retained office January 1977 might have witnessed a second South African invasion of Angola, with the collusion of France as well as the US. The closing months of 1976 saw several developments which appeared to foreshadow such a conflict. In mid-November government sources let it be known that a military attack on Namibia from Angola might be expected early in 1977. Simultaneously South Africa's Defence Minister called for military enlistment by middle-aged men, hinting at compulsion if the response was not good. This appeal for a 'Dad's army' was treated by many with positive derision. The army was surely strong enough? The Minister was simply trying to whip up a war psychosis to quieten demands for domestic reform. It was just a joke — the 'fat 'n' forty brigade', as it was called. Few sought to ask what the implications were if the Minister were really serious. Under what circumstances other than a massive extension of the present army's operations could such reinforcements be needed?

A further announcement on 8 December, by the Commissioner for South West Africa, Jannie de Wet, again seemed to suggest that Pretoria was trying to establish a *casus belli* in advance. In a remarkable reversal of previous policy de Wet openly suggested that South Africa might be provoked to strike into Angola.

> We are gearing ourselves for a massive infiltration early next year. We have information that SWAPO is planning to attack South West Africa on a scale unequalled before. They plan to strike far deeper into the territory and even to penetrate white areas. . . . The Cubans will definitely assist. . . . South African troops may be forced to follow SWAPO in hot pursuit and wipe out their bases in Angola.[1]

Meanwhile, in Nairobi UNITA's 'Foreign Minister', Jorge Sangumba, announced in early December that he was holding talks with FNLA, FLEC and the MPLA 'Active Revolt' splinter group with a view to forming a common front. The aim of the front, he said, would be to secure Cuban withdrawal as a prelude to setting up a coalition government of national unity. UNITA, he announced, was now willing to concede a very considerable degree of regional autonomy to Cabinda. The formation of such a front, Sangumba (quite unnecessarily) hinted, would be greatly in the interests of all those who wished

[1] *Daily Telegraph* (London), 29 November, 1976.

to see a more moderate, pro-Western government in Angola.
Meanwhile, it would be necessary for the front to continue a
military struggle to force the MPLA to concede to it.

Everything, in a word, seemed ready for the invasion of
which MacBride had warned. If such a plan existed, it too was a
casualty of the American election. South Africa might feel
extremely tempted, but there could be no guarantee that the
Carter administration would not leave her in the lurch.
Kissinger, in his last major speech in office (addressing the
NATO Foreign Ministers in December), pointed the way
forcefully enough to the new administration, drawing attention
to UNITA military activity in Angola and suggesting that 'It
seems to reflect the inability of the authorities in Luanda to
establish control even with the support of 13,000 Cuban
troops.' Kissinger denied that the US was supporting UNITA,
but the hint was clear enough. A ruthless Communist tyranny
was being established in Angola with the help of a foreign army
of occupation. Who could be surprised if the population
resisted, if that resistance should continue and grow; who could
say it might not be worthy of support?

In fact the events of early 1977 gave the strong impression of
a gathering siege against Angola. South Africa angrily
denounced the Angolan regime for refusing to allow her to send
her construction teams back into Angola to work on the
Cunene Dam. BOSS continued to train UNITA guerrillas and
launch them into action inside Angola. Luanda complained
that South African forces were, by March, making almost
regular daily incursions inside Angolan territory and that the
incursions were getting deeper and deeper. A zone of permanent
insecurity had been created in southern Angola.

Meanwhile, in mid-January FLEC re-emerged into view with
a raid in which they carried off three French engineers working
on the Brazzaville—Pointe Noire railway in the Congo. President
Ngouabi of the Congo angrily denounced the raid and suggested
that Paris should take responsibility for releasing the three men
since FLEC was entirely financed and organised from Paris
anyway. The French denied the allegation, but within two
weeks the three missing Frenchmen did indeed turn up
unharmed in Paris, the Elysée announcing that this happy result
had been achieved by steps taken by the French government
'with the authorities of the interested countries'. This was a
remarkable statement, for it was quite clear that neither Angola
nor the Congo could be meant.

By this stage it was becoming clear that Paris was bent on a
campaign aimed at the wholesale destabilisation of the Ngouabi

regime. Economically the regime depended on its potassium deposits, mined by the Congolese Potassium Company (CPC) in which the French hold the major share. In December 1976 all the French directors. both governmental and private, resigned *en bloc* from the CPC board, announcing that the deposits were 'no longer profitable due to over-investment'. How the world's largest potassium deposits could suddenly become unprofitable overnight went unexplained. Since the French, as majority partners, had had control over the investment programme, similar questions were posed as to how 'over-investment' could have taken place except at French behest, if take place it truly had. Meanwhile, the country's largest export and foreign exchange earner was immobilised. Shortly afterwards ELF—Congo suddenly announced that its exploitation of the Emeraude offshore oil field was proving uneconomic and would have to be wound up. Most of the Congo's future economic hopes rest on the field where, it was believed, recoverable proven oil reserves exceeded 700 million tonnes. ELF (which is French government-owned) now discovered that the water was too deep, the oil pressure too low, and that there were 'geological faults' in the ocean bed. As a result, ELF said, recoverable reserves must now be downgraded to just 7 million tonnes — which made the whole operation uneconomic.

These two withdrawals had the effect of paralysing the Congolese economy. At the same time the country was subjected to increasing harrassment from the FLEC guerrillas. This, too, was extremely odd: notionally FLEC was an Angolan movement — but almost all of its guerrilla activities took place in the Congo, not Angola, and seemed aimed principally at the Ngouabi, not the Neto, government.

After the January FLEC raid Neto met Ngouabi, and the two presidents agreed to co-ordinate their action against FLEC. Meanwhile tension continued to increase on the Zairean border with Angola with Mobutu again lending supporting to FNLA and FLEC. On 18 March a major blow to isolate Angola was struck by the assassination under mysterious circumstances of President Ngouabi. Most of the blame was laid by the Congolese authorities on the former premier and pro-French conservative, Massemba-Debat, who admitted his guilt shortly before being shot. There were strong hints that the SDECE (French intelligence) had also been involved. By early March President Neto was warning with some desperation against the state of siege in which he found himself. He also claimed to have proof of plans for a new invasion of Angola, 'Operation Cobra 77', which would see a second concerted attack from

South Africa and Zaire in September or October 1977. Information also came to light of the activities of a mysterious consortium of international financiers 'headed by a Canadian multi-millionaire who lives in Switzerland' which, apparently in co-ordination with Zaire and BOSS, was attempting to over-throw the Angolan regime. The consortium, whose aim was said to be the gaining of oil concessions in Cabinda, bought up millions of Angolan escudos in an attempt to undermine the country's currency. It also flew in regular consignments of arms and mercenaries to 'drive out the Cubans'.[1]

Apparently deciding to throw his enemies off-guard, Neto now launched the former Katangese gendarmes resident in Angola back into Zaire. The gendarmes — pro-Tshombe veterans of the early 1960s — had fought with the MPLA in the Angolan war, and Mobutu immediately claimed that they were being closely supported by the Cubans. Of this there was no evidence. Mobutu's army simply melted away rather than fight, and the rebels quickly took over most of Shaba province (the old Katanga). South Africa angrily denounced the invasion, and Pretoria spoke admiringly of the Chinese analysis of the action (the machinations of Soviet imperialism). The French rushed to Mobutu's rescue, prompting the Moroccans to send troops to help Mobutu. The CIA, perhaps constrained by the new Carter Administration, seems to have played only a peripheral role. Even so, this led to the angry resignation of the head of the CIA's Angola Task Force, John Stockwell, who disclosed (10 April) that the CIA was engaged in recruiting for Zaire 'the same French mercenaries the CIA sent into Angola in early 1976'. The Angolans, for their part, disingenuously attempted to dissociate themselves from the Zaire invasion and spoke with alarm at the sight of French and Belgian officers moving into action only a few miles from their border. Meanwhile there were reports of BOSS agents in Kinshasa arranging South African military assistance for the beleaguered Mobutu. Whatever the truth of the Katangese invasion, the fact remained that, more than a year after the end of the Angolan war, the coalition of forces which had fought the MPLA then was now wholly reassembled — in strength. It was a menacing picture.

[1] *The Observer* (London), 17 April 1977. It is difficult to believe that such a consortium can have been other than a front for the French SDECE. The sums required to buy up a currency are too vast for a private enterprise, and the necessary air-lift facilities and a friendly welcome in Zaire would similarly require official French backing. *The Observer* was surely naive in taking seriously the (thin) Swiss cover and the delightfully anonymous Canadian tycoon.

Conclusion: How Long Will South Africa Survive?

The White Establishment of South Africa which had so successfully weathered the crisis of Sharpeville in the early 1960s was, by the mid-1970s, gripped in a crisis of infinitely greater proportions. It seemed much less likely, moreover, that the crisis would this time be followed by a decade of prosperity and repressive calm. The year 1976 had, like 1960, posed in an acute form the great question which lies at the bottom of all debate over South Africa: how long can the whole structure of white power survive?

The question has, of course, a considerable history of discussion amongst South African whites, who take a fairly lively interest in their own fate. The government's answer is quite straightforward. The whites will survive as long as they retain the will to do so, a will they can best express by shunning all varieties of liberalism, communism and other heathen creeds, and supporting the government's separate development policies. For, if these policies are taken seriously and can be made to work, the argument goes, the question of white survival is hardly posed. Vorster was taking this view, for example, when he told the Israeli newspaper, *Ma'ariv*, in November 1976 that there *was* no black majority in South Africa. There was, instead, a white majority, alongside whom were found a mass of black workers who had voluntarily abandoned the homelands where they enjoyed political rights in order to gain the higher wages to be found in the 'white country'. This argument can, of course, be made juridically and even philosophically watertight, but it makes no reference to the question of the consent of the black majority to such arrangements. If pressed on this question there can be only one answer: the arrangement is, in the last analysis, guaranteed by force, not consent. (As Vorster told his Israeli interviewer, 'The Arabs don't consent to Israeli rule either.') The regime would be happiest, of course, if Africans did consent, but if not, well... It is known that Vorster and many other Afrikaners view the Bantustans very much in the perspective of the endless land-haggling between races which occupied much of South Africa's pre-twentieth century history.

287

Once Bantustans have been properly set up, it is thought, political debate can settle down to long and satisfactorily complex arguments over particular pieces of land. With 87% of the land to deal from, the whites should hold a good hand for an extremely protracted game.

In periods of calm and prosperity the government's arguments are, explicitly or implicitly, accepted by most whites. In periods of internal crisis — that is, when it is made glaringly clear, yet again, that non-whites do not consent to these arrangements, that naked force *is* required — anxious voices are raised within the white community to question both the system's clear impracticality and the morality or otherwise of using force to sustain it.

These discussions follow a fairly set path. Reference is made to the grosser inequalities of the Africans' condition, to the daily indignities consequent upon non-white status, and to the clear probability that these can only produce greater and greater explosions of discontent. Schemes for reform are unveiled. Typically (as with the Progressives) such schemes concentrate on the consolidation of a 'moderate' African middle class or upon the co-optation of the Asian and Coloured groups to a more privileged status. The objective is, openly enough, to bolster and secure white dominance (the overwhelming majority of Africans are left out of such schemes) by a small, though significant, redistribution of privilege. This is generally what is meant by 'reform'. Cries for reform are usually accompanied by urgent statements that 'time is running out', that it is 'five minutes to midnight', that it will soon be 'too late'. An oddity of such urgings is that, although they have been made for decades, it is never actually concluded that it is already 'too late'. The clock is stuck at 'five minutes to midnight'. It is at this point that reference is made to 'the vast fund of goodwill which still exists between the races'. African 'moderates', though fast losing patience, one is told, have still not actually lost it. Fairly soon after this one will frequently hear that the real hope of change comes from the stirrings among the Afrikaans intelligentsia, particularly in the Afrikaans churches. Similarly, these stirrings are always on the point of producing bold new initiatives but never quite get beyond that point. At this stage the argument will often drift off into professions of sympathy for the sad lot of the blacks, coupled with admiration for the sterling qualities of the Afrikaner. The Zulus and the Afrikaners, it is said, are the two strongest, proudest groups. Sooner or later the future will belong to a coalition between them. At this stage the discussion often becomes academic in the worst sense of the word.

This academic quality of much of the debate within the white community is almost its most distinctive characteristic. The lot of the Africans is discussed, but few whites indeed can speak from any real grounding of knowledge in the daily conditions of African life. The whites with the closest acquaintance with the realities of black township life are the police, who are not much given to empathetic investigation and, in any case, do not publish their results. Discussions of race relations are, accordingly, phrased in terms of high principles — 'separate freedoms', 'the right to nationhood', 'Western civilisation', 'Christian principle', 'non-racialism', 'human dignity', and so forth. At a popular level discussion is in less ethereal terms but still often strikes a superficial note, hingeing on the wisdom or unwisdom of 'petty apartheid' — whether mixed sport should be allowed, or mixed restaurants, even mixed scientific congresses. At the lowest level of all, of course, one can always return to 'would you like your sister to marry a black/ Coloured/Asian?', arcane historical discussions of whether whites or blacks were in South Africa first, and attempts to weigh the relative 'contribution' made by each group to South Africa's development (the white man has contributed his superior wisdom, the black his labour; the white man has 'raised the black man up', etc., etc.). One may frequently imagine oneself sitting on a plantation verandah in the ante-bellum American South, listening to a heated debate about the Negro condition among liberal and conservative slave-owners.

The unreality of the very terms of such debates is, perhaps, due to the fact that there is no white South African alive who has not lived his or her entire life within the comfortable security of white supremacy. Upon this fundamental fact a vast social and ideological superstructure has been erected which, it sometimes seems, has become more important than the base itself. The discussion can devote itself to 'social apartheid' — to mixing with other races in sport, swimming pools or matrimony — because whites have been able to take the basics (wealth, jobs, and power) for granted. When South African whites talk of making concessions to Western liberal opinion they mean it in this sphere alone: multi-racial rugby teams, not halving their standard of living in order to share wealth more equitably with the blacks. Such things are simply inconceivable and are not talked about. White reformers aim, rather, at broadening the base of white supremacy, while the government pretends it does not, properly speaking, exist at all.

1. History on the side of the verkramptes

One must have some sympathy with such discussions in one sense: South Africa *is* a unique historical case. There is no precedent in history anywhere of an ethnic minority of over 4 million people voluntarily dismantling the dominance they enjoy over more than 20 million ethnically different others. Anything other than white supremacy *is*, in this sense, unthinkable. Propagandists of the South African CP are much given to predictions of the 'historical inevitability' of an early socialist revolution in South Africa.[1] They may, of course, turn out to be correct. But, at least until now, historical inevitability would seem to lie on the side of Vorster, or even the *verkramptes* to his right, not on that of their opponents.

It is, of course, frequently argued that an advanced, urban, industrialised society of the type which has come to exist in South Africa is somehow immanently hostile to the crudities of ethnic differentiation and discrimination. This argument is difficult to sustain in the widest sense, for there is little to suggest that South Africa's industrial development has not been considerably assisted by the permanent depression of black wage rates, allowing high rates of profit and high consequent rates of capital re-investment. To be sure, a higher price than is at first apparent is in fact paid. In a sense, part of the businessman's wage bill is made up of taxes to maintain a large police and military apparatus — which in turn keeps wages down, by preventing labour organisation and repressing labour discontent. Business, with its high profit rates, has easily met the bill — or simply passed it on in higher prices. Much of the tax bill, after all, may be shifted on to the African workers themselves. In any case, the record of South African industrial development during the 'high period' of formalised apartheid is simply too overwhelmingly successful for it to be believed that apartheid and development do not go hand in hand. One might even argue, indeed, that South Africa is in the van, for most of the other developed economies, to show growth rates at all comparable to South Africa's during the 1960s — notably the

---

[1] See, for example, the extraordinarily confident predictions from historical 'inevitability' provided by Slovo ('South Africa — no Middle Road', in B. Davidson et al., *Southern Africa. The New Politics of Revolution*, op. cit.). When confronted by the fact that the greatest recent impetus to change in South Africa has been provided not by an internal development but by the exogeneous factor of the Portuguese coup, Slovo simply uses Engels' quotation about accidents being 'the form behind which necessity lurks'. Such formulae are useful not in providing analysis but obviating the need for it.

German, French and Swiss — were themselves developing labour-repressive practices based upon the existence of a large, underprivileged migrant worker force. The growth of European capitalism in this period came increasingly to resemble the South African pattern, not to diverge from it, as these most dynamic countries developed 'their' Bantustans — in Italy, Portugal, Turkey and Algeria — the homelands to which *their* voteless, single, and barracks or *bidonville*-accommodated workers were shunted back when the host economies no longer needed them.[1]

Nor, it must be said, can there be any simple argument from 'modernity' against the persistence of 'primitive' practices of ethnic discrimination. Rather, modern society has in general shown a striking capacity to adapt to, and to find room and uses for, pre-existing patterns of racial differentiation — as the examples of Jews in the Soviet Union or Poland, or of the French in Canada continue to prove. Indeed, South Africa, with her stress on separate ethnic and cultural development, might again be said to be in the van when one considers the explosive growth of Flemish, Scottish, Ukrainian or other 'national' movements in the advanced countries in recent years.

The argument may be rephrased, however, to suggest that what *is* repugnant to modern industrial capitalism is the permanent repression of an ethnically defined servile majority. This argument has, of course, been made before in connection with the alleged incompatibility in American history between the slave-owning ante-bellum South and the free North and West of the United States. The Civil War, it is said, was an 'inevitable' conflict, in that it pitted the forces of plantation slavery and industrial capitalism against one another, with no reconcilation possible between the two. It is worth quoting Barrington Moore's conclusions on this debate.

> The evidence indicates very clearly that plantation slavery was an obstacle to democracy, at least any conception of democracy that includes the goals of human equality, even the limited form of equality of opportunity, and human freedom. It does not establish at all clearly that plantation slavery was

---

[1] The first great 'breakthrough' to such a system was, of course, made in the Third Reich. See, for example, E. L. Homze, *Foreign Labour in Nazi Germany* (Princeton, 1967). The visitor to Munich may actually compare the old and the new by visiting the barracks at Dachau (preserved as a monument) and then those at the nearby B.M.W. works, outside which stand baton-carrying company guards.

an obstacle to industrial capitalism as such. And comparative perspective shows clearly that industrial capitalism can establish itself in societies that do not profess these democratic goals or, to be a little more cautious, where these goals are no more than a secondary current. Germany and Japan prior to 1945 are the main illustrations for this thesis.[1]

Rather, Moore suggests, 'Labour-repressive agricultural systems, and plantation slavery in particular, are political obstacles to a *particular kind* of capitalism, at a specific historical stage: competitive democratic capitalism, we must call it, for lack of a more precise term.'[2]

Undeniably, there is a latent conflict between what Moore calls 'competitive democratic capitalism' and a strongly repressive labour system such as that enshrined in South African apartheid. The tensions between the business and political leaderships of the White Establishment, between Oppenheimer and Vorster if one takes ideal types, is real enough and has never been difficult to descry. The strong traditional hostility among the English-speaking business classes to the Nationalist government, as also the traditional anti-capitalism of Afrikaner nationalism, bear witness to this 'conflict of civilisations'. In the American case these latent tendencies towards conflict were actualised in the Civil War, in the South African case they were, rather less clearly, present within the conflict of the Boer War. Both wars may be said, with some meaning, to have constituted critical phases in a 'capitalist revolution' in these countries. The differences between the two countries' experience are several-fold. First, and most obviously, the victory of English-speaking business civilisation in the South African Boer War did not result in the same profound change of status among the black majority that occurred during the American Civil War in the case of the Southern slaves. Second, this victory of English business in the Boer War was fairly quickly qualified by at first a partial and then a complete political come-back by the forces of rural Afrikaner nationalism. Within five years of the South African war a Boer general, Louis Botha, had taken office as prime minister. In the US, the Southern whites, once defeated, stayed defeated. The full political re-integration of the old (and now transformed) Deep South was symbolically achieved only in 1976, with the election of a Georgian, Carter, to the

---

[1] Barrington Moore, *Social Origins of Dictatorship and Democracy. Lord and Peasant in the Making of the Modern World*, (London, 1967), p. 152.
[2] Ibid.

presidency. Thirdly, the conflict between these two 'types of civilisation' in America took place in the context of the almost total isolation from external political threats or even influences which the US enjoyed in the mid-nineteenth century. One can hardly imagine such a conflict taking on even a very sharp political form in the context of contemporary South Africa, hemmed in on all sides by what it perceives as major political and military threats. The present-day White Establishment in South Africa is keenly conscious that it cannot afford to disregard the national motto, 'Unity is Strength'. It will stand together because it feels it has to. Tendencies towards conflict within the White Establishment will remain mere tendencies, it is safe to predict. 'Business civilisation' may find apartheid repugnant, but it will not risk a major political fracture within the white bloc in an attempt to get its way. The Anglo-American and De Beers sheep have long ago learnt to lie down, however irritably, with the wolf of Afrikaner nationalism. (Each side would, of course, see the other as wolf, itself as sheep.) In any case, the rise of a new class of Afrikaner businessmen has helped further to unify the White Establishment, whose economic and political elites increasingly interpenetrate one another.

The political victory of Afrikaner nationalism and the social forces it represented goes a good way to explaining the uniqueness of the South African example. What, after all, would have happened had the South won the American Civil War? Again, Moore is a useful guide.

> One need only consider what would have happened had the Southern plantation system been able to establish itself in the West by the middle of the nineteenth century and surrounded the North East. Then the United States would have been in the position of some modernizing countries today, with a latifundia economy, a dominant and antidemocratic aristocracy, and a weak and dependent commercial and industrial class, unable and unwilling to push forward toward political democracy. In rough outline, such was the Russian situation . . . in the second half of the nineteenth century.[1]

It would not do, of course, to push any of these historical parallels too far: slavery and apartheid are *not* the same, the Boer War and the Civil War were very different, both in their

---

[1] Ibid., p. 153.

conduct and their outcome; South Africa *is* unique. None-theless, it is of some interest that the American comparison above has, in the end, led us back via Moore to Russia, for we have already noted in this book the not inconsiderable political parallels between contemporary South Africa and pre-1917 Russia.

Such a parallel would doubtlessly be relished by many of the Pretoria regime's revolutionary opponents, particularly, of course, the CPSA. In fact the comparison might serve at least as well as a warning against the likelihood of revolutionary change as a prediction of it. The typical forms of social unrest produced by pre-revolutionary Russia were anarchistic sabotage and assassination, strikes by urban workers, and sporadic peasant *jacqueries*. The regime weathered them all, just as the Pretoria regime has weathered them. The Czarist regime even weathered 1905. Peacetime Czarist Russia seemed unlikely to generate a more total or threatening challenge than that. At worst the situation might produce more '1905s'. South Africa, we have argued, weathered its 1905 at Sharpeville — there is even an uncanny resemblance between the political pattern of Russian and South African events to strengthen the comparison. The Soweto and Cape Town riots of 1976 were hardly a mere repetition of Sharpeville — they went on longer, were much bloodier, saw a much greater participation by urban workers, and were simply a much more bitter, less naive event. They nonetheless clearly constituted 'merely' another '1905'. South Africa may well experience yet more '1905s' without a '1917' ever arriving.

It is important to realise, pursuing our Russian analogy, that the mere fact of a '1905' does not pre-determine the arrival of a 1917. For all its internal contradictions there was no sign of the impending collapse of the Czarist state until it was drawn into an external war which partly destroyed, partly revolutionised, but, above all, simply removed its army — the means of internal repression; a war which, moreover, tested the economic and social fabric of the state to and beyond its breaking point. Without such a war the Czarist state might well have survived, perhaps even to this day. Japan, after all, presents the spectacle in this century of an absolutist feudal state which was able to manage both capitalist industrialisation *and* the defeat of social revolution. It too was only brought down ultimately by overwhelming military defeat. Even then the reformism — not social revolution — which triumphed was sponsored by a foreign army of occupation and took place within a still recognisably feudal context. For all the differences between it and Czarist

Russia or Imperial Japan, such examples ought to still any blithe confidence among revolutionaries in some 'inevitable' 1917 lurking in the wings for South Africa.

What, after all, are the challenges to the White Establishment likely to be generated by the discontents of South Africa's non-white population? The events of the past two decades suggest that the challenge may come from three possible groups: urban workers, the urban unemployed, and rural Africans.

There is not much doubt that, of the groups, the black urban working class is potentially by far the strongest. There are now perhaps 4.5 million Africans living in 'white' urban areas (though not all are workers) — as many as the whole white urban population. Whatever government policy may be they are not going to go away and, indeed, their numbers are bound to grow rapidly. This group is increasingly literate, informed and organisationally resourceful. Each day the demands of work place such people in key positions within the white citadel, and the whole 'white' economy would seize up immediately should they withdraw their labour. Moreover, this group, however miserable its objective condition of life may be, includes many who have made not insignificant gains in economic terms and in their style of life. Having gained a little they are — as any student of de Tocqueville would anticipate — eager to gain more. Their new assertiveness — visible since at least the strike wave of the early 1970s — creates a climate in which political consciousness is likely only to grow. Although recent years have witnessed the luxuriant growth of a somewhat inchoate and formless 'black consciousness' ideology, there is no reason to believe that this group will not again become receptive to the vulgar marxism of the ANC and CPSA. These organisations may not have much to offer but the prestige of the former, at least, remains considerable and even the most vulgar marxism does provide a coherent ideological framework within which a classically oppressed urban working class may understand its present and descry its possible future. In the end the barrenness of CPSA marxism may not matter very much, and its very *deus ex machina* exile position may even assist the Party in its ambition to become the provider of an ideology to a movement which, after Soweto, is very much in search of it. In the wake of Soweto the 'black consciousness' movement was dealt a series of heavy blows from which it may not recover. In any case, inasmuch as the current of black consciousness was responsible for leading the young black radicals into the valley of death at Soweto — a confrontation without much positive result — it

may anyway lose some of its original thrust and influence. The
CPSA—ANC alliance is extremely unlikely to provide a cogent
or coherent marxist analysis of the situation; it is likely to
remain a by-word for bureaucratic manipulation; and it will
doubtless remain a target of black suspicion given the influence
of white communists within it. But in the end there may be so
much going for it in the urban black milieu that it will pass
muster, ideological crudities and bureaucratic malformations
notwithstanding.

The black working class, then, is an already powerful group
which will get stronger, possesses a crippling weapon in the
mass strike, and may very well acquire the militant socialist
ideology which would help it make the most of its strength. It
seems, nonetheless, somewhat unlikely that this working class
will play a decisive role in any South African revolution or,
at least, not under the normal conditions of peacetime South
Africa. For, great though its strengths may be, so too are its
weaknesses. It lacks trade union organisation and what organisations it has are weak and penetrated by police informers. It is
deeply divided between urban resident workers and the single
migrants from the homelands — divisions which are frequently
overlaid with ethnic and linguistic differences. It is, moreover,
conscious enough of its relatively privileged position and of the
fact that it has something to lose. Like any other working class
it is most prone to strike action in a period of prosperity and of
a relatively tight labour market — when it can most easily be
bought off. A period of high and threatening unemployment
will tend to make it, like any other working class, cowed,
cautious and conservative. The system is, in any case, perfectly
well able to cope with sporadic and localised strikes. Even
during the height of the 1972—3 strike wave South Africa still
enjoyed one of the lowest rates of industrial disputes in the
world.

In order to extend the perspective of black working class
action beyond the point of local wage disputes it is necessary to
start conjuring with notions of a concerted general strike
leading to a violent confrontation between workers and the
state. Such notions, it may be seen, have more to do with the
wilder flights of Sorelian revolutionary syndicalism than with
the more mundane expectations suggested either by traditional
marxism or historical experience. Labour history elsewhere in
the world suggests strongly, after all, that the myth of the mass
general strike *is* a myth. Even should such an initiative be
launched it is difficult to see how it could be victorious. The
workers lack co-ordinating organisation. They do not have

funds to support a long strike. There are blacklegs a-plenty.
The townships will be sealed off by the police — they have been
built to specification to allow tight surveillance and control by
small numbers of police from prepared, strategic positions.
Attempts at violent confrontation will be met with the full
force of the state's repressive machinery. As yet little of this has
been deployed — there is much more in reserve. The Soweto
disturbances saw the widespread use of armoured cars and
helicopters against the rioters. Pretoria has tanks and jet fighters
too. How long will even the most determined workers' protest
march last if it is being strafed by Mirages? Black workers —
who are not fools — have understood this equation better than
many of the revolutionary enthusiasts who would urge them
towards fresh confrontations. Their political and industrial
activity is likely to take such facts well into account. They may
risk such confrontation if pressed, if desperate, or just possibly
as part of some broader black movement of protest (as seems to
have been the case at Soweto, where their action seems to have
been one of communal rather class solidarity). They are
unlikely to take such action out of revolutionary élan or mere
principled loathing of white supremacy.

It seems not unlikely that the frustrations of black workers and
unemployed may find outlets in attempts at urban guerrilla
warfare. Towards the end of the Soweto events there were,
indeed, signs of such a development with petrol-bombing forays
into the white suburbs and arson against white business
establishments. There is no doubt that urban guerrillas could
wreak very great havoc and that there is no shortage of either
targets or opportunities for such a movement. It is worth pointing
out, though, that an urban guerrilla movement is constitutionally
incapable of generating a mass movement behind it. A small
number of militants act stealthily; their actions are as likely as
not to have uninvolved blacks directly among their victims, and
will quite certainly make them victims of the likely mass
reprisals. For such reasons urban guerrillas have never led a
successful campaign anywhere in the world. This tactic has
failed throughout Latin America and it also failed under the
more 'promising' conditions of colonial Algiers. All the evidence
suggests it would be a bloody dead-end in South Africa too.

To date the greatest power of the urban Africans, has, as we
have noted, been felt in the international money markets. Black
protestors may not be able to stop the factories or mines for
long, if at all, but they can interdict the flow of foreign capital
into South Africa on which the economy depends. Thus, it
could be argued, black protest may become a vicious spiral,

with each fresh outbreak triggering further foreign disinvestment, producing deeper recession, mounting unemployment and a continual shambles of repression — in a word, an endless succession of Sowetos. Such a scenario is, however, too mechanical. For the second group — the urban unemployed (the key actors at Soweto) — are merely workers out of work and are subject to the same constraints which apply to other workers. The unemployed are, moreover, frequently a direct threat to the employed, and solidarity between the two groups can hardly be taken for granted. At the same time it is difficult to see how the unemployed can play any sort of independent role for long, for they are in practice the dependents of the workers. They live in the townships either by the direct charity of the workers — as their children and kin — or by parasitism upon them in the form of robbery, protection rackets and so forth. The unemployed are, too, a permanently shifting group. The Soweto rioters, after all, hardly provide a steady social base to sustain a continuing movement. Of those who participated in the events of 1976 many are now dead, others in prison, underground, in exile, or back in the homelands, while others again may by now have joined the 'privileged' ranks of the work force. Those who remain in Soweto, still unemployed, can at most congratulate themselves on having won a few small concessions for the workers and the African middle class — not for themselves. They have taken the brunt of police repression and have many losses to count and mourn. They have, in effect, been the losers in a small civil war. Historical comparisons both in South Africa and elsewhere (Greece, Spain) indicate a period of quietus and bloodied calm after such losses.

There is an even more fundamental point omitted in the simple assumption of rising black unemployment producing rising black discontent. What was explosive in 1976 was the *fear* of unemployment among a younger generation of Africans, cruelly cutting short the heightened expectations generated by a period of prosperity and upward movement. The experience of *actual* long-term unemployment is likely to have rather different effects, certainly if labour history elsewhere in the world is anything to go by. The long-term unemployed tend to be a cowed, weak, helpless and resigned group, not a militant one. Their plight may — and usually does — make them bitter, but it also makes them pliant. A first sign of this was already evident in the later stages of 1976, in the increased success experienced in recruiting South African blacks (particularly from the Transkei) to work on the mines as the supplies of foreign labour began to dry up. During the height of the disturbances in the mining compounds it was strongly argued by many observers that conditions there were so repugnant to South African blacks that they would refuse mining work under almost any circumstances, virtually regardless of what wage-levels were set. This may have been true — positive incentives seemed to achieve little at the time. But negative incentives — such as the fear of starvation by oneself or one's children — have a power all of their own.

Some of the same considerations apply to the possibilities of political action by rural Africans. These fall into two groups — those in the 'white' countryside, and those in the homelands. The first group — perhaps 4 million strong — is politically invisible but not unimportant. For as white farms grow in size to become great agri-corporations and whites drift ever more to the towns, the *de facto* black preponderance in the countryside has become overwhelming. A considerable question mark hangs over this group. As white farms become increasingly mechanised their labour is required less and less, a fact which, in the government's eyes, provides a compelling reason for shunting this 'surplus' population where it properly belongs — the homelands. Between 1960 and 1970 around a million rural Africans were thus uprooted. At some point the fear of starvation in the homelands may become so great that rural Africans, historically a politically quiescent group, heavily dependent upon their white farmer employers, may be pushed into open and violent resistance. The prospects for such a movement of resistance are, it must be said, extremely poor. The farmers themselves have a legendarily heavy hand with 'awkward' Africans — among the African population in the towns rumours of horrific atrocities on the farms circulate continuously. In case of 'trouble', the farmers would receive the full backing of the police against Africans who are usually illiterate, unorganised and only parochially conscious. For all their *de facto* preponderance in the 'white' countryside such rural Africans have no land there of 'their own' to retreat to. The possibility of rural risings against individual white homesteads can hardly be ruled out, but such activity would have a short life indeed unless it were part of a much more general movement of insurrection.

Finally, what of the prospects of political activity amongst the 'homeland' Africans? One feature of the government's policy is, ironically, to break down the political and social isolation of these areas. Inasmuch as the homelands function effectively as labour reservoirs for the urban areas there results a continual process of movement between town and homeland, with ex-urban workers relaying back political and other information to those who stay in the homelands. Thus the government has, foolishly perhaps, guaranteed that the heightened political consciousness of urban blacks will not stay dammed up in the townships but will lap into the homelands fairly quickly. The potential consequences of such a process have not yet become visible, and are indeed, incalculable.

There are, of course, extremely limited possibilities for black political action in the homelands, as was evident from the first Transkei election of 1963. The moderate, even conservative anti-Bantustan party won a clear majority of the African popular vote (despite a grotesquely corrupt and partially rigged election), but its representatives were automatically out-voted by the built-in majority of appointed chiefs under the Bantustan leader, Kaiser Matanzima. Other Bantustan leaders — most notably Chief Buthelezi of KwaZulu — are less unpopular than Matanzima but all are critically dependent on the Pretoria government and are conservatives who pose little real threat to the established order. (Buthelezi's foundation of a Black Unity Party in December 1976 was greeted with bitter derision by the Soweto radicals.) Within the Bantustans such leaders are supported by a small privileged stratum of chiefs, officials, traders, and larger landowners, the latter deliberately created by the government's policy of land consolidation.

The question mark which hangs over the political activity of homeland Africans is not so much the chance that they may democratise the political systems of the Bantustans themselves, but whether the homelands in time will become the *foci* of guerrilla action threatening the white towns and countryside. There is no doubt that the build-up of a large, starving population, gradually radicalised by the experience of migrancy, poses such a threat.

Again, it must be said, the prospects for such action are rather poor. The homelands are bled of their young and active men. Only 42% of the population there is male; 49% are under 15 and a further 5% over 65.[1] Secondly, one must not reason simplistically from starvation to revolt any more than one should argue from unemployment straight to urban protest. An overcrowded population at or beyond the edge of starvation does not necessarily provide a comfortable base for guerrilla action. Those who starve only sometimes rebel in anger; more frequently they die quietly of starvation, or live pleading for succour. Third, any such movement will, of course, have the

[1] By comparison, in the black urban population the under-15s constitute only 30.6% and the over-65s 2.3%.

power of the White Establishment with which to reckon — and, inevitably, the hostility of the Bantustan authorities themselves.

This last point is fairly crucial, for it means that such a guerrilla movement would not be able to regard the Bantustans as sanctuaries. There is no recorded instance of a guerrilla war being successfully waged without the benefit of a sanctuary. (Even the Cubans had the Sierra Maestra.) The sanctuary must provide not merely a place to which to retire after combat, but food, access to arms, and military training. In a number of recent guerrilla wars — the Vietnamese case is the most striking — the sanctuary has also provided a strongly supportive host government which supplies help in the most tangible form of all: its own professional army. A glance at the map, moreover, will show that most of the Bantustans are broken up into a multitude of small, unconnected fragments of land and that many are overshadowed by neighbouring centres of white power. They could provide some sanctuary — but not much.

There is, finally, the point, argued by many, of the inevitability of the collapse of the White Establishment due to the sheer and growing numerical preponderance of the non-whites. The picture produced by setting recent population estimates and projections alongside one another is summarised in the table below.

TABLE 3. *South Africa's Population: Present and Projected (millions)*[1]

	1974	2000	2020
WHITES	4.2	6.8	9.2
ASIANS	0.7	1.2	1.6
COLOURED	2.3	4.1	7.7
BLACKS	17.7	37.3	62.8
TOTAL	24.9*	50.2[+]	81.3[+]

(Population figures include Transkei, which became independent in October 1976)
*Official Estimate
[+]Projection

To such figures one might add that if present projections of urban growth are fulfilled, by the year 2000 the total population of the 'white' urban areas will grow from 12 million

[1] Figures from The *Economist* (London), 1 January 1977.

to 40 million. That 40 million will include virtually all the expected 6.8 million whites — and 33 million non-whites, of whom Africans will make up almost 28 million. In other words, the present situation of rough parity between Africans and whites in urban areas will change to one where the Africans outnumber the whites by 4:1.

Such projections may, of course, turn out to be wrong, even badly wrong. Demographers can only predict on the basis of the past — they do not know the future. The greater the degree of African overcrowding in the homelands, for example, the higher the already horrific rate of infant mortality is likely to climb. Nonetheless, the general pattern is so clear that such objections amount to little more than cavilling: the non-white, and particularly the African predominance is bound to grow, and the growth is likely to be at its most rapid in the most sensitive areas, the 'white' cities. Such projections, moreover, assume an annual inflow of 30,000 white immigrants which may, under some possible future circumstances, be a somewhat optimistic figure. The picture does not, however, in any important degree, depend on white immigration. If one projects a 60,000 annual rate of white immigration to 2020 this produces another 1.32 million whites. If one assumes a rapid rate of natural increase among such immigrants one might add perhaps as many as 2 million to the total white population. Even such a development would see a steady rise in the ratio of Africans to whites from 4.2:1 in 1974 to 5.6:1 in 2020 (the actual projections predict a 6.8:1 ratio in that year). Moreover, talk in terms of such ratios implies that the rapidly growing Coloured population may somehow be left out of account — while the events of 1976 suggest strongly that they ought perhaps to be counted on the African 'side' in future.

Such figures appear to have a remorseless logic all of their own, and there can certainly be no doubt that at least many of the 'social' aspects of apartheid must collapse in the face of the transformation of South African society which these figures foretell. Nonetheless, one must again warn against any simple jump in logic from such figures to the assumed inevitability of black majority rule in South Africa. There have been other white regimes in Africa and many have survived for years in the face of adverse black—white population ratios much greater than the 6.8:1 predicted for 2020 (or 9:1 if the ratio of all non-whites to whites is preferred). At the time of writing, the Smith regime in Salisbury survives despite a ratio of blacks to whites of at least 20:1. The mind may well boggle at the prospect of over 70 million non-whites being held in varying degrees of subjection by 9 or 10 million whites in the year 2020. The human costs of such a holding operation would be higher (they are high now), if only because there would be more humans, but there is nothing in historical experience to suggest that such a picture is inherently impossible. The figures can, of course, be projected onward to 2100 or beyond; at some point they must, doubtless, become conclusive on their own of black majority rule. But the history until now of white regimes in Africa does not suggest that the population ratio for, say, the next 50 year period provides an insuperable obstacle to continuing white supremacy. Rather, the history of such regimes very strongly suggests that the continuation of white supremacy for such a period is more likely than not. History, in a word, is again on the side of the *verkramptes*.

Mention of the other white regimes in Africa poses a further series of questions. South Africa, we have said, is historically unique — but surely it is simply a fullblown example of what now exists in Rhodesia, or what once existed in Mozambique, Angola, Kenya or Algeria? And surely the fate of such regimes — all have gone save the Rhodesian regime which, one way or another, is clearly doomed — suggests that South Africa's White Establishment must, ere long, pass away? The history of such regimes does indeed hold some lessons for South Africa, but they are not as simple as that.

First, although all such regimes have given way (or, in Rhodesia's case, will give way) to black (or other indigenous) majority rule, none of them have managed this process peacefully. Whether in the form of Mau Mau, ZANLA, FRELIMO, the Algerian FLN, or the MPLA, Africans have had to take up arms for a protracted period of years to achieve what they wanted. True, several of the white regimes experienced what may be called the 'reform cycle', during which attempts were made to make a peaceful transition to at least a wider sharing of power between the races. In some cases it was even possible for white political leaders to gain (short-lived) mandates from their own electorates for such change. But such schemes always ran well behind what African aspirations had already come to demand and refused to be denied — they were too little far too late. Moreover, the onset of actual change — not just the prospect of it — quickly led to a white reaction so fierce that the would-be reformers not only lost their mandate but saw progressively more and more hard-line politicians (and generals) succeed them. The last state was actually more extreme than before, so that by the end of the cycle reform was more distant than ever. Attempts at 'reform' within the South

African context must be expected, if history is our guide, to meet a similar fate — to the benefit of the *verkramptes.*

Secondly, this process of reaction saw the formation of a white political bloc of monolithic proportions, with hitherto existing social divisions within the white community simply submerged. The formation of such a bloc has considerable importance, for it robs the established economic and political elites of any possibility of independent room for manouevre. The result has been, even though all of these societies have been full-bloodedly capitalist, that the business elites which one would normally expect to be predominant have been rendered virtually impotent. These elites tend to include most of those whites who have a long-term interest in 'reform' — who have made investments they wish to protect and who have the economic power to immunise themselves against the consequences of all but the most dramatic social changes. The formation of this solidary white bloc neutralises them almost completely. This stage was reached long ago in Rhodesia and is already a long way towards completion in South Africa. As the bloc solidifies further there — and it seems likely to — the somewhat extravagant hopes placed in the liberal intentions of *verligte* businessmen (merely on the peculiar grounds that they speak Afrikaans) are likely to be disappointed.

The third point to be made about the demise of other white regimes is that most commonly made by South African whites themselves. 'They', they argue, 'had somewhere else to go. We don't.' This point is actually not as strong as it seems. The mass departure of more than a million Frenchmen from Algeria or perhaps 800,000 Portuguese from Mozambique and Angola constitutes one of the most rapid and striking migratory phenomena of recent time. To be sure, there are far more whites in South Africa than there were even in French Algeria. Nonetheless, if civil strife in South Africa developed beyond a certain point, the history of other white societies in Africa warns that one should indeed expect a breathtakingly large emigratory movement among whites there too. At least, the instinct to emigrate away from bloodshed seems fundamental enough. The question is, where to go? Once-welcoming countries, such as Australia, are less open havens now than hitherto. And — what is most crucial — South Africa does not possess the relationship with a metropolitan state enjoyed by all of these other white regimes. Many English-speaking South Africans might be able to look to Britain or the Commonwealth, but the Afrikaners — a full 60% of the whites — cannot.

This is, indeed, the nub of the comparison with the other

white regimes of Africa. All of them were colonies, which South Africa, in any meaningful sense of the word, is not. Ultimately the transition to black majority rule in colonies settled by whites took place, as we have seen, after a period of armed black insurrection. At a certain point the whites within the colonies required the metropolitan army to protect them, for they could no longer secure their safety by their own efforts alone. The war for black majority rule continued but, in order to win, the guerrillas did not need to achieve military victory. All the insurgents had to do was to make it clear to the colonial power that it was fighting an endless and unwinnable war. Sooner or later, the colonial power decided to cut its losses. At this point the colonial power was faced with the (unpleasant) necessity of making the local white population swallow the prospect of black majority rule which it had resisted so mightily. In every case the local whites reacted with bitter hostility against the decolonising power (even launching the OAS in Algeria). Their cause was a lost one, however, because the colonial power had acquired a crucial leverage through its provision of military protection. In the last analysis it could threaten to deprive the local whites of their only possible safeguard against an indigenous rebellion they could not themselves quell. This threat was so fundamental and so compellingly persuasive that there could not be much further argument. (In the Rhodesian case, as we have seen, South Africa has willy-nilly moved into the role vacated by Britain; it too came to apply the leverage of military withdrawal in 1976; and that, at least, was successful with Smith in a way no earlier pressures had been.)

The lesson for South Africa seems clear enough. The whites do not depend on a metropolitan army to protect them from the discontents of their local blacks. The South African state is incomparably stronger than that of any earlier white society in Africa. In the face of possible internal rebellion, at least, white South Africa can look after itself. There is every future prospect that it will continue so to be able. There is no metropole to which to flee, or on which to depend militarily. There is no colonial power to exercise leverage towards black majority rule. The laager is intact and can be defended.

2. The Frontier Problem

Thus far we have discussed the problems of the survival of white supremacy as if South Africa was able to conduct her affairs in splendid isolation. Such a strategem is useful for the sake of argument but it does not, of course, answer to the facts. For South Africa's northern buffer is gone. She faces radical regimes in Angola and Mozambique, and, to some degree as a consequence, the necessity of decolonisation in Namibia and Rhodesia.

We have seen in earlier chapters of this book how this attempt at decolonisation on her borders has involved South Africa in a series of contradictory and often ironic positions. We have seen the whites of Namibia — and few groups have been more utterly loyal to apartheid doctrine than they — forced under strong pressure from Pretoria to accept the racial integration of cinemas and restaurants (though not of their suburbs or schools, it might be noted). We have seen Vorster speak of his unwillingness to exercise pressure on Rhodesians 'who are proud people' — clearly referring to the white 5% — and, in the next breath, speak of the need for government acceptable to all 'the peoples of Rhodesia'. Perhaps most richly comic has been the sight of Pretoria intimating in no uncertain terms to Salisbury that it will view any attempted devolution of power to South African-style Bantustan chiefs as a shifty and unacceptable attempt to get round the need for a realistic and just settlement.

The dilemma which South Africa faces on her frontiers may be stated fairly simply. On the one hand Pretoria must seek to instal in Namibia and Rhodesia governments which are sufficiently conservative in hue to present no long-term threat to her (by, for example, being willing to provide sanctuary for guerrilla movements aimed against her). On the other hand she must also find the political strength and will to impose on those countries governments which are not unambiguously puppet regimes, for such regimes will fail to gain international or wider African recognition and will, accordingly, be permanently subject to destabilisation via their radical neighbours in Angola and Mozambique.

As we have seen, South Africa has not yet been able to achieve this delicate compromise, and the case of Rhodesia has proven most particularly difficult both because of Smith's in-built resistance to decolonisation and to the political constraints represented by *verkrampte* forces within South Africa. At the time of writing the situation is still finely balanced and one can do no more than set out the alternatives

First, South Africa may fail to achieve this compromise or, in the Rhodesian case, may fail to achieve it in time (i.e. before the guerrilla movement has achieved such strength that it becomes the automatic arbiter of the future Zimbabwe *however* the transition to majority rule is managed). In this case South Africa will be faced with the prospect of the Rhodesian and Namibian (white or puppet) regimes collapsing before the onslaught of left-wing guerrilla armies. This is not a prospect which she can afford to accept, not merely because the regimes which will then come to power will pose a direct threat to her, but because the very manner of such a collapse would have an explosive (and diametrically opposite) effect on black and white opinion within South Africa itself. The impact made by the collapse of white rule in Angola and Mozambique has been severe enough but it may safely be said that this would be as nothing compared to the sight of, for example, Smith fleeing in the style of Marshal Ky or General Thieu from the victorious armies of a Tongogara or a Mugabe. In order to avert such a possibility Pretoria is likely to intervene militarily herself. Such intervention could only lead — fairly quickly — to war between South Africa and Mozambique and/or Angola.

Secondly, whatever success South Africa achieves in her decolonisation of Namibia and Rhodesia she may nonetheless find herself subjected to attack by guerrilla movements which are able to enjoy sanctuary in countries on her borders. The possibilities of sanctuary for such movements extend from Mozambique to a (radicalised) Swaziland, an independent Zimbabwe, Botswana, and an independent Namibia — with Mozambique clearly the most obvious and significant candidate. At this point it is worth pointing out that although the possibilities of the Bantustans providing sanctuary for guerrillas are, in general, poor, this may not apply so strongly to those Bantustans lying on or near the borders of these foreign states. A guerrilla movement raiding into northern Natal might not be able to rely on the support or welcome of Buthelezi's KwaZulu but, if the pressures were great enough, it might succeed in using his Bantustan as a transit route to southern Mozambique. The Bantustans of the north-eastern Transvaal and even possibly the Bophuthatswana Bantustan strung along the Botswana border could come to play a similar role. Similarly, if South Africa allows Namibia to 'fall' to a sister regime of that currently existing in Angola, the Namibian 'Bantustan' could become a potent focus of guerrilla activity in the whole of the western Cape. Again, the development of such guerrilla activity would very likely have as a fairly immediate consequence the widening of the conflict into a direct convential war between South Africa and her independent neighbours.

Thus two of the alternatives — and they are independent of one another — have as their outcome a likely war encompassing most or even the whole of the southern African region. It is doubtless such calculations as tnese which have caused Pretoria to weigh, and weigh again, the pros and cons of a pre-emptive strike into Mozambique and Angola. As we have seen, it seems not unlikely that such an attack on Angola was planned, with French and American co-operation, for early 1977. If so, the result of the US presidential election caused the plan to be frozen or, as some of the events of early 1977 suggest, to go off at half-cock.[1] By April 1977, with South African troops poised on the border — and crossing it frequently in hot pursuit, a continuing pattern of UNITA activity in southern Angola and the establishment of a direct French military presence in Zaire,[2] the prospects of such an invasion had hardly receded. Even should this latest bout of activity not result in another Angolan conflict, the possibility of war cannot but remain on Pretoria's agenda.

As Pretoria weighs her military options it is possible that she may come to believe that her previous strategy of military non-intervention was mistaken. Quite possibly it was. Had Pretoria committed herself openly and heavily to the defence of white rule in Angola and Mozambique when there were still large white settler populations in those countries she would doubtless still be holding the ring there. But it is too late for such options now — the settlers have largely gone. Had Pretoria

[1] It is not impossible that South Africa 'let down' the French by drawing back from such a plan on the morrow of the US election. Those who would have had responsibility for planning such an attack on the American side — the CIA — would undoubtedly have hesitated to risk their necks by precipitating a 'Bay of Pigs' on to an indignant Carter Administration in its first months. It is worth noting that Paris abruptly announced on 9 November 1976 (a week after the US election) that it would supply no more nuclear reactors to South Africa. This was strange: Paris had agreed to supply the first two such reactors, amidst gales of international protest, as recently as May 1976 — at which point, we have seen, a Paris—Pretoria rapprochement may have been taking place as a prelude to the re-opening of the Angola invasion question. In August the 86 non-aligned nations, meeting in Colombo, had threatened France with oil sanctions over the decision and Paris had taken no notice. Just as her decision to limit future arms sales to South Africa in August 1975 may have been the result of French resentment at Pretoria's failure to commit herself more deeply in Angola then, the November 1976 parallel may suggest a similar cause.

[2] Giscard did not wait for the Moroccans to take the intitative but went to them, offering French airlift facilities. Defending his action to the French electorate he promised that the operation would not lead to a 'new Vietnam'. In one sense, of course, it was precisely that, since the initiative was launched by presidential fiat, without the legislature's prior consent. South Africa would do well to consider how unrewarding the role of supporting ally was to the Australians and others in Vietnam.

intervened earlier, she might well have been able to inflict such losses on FRELIMO and the MPLA that it would have been possible to withdraw leaving acceptably 'moderate' African regimes in their place. As Pretoria toys with the attractive possibility of a UNITA—FNLA government in Luanda the might-have-beens of the past must seem bitter indeed.

They are, nonetheless, might-have-beens. Few things could be more dangerous to the future of white rule in South Africa than military involvement beyond her borders now. First, and most obviously, both Angola and Mozambique now have treaties of friendship with the Soviet Union. This does not reflect the ideological options of these regimes (the ideologically indistinguishable regime of Guinea-Bisaau has no such treaty) so much as their fear of South African invasion. It is extremely difficult to see how the Soviet Union could now allow either of these regimes to collapse under the weight of such an invasion. True, the Russians possess very limited means for making their strategic weight felt in southern Africa, even when the presence there of their Cuban allies is taken into account. It was a consciousness of this essential weakness of the Soviet position which probably furnished the key motive for the visit of President Podgorny to the region in early 1977. The Russians must hope that the symbolic fact that the President of the Soviet Union, no less, has visited Maputo and Luanda as a positive gesture of support for the regimes there may pre-empt the awkward possibility of the USSR having to face up to supporting them militarily in an emergency. How far the Soviet Union would go in such an emergency — whether she would actually jump straight to the threat provided by her nuclear capability — must remain a matter for some doubt. It would, however, be a terrible gamble for Pretoria to force the Russians to make up their mind on the issue.

Secondly, even if the Russian factor is left out of the equation — if it is assumed that they would, in the last analysis, back down from a full-scale commitment — the results of such an extra-territorial military involvement would still be disastrous for South Africa. Should South Africa intervene and displace FRELIMO and/or the MPLA from power there is little prospect that she could withdraw, leaving matters at that. For these movements, having now tasted power, will certainly not give up. They would, rather, be in the position of the South Vietnamese National Liberation Front after 1955, when the French forced them to lose the fruits of earlier victory and take to the hills again. There is no reason to believe that FRELIMO and the MPLA would not take to the bush again too. Both have a long and formidable record in guerrilla warfare and would dig in for a protracted struggle against the puppet regimes left in their place. Before long South Africa would find herself having to maintain a large and permanent military commitment at arm's length. It is precisely in such circumstances that the '1905s' which threaten her internally might well give way to a '1917'. Then, indeed, the Russian analogy would become almost perfect. The military strength of the state would be worn away in foreign wars; the wars would consititute a huge extra strain on the economy (even South Africa's current level of military activity does that); dislike of the war would help trigger insurrection at home; and the state's repressive apparatus would be neither intact nor in place to meet such a threat. Large-scale military intervention by Pretoria in Angola, Mozambique, or even, ultimately, Rhodesia, is a recipe for social revolution in South Africa. It may be seen that it is not necessary to bring states such as Botswana and Zambia into such a reckoning. In the convulsion which would grip the whole southern African region in such an eventuality they would be frail rafts indeed, little more than corks bobbing in the storm. The political versatility of a Banda or a Kaunda is, in any case, a proven quantity: they would accommodate themselves, chameleon-like, to whatever final environment resulted — finding, of course, reasons of strong principle for doing so.

These are, however, only two of the possibilities which face South Africa in her frontier region. There are others. As we have seen, Pretoria's best interests would best be served by installing compromise regimes in Namibia and an independent Zimbabwe — politically moderate regimes which are not her puppets: in a word, other Zambias. Such a compromise may be difficult to achieve but it is not impossible. Both Britain and the US (and other Western powers) may be relied upon to give South Africa the fullest possible support in establishing such regimes — indeed they will exert strong pressure on her to do so.
    That such pressure should be required at all may seem odd — it is first and foremost in South Africa's interest to achieve the installation of such regimes. Yet South Africa perseveres with a 'hands off' policy on Rhodesia, and on 9 March 1977 the Turnhalle conference completed its work by proposing an interim government for Namibia with a peculiar form of ethnic representation — a white premier (the Nationalist leader, Dirk Mudge) and Chief Kapuuo as president. Under this constitution Pretoria will continue to exercise power over defence, foreign affairs, transport, foreign exchange, finance, the police, the SADF and telecommunications. In

addition, the president of Namibia will be appointed and dismissed at will by the South African president. The Western nations, appalled at the prospect of having to defend such grotesque puppetry at the UN, quickly made it clear that this was entirely unacceptable. Pretoria replied that as far as she was concerned all options were still open in Namibia. The same, doubtless, applies to Rhodesia. That is, Pretoria has decided — for the moment, at least — to play 'hard to get', doubtless hoping to exact further deals from the West for her collaboration. After all, if a few months' pressure on Rhodesia in 1976 could win an extra $50 on the gold price, what might not a Namibian settlement acceptable to the UN be worth? It is a somewhat dangerous game in which Pretoria threatens to cut off her nose to spite her face, but it makes sound domestic political sense — the proposed Namibian state will be in line with apartheid doctrine, if nothing else. If Western pressure — and concessions — are great enough, however, Pretoria will doubtless consent in the end to be the horse led to the trough and 'made' to drink. All she has to imbibe, as we have said, is another Zambia in Zimbabwe and another Botswana in Namibia.

It is still not too late for such a settlement — one which would place Muzorewa or Nkomo (or even Sithole) in power in Zimbabwe and produce a similar regime in Namibia. Vorster may have a strong personal aversion to the SWAPO leader, Nujoma, but he could still conceivably play such a role — at least, his opportunism in the past supports such a view.[1] The difficulties in the way of such settlements lie partly in the resistances of Rhodesian and Namibian whites and partly in *verkrampte* sympathy for them inside South Africa. Vorster's success in overcoming the resistance of the former and, to date, in holding off the challenge of the latter augur reasonably well for such settlements — provided the Nationalist regime and Vorster himself are willing to forsake the line of consistent ideological principle. It does not seem too high a price for what it can probably buy, and is, accordingly, perhaps still the most probable outcome.

In the eventuality of such a decolonisation process being successfully achieved, South Africa will gain a considerable

[1] Ironically, Nujoma seems to have thrown in his lot with the MPLA and the supporting Cubans in some measure to make himself safe from the criticisms of the SWAPO radicals held in Nyerere's jails in Tanzania. But if Nujoma decided to cling to this alliance it should still not be difficult for Vorster to come to terms with SWAPO's internal wing if he shows himself willing to allow them a share of real power in Namibia.

breathing space. For then, it should be seen, South Africa would have negotiated her passage through the worst and most immediate effects of the collapse of Portuguese colonialism. A new status quo would be established and no further threats emanating from the north would need to be weathered for some time to come.

The Angolan and Mozambiquan regimes, after all, show no signs of looking for a fight — rather the reverse. The MPLA regime has made not a few solicitous overtures to the West; it has not disturbed Gulf's tenure (indeed, Cuban soldiers guard Gulf's oil installations from harm); and has much to preoccupy it internally for years to come. Both Angola and Mozambique, after all, must look to repair the ravages of many years of bitter colonial and civil war. Their economies are staggering under the effects of the mass departure of the Portuguese settlers. MPLA must hope to cultivate and woo the support of the peoples of southern Angola for a long time to come, just as FRELIMO must continue to bid for support in southern Mozambique where its popularity is fragile and where it was never militarily strong. Angola is far away from South Africa and, after 1975–6, would like to keep her distance. Mozambique is still economically integrated with and dependent upon South Africa. The FRELIMO regime naturally feels ambivalent about such ties, but it has little real option but to continue them. Cabora Bassa symbolises the situation fairly well. For years the anti-apartheid movement in the West campaigned against the construction of this hydro-electric complex because it would produce power for South Africa. Now the FRELIMO regime is glad to have it and sells power to South Africa. Anglo-American have made their peace with both FRELIMO and the MPLA and have even begun new projects in Mozambique since independence. There is, moreover, no indication that the Soviet Union would like to push these states into confrontation with South Africa. Again, the reverse appears to be the case. The Soviet Union seems alarmed by the possibilities of the need for a greater Soviet commitment to the region at this point and would like to see strong, viable 'socialist' regimes erected in Angola and Mozambique. During Podgorny's visit to Maputo in March 1977 he was widely reported to have counselled Machel quite strongly against the discontinuation of economic links with South Africa, suggesting in particular that Mozambique should continue to send her migrants to work on the Rand mines.

Thus, if a compromise settlement can be achieved in Rhodesia and Namibia, and if South Africa does not intervene militarily beyond her borders, the prospects are that her neighbours will be willing enough to leave her alone. If this period of respite is to last until the MPLA and FRELIMO have built strong, viable states and economies in Angola and Mozambique one could well be talking in terms of a period of at least ten and perhaps twenty years. The record of economic development achieved thus far by radical regimes in Africa is sufficiently poor, indeed, to cast doubt upon even such a term of years. Samora Machel has said that he sees inspiration for Mozambique in the impressive record of economic growth and self-reliance achieved in East Germany. Saying this in no way guarantees that we are about to see a new German Democratic Republic arise in Mozambique. In fact the country will have to find its way through a situation much more closely approximating that experienced in such states as Guinea (Conakry), Mali, Tanzania or Congo (Brazzaville) than that of the GDR. A new brand of rhetoric or ideology will do nothing to change that — though, in the case of Angola, the simple fact of oil might. But of the two it is Mozambique, with its close proximity and its long borders with South Africa, that matters from the point of view of future guerrilla activity aimed at the Republic.

The development of the forces of the South African revolution will not, of course, wait patiently upon the development of a strong state and viable economy in Mozambique. Long before then one can safely predict that would-be South African — or, as they will call themselves, Azanian — guerrilla movements will want to set up house in Mozambique and use that country as a sanctuary from which to launch their raids. All that one can safely say is that the Mozambique regime is unlikely to be in any hurry to allow this to happen. CPSA leaders briefly put in an appearance in Maputo in late 1976 and one isolated incursion did apparently take place then. But the CPSA leaders departed again and there have been no sequels to date. One may also safely predict that the Soviet Union will use its influence in Mozambique to delay the launching of such a guerrilla initiative for a long time to come. There is no doubt that the launching of such a campaign will immediately threaten a direct and conventional war between South Africa and Mozambique — something the latter cannot possibly survive unless backed to the hilt by the Soviet Union. For this to occur the whole pattern of Soviet strategic commitment will have to alter very dramatically indeed — the USSR will have to lend to its African allies a degree of direct military support which it has not, for example, ever seemed tempted to offer to its friends (Syria, Nasser's Egypt) in the Middle East.

Such a guerrilla initiative is, nonetheless, likely to come in the end. Reportedly the South African army already has contingency plans which envisage that areas such as the north-eastern Transvaal and northern Natal may need to be abandoned as zones for free-fire operations. Even more fantastical schemes — for the withdrawal of the white population to a laager in the Cape, for example — are sometimes spoken of but may, effectively, be dismissed. The moment of truth comes long before that — if and when the great concentration of power, wealth and population in the Pretoria—Johannesburg area comes under threat. White South Africa cannot abandon that and survive. The crucial battles of a South African guerrilla war, one may fairly safely predict, willl take place amongst the lions and zebras of the Kruger National Park and along the northern chain of the Drakensberg Mountains. The game reserves of northern Natal would seem equally likely areas of combat but they are strategically less significant.[1]

To sum up, the position which faces South Africa in her frontier region is still extremely uncertain and one cannot predict with any confidence which direction events there may take. All that one may say is that the future of white supremacy in the Republic is likely best to be served by retaining the strategy of military non-intervention for as long as possible. This does not 'solve' the long-term problems posed by the frontier balance but it would mean not having to face them fully for some time to come. To put it bluntly: if the Pretoria regime adopts a sufficiently ruthless and brutal policy at home it may be able to repress black rebellion well into the twenty-first century; if it is willing to be sufficiently tough and flexible over Rhodesia and Namibia (allowing truly representative regimes to emerge there) *and* it is wise enough to keep its troops at home, its future would seem secure enough well into the 1990s. The margin is narrower but it is still considerable — and, of course, a 10—20 year period of respite places the decisions to be faced then comfortably beyond the time-horizon of working politicians now.

---

[1] Truth, by hallowed convention, is the first casualty of all wars but, as wildlife-lovers will already have noted, game animals look likely to be a close second in such a conflict.

3. *South Africa and the International Order*

We have moved outward from a consideration of South Africa's internal balance to a consideration of the balance of forces on her frontier. Even as we examine these questions of the second tier, however, it is necessary to introduce such factors as Soviet, American and even British intentions into our conspectus. Our final concentric step must be to take into fuller consideration the international order of which South Africa is a part.

Such a step poses all manner of difficulties. Just as the uncertainties and possible outcomes increase as we move outward from South Africa to her frontier region, so the uncertainties multiply at an exponential rate as we go further outwards still. Many of the factors which will affect South Africa at this level are quite beyond prediction. This will be obvious enough from what has already been said in this book of the play of factors in the international order upon South Africa in the period since Sharpeville. To take only a few examples: among the factors which have most affected South Africa in that period have been the running down of the Texan oil reserves (creating the conditions for OPEC's existence), the 1973 Yom Kippur War (bringing the Afro—Arab and the Israeli—South African alliance), Pompidou's acceptance of Britain into the EEC (cutting South Africa off from the British market and hastening the fall of the Portuguese empire), the discovery of oil in Nigeria (producing the first real rival and counterweight to South Africa on the African continent), the Franco—American war over gold, the post-1973 world recession — the list is endless. In the future doubtless other such 'random' events will play a major role too. A coup in Tehran, for example, would now threaten South Africa almost as much as the coup in Lisbon did (if it cut off her oil). A real peace in the Middle East might be equally disastrous, for Israel might then forsake her alliance with Pretoria in order to regain the goodwill of the Afro—Arab bloc. The Left might win the French elections and reverse French policies in Africa. Again, the list is endless and there is little point in attempting predictions.

Nonetheless, we can hardly neglect the impact of the international political and economic order upon South Africa. It has, indeed, been a principal theme of this book that such factors have in the past been taken too little account of. South Africa has become steadily more involved — partly against her will — in these world orders. This has not, though, been an accident — indeed it has been inevitable. To sum up the situation crudely: the White Establishment, that is South

African capitalism and the South African state, found in the need to provide for its own survival, stability and expansion, compelling arguments for economic growth. This growth, as also its military security, could be guaranteed only by gaining South African access to the advanced technologies of the West. It was this which South Africa was 'buying' by opening her economy to massive foreign penetration and by rewarding such foreigners so handsomely. The 'price' which South Africa had to pay — the 'dominant contradiction', if one prefers such terminology — was her own ever-increasing involvement in (and thus vulnerability to) a world economic order over which the Republic had scant control and whose own gyrations and conflicts might, and eventually did, react back upon South Africa in a most alarming and unpredictable way.

The chain of causality behind these crises is long and complex and there are no true 'first causes'. We may, if we like, see such crises as the inevitable contradictions of the world capitalist system, though not a lot is gained from using such a phrase and something is lost if we are thereby led to believe that such terminology enables us to make confident predictions of the future.

If we are to examine international factors, then, it would be best to select trends at a fairly general level. First, and perhaps most important, one must take into account the likelihood of continuing economic recession in the capitalist world. The recession which began in 1973 has all the hallmarks of a long-lasting trough. By 1977 — after four years — it is clear enough that we are experiencing more than a short-term cyclical downturn, and there is no real recovery in sight. The last great depression in the 1930s was ended only by war and was thus, in a sense, artificially and politically cut short. If we wish to find a historical analogy for our present period we might perhaps be better advised to have regard to the great world recession of 1873—96. We may, in other words, be in for a trough several decades long.

If this did turn out to be the case — at present it seems rather more likely than not — then we may expect two major consequential developments which could have a fatal bearing on South Africa. First, though the communist world is not entirely immune from the effects of the world recession, it is nevertheless not a victim of it. The Soviet Union and Eastern Europe still manage full employment, low inflation and high, steady rates of economic growth. If the recession continues (and even, perhaps, if it doesn't), one must anticipate a continuing growth in the economic and political power of the communist bloc relative to the West. Quite apart from the fact that her socio-economic system tends to immunise her from the worst effects of recession in the capitalist world, the USSR's possession of prodigious mineral and raw material sources will alone give her an increasingly commanding position — she already has the world's largest natural gas reserves, she has more oil than even Saudi Arabia, the raw materials of Siberia have not yet been fully prospected, let alone tapped. Her agriculture, for all its ups and downs, has been on a steadily rising upward trend and the average growth rate of her food outputs easily outstrips her population growth. One need not go on, for the point will be fairly clear. The West may stagnate or grow slowly, the Soviet bloc will grow faster and, every year, will catch up a little more. It must be expected that Soviet political and military power relative to the West will grow commensurately and that in these spheres too the recession in the capitalist world will enable the Soviet bloc to catch up more quickly. There is no natural order of things to prevent such a development — indeed one would probably argue from history that Western dominance has had an unusually long run.

It is to be expected that the continuation of recession in the capitalist world plus the sight of the Soviet bloc catching up will generate deep anxieties in the West, all the same. Long before the Soviet bloc remotely catches the West in economic terms (there is a very long way to go) — and in part because the USSR, spending far more of its GNP on arms, will catch up militarily first — detente will become unpopular with many in the West and there will even be those who argue for taking a (military) stand against Soviet power before the rot goes any further. The frustrations born of recession will, as in the 1930s, make such military posturing a satisfying psychological exercise for many. One must expect a powerful pressure group to develop in the West that sees the 'battle for southern Africa' as a sort of last stand which the West cannot afford not to take.

Should such a school of thought gather real strength — it already has its influential spokesmen, as we have seen — it will augur well for the future and survival of white supremacy in South Africa. Attention will be drawn particularly to South Africa's undoubted mineral wealth which the West cannot affort to 'lose' (an odd conception since even a revolutionary black regime in South Africa would be keen to sell it). There will be mention of the likelihood of a world uranium shortage by 1985 and the fact that South Africa has large supplies of the material. The importance of the Cape sea-route will be stressed,

in true nineteenth-century fashion. For these and other reasons
the West will be urged to take a stronger protective role,
reinforcing the Pretoria regime against internal and external
threat. These pressures are likely to be successful at least to the
extent that the Western powers — particularly the US — are
likely to become increasingly involved and committed in the
region. There may be economic reasons for greater involvement
too, but these are less likely to be crucial than the political
ones.[1]

At the same time one must anticipate that the Afro—Arab
bloc will grow in economic strength and political influence, if
only because of oil. This rather amorphous bloc may be
expected to maintain and increase its pressures for the ending of
white supremacy in South Africa. As yet the pressure of the
non-aligned nations on the West over this issue has been
relatively weak, but one must expect both this bloc's bargaining
strength, as also its use of it, to increase. The Colombo
conference of August 1976 was, in this respect, a major
landmark, for it saw the formal initiation of threats to use
Afro—Arab economic power against third parties (Israel and
France) over their support of South Africa. Since then the
threat of this indirect weapon has become more prominent still.
At the same time there is growing pressure against the extension
of Western loans and credits to South Africa. In a period of
world recession South Africa will need such loans for the whole
of the forseeable future, which makes this a potent weapon too.

One particular irony of the pressure of the non-aligned and
Soviet blocs against South Africa should be noted: while
pressure is exerted against deeper Western involvement in South
Africa, the very refusal of economic ties with South Africa by
the non-aligned and Soviet blocs has the effect of pushing South
Africa into a deeper and more exclusive involvement with the

---

[1] The US is not critically reliant upon the minerals supplied to her by
South Africa. Such, at least, was the conclusion of a special report by
Charles Rivers Associates, commissioned by the US Department of
Commerce. The report, released in December 1976, was specifically asked
to include within its brief an evaluation of the effect on US mineral
supplies of a revolt in South Africa. It concluded that such an event would
lead to short-term disruptions of supplies only, together with a brief
period of higher prices, but that long-term supply flows from other sources
would be easy enough to procure without the US having to pay
significantly more for them. James C. Burrows, who headed the study
team — which surveyed the outlook for chromium, manganese, platinum,
bauxite and cobalt — added that the US wasn't 'vulnerable' at all and that
'there has been too much of a crisis atmosphere in discussions about these
commodities'. *Financial Times*, 30 December 1976.

West. If one is to isolate a single critical turning point for the South African political economy since Sharpeville, there is little doubt that this has been the general refusal of independent Africa to trade with her. Almost all of South Africa's economic difficulties flow from this. Had she been able to flood the African continent with her manufactured goods she might well have no trade deficit, would not be dependent on foreign investors, and would be less dependent on gold. Instead, her reliance upon (and vulnerability to pressure from) Europe and America has increased. The development of her third-party relationships with Israel and Iran do not offer an escape from this — indeed, they are in good part valuable to her because they may allow her back-door access into the EEC. She has, moreover, been forced into an 'Australian model' of development. That is, having developed her manufacturing base in order to become a ranking industrial power, she has been forced to step back a stage and concentrate again upon production of primary raw materials for export.[1] Thus present plans envisage that between 1976 and 1979 South Africa will increase her annual exports of coal from 4 million to 12 million tonnes, that she will export an extra 21 million tonnes of iron ore a year, a further 4.9 million lbs of uranium, plus equally large increases in her exports of titanium, beach sand, platinum, copper, diamonds, ferrochrome, rutile, zircon, nickel, rhodium and palladium. So great is her increase of planned exports of such materials (an extra R1,120 million per year worth by 1979 over 1976) that by 1979–80 the value of such mineral exports is likely to equal or even overtake that of gold. South Africa's long attempt to escape from the colonial role of purveyor of raw materials — and with it the vulnerability to the wild price fluctuations suffered by such commodities — will thus have failed. The mining of such materials, as also the construction of rail and port export facilities, and any possible construction of semi-processing plants for them in South Africa all require huge amounts of capital — for which, again, she must turn to the West.

Nor, as we have seen, has she been able to escape from her dependence on the West for advanced military technology.

---

[1] The Australian case may suggest there is something 'natural' about such a development. But Australia's problem has been her proximity to the vastly superior manufacturing capacity of Japanese industry and its satellites in South Korea, Taiwan and Singapore, together with the lack of access to a large nearby market. South Africa had the large nearby market and she did not have any competitors in Africa of Japan's calibre.

True, South Africa's own arms industry makes her self-sufficient in many low and medium-calibre arms and she can acquire some useful extra items from Israel. But for her next generation of jet fighters, for counters to SAM missiles, for advanced radar and surveillance equipment, for answers to the 'Stalin organs' she can look only to the West. As we have seen, her hopes of acquiring the Israeli Kfir fighter depend entirely on American permission (the vetoing by the Carter administration of the delivery of 24 Kfirs to Ecuador in March 1977 made the point clearly enough). Israel also makes the Quito 24 Nesher (Eagle) jet — like the Kfir, essentially a development of the Mirage. But there is no escape from the need for Western permission here either: just as the Kfir depends on US General Electric engines, so the Quito uses the French Dassault engines.[1]

If we take these trends together — the growth of Soviet power, the increasing use of Afro—Arab economic pressure on the West (in a period of recession), and South Africa's growing military and economic reliance on the West — there is the possibility that the West (and in practice it comes down to the US) will gradually come to assume, however informally, a 'metropolitan' role *vis-à-vis* South Africa. In our examination of the fate of other white regimes in Africa we saw how crucial to the transition from white supremacy to black rule was the key role of the metropolitan power. First it protected the whites from the military threat of black rebellion — and then used the leverage so acquired to force the whites into acceptance of majority rule. South Africa, we have said, was unique in good part because she lacked any relationship to such a power. But, if all the trends above continue, she may acquire one with the US. As Soviet power grows, so South Africa will feel increasingly threatened; at the same time she will be driven into ever greater dependence on the West militarily and economically; and the West will be under ever greater pressure from the Soviet bloc and the non-aligned states to use her leverage to ensure black majority rule in South Africa. That is, the US will find herself placed in relation to South Africa as South Africa is now placed in relation to Rhodesia. It is exceedingly unlikely that America will ever play a metropolitan role to the extent of

[1] Interestingly, after the US had interdicted the Ecuador deal Israel turned to Paris, offering the French a share in the profits if they allowed the sale of the Quito to Ecuador instead. Should the French concur this may provide a model for a continuing 'back-door' supply of French arms to Pretoria.

actually providing troops to stand between South Africa's whites and their black opponents internally or on the frontier. All else apart, the US army now consists quite largely of the black unemployed: no US president in his right mind would risk sending such forces to protect a white supremacist regime. But the US has no shortage of other and almost equally direct forms of leverage on South Africa — as the events of 1974–6 showed only too clearly. The historical significance of the Kissinger diplomacy of 1976 may, indeed, be that it initiated the US into a series of escalating squeezes on South Africa — with the difference that later squeezes will be applied not over Namibia or Rhodesia but against the apartheid system itself.

There are considerable problems with such a model — not least that South African political resistance to such direct pressures will be bitter indeed, and that it will be difficult to provide the White Establishment with what it will regard as satisfactory *quid pro quos* for the surrender of white supremacy: in the eyes of many whites such a surrender means giving up everything.

Indeed, one must have regard to the history of what we have called 'the reforming cycle' in the case of other white regimes in Africa. Those who exert such pressure must face the problem that within South Africa its political effect may be merely to strengthen the *verkrampte* elements yet further. If destabilisation brought Pinochet to power in Chile it might, in South Africa's case, result in power falling into the hands of BOSS and the formidable military—police establishment built up over the years. In one sense this might even be a good bet, for the regime charged with the awkward job of forcing black rule on white South Africa is going to need to use against rebellious whites the same brutality and ruthlessness hitherto mainly employed against blacks. This idea, as we have noted, has already occurred to Vorster's *verkrampte* opponents. Vorster, for his part, has the political authority to force through more such changes than most — although he shows no sign of wanting to do so. Any successor to Vorster will probably have less room for manouevre for several years at least. If one is looking for a white civilian politician who is sufficiently tough to force through majority rule and sufficiently right-wing to retain conservative confidence while he does it, perhaps Andries Treurnicht is the man.

However one looks at the problem, though, there is no doubt that the West, if its object is nothing less than the abandonment of white supremacy, will face very considerable difficulties in exercising pressure on South Africa. To play the classic metropolitan role the US would have to threaten to leave South Africa defenceless before the mercies of Soviet-backed black guerrilla armies. But it would be difficult for the US to make such a threat and for South Africa to believe that the threat was real. It may be that the threat of economic blockade would work instead (as used, in part, by Vorster on Smith via the railway holdups), but the record of such attempts is not very successful. In the end the threats to which white regimes have responded have been military. If this were again to be the case with South Africa one should not expect US pressure to become effective until South Africa is threatened by a very considerable deterioration in the military position which she enjoys today. It is difficult to see this deterioration taking place without the help of a greatly strengthened Soviet presence in the southern African region. But, of course, the stronger the Soviet presence becomes the less the US will wish to weaken her strongest ally in the region. Yet there is not much point in expecting the US to pre-empt such a situation by acting firmly before she 'needs' to. Democratic politicians, in the US as elsewhere, seldom act before they are forced to and do not, on the whole, go looking for trouble.

If the US lets sleeping dogs lie longer the position might come to resemble the Middle East crisis of 1973 when, essentially, a deal was done between the US and the USSR which then had to be forced on their respective clients. The Russians, who got the worst of this particular deal — the US ended up with Egypt *and* Israel as clients — may be expected to play their hand for all it is worth next time. Meanwhile the prospect of becoming either a protectorate of one of the big powers or a bone of contention between them has occurred to South African politicians. They do not like it, and are already beginning to strike heroic, 'go-it-alone' stances. This does not necessarily mean very much — Smith did it in 1965. In the end reality has to be faced.

It has to be faced in the West too, particularly in the US. In the long run there are only two alternatives. Either the West must dig in and support white supremacy in South Africa or it must exercise a general pressure for its 'reform', and, ultimately, its complete dismantlement. It is, as yet, too soon to know what the Carter administration's policies will be — the temptation, of course, will always be to work for piecemeal adjustments, not general change. All that one can say is that the coalition which brought Carter to power and on which he must rely for the next eight years is almost ideally suited to providing backing for such pressures for general change.

There are, of course, other possibilities. Israel now almost certainly possesses nuclear weapons, and Pretoria too has boasted of a 'nuclear capacity'. Whether by her own direct efforts or as a result of a deal with Israel, South Africa might well be in a position to threaten the use of nuclear weaponry against her foes. Such possibilities seem small. South Africa is hardly likely to gain US approval for the use of such weapons and rather unlikely to use them without it.

If, however, one is to take one's courage in both hands and attempt a prediction — on the basis of what is known and what is, on the whole, most likely — then one should, perhaps, expect something like the following scenario.

First, the South African economy is in for several hard years at least. The gold price has gone up, but not enough. It hit $200 in December 1974. Since then, inflation has been of the order of 25—30%. This means the present $150 price is worth only about $110 in December 1974 terms — an overall fall of 45%. Foreign investors have been thoroughly scared off, and though there is in fact every prospect of a quick killing in the markets for those who bought in at post-Soweto lows, it may well be that the country will never again benefit from the same degree of foreign investor confidence it enjoyed in the 1960s. The country will need loans, but remains a good credit risk and should get them. The problem is that it will be exceedingly difficult to acquire long-term investment from any source, and both private and public foreign investors will require high rates of return and copper-bottomed guarantees for whatever risks they take. The government is likely to spend even more on defence, to maintain white employment in the para-statal sector, to squeeze imports, and to pursue deflationary policies as far as these other objectives allow.

The likely results are high and rising African unemployment, a moderate redistribution of resources within the white community, and a gradually stabilising economic situation presaging at least a minor (and possibly major) boom in mineral exports in the late 1970s and early 1980s. The economy may well appear to tremble on the brink of the apocalypse but it is too fundamentally strong not to pull through by the simple expedient of off-loading most of the costs of recession on to the blacks. It is possible (though by no means certain) that we shall witness further revolts by the black unemployed or even the peasantry under such circumstances. These revolts could take almost any form, with urban guerrilla action perhaps marginally the most likely. What is certain (not just possible) is that such revolts, if they take place, will be thoroughly and effectively repressed.

In its frontier region South Africa will move towards a majority rule settlement in Rhodesia/Zimbabwe and, in the long term at least, in Namibia too. She will be continually tempted to intervene militarily beyond her borders but is unlikely actually to do so (other than to destroy SWAPO bases in Angola) unless the US agrees to co-sponsor such action. It is doubtful whether the electoral alliance which put Carter in the White House would stomach such a policy, and it is unlikely that Pretoria will intervene merely at the behest of the French. The latter simply lack the bargaining power of the US, and the Quai d'Orsay's schemes have a better record for imagination than success.

Within the Western bloc there will emerge strong and clamant voices urging a greater political and military commitment to South Africa. The tune will be familiar and is typically sung in two stanzas: 'We find the Ky/Syngman Rhee/Franco/ Salazar/Pinochet or, in this case, Vorster, regime distasteful, but it is a bulwark against communism'; and the subtler 'Their way of doing things may not be ours but one must have some respect for the unique historical experiment and sheer stability of Falangism/guided democracy/dictatorial machismo or, in this case, apartheid.'

Western governments will come under strong pressure from such voices, but this is likely to be at least counter-balanced by the growing pressures and even boycott threats emanating from Third World countries against Western nations which 'support apartheid'. Most Western governments will seek to satisfy both groups and will placate neither. They will take a 'middle road' of publicly urging 'reform' in South Africa while maintaining whatever economic or military involvement they have there. They will issue occasional tough warnings to the Russians to 'keep out of Africa' (in order to placate cold warriors at home — the Russians are hardly expected to take any notice). They will exert continual pressure on Pretoria for at least cosmetic reforms, mainly in the field of 'petty apartheid', in order to reassure the Third World countries that some progress is being made. Their actions will guarantee a steady diet for all those to whom the exposure of moral hypocrisy is meat and drink. But they are unlikely to do more. The West effectively ignored the Rhodesian 'problem' until the rise of a black guerrilla movement grew to offer a 'solution' they liked even less than they did Smith. It is likely to be the same story with South Africa. While the regime remains strong, profitable involvement and (deliberately) ineffectual abhorrence will go hand in hand. But the emergence of a real threat to the regime will concentrate minds quite wonderfully.

Such a threat is most likely to arise when a viable Azanian guerrilla movement emerges, with sanctuary in Mozambique. But Mozambique is not likely to be in any haste at all to offer such facilities, especially since South Africa is intent on making herself a model and indispensable neighbour. Even should the Mozambiquans feel tempted by ideological or 'solidarity' considerations to lend such support, they will not do so while Rhodesia remains to be settled, or while it seems likely that they will be alone in so doing. The Russians, moreover, are likely to stay their hand still further. Once Maputo commits itself, the Russians will find their prestige at stake in a struggle against a coalition of superior strength in a land far away where their strategic might barely reaches. They can hardly be expected to be in any sort of hurry for such a confrontation.

Russia's disinclination to find itself thus committed is likely to exercise a definitively restraining hand on the CPSA, which is nothing if not loyal to Moscow. Via the CPSA the same restraint will be exercised on the ANC. This is of some importance, since it is the Congress Alliance which at present seems the most likely progenitor of a guerrilla movement. The situation will thus resemble somewhat that obtaining in Vietnam in 1955. On that occasion both Chou En-lai and the Russians strongly counselled Ho Chi Minh against continuing the war in the South, arguing the principle of unripe time. Ho Chi Minh in turn advised the South Vietnamese NLF against all further guerrilla activities. In the end the latter, responding to their own internal pressures, disobeyed these injunctions. The war began in the South; the North found itself committed willy-nilly to the NLF, and both the Russians and Chinese found themselves similarly committed to the North. It was domino theory with a vengeance.

The South African case is quite likely to follow the same pattern. That is, at some point — perhaps as a result of some further Soweto — South African non-whites outside the political hold of the Congress Alliance will initiate guerrilla action, and will throw themselves on the mercy of the Maputo regime by fleeing from SADF troops across the Mozambique border. Maputo will refuse to hand over its guests to Pretoria but, unless it actually wishes to imprison the guerrillas, may then find they have launched a new attack by slipping back over the border. Mozambique, perhaps against its will, could thus simply become a guerrilla sanctuary without ever taking a conscious decision in the matter. At this point the CPSA will, as in the sabotage campaign of the early 1960s, find itself uncomfortably outflanked on its left and will wish to start its 'own' guerrillas. Or, if its sticks to the Soviet line and refrains from such action, it may find the ANC splits from it over the issue. Either way it cannot be long after that point that all the established exile groups attempt to move into the guerrilla business on their own account. This is precisely what has happened in Rhodesia — with ZANU turning the tables on its senior movement, ZAPU, by being first in the field with a significant guerrilla movement.

Fairly soon thereafter Pretoria will find itself faced with the decision as to whether to launch major retaliatory strikes into Mozambique. The US will attempt to restrain Pretoria's hand, in just the same way that Pretoria attempted to restrain Smith's in 1976. The only *quid pro quo* acceptable to Pretoria (as to Smith) will be a cessation of the guerrilla attacks. This the US will attempt to obtain via the good offices of the Soviet Union and, presumably, will fail. Not long after the first such strike the Russians should be able to ensure that the Mozambique regime is endowed with such defensive (missile) capability that all further such strikes become quite prohibitively expensive to Pretoria. (If one imagines this scenario as taking place in, say, 1990, and assumes a continuing Western arms ban on South Africa, one must also assume that Pretoria's Mirages (or Kfirs?) will be quite obsolete in comparison to the weapons the USSR could provide to Mozambique.)

At this point Pretoria will reach the same moment of truth experienced by Smith in 1976: that it faces an endless guerrilla war which can only get worse, and that its capacity to deprive the guerrillas of sanctuary is both limited and weakening. It is rather more likely than not that, if the guerrilla war reaches this critical stage, it will be accompanied by a rising tempo of unrest among urban blacks inside South Africa. The Pretoria regime will find itself threatened on all sides at once and in desperate need of help. At this point (and *only* at this point) the US will gain the same leverage over Pretoria that Pretoria held over Smith in 1976. The US, for its part, will wish to 'save' South Africa for the West at all costs and will presumably attempt to force South Africa to accept majority rule as the price of a major US commitment to South Africa — perhaps in the form of the SATO agreement always hungered after by Pretoria. The US is unlikely to press for anything less than majority rule. Nothing less would be acceptable to the Third World, nor to certain sections of American domestic opinion. Moreover, just as universal suffrage in Rhodesia in 1976 would probably have brought Muzorewa, not Mugabe, to power, so the US will doubtless hope (and the CIA will seek to ensure) that Buthelezi or his equivalent will emerge victorious in South African elections.

Such, at least, is one possible scenario. The main 'disadvantage' of most of the alternative scenarios one can produce is that they spiral fairly rapidly towards a world war between the super-powers. This hardly makes them impossible, though it may make them a little less likely.

As will already be evident, pondering the future of South Africa's White Establishment is no easy task. It would seem a historical certainty that it must eventually pass away or fall. Yet to ask 'how long will (white) South Africa survive?' is, in Herman Kahn's famous phrase, to 'think about the unthinkable'. So many factors are relevant. Most are complex, many are humanly repugnant and some not a little frightening. One has to think about them all the same.

List of Acronyms and Terms used in the Text

ANC, African National Congress (South Africa)

ANC, African National Congress (Rhodesia) — no connection with ANC (SA)

BOSS, Bureau of State Security (South Africa)

CFP, Compagnie Française de Petroles

CPSA, Communist Party of South Africa

CPSU, Communist Party of the Soviet Union

CREEP, Campaign to Re-Elect the President (Nixon)

CSO, Central Selling Organisation

EFTA, European Free Trade Area

ELF, Subsidiary of CFP

FLEC, Front for the Liberation of the Enclave of Cabinda

FNLA, National Front for the Liberation of Angola

FO, Foreign Office (UK)

FRELIMO, Mozambique Liberation Front

GDP, Gross Domestic Product

GNP, Gross National Product

GOP, Republican Party ('Grand Old Party') (US)

GRAE, Government of the Republic of Angola in Exile

HNP, Purified National Party (South Africa)

MPLA, People's Movement for the Liberation of Angola

NLF, National Liberation Front (South Vietnam)

NP, National Party (South Africa)

NSC, National Security Council (US)

NUSAS, National Union of South African Students

OAS, Secret Army Organisation (Algerian settlers)

OAU, Organisation of African Unity

OFS, Orange Free State

OPEC, Organisation of Petroleum Exporting Countries

PAC, Pan African Congress (South Africa)

PAIGC, Party of Independence for Guinea-Bissau and Cape Verde

PDRY, People's Democratic Republic of Yemen

PRP, Progressive Reform Party (South Africa)

SAAF, South African Air Force

SABC, South African Broadcasting Corporation

SADF, South African Defence Force

SAM, Surface to Air Missile

SAP, South African Police

SAR(and H), South African Railways (and Harbours)

SASOL, South African Coal, Oil and Gas Corporation

SATO, South Atlantic Treaty Organisation

SDECE, Service de Documentation Extérieure et de Contre-Espionage (French intelligence agency)

SPD, Social Democratic Party (West Germany)

SWAPO, South West African People's Organisation

UDI, Unilateral Declaration of Independence

UNCTAD, United Nations Conference on Trade and Development

UNIP, United National Independence Party (Zambian)

UNITA, Union for the Total Independence of Angola

UP, United Party (South Africa)

UPA, Union of the Populations of Angola

verkrampte, (lit. 'narrow') — refers to HNP and right wing of NP

verligte, 'enlightened' wing of NP

ZANLA, Zimbabwe African National Liberation Army

ZANU, Zimbabwe African National Union

ZAPU, Zimbabwe African People's Union

ZIPA, Zimbabwe People's Army